THE CLINICAL INTERPRETATION OF THE *MMPI–2*

A Content Cluster Approach

THE CLINICAL INTERPRETATION OF THE *MMPI-2*

A Content Cluster Approach

Edward E. Gotts
Thomas E. Knudsen

LEA LAWRENCE ERLBAUM ASSOCIATES, PUBLISHERS
2005 Mahwah, New Jersey   London

Lawrence Erlbaum Associates, Inc., Publishers
10 Industrial Avenue
Mahwah, New Jersey 07430
www.erlbaum.com

Cover design by Kathryn Houghtaling Lacey

Library of Congress Cataloging-in-Publication Data

The Clinical Interpretation of the *MMPI–2*: A Content Cluster Approach,
by Edward E. Gotts and Thomas Knudsen

ISBN 0-8058-5033-3 (cloth : alk. paper).

Includes bibliographical references and index.

Copyright information for this volume can be obtained by contacting the Library of Congress.

Dedicated to the loving memory of our fathers,
Edward T. Knudsen, Jr., and Earl Gotts,
who were still with us when this work began.

Contents

4   SYNOPSIS OF THE SPECIAL SCALES: SOURCES AND INTERPRETATION

5   OVERVIEW AND RESULTS OF A CLINICAL RESEARCH PROGRAM

6   RENEWING THE OLD: SCALE RECOVERIES AND LOSSES

7 NEW DEVELOPMENTS FOR *MMPI–2*   102

8 THE *DSM* AND AXIS I CONDITIONS   133

9 CLUSTERS, PERSONALITY TRAITS, AND DISORDERS   153

Preface

When Eugene E. Levitt was preparing his manuscript for the book, *The Clinical Application of MMPI Special Scales* (1989), a major revision of *MMPI* was concurrently being finalized (Butcher, W. G. Dahlstrom, Graham, Tellegen, & Kaemmer, 1989). Levitt's objective was to present in a single source a collection of scales that he and colleagues at the Indiana University Medical Center had found to be clinically useful. Among them were a small number of original scales styled as the *Indiana Rational Scales*. These had been developed to cover clinical features that were insufficiently sampled by existing scales (Levitt, 1989, pp. 43–47).

A revision of that work was commenced in 1993 by Levitt and Gotts (1995). It was based, to a considerable extent, on applications and extensions of the earlier work that the authors conducted collaboratively from 1986 to 1994 at the Madison State Hospital, Madison, Indiana, during monthly consultation and work sessions. When this joint effort began, *MMPI* was still widely used in clinical settings. *MMPI–2* was, however, unquestionably replacing the aging *MMPI*. By 1995, when the revised edition of Levitt's book appeared, it was close to becoming an anachronism in view of the increasingly widespread adoption of *MMPI–2*. Levitt passed away in early 1995, at which time the book was still in press. He, thus, never saw the final product or witnessed its reception by the psychology community.

The time had come to retool for a fresh beginning when the *MMPI–2* was adopted. The challenge was to reappraise the prior work as well as to incorporate new scales and perspectives. Reappraisal meant using our considerable patient database to retest scales that had lost items in the *MMPI–2* revision or that had not been subjected before to sufficiently close empirical scrutiny. The results of this reexamination are reported as a firm basis for clinical applications.

A second burden is to reframe clinical inferences within a framework of psychosocial crisis issues, thereby covering both positive personality attainments and psychopathology. To this end, applications are made here with *MMPI–2* of Erikson's (1963) perspectives on normative crises of the life cycle. The psychosocial framework is then interwoven with clusters of clinical and Content scales. The clusters, in turn, serve to describe the clinical state of the patient while defining those larger dynamic issues that need to be considered when formulating a plan of treatment.

Furthermore, patient responses to certain *MMPI–2* items require further direct inquiry. Critical inquiry methods are, therefore, presented and an inquiry instrument is provided. Some clinical situations call for administration of *Rorschach* psychodiagnostics together with *MMPI–2*. These applications, along with questions of when this may provide needed guidance, are considered.

Additionally, this clinical research program has, in certain respects, been a kind of salvage operation. It brings into focus older scales that are not typically scored from the *MMPI–2* record, it edits some frequently used scales to improve their reliability, it follows up on leads from Levitt's earlier work (1989; Levitt & Gotts, 1995) that were not adequately developed and tested, and it attempts by critical analysis to improve on important Validity scales. All of this work exposed measurement gaps that did not seem either inevitable or desirable. Accordingly, for example, scales have been developed that measure components of impulsivity. This book covers the status and properties of any new scales. An examination of the Restructured Clinical Scales (Tellegen et al., 2003), a radical and promising tool, justifies these efforts to improve on the uses of the *MMPI–2*.

ACKNOWLEDGMENTS

Thanks to the University of Minnesota Press for permission to refer by name to its copyrighted scales, to reproduce the *MMPI–2* acronym, and to make applications based on itemmetrics included in Appendix G of its manual. We thank Lawrence Erlbaum Associates for permission to use copyrighted material from Levitt (1989) and Levitt and Gotts (1995). Thanks to Dr. Kenneth B. Stein for permission to use the *TSC* cluster scales. Thanks to Dr. Jerry S. Wiggins, Dr. David Lachar, and the American Psychological Association for permission to update the Wiggins Content scales and to adapt interpretations of them.

Special thanks to the Madison State Hospital for continued support of this research program over a period of years by funding the stipends of summer students who performed research assistant duties. We are grateful for the insights of the many predoctoral psychology interns who, by using the content cluster approach during their training program at the Madison State Hospital, helped us to reach this point of presenting it to a broader audience in order that it may be further refined and improved on. We express our appreciation to the memory of Gene

Levitt, who accompanied us along another path that in the course of events branched to this one.

LOOKING AHEAD TO IMPLEMENTING CONTENT CLUSTER SCORING

The interested reader may be wondering how to use the many new and revised scales. Anticipating the need of potential users for help in implementing use of these scales, we have experimented over the past 3 years with computer scoring solutions. We have designed software solutions that will score the new and revised scales, make it possible to merge them with scores obtained from Pearson Assessments (formerly NCS) or from their hand scoring keys, arrange all scores in the content cluster arrays, display them in an easy-to-read profile format, and list, by critical inquiry groupings, the numbers of those items that invite further inquiry. As a follow-up to the publication of this book, we plan, by providing our scoring solutions, to support others who desire to implement a content cluster approach.

In order to begin use of the content cluster approach sooner, an interim arrangement is needed. So, those who wish to use the content cluster method are hereby authorized to prepare for their personal use hand scoring keys, based on Appendix A. This may be done for only those new scales that were developed during this research or for familiar scales that have changed scoring due to their revision. Hand scoring keys must not be made for those scales whose scoring is currently available through Pearson Assessments or other vendors.

For example, hand scoring keys may be prepared for the Psychosocial Development Scales and the Impulsivity Components Scales. They may not be made for those Harris–Lingoes scales that were unchanged by item analysis. The Harris–Lingoes scales *D4/2MD* and *D5/2B* are examples of scales whose scoring is unchanged and that thus may not be reproduced in this manner. Those who desire guidance in the mechanics of preparing hand scoring keys may direct their inquiries to P.O. Box 856, Madison, IN 47250-0856.

Edward E. Gotts, Ph.D.
Thomas E. Knudsen, Psy.D.

Guide to Scale Names Referenced in Text

Psychosocial Development Scales		
Abbrev	*Issue*	*Name*
Cared for vs. Neglected	Trust	Feels Cared for/Loved vs. Neglected/Disliked
Autonomous vs. Doubting	Autonomy	Autonomous/Self-Possessed vs. Self-Doubting/Shamed
Initiating vs. Guilt Prone	Initiative	Initiating/Pursuing vs. Regretful/Guilt-Prone
Industrious vs. Inadequate	Industry	Industrious/Capable vs. Inadequate/Inferior
Ego Identified vs. Confused	Identity	Life-Goal Oriented/Ego Identity Secure vs. Directionless/Confused
Involved vs. Disengaged	Intimacy	Socially Committed/Involved vs. Disengaged/Lonely

Impulsivity Components Scales		
Abbrev	*Cluster*[1]	*Name*
Imp-B	X	Behavioral Impulsivity
Imp-I	X	Ideational/Attitudinal Impulsivity
Imp-A	X	Affective Impulsivity
Imp-T	X	Impulsivity Total

Critical Inquiry Scales		
Abbrev	*Cluster*[1]	*Name*
NeurPsy	V, VI	Neuropsychological Signs
AA	X, XVIII	Addictive Activities
Suic-S	II, XVIII	Suicide Subtle
Suic-O	II, XVIII	Suicide Obvious
Suic-T	II, XVIII	Suicide Total
Panic	III, XVIII	Physiological Reactivity/Panic
Sadist	IX, XVIII	Sado-Masochistic Signs

Indiana Personality Disorder (PDO) Scales

Abbrev	Cluster[1]	Name
ANTI	XVII	Antisocial *PDO*
PRND	XVII	Paranoid *PDO*
NARC	XVII	Narcissistic *PDO*
HIST	XVII	Histrionic *PDO*
PAAG	XVII	Passive–Aggressive *PDO*
DPND	XVII	Dependent *PDO*
OBCP	XVII	Obsessive–Compulsive *PDO*
AVDT	XVII	Avoidant *PDO*
SCZY	XVII	Schizotypal *PDO*
SCZD	XVII	Schizoid *PDO*
Dist	XVII	Distress (*PDO* Disturbance)

Indiana Rational Scales

Abbrev	Cluster[1]	Name
I-RD	IV	Severe Reality Distortions
I-DS	IV, V	Dissociative Symptoms
I-OC	III	Obsessive–compulsiveness
I-Do	XVI	Dominance
I-De	XVI	Dependency
I-SC	VII	Poor Self-Concept
I-SP	XV	Sex Problems Inventory

Validity Scales Group

Abbrev	Cluster[1]	Name
L	I	Lie
F	I	Infrequency
F_B	I	Back F, Back Infrequency
Fp	I	Infrequency Psychopathology
K	I	Correction
VRIN	I	Variable Response Inconsistency
TRIN	I	True Response Inconsistency
TR-T	I	TRIN True
TR-F	I	TRIN False
TR-S	I	TRIN Sum
RCon1	I	Response Consistency 1st Half
RCon2	I	Response Consistency 2nd Half
RCon +	I	Self-Enhancing Consistency
RCon −	I	Self-Effacing Consistency
RIncon	I	Self-Inconsistent
ME	I	Mean Elevation
Sd	I	Social Desirability–Wiggins
So	I	Social Desirability–Edwards
ODecp	I	Other Deception
S	I	Superlative Self-Presentation
S1	I	Beliefs in Human Goodness

S2	I	Serenity
S3	I	Contentment with Life
S4	I	Patience and Denial of Irritability and Anger
S5	I	Denial of Moral Flaws
CLS	I	Carelessness
TR	I	Test–Retest

Tryon, Stein, and Chu (TSC) Cluster Scales

Abbrev	Cluster[1]	Name
TSC/A	V	Autism & Disruptive Thoughts
TSC/B	VI	Body Symptoms
TSC/D	II	Depression & Apathy
TSC/R	IX	Resentment
TSC/I	VIII	Social Introversion
TSC/S	IX	Suspicion & Mistrust
TSC/T	III	Tension, Worry, & Fear

MMPI–2 Basic Scales

Abbrev	Cluster[1]	Name
Hs or 1	VI	Hypochondriasis
D or 2	II	Depression
Hy or 3	XI	Conversion Hysteria
Pd or 4	X	Psychopathic Deviate
Mf or 5	XV	Masculinity–Femininity
Pa or 6	IV	Paranoia
Pt or 7	III	Psychasthenia
Sc or 8	IV	Schizophrenia
Ma or 9	XII	Hypomania
Si or 0	VIII	Social Introversion

Harris–Lingoes Subscales

Abbrev	Cluster[1]	Name
2SD, D1	II	Subjective Depression
2PR, D2	II, XII	Psychomotor Retardation & Suppressed Anger
2PM, D3	VI	Physical Malfunctioning
2MD, D4	II, V	Mental Dullness
2B, D5	II	Brooding
3DSA, Hy1	XI	Denial of Social Anxiety
3NA, Hy2	XI	Need for Affection
3LM, Hy3	II	Lassitude–Malaise
3SC, Hy4	VI	Somatic Complaints
3IA, Hy5	X	Inhibition of Aggression
4FD, Pd1	XIII	Family Discord
4AC, Pd2	XII	Authority Problems or Conflict
4SI, Pd3	VIII	Social Imperturbability
4SOA, Pd4	XIV	Social Alienation
4SA, Pd5	II, III	Self-Alienation

6PI, Pa1	IV	Persecutory Ideas
6P, Pa2	XIV	Poignancy, Social Vulnerability
6N, Pa3	XI	Naiveté
8SOA, Sc1	XIV	Social Alienation
8EA, Sc2	II	Emotional Alienation
8COG, Sc3	V	Lack of Ego Mastery, Cognitive
8CON, Sc4	XVIII	Lack of Ego Mastery, Conative
8DI, Sc5	X	Lack of Ego Mastery, Defective Inhibition
8BSE, Sc6	IV, V	Bizarre Sensory Experiences
9AMO, Ma1	X, XI	Amorality
9PMA, Ma2	XII	Psychomotor Acceleration
9IMP, Ma3	VIII	Imperturbability
9EI, Ma4	X	Ego Inflation

MMPI–2 Content Scales

Abbrev	*Cluster*[1]	*Name*
ANG	IX	Anger
ANX	III	Anxiety
ASP	X	Antisocial Practices
BIZ	IV	Bizarre Mentation
CYN	IX	Cynicism
DEP	II	Depression
FAM	XIII	Family Problems
FRS	III	Fears, Phobias
HEA	VI	Health Concerns
LSE	VII	Low Self-Esteem
OBS	III	Obsessiveness
SOD	VIII	Social Discomfort
TPA	IX, VI	Type A
TRT	XVIII	Negative Treatment Indicators
WRK	XVIII	Work Interference

Wiggins Content Scales

Abbrev	*Cluster*[1]	*Name*
W-AUT	X	Authority Conflict
W-DEP	II	Depression
W-FAM	XIII	Family Problems
W-FEM	XV	Feminine Interests
W-HYP	XII	Hypomania
W-HOS	IX	Manifest Hostility
W-ORG	VI, V	Organic Symptoms
W-PHO	III	Phobias
W-HEA	VI	Poor Health
W-MOR	VII	Poor Morale
W-PSY	IV	Psychoticism
W-SOC	VIII	Social Maladjustment

Other Individual Scales

Abbrev	Cluster[1]	Name
A	III	Anxiety Factor/Demoralization
APS	X	Addiction Potential Scale
Cn	XVIII	Control
5C	XI	Conventionality
RCd	I	Demoralization (RC1–4, 6–9, see Basic scales)
Depnd	XVI	Dependency/Self-Doubt
D-S	II	Depression, Subtle
Do	XVI	Dominance/Self-Confidence
Es	XVIII	Ego Strength
S+	IV	Extreme Suspiciousness
GF	XV	Gender Role–Feminine
GM	XV	Gender Role–Masculine
Ho	IX, VI	Hostility
Impert	VIII	Imperturbability/Denial of Social Anxiety
Sexual	XV	Sexuality/Intimacy Failure
MAC-R	X	MacAndrew Alcoholism Scale–Revised
O-H	IX	Overcontrolled Hostility
Pe	XV	Paraphilia/Pedophilia
PK	III	PTSD–Keane
PS	III	PTSD–Schlenger
R	X	Repression Factor/Suppression
Rage	IX	Psychogenic Rage Reaction
Si1	VIII	Shyness/Self-Consciousness
Si2	VIII	Social Avoidance
SoAlien	VIII	Social Alienation
Re	X	Social Responsibility
True	I	Total True Answers
Trust	XI	Trustworthy/Trusting

[1]Key to clusters appears in chapter 1.

1

A Content Cluster Approach to *MMPI–2* Interpretation

For some contemporary users, *MMPI–2* interpretation involves reviewing the patient score profile in conjunction with an expertly crafted, computer-generated report. The algorithms underlying interpretive reports variously draw on actuarially derived information. Other users begin with an extended profile of scores obtained either by computer scoring or hand scoring, after which they apply an interpretive strategy based on their training or on a defining text or both. Still others approach the task more or less intuitively, perhaps even idiosyncratically.

The content cluster approach was derived almost exclusively by study of an inpatient population that is typical in many ways of the severely and persistently mentally ill and/or chemically dependent patients encountered in state-supported care settings. Its application to patients from other settings may require retuning and adjustment.

A *cluster* refers to a group of scales that correlate more strongly with one another than they do with scales assigned to other clusters. Scales within a cluster also share content characteristics that make them recognizable as differing ways of measuring aspects of a common domain. Because the manifest content of many of their items tends toward being transparent, they may be subject to the influence of response styles. Nevertheless, Content scales contain other items that are less transparent and, consequently, less subject to response style influence.

Clusters in use draw on scales of diverse origin: standard clinical scales and new Content scales (Butcher et al., 1989); Indiana Rational Scales (Levitt, 1989); Tryon, Stein, and Chu Cluster Scales (Chu, 1966; Stein, 1968; Tryon, 1966); Wiggins Content Scales (Wiggins, 1966); Harris–Lingoes Subscales (Harris & Lingoes, 1968); Indiana Personality Disorder Scales (Levitt & Gotts, 1995); and a number of individual or stand-alone scales. In addition, clusters contain the fol-

1

lowing groupings of scales that make their initial appearance here: Impulsivity Components Scales and Critical Inquiry Scales. The Psychosocial Development Scales are of a different order, penetrating and permeating the content clusters.

Clusters are arranged and labeled in the following manner:

I.   Validity
II.   Depressive Spectrum Conditions
III.   Anxiety Spectrum Conditions
IV.   Thought Process Disorders
V.   Cognitive Disorders
VI.   Somatic Concerns
VII.   Self-Esteem
VIII.   Social Maladjustment & Social Anxiety
IX.   Anger, Hostility, Suspicion, Cynicism, Resentment
X.   Behavior Controls & Norms Violations
XI.   Virtue & Morality
XII.   Stimulus Seeking & Drive
XIII.   Family Relationship Issues
XIV.   Social Vulnerability & Alienation
XV.   Gender & Sexuality
XVI.   Dependency-Dominance
XVII.   Personality Disorders
XVIII.   Prognosis & Risk Management

The residues of past psychosocial crises appear in six new scales that reliably examine Erikson's (1963) psychosocial crises using *MMPI–2*:

Feels Cared for/Loved vs. Neglected/Disliked (*Cared for vs. Neglected*)
Autonomous/Self-Possessed vs. Self-Doubting/Shamed (*Autonomous vs. Doubting*)
Initiating/Pursuing vs. Regretful/Guilt-Prone (*Initiating vs. Guilt-Prone*)
Industrious/Capable vs. Inadequate/Inferior (*Industrious vs. Inadequate*)
Life-Goal Oriented/Ego Identity Secure vs. Directionless/Confused (*Ego Identified vs. Confused*)
Socially Committed/Involved vs. Disengaged/Lonely (*Involved vs. Disengaged*)

The Psychosocial scales are shown in later analyses to offer a latticelike framework within which to view the varieties of normality and psychopathology. In some instances, they may offer insights into the origins of particular disordered patterns of thinking, feeling, and behaving. Next, consider the research activities and results that support the foregoing assertions.

PREVIEWING UPCOMING CHAPTERS AND APPENDICES

Chapters 2–4 review the literature, including the interpretation of scales in isolation from one another. Chapters 5–7 present the methods used in the present study, scale updates and revisions, and new scales created for *MMPI–2*. Essential results of that work appear as Appendices A–C. Chapters 8–10 explore what is known clinically in terms of the psychosocial framework at its points of intersection with the content clusters. These latter chapters further expose limitations of the *DSM* approach vis-à-vis the *MMPI–2*. As a result, a selected subset of *DSM* findings for the database sample is set apart in Appendix D. Chapter 11 juxtaposes *Rorschach* findings with those available from *MMPI–2* and other data sources and identifies occasions when their conjoint use can clarify patient condition. Chapter 12 pulls into unified focus the pragmatics of applying the content cluster approach.

2

Assessing the Quality
of the Test Record:
The Validity and Response
Style Scales

The Validity scales are some of the best known and most widely used scales for the *MMPI–2*. Before a test profile is analyzed, the clinician uses the Validity scales to lay the foundation for building the psychological profile from the remaining clinical and special scales. The term *validity* is somewhat misleading. Validity in psychological testing refers to whether the tool measures what it claims to measure (Greene, 2000). The Validity scales on the *MMPI–2* capture the respondent's response style. These scales help the examiner to determine if the respondent exaggerated or underreported psychopathology, attempted to fake bad or fake good in the answers, or answered in an inconsistent or random manner. Many reasons exist for the myriad of response styles. A respondent could be trying to appear more pathological to receive disability compensation. In another scenario, respondents could attempt to minimize their pathology in a child custody evaluation to appear more stable and psychologically healthy. The Validity scales have become more than a measure of test accuracy. They provide useful clinical data on the individual respondent.

Hathaway and McKinley (1940) were aware that dissimulation might occur on a verbal inventory. They attempted to develop several validity indicators via internal measures that would point to an individual who was not responding honestly. Sixty years later, this approach is still being touted as one of the cornerstones of the *MMPI–2*. In fact, the Validity scales have become a powerful tool in diagnostic measurements. In a study by the American Psychological Association's Psychological Assessment Work Group (Meyer et al., 2001), effect sizes were compared between psychological assessments and medical assessments. The popular assumption would seem to be that medical tests would far outweigh the validity of psychological measures. However, this was shown to be untrue: The *MMPI–2*

Validity Scales demonstrated some of the largest discriminative abilities of the measures compared. The validity measures on the *MMPI–2* for identifying malingering of psychopathology produced an effect size of .74, whereas the effect size of an exercise electrocardiogram to diagnose coronary artery disease was only .58. Users of the *MMPI–2* can be confident of impressions formed based on the Validity scales in both the clinical and forensic settings.

This chapter overviews the traditional Validity scales: *L*, *F*, *K*, and Cannot Say (*?*). The Mean Elevation (*ME*) of the Clinical scales has had past use, but is not commonly used in modern validity profiles. It is updated here. The *MMPI–2* brought further improvements, including Variable Response Inconsistency (*VRIN*; Butcher et al., 1989), True Response Inconsistency (*TRIN*; Butcher et al., 1989), and Infrequency Back (*F_B*) for the second half of the questions (Butcher et al., 2001) and Infrequency-Psychopathology (*Fp*; Arbisi & Ben-Porath, 1995). Some older measures of response style are reexamined for their value along with more recent ones. These include the Wiggins (1959) Social Desirability Scale (*Sd*) and the Edwards (1957) Social Desirability Scale (*So*). New approaches to consistency measurement are treated at the end of this chapter.

TRADITIONAL VALIDITY MEASURES

Lie Scale (*L*)

The Lie (*L*) scale was constructed by the developer of the *MMPI* on a completely nonempirical, rational basis. It consists of 15 statements whose content is such that a truthful respondent has a high probability of responding "True" to any one of the statements. The intent of the *L* scale was that it should provide an index of the extent to which patients attempt to answer the *MMPI* items by selecting those responses that represent them most favorably to others (Hathaway & McKinley, 1951). However, the gambit is rather obvious to anyone with at least average intelligence and a somewhat developed amount of psychological mindedness. Normative studies have indicated that the average raw score is between 3 and 5 (Greene, 2000). The *L* scale is, however, not an effective measure for detecting underreporting of psychopathology in psychologically sophisticated persons.

An investigation by Lebovits and Ostfeld (1967) showed that *L* scale scores and educational level are negatively correlated. The same can be seen with respondents of lower socioeconomic (SES) status (W. G. Dahlstrom & Tellegen, 1993). The respondent from within a low SES and/or low education group may not be purposefully trying to falsify their scores when the *L* scale is elevated. Thus, interpretation must be formulated within its proper cultural context.

Interpretation of the *L* scale requires sensitivity to the assessment context in which it was given. Use of the *MMPI–2* is common for forensic reasons (e.g., child custody evaluations) or employment selection (e.g., airline pilots). These contexts promote elevated scores on the *L* scale (Friedman, Lewak, Nichols, & Webb, 2001). The response style in such circumstances is naturally self-enhancing. When respondents score low in these circumstances, interpretation needs to explore why they failed to present themselves more favorably.

Those with average educational backgrounds who have elevated *L* scale scores (> T70) in other than forensic and employment settings are most likely using a simplistic form of denial and lack psychological mindedness. These individuals may be highly conforming to social or religious norms, and lack insight. Other scales that may also be elevated include those that draw on histrionic or somatic symptoms (*TSC/B, 2PM, 3SC, HEA, W-ORG, 3DSA, 3NA, HIST*). A respondent with clearly paranoid ideation may also score high on the scale (Friedman et al., 2001; Greene, 2000).

In summary, an elevated score on the *L* scale can be seen as an accurate gauge of underreporting of psychopathology (Baer, Wetter, & Berry, 1992). That is only a preliminary conclusion. Careful examiners will seek to uncover reasons for underreporting within the context of SES, education, test setting, and those forms of psychopathology that favor perfectionism in self-presentation.

Low scores can also provide information concerning the test-taker's attitude. Low scorers may be trying to enlarge the picture of psychopathology for secondary gain (i.e., malingerers). However, interpretation of a low *L* score requires the joint use of the other scales of overreporting (high on *F*, F_B, & *Fp*, and low on *Sd* & *So*). Although the *L* scale is not a comprehensive measure of the *MMPI–2*'s validity or accuracy, it can offer useful information on respondents' general test-taking attitudes.

Infrequency Scale (*F*)

The *F* scale is composed of 60 items that evoked responses in the deviant direction by 10% or less of the segment of the Minnesota standardization sample that was collected prior to 1940. Like the *L* scale, the original authors' intent was to create a scale for validity of the record. A high score (> T70) indicated that other scales in the record were likely invalid. This could be because the patient was careless or had limited comprehension. It could also be due to clerical and processing errors. A low *F* score was originally viewed as indicating reliably that the respondent was behaving coherently relative to the items' obvious meaning (Hathaway & McKinley, 1951). The detection of overreporting or exaggeration of symptoms and distress (i.e., faking bad) was not originally mentioned as the purpose of the *F* scale. The scale's meaning has been clarified by years of research, the results of which suggest that this scale is more useful for the diagnosis of malingering and less for use as a general validity of the profile.

F scale items represent a wide range of clear and obvious content. It follows that a circumscribed tendency or pattern by a respondent would not necessarily result in a scale elevation (Meehl & Hathaway, 1946). The obviousness of the item content allows perceptive respondents to easily change their score if desired (Greene, 2000). Thirteen items deal with hallucinations and delusions. Fifteen are found on Scale *8*; 6 on Scale *6*; and 10 on the *I-RD* scale (see chap. 6). The correlations between the *F* scale and Scales *6*, *7*, and *8* are substantial (W. G. Dahlstrom, Welsh, & L. E. Dahlstrom, 1975). Consequently, elevated scores on the *F* scale correlate with elevations of the Clinical scales.

Hathaway and McKinley's original cutoff score of T70 does not fare well in light of the many investigations demonstrating that elevated *F* scale scores are often obtained by individuals with severe mental illness (Friedman et al., 2001; Greene, 2000). An elevated *F* scale, therefore, could be the respondent's accurate description of their own psychopathology. This relation is not specific only to psychotic disorders, but also holds for characterological and behavioral problems. Treating clinicians should seek respondents who have moderate to moderately high elevations (T59–T80) on the *F* scale as indications both of overall level of psychopathology and of respondents' awareness of such (Graham, 2000). In a meta-analysis by Berry, Baer, and Harris (1991), 28 studies were examined that used the *F* scale as an indicator of malingering. The result suggested that the *F* scale was clearly able to catch the malingering respondent. Friedman et al. (2001) added the precaution that all measures of overreporting of psychopathology need to be understood before assigning a diagnosis of malingering.

Differences in *F* scale scores have been found with African American respondents, depending on geographic location (Gynther, Lachar, & W. G. Dahlstrom, 1978). The Gynther group developed a more culturally sensitive *F* scale, but little research has been done in support of this venture. Greene (2000) offered an extensive discussion of the effects on demographics on *MMPI-2* scores. This excellent discussion should be referenced when using the *MMPI-2* with ethnic minorities.

In conclusion, it is difficult to specifically provide a cutoff score on the *F* scale that may indicate an invalid test due to the myriad of reasons the *F* scale could be elevated. The scale appears to be a strong measure of response style and respondent attitude. Low scores (< T45) may indicate a denial of problems or difficulties. Moderate to moderately high elevations (T59–T80) can suggest a "cry for help" and need for supportive and therapeutic interventions. Even at marked elevations (e.g., > T80), the *F* scale provides information on either malingering or extreme psychopathology when there is no motivation for malingering.

Correction or *K* Scale

The original purpose of the *K* scale was to identify the presence of a defensive style that resists admitting psychological weakness. Its developers viewed elevated *K* as suggesting a deliberate kind of distortion that is intended to make the person seem normal (Hathaway & McKinley, 1951).

The selection of *K* items was based essentially on a group of 50 psychiatric inpatients, all of whom obtained *MMPI* Clinical Scale profiles (uncorrected by *K*, of course) that had no scale above a *T*-score of 70. A second qualification was that each had an *L* scale *T*-score of at least 60. The perspective taken was that such individuals, who were identified as seriously ill by reason of hospitalization, were evidencing defensiveness by producing low ranging *MMPI* records. With some additional corrections, the result was a 30-item scale that measures subtle forms of defensiveness.

Meehl and Hathaway (1946) sought to reduce the number of false negatives in the profile by correcting the Clinical relative to the *K* scale. Their goal was to accentuate the discriminate ability of the Clinical scales with their respective criterion groups. They examined how the *K* scale can affect certain Clinical scales. The result was their assignment of specific proportions of the *K* scale to be added to the raw score of the Clinical scale before the *T*-score conversion. This became known as the *K*-correction.

Unfortunately, the *K*-correction does not have research supporting its use in this way (Friedman et al., 2001; Graham, 2000; Greene, 2000). The research results have been mixed at best, with many studies suggesting that *K*-correction does little to improve the diagnostic acuity of the *MMPI–2*. Greene cautioned about use of *K*-corrected scales in clinical settings and suggested an all out dismissal of its use when working with normal groups. However, clinical users have acquired the habit of using the *K*-correction because much of the clinical data generated from *T*-scores is based on *K*-corrected Clinical scale scores. Thus, not using the corrections may lead to inappropriate projections from the clinical scores. In the face of this unsupported practice, clinicians should plot both corrected and noncorrected Clinical scale scores in order to evaluate the extent to which the *T*-scores are caused by scale item content versus the *K*-correction (Greene, 2000).

Further research into the *K* scale suggests that it is more a measure of coping skills, adjustment, and overall stability of the personality (Heilbrun, 1961). This seems to be contrary to the original intention. Denial, like other defense mechanisms, can exist on a pathological level, but it can also be an adaptive strategy. Indeed, denial is probably the most common defense mechanism used by normal people (Levitt, 1980b). Is the high *K* scorer deliberately concealing psychopathology or is the individual more free of symptoms? It depends. As Greene (2000) suggested, the *K* scale measures normality among normal persons and defensiveness among the maladjusted. The distinction is appealing, but it has little empirical backing. In any event, the population to which the respondent belongs is often unknown. Indeed, the very purpose of the administration of the *MMPI–2* may be to determine the population to which the respondent belongs.

Thus, moderately high scorers (T65–T80) can easily be seen as those who show more sophisticated defenses and may be members of high standing in their respective communities. These respondents exert a high level of defensiveness as a means of maintaining a sense of self and importance (Butcher et al., 2001). Extremely high respondents on the K scale (> T80) may be deemed as those individuals who take a more defensive stance and refuse to admit to any difficulty in their life (Friedman et al., 2001).

Respondents who score low on the K scale may be exhibiting very low coping skills and expressing a high level of stress. Further inquiry is necessary to determine if these respondents are exaggerating their problems for secondary gain. In studies by Graham, Watts, and Timbrook (1991) and Wetter, Baer, Berry, Smith, and Larson (1992), respondents with clear psychiatric disorders actually scored higher on the K scale than normal respondents who attempted to falsify their responses by simulating pathology. Low and extremely low scores should be treated with caution and interpreted in the context of respondents' clinical interviews and backgrounds. The *F–K Index* (Gough, 1950) adds nothing.

Cannot Say (*?*)

When measurement requires that the subject respond true or false to a fixed number of items, common sense suggests that the accuracy of assessment depends on how many are actually answered. Accuracy will be impaired if the person fails to respond to some number of items. The number of items to which the subject failed to respond is usually represented by using the question mark (*?*). The *MMPI*'s creators recognized early in the test's development that this datum could be used to evaluate the validity of a test record. Deciding how much damage has resulted from omitted items, however, is no simple matter.

The concept itself was obviously incontestable. But, the number of omitted items that would invalidate a record completely was unknown, and Hathaway and McKinley (1940) did not have an empirical method for making this determination. The use of *T*-scores made no sense. The Minnesota normative sample omitted a mean of 2.83 items with a standard deviation of 1.5. The omission of a little more than 0.5% of the inventory's items would hardly seem to invalidate a record. Instead, Hathaway and McKinley suggested quite arbitrarily that omissions exceeding 30 should be viewed with suspicion. A fair amount of evidence shows that, except for a population defined by serious deficiency in reading comprehension or by intellectual deficit, no group averages more than 5 omissions.

A study of Clopton and Neuringer (1977) assessed the impact of omitted items on high-point codes. They found that a little more than 25% of code types were altered by the omission of 30 items. Looking at the other side, more than 40% of the high-point codes were unchanged by the omission of as many as 120 items. The applied significance of this study is unclear but, in any event, it has no practical relevance for the clinician who is diagnosing with special scales rather than Clinical scales.

Invalidity due to item omissions is not a serious problem for *MMPI–2* clinicians as long as they remain aware of the impact of comprehension on test validity. Butcher et al. (1989) recommended an eighth-grade reading level and Butcher et al. (2001) indicated a sixth-grade reading level as a requirement for completing the *MMPI–2* validly. Among those with no intellectual limitations, clinical experience indicates that less than 1 in 20 will have as many as 10 or more omissions.

Relatively more ambiguous items and those with higher lexiles (see *MMPI–2 Manual*, Appendix G) may be omitted because of the comprehension problems that they present. Moreover, if the patient has no experience with the area covered by the item's content or has no opinion when one is requested, then further omissions may occur. Occasionally, items are inadvertently omitted. Clinicians who review the answer form for omissions find that patients usually comply when asked to go back and complete them.

Certainly records are affected by omitted items, but they are almost never totally invalidated. Any scale that is elevated despite omissions is, for that reason, all the more significant. It is more important for the clinician to know which, rather than how many, items have been omitted. Any remaining omissions should be reviewed to determine if they represent a focal area that the patient is avoiding. A cluster of omitted items dealing with the same matter, such as family problems or antisocial behavior, has evident clinical significance.

NEWER VALIDITY MEASURES OF OVERREPORTING

Back Infrequency (F_B)

The F_B scale was developed in the same manner as the F scale, but with the items drawn from the latter half of the *MMPI–2* booklet. The new Content scales and many other special scales use items from the complete item pool. Consequently, the F_B can be a valuable tool in the interpretation of these scales.

Although F and F_B are similar in design, the differences are worth noting (Greene, 2000). Both scales were developed to be composed of items that the normative sample endorsed only 10% of the time. The F_B scale used the normative sample from the *MMPI–2* development. What occurred is that the modern sample endorsed more than 10% of some F items. Thus, the F_B is composed of items endorsed less frequently than the F scale (Arbisi & Ben-Porath, 1995). The content of the F scale taps atypical and bizarre experiences that can include psychoticism. The content of the F_B scale contains more depression and hopelessness items (Nichols & Greene, 1995). It also includes items that ask about suicidal ideation, chemical abuse and dependency, and significant relationship problems.

Interestingly, the F_B scale may be more elevated than the F scale within an individual record. The reasons for this event are varied. It may simply be due to fatigue from the test-taking process (Friedman et al., 2001). Alternatively, respondents may become more comfortable and less defensive with their later responses. Respondents who are more depressed than psychotic or hysterical may in fact produce a valid protocol with the F_B scale being higher than the F scale due to endorsement of different item content that is more prevalent in the second half of the test. However, extreme differences could possibly mean there is random or malingered responding in the latter half of the test. Thus, if this problem is verified, then Content and other special scales that draw from the latter half will need to be interpreted with caution. In turn, if F_B is in a valid range with a significant elevation on the F scale, then the Clinical and the Harris and Lingoes Subscales will require more cautious interpretation. Those Content and special scales whose items appear primarily in the back of the test can possibly be interpreted with greater confidence.

Greene (2000) advocated the use of the absolute value of the differences between the two Validity scales as a tool for determining consistency in the response style. Even though the F and F_B scales are measures of infrequency of endorsement, the comparison allows the clinician to see the consistency through the entire test. Greene extensively studied the difference index $(F - F_B)$ and reviewed the literature on this matter. He concluded that $(F - F_B)$ would be most useful if it were used in conjunction with $VRIN$, F, and F_B in those cases when they fail to deliver a clear answer about the consistency of item responding. An alternative approach to using the $F - F_B$ index is discussed in terms of Response Consistency Pairs (*RconPr*) at the end of this chapter.

Similar to the use of the F scale in identifying overreporting of symptoms, the F_B scale has shown efficacy with this as well (Wetter, Baer, Berry, Robison, & Sumpter, 1993). The F_B is a relatively new scale that appears to show excellent stability and interpretative power. However, research has not yet concluded what are appropriate cutoff scores for interpretation. The general consensus is to use the same cutoff scores as for the F scale (Friedman et al., 2001; Graham, 2000; Greene, 2000). Unfortunately, as discussed earlier, the F scale cutoff scores are rather indeterminate as well and must be adjusted to setting (Butcher et al., 2001).

Infrequency Psychopathology (*Fp*)

As mentioned previously, an elevated F or F_B scale may not be due to overreporting of psychopathology but instead to actual psychological distress experienced by the respondent. Thus, to aid in better identifying overreporting symptoms, Arbisi and Ben-Porath (1995) developed a scale of 27 items that were infrequently endorsed by psychiatric inpatients. Items on the F and F_B scales were endorsed about 10% or less of the time in the normative sample, whereas items on the Fp scale were endorsed under 20% of the time by the normative sample and by two large psychiatric inpatient samples. In theory, elevated F and F_B scores can be attributed to true psychopathology when the Fp score is below a T-score of 100. On the other hand, when Fp is elevated along with F and F_B, the clinician needs to evaluate the possibility that malingering or overreporting of psychopathology is present.

This is a young scale that shows some potential. Unlike the *F* scale, it traverses all the *MMPI–2* items. Arbisi, McNulty, Ben-Porath, and Boyd (1999) suggested dividing the *Fp* scale into a front and back to allow for comparison similar to that of *F* and F_B. Furthermore, elevations in either *F* or F_B could then be compared to either *Fp-1 or Fp-2*, respectively, to help better differentiate malingering from expressions of true pathology.

Another property of the *Fp* scale is that it has heterogeneity of item content reflecting many different pathological symptoms. Interestingly, the diagnosis of the respondents did not appear to affect scores on the *Fp* scale (Arbisi & Ben-Porath, 1997). A study by Ladd (1998) demonstrated that respondents with antisocial behavior or drug dependency did not elevate the *Fp* scale. Thus, the scale may be useful in these types of settings without it being artificially elevated. Accordingly, Friedman et al. (2001) made the important suggestion that the content of endorsed *Fp* items should be examined during the process of deciding if symptom exaggeration is present.

RESPONSE CONSISTENCY–INCONSISTENCY

Much early work on the Validity scales concerned itself primarily with the issues of over- and underreporting of psychopathology (i.e., *F*, *L*, and *K*). Yet, for many years, the occurrence of inconsistent responding also was thought to be a major source of invalidity (Buechley & Ball, 1952). Levitt and Gotts (1995) addressed inconsistency by using the Carelessness (*CLS*) scale (Greene, 1978) and Test–Retest (*TR*), a scale based on the 16 pairs of item duplicates in *MMPI* (Buechley & Ball, 1952). These two scales are discussed briefly next in order to clarify how they were designed as a means of detecting inconsistency.

Test–Retest (*TR*)

One of the original attempts at measuring inconsistent responding was the Test–Retest (*TR*) scale for the *MMPI*. *TR* was an unplanned possibility. It came about when the *MMPI* card form was superseded by the group booklet form. With this change, machine scoring also was introduced. In order to facilitate alignment of the answer forms for machine scoring, 16 duplicate items were added, bringing *MMPI* to 566 items. This addition had no other purpose originally. Interestingly, when the 16 items were no longer necessary for machine scoring, the 566-item form persisted.

Buechley and Ball (1952) recognized the possibility inherent in the 16 pairs of duplicate items relative to assessing response consistency. They then scored the duplicated items for response inconsistency as a way of checking on the validity of the record. They assumed that, in a valid record, each item of a pair would be answered identically. To the extent that responses to identical items were not the same across the pairs, invalidity was suggested. *TR* ceased to exist when *MMPI–2* dropped the repeated items in the interest of adding new items.

Carelessness (*CLS*)

Greene (1978) devised the Carelessness (*CLS*) scale as a validity indicator that consisted of 12 item pairs. Seven of the pairs should be answered in the same direction on logical grounds and 5 should be answered in an opposite direction. For example, thoughtful, clear-minded individuals should respond to an item in a certain way that suggests dysphoric mood, and they should respond in the opposite way to a paired item that suggests euphoria or happiness. The *CLS* scale lost *MMPI* items 63 and 425 in the test's revision, reducing it from 12 to 10 pairs. *CLS* is replaced in current usage by *VRIN*, which follows a similar logic-based scoring rationale.

Variable Response Inconsistency (*VRIN*) Scale

Fortunately, Butcher et al. (1989, 2001) developed alternative scales when *TR* and *CLS* became unavailable. One of these was *VRIN*. The *VRIN* scale is composed of 67 pairs and resembles in construction the earlier *CLS* (Greene, 1978) scale. Each *VRIN* pair presents a logical-semantic content linkage between two items. These items thus gauge responses to be consistent if answers to the pair are congruent with the logical content or semantic linkage. When the answers fail to match, responses to the pair are coded as inconsistent and one raw score point is added to *VRIN* (Butcher et al., 2001). Consequently, as the *VRIN* raw score increases, the profile begins to appear inconsistent.

   VRIN was developed based on the scoring direction of the *MMPI–2* normative sample. Thus, there may be other logically or semantically paired items for which there could be contradictory responses. If these exist, then the pairs did not become part of the *VRIN* scale (Friedman et al., 2001). There could be several reasons for an inconsistent response style: confusion, poor reading ability or verbal comprehension, and carelessness. In some instances, however, pairs may be answered inconsistently but accurately based on detailed semantic distinctions made by respondents. Nevertheless, the total number of pairs judged inconsistent in such cases usually will be small and will not result in false positives for inconsistent responding.

   A number of studies have demonstrated the value of the *VRIN* scale for recognizing inconsistent responding on the *MMPI–2* (Berry, Wetter et al., 1991; Berry et al., 1992; Gallen & Berry, 1996; Wetter et al., 1992). The *VRIN* appears superior to the *CLS* based on its greater length (i.e., 67 item pairs vs. only 10 remaining on the *CLS*). Thus, the *VRIN* scale is useful in determining whether the patient has responded to the 567 questions in a consistent manner.

VRIN also helps in determining the reason for a high *F* scale. As reviewed be-fore, all of the infrequency scales (*F*, F_B, *Fp*) can be elevated with inconsistent re-sponding. Consequently, if the *VRIN* scale is normal and the infrequency scales are elevated, then the clinician could conclude that the elevations are not due to inconsistent set. However, if *VRIN* is elevated (> T85) along with the infrequency scales, then the likelihood of an invalid protocol due to inconsistent or random re-sponding is very high. In these cases, the clinician can use this data to further eval-uate whether or not there is confusion, cognitive or learning difficulties, or possi-bly noncompliance in following directions on the part of the respondent. Transcribing and hand scoring VRIN's 67 item pairs is time consuming and sub-ject to errors, so machine scoring is advised.

True Response Inconsistency (*TRIN*)

TRIN is another scale aimed at measuring inconsistency in the protocol and, fur-ther, detecting a proclivity to respond either True or False (Butcher et al., 2001). The 23 pairings that comprise the scale are scored only if the respondent answered both members of a pair in the same keyed direction. Each item of a pair is similar in content. Items within each pair are phrased to be answered in opposite direc-tions for consistency. For example, one hypothetical item might say, "I see my doctor often," and its paired item might then say, "I seldom see my physician." Thus, this would signify inconsistent responding if both are answered either True or False. Other pairings are scored only unidirectionally (i.e., they count only if either both are answered True or only if both are answered False).

When scoring *TRIN*, one point is added to the raw score for each True response pair. One point is subtracted for each False response pair. Three of the pairs are scored for both True–True and False–False, whereas the rest of the pairs are scored for only one of these possibilities. Thus, although there are 23 pairings, these are comprised of only 20 different pairs of items. After obtaining the alge-braic sum for the 23 pairings, 9 points are added to the raw score to eliminate the possibility of assigning a minus value score. Raw scores of less than 9 suggest that the respondent was prone to answer in an inconsistent False direction, whereas re-spondents with raw scores above 9 tended to answer True inconsistently. More-over, conversion of the resulting raw score to a *T*-score is confusing. There is no score below T50. Thus, raw scores below 9 would have an inverse effect on the *T*-score (the smaller the raw score, the higher the *T*-score). Raw scores above 9 would use the traditional linear *T* formula. Therefore, because of its complexity, transcribing and scoring *TRIN* by hand is not recommended.

Research on *TRIN* is needed to justify its use in determining the consistency and validity of an *MMPI–2* protocol. In fact, the current research project has raised important questions about the manner in which *TRIN* combines True and False pairings. Findings reported in chapter 7 (see discussion titled "Exploring *TRIN*'s Composition") suggest that only *TRIN*'s True pairings are reliable and that combining them with the False pairings actually decreases the reliability of *TRIN*. See Appendix B for reliabilities of *TRIN* components. The present work may stimulate further study of *TRIN*. Much more is needed.

Combining Validity Measures: The *AdjAll* Variable

TRIN, *VRIN*, *F*, F_B, and Mean Elevation (*ME*; see discussion of *ME* in next section) serve the purposes of evaluating either the consistency or the overreporting of psychopathology. It may thus be convenient for some purposes to consolidate them into a single index. A method was developed for combining these (chap. 6) in an index that was called Adjusts All (*AdjAll*). Because of subtle nuances that should be considered in the application of *L* and *K*, they were not included.

REVIVAL OF OLDER VALIDITY MEASURES

Mean Elevation (*ME*)

One of the early research reports on the *MMPI* (Modlin, 1947) suggested that the average elevation of the nine scales then in existence (including Scale *5*, but not Scale *0*) could be used as a rough index of psychopathology. Modlin believed that an average elevation of T70 or above (uncorrected for *K*, which was not proposed as a correction until 1948) indicated "major pathology."

No one appears to have taken seriously Modlin's notion that an agglomeration of *MMPI* Clinical Scales scores might be used as a screening index, and its use as a general index is infrequently reported (e.g., Cernovsky, 1986). The nature of the faking bad profile does, however, suggest a potential use for the average elevation of the Clinical scales (*ME*). Because Scales *5* and *0* are most often uninvolved in the faking bad tactic, the diagnostic capacity of *ME* is sharpened by basing it on the remaining eight scales (i.e., the Clinical scales).

It is generally agreed that the vast majority of *MMPI–2* clinical profiles can be classified as having a high-point pair or high-point code, in the conventional parlance. For a discussion of this connection, see Friedman et al. (2001, chap. 6) and Greene (2000, chap. 7). In the psychiatric patient, the high points may be expected to exceed T70. Other scales' elevations might reasonably range from T55 to T69. In a large majority or records, this distribution would yield an *ME* below T70. For example, two scales at T75, four scales at T65, and two at T60 would produce an *ME* of 66. Even if the high-point pair were at T80, *ME* would be below 68.

However, it is difficult to attain an *ME* of 75 without diffuse elevation of the Clinical scales. For example, even if the high-point pair were at T90, the remaining scales would have to average T70 in order to produce a *ME* of T75. Even with three scales at T90, the remaining scales would need to average T66. With three scales at T80, the remaining scales must average T72 in order to yield an *ME* of T75. These combinations illustrate how unlikely *ME* is to be T75.

Two diagnoses are suggested by a record with an *ME* of T75 for *K*-corrected profiles for T70 for uncorrected profiles: an acute psychotic episode, a condition so obvious that psychological evaluation is rarely called for; and Borderline Personality Disorder (Levitt & Gotts, 1995). Clinical experience dictates that, more often, such profiles are a consequence of confusion, inadequate reasoning, poor comprehension, or a faking bad response set.

For comparative purposes, approximate *ME* scores for *K*-corrected fake bad records are: females, 93.50; and males, T90.50. Right-sided elevation of fake bad profiles is prominent. The nature of the response set will be obvious to the examiner. Randomly marked records have *ME* for females of about 74.50 and for males of about 76.50. Again right-sided elevation surpasses that on the left. These also will be easily detected by their failure to match known patient characteristics based on other data. Simple visual inspection identifies both all True and all False response records. Even though the all True records are less elevated (females, 69.50; males, 72.00), great disparities appear in profile slope with the right side towering above the left. Next to fake bad records, all False records are the most elevated (females, 81.50; males, 83.50), with the left side of the profile being more elevated. All approximations are based on interpolated readings of Graham's (1990) graphic representations. These estimates show that the *ME* scale readily identifies nearly all of the bogus records, except for those with all True responses. The *True* responses variable used in the present clinical research can be used to bypass the wasted effort of profiling all True and all False profiles. Current clinical research findings on the *ME* scale appear in chapter 6.

Wiggins Social Desirability (*Sd*)

Wiggins (1959) developed a 40-item scale to measure respondents' efforts to present themselves in a socially desirable manner. The scale was empirically derived from a sample of college students who were asked to answer the protocol in a socially desirable manner. The results were compared with a control group and the items that were able to discriminate the two became the *Sd* scale.

Recently, several studies have established validity for the use of the *Sd* scale. Baer, Wetter, Nichols, Greene, and Berry (1995) determined that the Wiggins Social Desirability Scale added to the validity outcome for identifying underreporters of psychopathology. In fact, when used along with the Superlative Scale (Butcher & Han, 1995), it may be superior to *L* and *K* for this purpose. In a later study, Bagby, Nicholson, Buis, Radovanovic, and Fidler (1999) concluded that this was also true in family custody and access evaluations. Bagby et al. (1997)

found that *Sd* appeared to be more appropriately used with normal than with clinical populations.

High scorers tend to endorse positive attributes rather than suppressing pathology (Friedman et al., 2001). They are more conventional and seem to think that they are more virtuous and moral than others. Scores above T65 should be considered as an alert to underreporting of pathology. The *Sd* scale should be compared with other Validity scales to establish a complete picture. Low *K* scores with elevated *L* and a high *Sd* increases the likelihood that this person is trying to appear desirable and appealing, and that remaining scales should be interpreted in this light. However, high *K* scores with a low *Sd* and *L* may indicate an educated person with strong coping skills who is not attempting to underreport pathology.

Thirty-three *Sd* items remained after the *MMPI–2* revision. As a result of the present research, only 20 of the 33 were retained following item analysis (Appendix A). The 20- and 33-item versions correlated .88 with each other for both females and males. The revised *Sd* scale shares 6 items with *L* and 3 with the *S* scale. More tellingly, all of its remaining 20 items are found in the Other Deception (*Odecp*) scale (Nichols & Greene, 1991). Four of the items that were rejected by item analysis (133, 194, 356, all coded True; 232 coded False) also appear in *Odecp*, in which all of them except Item 194 also were noncontributory to that scale's reliability among this patient sample. *Odecp* contains bolder, cheekier self-attributions (e.g., Items 239, 261, and 350) and does a thorough job of denying worry. The revised *Sd*'s items convey the somewhat less forceful, more socially conforming and conventional aspects of *Odecp*'s item pool.

Edwards Social Desirability (*So*)

A. L. Edwards (1957) established a 39-item scale based on expert judges unanimously agreeing on socially desirable responses on the *MMPI*. Edwards was more statistician than a clinician and used his scale to understand social desirability theory in personality testing. A. L. Edwards and L. K. Edwards (1992) completed factor analysis on the basis of which they confirmed that the Edwards Social Desirability Scale loaded strongly and negatively on the first factor of the *MMPI*. That is, it was located at the pole of the factor opposite to A. They concluded that much of the variability on the *MMPI* and personality scales, in general, boils down to presentation of social desirability. Although this conclusion is not widely accepted, *So* adds anchoring focus to the Validity scale cluster for *MMPI–2*.

Bagby et al. (1997) examined many scales that identify underreporting of psychopathology and compared the advantages of each. In a sense, like *Sd*, *So* measures the respondents' attempts to appear less pathological and more socially acceptable. They differ, however, in that *Sd* aligns more positively with the scales *L* and *Odecp* (of which revised *Sd* is a subset—see preceding section), whereas *So* relates more positively to K, Es, and S, and negatively to the A factor. These, thus, form two social desirability responding subsets that are believed to affect under-reporting by different processes: a more intentional one in the case of Sd that serves the interest of impression management and a more automatic one in the case of So that Paulhus (1984, 1986) identified with self-deception. This distinction is usefully discussed by Friedman et al. (2001). The discriminative ability of this scale in more normal populations suggests that it can be useful when working on forensic or placement issues with individuals who have had some treatment history but are not manifesting major forms of psychopathology.

Dominance (*Do*)

In an effort to capture certain positive traits of *MMPI* respondents, Gough, McClosky, and Meehl (1951) brought together 60 items that appeared to isolate the traits of someone who is self-confident, assertive, and exercises leadership. The items were based on the response patterns of high school and college age subjects identified by their peers as either exhibiting these qualities or lacking them. Only 28 of these 60 items were on the original *MMPI*, with only 25 surviving the *MMPI-2* revision that now comprises the Dominance scale.

The scale draws items from only a few other scales, possibly because it is a scale of positive rather than pathological traits. Many of the shared items are scored in the opposite direction. Most items scored are in the false direction, thus if *TRIN* indicates a false proclivity, the *Do* scale may be inflated (Greene, 2000).

There is limited research with the *Do* scale, especially in the clinical population. This current research project appears to be the most extensive with a patient population. However, Hedayat and Kelly (1994) studied the scale with a patient population and claimed that the Do scale was useful to identify those patients more likely for independent living. It is surprising that this study has not been replicated or expanded on. A scale that could be an objective source to aid in placement of patients would seem to be a valuable money and resource saving tool.

In nonpatient populations, few studies have been conducted to clarify the validity of the Dominance scale. Knapp (1960) used the scale for military personnel. This study concluded that officers had higher scores than enlisted personnel, which is consistent with the original authors' intentions. Conversely, Olmsted and Monachesi (1956) were unable to find differences between firefighter captains and other lower ranking firefighters. Clearly, the *Do* scale could benefit from more research to help establish its usefulness.

Using the Gough et al. (1951) definition for the scale, high scorers would be individuals who display self-assurance and leadership qualities. These individuals appeared to be confident in their own abilities and this confidence is reciprocated by peers. In addition, high scorers may be more successful in leadership positions. For psychiatric patients, they may be more successful at independent living. Low scorers, by theory, may appear more dependent and less confident. They may be more like followers than leaders and do better if they have authorities make decisions for them.

This scale can also be a powerful tool to look for convergent and divergent data when used with K, Es, $Depnd$, and Dependent PDO. When a respondent scores high on the K scale with $TRIN$ appearing normal, an elevated Do would suggest that this profile was due to the respondent's sense of self-assurance and confidence rather than a faking good or a defensive stance. Furthermore, low Do and Es, along with high $Depnd$ and Dependent PDO, scores would paint a picture of a dependent style lacking in confidence. The current item analysis substantially shortened this scale (Appendix A), while making it more reliable (Appendix B).

A NEW APPROACH: RESPONSE CONSISTENCY PAIRS ($RConPr$)

The Response Consistency Pairs (chap. 7 & Appendix A) were developed in the current research program as complements to $VRIN$. Second, they provide tools for comparing response consistency between the first and second halves of the $MMPI–2$. That is, they represent an alternative approach to studying what is presently defined empirically by the difference between F and F_B ($F - F_B$). Third, they are used to unravel the contributions of various components of TRIN to that scale's reliability (chap. 7 & Appendix B).

The 43 Response Consistency Pairs are combined in various ways that result in five different consistency scales whose compositions and reliabilities are reported. Three of the five scales employ the items arranged in pairs that index response consistency for self-enhancement ($RCon+$), self-effacing tendency ($RCon-$), and inconsistency ($RIncon$). The structural basis for these pairings differs from that used for $VRIN$, enabling study of these differing approaches. The same three scales support a conceptual reexamination of components of $TRIN$. Two of the scales derived from these items represent the individual halves of $MMPI–2$: first half ($RCon1$) and second half ($RCon2$). The difference between them ($RCon1 - Rcon2$) parallels the goal of the index $F - F_B$, but it arrives there by a different route. Thus, new windows are opened on the issue of inconsistency.

$VRIN$ is strong in the logical-semantic connection between items in each pair. By contrast, Response Consistency Pairs lack a similarly strong inherent logical connection, although they do share a content connection. On the other hand, each Response Consistency item of a pair is well balanced probabilistically with the pair's other item in terms of their respective favorabilities. The pairs of $VRIN$ are not well balanced in this regard. Thus, responses to $VRIN$ items may at times appear inconsistent only because of the greater extremity or polarity of one item or the other in a pair. The complementarity of the two approaches thus derives from the differing bases of their construction (i.e., a logical and semantic basis in the case of $VRIN$, and a probabilistic one for Response Consistency Pairs). Ultimately, both of these kinds of pairings may offer certain advantages for evaluating the consistency of a record.

THE VALIDITY STORY IN REVIEW

Early *MMPI* users were aware of the Cannot Say item count as a means of evaluating the completeness of the record. They further had a reasonably effective measure of validity relative to overreporting of psychopathology in the form of the *F* scale. Although Modlin (1947) suggested Mean Elevation as another useful indicator of overreporting, the *ME* was never widely used. However, the Gough (1950) *F–K* Dissimulation Index became more widely adopted, even though it has been shown that *F* alone is equally, or more, effective than the *F–K* Dissimulation Index.

The *K* scale addressed underreporting for selected scales, but was never adequately validated for that purpose. *L* was also available. Other early scales were potential candidates for assessing underreporting, for example, Barron's (1953) Ego Strength and the Gough et al. (1951) Dominance Scale. These, however, were mainly used to measure personality traits—certainly a valid application but one that ignored their other possibilities. Both A. L. Edwards' (1957) and Wiggins' (1959) Social Desirability Scales received considerably more attention, but failed to permeate clinical practice, which continued to use *L, K,* and the *LFK* profile.

The situation regarding response consistency–inconsistency was the least satisfactory. It was virtually ignored. When the scoring of *TR* as an index of inconsistency became possible, Buechley and Ball (1952) demonstrated its practical feasibility. It was adopted 20 years later by W. G. Dahlstrom, Welsh, and L. E. Dahlstrom (1972) in the *MMPI Handbook*'s revised edition. Thereafter, it was used at clinicians' discretion, but its use did not become a standard assessment practice. Greene's (1978) Carelessness Scale was introduced somewhat later and appears, from its use in published studies, to have gained wider acceptance. Once again, however, its use did not become a standard assessment practice.

The scene now jumps to 1989 and the introduction of *MMPI–2.* Cannot say, *L, F, K,* and (*F – K*) continued to be standards in the sense that they were featured in the body of the new *MMPI–2 Manual.* Other assessment standards were in effect created by the inclusion there of the new scales F_B, *VRIN, TRIN,* plus the recommendation that discrepancies between *F* and F_B be viewed as evidence of another kind of response inconsistency.

Subsequent to *MMPI–2*'s publication, the addition of an Infrequency Psychopathology (*Fp*) measure (Arbisi & Ben-Porath, 1995) to the standard Validity scales further strengthened the clinician's capacity to assess overreporting. Likewise, Nichols and Greene's (1991) updating of an earlier scale that they called Other Deception enhanced the capacity to assess underreporting. Publication of the Superlative Scale and its subscales (Butcher & Han, 1995) greatly expanded the corpus of scales available to assess underreporting of psychopathology.

Even this cursory examination of *MMPI* Validity Scale developments from their humble beginnings attests to a healthy ongoing process of refinement. Clinicians are now in a far better position to appraise the validity of a record than they ever were before. The validity story is, of course, a never ending one. The present research constitutes just one more skirmish with uncertainty. Its only claim to significance is that it introduces new clinical possibilities by nibbling away at the boundaries of what is known and what researchers only think they know. If fortune favors, then some of these new directions will be pursued by others who likewise recognize that, although the validity story's plot has become clearer, this is not the final chapter.

3

Status of the Basic Scales

Kuhn (1970) defined a scientific paradigm as a developing school of thought that gathered "adherents away from competing modes of scientific activity (and) . . . was . . . open-ended (leaving varied) problems . . . to resolve" (p. 10). In the paradigmatic system of objective personality testing, few have survived the test of time and rigorous research. The *MMPI–2* has unequivocally become the quintessential flagship of objective personality testing in clinical and research psychology (Friedman et al., 2001). Thus, the use of the *MMPI–2* can easily be conceptualized in terms of Kuhn's paradigm analogy. The original premise and theories rest on the use of the empirically validated scales. Clearly, the development of the *MMPI* and the original use of the Clinical scales attracted many researchers and practitioners and allowed for unique diagnostic and empirical questions to be answered for years to come.

Hathaway and McKinley's (1940, 1951) development of the original *MMPI* and the subsequent Clinical scales moved the science of objective personality testing years ahead. Today, the *MMPI–2* is used for psychological assessment in many different areas, including forensic assessment, child custody evaluations, personnel assignment, and clinical diagnosis. The practical and research value of the Clinical scales has been clearly demonstrated. Many prospective practitioners and researchers are trained to use primarily the Clinical scales, with little attention being given to the special scales. The *MMPI–2 Manual* (Butcher et al., 2001) contends that the empirical basis for the Clinical scales allows for more accurate inferences because interpretation derived from item content may be problematic. Respondents may not interpret item content in the same manner, thus reducing the validity of the scale. The Clinical scales were empirically keyed and avoided this dilemma (Hathaway & McKinley, 1951). A set of items that differentiated a criterion group from a normal group qualified for the scale named for the criterion group (e.g., Depression). The content of the individual item was not deemed determinative at that time. The individual Clinical scale could encompass diverse item content, yet maintain its empirical functioning (Greene, 2000).

PROBLEMS WITH THE CLINICAL SCALES

Kuhn's (1970) explanation of the scientific paradigm further describes a phenomenon that occurs when the results of new empirical research begin to challenge the original premise of the paradigm. Often, this is initially met with resistance (and sometimes all out hostility), but eventually there comes what he called a *paradigm shift* when a school of thought reorganizes the original theory in order to accommodate new data. The rationale behind the applications of the *MMPI–2* Clinical Scales has not been sheltered from the possibility of paradigm shift. Mounting data that question the usefulness of the Clinical scales needs to be resolved and assimilated into psychological assessment theory. That could mean displacing the Clinical scales from primary use and making them a more peripheral feature in *MMPI–2* profile interpretation.

Through the years, conflicting empirical research and theoretical analysis began to develop concerning the use of the Clinical scales with the *MMPI/MMPI–2* (Faschingbauer, 1979; Levitt & Duckworth, 1984). Faschingbauer observed that the Clinical scales share many items and, as a result, are often capturing many of the same traits across all scales. Furthermore, the Clinical scales ignore over 100 items that could provide other useful clinical information. Norman (1972) made more radical statements by calling the Clinical scales "inefficient, redundant, and largely irrelevant for their present purposes" (p. 64). He further claimed that the methods of "combining scale scores and . . . profile interpretation are unconscionably cumbersome and obtuse" (p. 64). Norman summed up his assessment of traditional *MMPI* methods by asserting that they are unbelievably ill-suited and inappropriate "for their current uses in profile analysis, and interpretation and typal class definition" (p. 64). Archer and Krishnamurthy (1993b) theorized that the general absence of correlation between the *MMPI–2* and the *Rorschach* is due to the multidimensional nature of the Clinical scales.

Wiggins (1966) addressed the heterogeneity of the Clinical scales by contending that they are composed of impossibly comingled combinations of content. This results in high scores whose meaning is so ambiguous that they are subject to multiple and conflicting interpretations. Thus, they cannot provide evidence of stable traits or structures of personality. Indeed, the libraries of interpretative statements that have been proposed for high scores on Clinical scales can lack precision and clear description. Graham (2000) listed over 30 interpretative statements that are indicated by a high score on Scale *4*. A high score on Scale *9* has over 40 interpretative statements. In critiquing these scales, Clopton (1979) observed that respondents can achieve identical raw scores on the Clinical scales by endorsing entirely different item subsets.

The *MMPI–2* (Butcher et al., 1989) revision sought to update and restandardize the well-established *MMPI*. The revision accomplished some notable objectives: It included more representation of ethnic minorities in the normative group, modified sexist and antiquated language of the original, eliminated items that respondents found objectionable, added valuable new content, and developed uniform *T*-scores for the primary scales. Through all of the process of change, a central goal was for the Clinical scales to remain intact, including retention of their items. Thus, the paradigm remained. Yet, growing concern over the use of the Clinical scales continued (Duckworth & Levitt, 1994).

RESTRUCTURED CLINICAL SCALES

There are signs that the Clinical scales may be headed toward a paradigm shift due to the mounting weight of clinical evidence. A notable development in this regard is that central figures from the *MMPI–2* revision team have collaborated in an innovative effort to improve on the traditional Clinical scales. In doing so, they have sought to "preserve . . . descriptive properties of the . . . Clinical Scales while enhancing their distinctiveness" (Tellegen et al., 2003, p. 1). They have accomplished this by developing the *MMPI–2* Restructured Clinical (*RC*) Scales.

These scales parallel the eight Clinical scales and add a ninth scale that is described further later. Although the Basic scales *5* and *0* were studied, no scales were developed for them. An especially novel feature of this work grew out of the group's acknowledgment of troublingly large correlations among the present scales. They recognized that these result partly from their many overlapping items. They have eliminated that problem by avoiding all overlaps. More importantly, Tellegen and his associates decided to focus their efforts on another property that is shared among the Clinical scales: The Clinical scales are saturated with a property that they have labeled *Demoralization*. That is, in addition the distinctive or focal variance that gives each Clinical scale its recognizable meaning, the scale also carries a loading of this negatively toned variance. Demoralization variance combines with the focal variance of Clinical scales, making it difficult to tell why particular scores elevate.

The group proceeded to develop a measure of Demoralization (*RCd*) that resembles the often replicated first extracted *MMPI* factor (Welsh, 1956). They then isolated the focal properties of each of the 10 Basic scales by removing from them the variance associated with Demoralization. They continued on through a series of steps to develop scales corresponding to Clinical scales (*RC1* through *RC4* and *RC6* through *RC9*). The *RC* scales closely resemble the focal variance of the original Clinical scales minus the heavy loading of Demoralization. The result has been a reduction in the intercorrelations among the *RC* scales, as compared with those for the Clinical scales, thereby implying greater emphasis on their focal clinical properties. Encouraging early results suggest that the external validity for the *RC* scales will equal or surpass that for the *MMPI–2* Clinical Scales (Tellegen et al., 2003). If the preliminary results hold up in replications by others, then the threat of Welsh's (1956) Factor One to *MMPI–2* discriminant clinical validity will have been blunted.

Whereas this does not represent a complete paradigm shift (Kuhn, 1970), it is admittedly a major shift within a paradigm that has remained in place since Hathaway and McKinley (1940, 1951) launched the *MMPI*. By the 1980s, *MMPI* rested on a respected paradigm with an international following. The *MMPI* paradigm was too pervasive to redirect when the decision was made to revise *MMPI*. Consequently, even a superficial analysis will show that the paradigm both steered and constrained the *MMPI* revision (Butcher et al., 1989).

Because of MMPI's popularity, reputation, and voluminous empirical base, the Restandardization Committee thus was obliged to preserve fairly intact the most familiar and widely used features of the original version. They must have considered that failure to do so would have virtually guaranteed rejection of their efforts by many. In that event, *MMPI* and *MMPI–2* would long have occupied competing places in the marketplace—hardly a desirable outcome either for continued development of the science or for the publisher.

All the knowledge and procedures necessary to create the *RC* scales actually existed prior to the preparation of *MMPI–2*. But, if this shift within the paradigm had been introduced in 1989 together with the much revised test, an outcry of anguish among users would have been predictable. Close adherence to the original paradigm likely accelerated acceptance of *MMPI–2* by the psychological community and hastened the demise of *MMPI* use. Even with the basic paradigm preserved—and, perhaps partly because it was, a contingent of holdouts was evident (Webb, Levitt, & Rojdev, 1993).

The introduction of the *RC* scales seems less likely to create a stir now that *MMPI–2* is well established. Notably, the timing of the *RC* scales' arrival in some ways is comparable to that which obtained when Wiggins (1966) introduced his Content scales. First, new arrivals appeared within the framework of an established, accepted test. Second, neither challenged the test's existence nor proposed to subtract from it. Third, each instead proposed accretions based on clear rationales and methodology. Fourth, in both instances, the proposed additions arose from motivations to improve the clinical usefulness of the test. Fifth, they were products of solid empirical challenge to the status quo.

Lest their intention be misconstrued, Tellegen et al. (2003) reassuringly stated that the *RC* scales are designed to preserve the essential meanings of the Clinical scales—not to bury them. They further welcomed use of the *RC* scales to sharpen understanding of other special scales and possibly to play a part in the development of new ones. Thus, a reorientation of the original paradigm has been set in motion. Inasmuch as the content cluster approach presented in this book mainly adds to the *MMPI–2* repertoire, it too can be viewed as accretionary building within the paradigm. Whether the reception of the *RC* scales will result in revolution rather than a reorientation, it is clear that the Demoralization issue will receive renewed attention. This is, of course, the business of science.

BASIC SCALES REVIEWED

Many well-respected works are available that outline in detail interpretative statements and diagnostic scale combinations (Friedman et al., 2001; Graham, 2000; Greene, 2000). A detailed review here would duplicate unnecessarily these fine in-print resources. Nevertheless, to establish a context for the focus here on special scales, the Clinical scales and high-point combinations will be reviewed briefly. The Clinical scales *1–4* and *5–9* use the uniform *T*-scores that were adopted by the *MMPI–2* Restandardization Committee (Butcher et al., 1989). The uniform *T*-score allows for the scale elevation to be compared across scales and between male and females. The Basic scales *5* and *0* continue to use linear *T*-scores.

Scale *1*—Hypochondriasis (*Hs*)

McKinley and Hathaway (1940) defined *hypochondriasis* as the preoccupation over bodily functioning and poor health. Members of the criterion group used to develop the items on this scale were assessed to have uncomplicated hypochondriasis based on this definition. However, the current *Diagnostic and Statistical Manual of Mental Disorders* (*DSM*; American Psychiatric Association, 2000) defined *hypochondriasis* as an exaggerated fear of having a serious illness with disregard of well-founded reassurances. Thus, interpretation based on the original definition should be kept in mind (Greene, 2000).

Graham (2000) offered over 20 statements of interpretation that range from the preoccupation with bodily functioning to the expression of hostility. Comrey (1957) performed a factor analysis on the items on the Hypochondriasis scale and determined that most of the variance can be accounted for by a general complaining of poor health or a denial of being in good health. Studies have found that respondents with chronic pain and legitimate physical illness can also have moderate elevations of Scale *1* (Friedman et al., 2001). Duckworth (1979) reported that transient physical illness, such as influenza or other infections, can elevate this scale. Furthermore, a general lack of psychological mindedness can elevate this scale, thus enhancing its relation to the *L* scale.

Although the scale has myriad possible explanations for elevations, item content is surprisingly homogeneous (Graham, 2000). Thus, interpretations of elevated scores (> T65) recognize that individuals are preoccupied with their current health and body functions, either real or imagined. Extreme scores (> T80) may indicate bizarre somatic complaints that require clinical diagnosis.

Scale 2—Depression (D)

Like the term *hypchrondriasis*, Hathaway and McKinley's (1951) use of the word *depression* does not conform to modern clinical use. In fact, their criterion group consisted of those diagnosed with bipolar disorder with psychotic features (then called manic depressive psychosis). The group was determined to be individuals in the depressed phase of that illness. The intention was to have a clear and extreme criterion of depression (Greene, 2000). However, the scale has been found to measure more global emotions of poor morale, hopelessness, and self-dissatisfaction (W. G. Dahlstrom et al., 1972). The scale also taps some physical symptoms that can be concomitant with a general malaise (Friedman et al., 2001).

The Depression Clinical scale has been found to be heterogeneous in item content. Two respondents can have equal scale elevations and yet endorse a different set of content items (Clopton, 1979; Wiggins, 1966). Although high scorers (> T80) can be determined to have depressive features, it is not recommended to use this scale alone to diagnose depression (Greene, 2000). The special scales will be needed to ascertain the nature and quality of the depression (see chaps. 8, 12). Moderate elevation (T65–T70) may indicate a more transitional dissatisfaction with current events, poor motivation, or dysthymia.

Scale 3—Hysteria (Hy)

The term *hysteria* is a holdover from Victorian era diagnoses and psychoanalysis. It is difficult to conceptualize in modern terms due to the changes in nosology. Symptoms of hysteria describe a pattern of converting emotional reactions into psychogenic physical complaints (Graham, 2000). This is similar to the modern diagnosis of a Conversion Disorder and resembles other somatoform disorders (American Psychiatric Association, 2000). The scale only minimally resembles Histrionic Personality Disorder. That would require the scale to measure components of emotional regulation, impulsivity, and ego identity. Duckworth and Anderson (1995) described the scale as denoting denial and repression in the respondent. The scale seems to identify a broad spectrum of symptoms, such as denial of mental health issues, low social anxiety, and specific somatic complaints.

The scale consists of 60 items of the *MMPI–2* item pool and, of those items, only 13 are unique to the scale. The remaining items are shared with the other Clinical scales. A significant number of items are shared with Scale *1*. Item content falls into two main categories that Wiener and Harmon (Wiener, 1948) described as the subtle and obvious items of the scale. The first group describes specific somatic symptoms of the respondent (obvious) and the second group describes respondents who saw themselves as lacking problems and enjoying social activities (subtle). In order to make any inferences from this scale, the clinician will need to determine if the respondent especially elevated the scale within one of these fairly mutually exclusive categories (Greene, 2000).

Graham's (2000) list of interpretive statements ranges from persons who are outgoing to those that are self-centered and egotistical. Thus, wading through the variations of possible interpretations, high scorers on Scale 3 (> T80) can be seen as those who react to increased emotional turmoil with physical problems. They can lack insight into their own difficulties and may be psychologically immature (Greene, 2000). Moderate scorers may simply be outgoing and friendly individuals. Furthermore, moderate scorers may have actual physical difficulties. This scale is most useful after analyzing the content of the items that were scored in the deviant direction and, further, reviewing it in light of other scales. The conversion diagnosis may be more confidently diagnosed in combination with Scales 1 and 2 (see scale combinations).

Scale 4—Psychopathic Deviate (*Pd*)

Scale 4 can be considered one of the stronger clinical scales. The term *psychopathic deviate* refers to a stable spectrum of behaviors that have retained their meaning through the era of development of both *MMPI* and *MMPI–2*. The criterion group consisted of young adults involved in the judicial system due to delinquent behaviors (Greene, 2000). Duckworth and Anderson (1995) saw the scale as measuring someone who is in conflict with societal norms or interpersonal relationships. Overall, the scale can be seen as a general measure of rebelliousness without necessarily including psychopathy.

Fifteen of the 50 items comprising Scale 4 are unique. The remaining clinical scales share the other items. As with many other Clinical scales, the item content is heterogeneous and appears contradictory (Greene, 2000). Elevations may come from a respondent who is confident and socially posed but had dysfunctional childhood family patterns. Many items tap abuse or family problems. Their inclusion relates to the notion that an abusive and dysfunctional childhood breeds impulsiveness and rebelliousness in adulthood (Friedman et al., 2001). Scale 4 is also sensitive to situational stress (Butcher et al., 2001). Furthermore, dysphoria and boredom in the respondent may elevate the scale. The subjects in the criterion group were in trouble and some were in jail at the time the scale was created. Thus, the situational stress involved in this may have been a confounding influence (Greene, 2000).

Nonetheless, the Psychopathic Deviate scale can prove useful when the *MMPI–2* is used in forensic settings, especially when combined with other scales (*ASP*, *W-AUT*, Scale 9) and external measures of psychopathy (*PCL-R*: Hare, 1991). High scorers (> T65) tend to be nonconforming, rebellious, impulsive, and lack sensitivity to the needs of others (Butcher et al., 2001). There may be conflict within their family, personal relationships, or with society's authority. Extreme scorers may be aggressive and hostile. Moderate elevations (T50–T65) may indicate a respondent who is extroverted, confident, and assertive. Low scorers (< T45) can be seen as conforming and rigid (Greene, 2000).

Scale 5—Masculinity–Femininity (*Mf*)

Scale *5* was developed after the original Clinical scales were formed. In fact, many early users did not accept the inclusion of Scale *5* (as well as Scale *0*) into the canon of Clinical scales. Hathaway and McKinley (Hathaway, 1956) wanted to develop a scale to measure homosexuality in men. Not surprisingly, the group of homosexual individuals gathered was heterogeneous in their item responses; thus, a set of items that differentiated them from the normative group could not be constructed. However, Hathaway and McKinley discovered several subgroups within the homosexual criterion group and decided to use only the subgroup described as "homosexual inverts" (Greene, 2000). Those classified as homosexual inverts were men who had feminine characteristics and participated in homoerotic behavior, but who did not feel free to express their sexual orientation overtly. Unfortunately, there were just 13 men in the criterion group.

Because of difficulty in creating a scale to identify homosexuality in men, Hathaway and McKinley (Hathaway, 1956) reconfigured the scale to differentiate traditional male and female characteristics in respondents. However, this leads to another problem with this scale. Hathaway and McKinley conceptualized masculine and feminine traits as being opposites, or a bipolar dimension (Constantinople, 1973), but these traits can be viewed as basically different. For example, the male who does not exemplify the traditional masculine role may not necessarily be feminine. Conversely, the female who does not present a traditional feminine role may not be masculine in character. Furthermore, men with higher education or certain occupations tend to elevate Scale *5*.

High scores (> T65) suggest men or women who reject traditional sex-based roles and have varied interests (Friedman et al., 2001; Greene, 2000). It is not recommended to use this scale to try to identify respondents' sexual orientation. On the other hand, some homosexual males who are comfortable with their orientation will score above T65. Clinical experience shows that males who practice transvestism or who are seeking sexual reassignment can register exaggeratedly high scores on this scale. Other male high scorers may be introspective, passive, and sensitive. Moderate elevations (T55–T65) may indicate men who find value in the fine arts and are less aggressive than their average male counterparts. Women rarely score above T65, but elevated *T*-scores for women suggest that they tend to deviate from traditional feminine roles.

Scale 6—Paranoia (*Pa*)

The Criterion group used to develop Scale 6 was never described (Friedman et al., 2001). The scale was originally experimental and was not meant to become part of the final Clinical scales. It is assumed that Hathaway and McKinley developed this scale in the same manner as the others to be empirically derived. Thus, the nature of the paranoia or the diagnosis associated with the subjects in the criterion group remains unclear. However, early research indicated that the scale was able to identify paranoid subjects with few false positives.

Twelve out of 40 items on Scale 6 are unique. Items on the scale overlap less with the content-based paranoid scales, such as the Bizarre Mentation Content Scale (*BIZ*; Butcher, Graham, Williams, & Ben-Porath, 1990); the Tryon, Stein, and Chu Suspicion Scale (*TSC–S*; Stein, 1968); and the Wiggins Psychoticism Scale (*W–PSY*; Wiggins, 1966). Greene (2000) suggested that this is due to the heterogeneity of Scale 6. This may be true because item content appears to tap three distinct areas: disturbed thinking, feeling mistreated, and resentfulness. Nichols and Greene (1995) suggested viewing this scale as a measure of respondent attribution of difficulties onto others (i.e., projection). All of these areas may be included in the paranoid spectrum, but scale elevations can occur without respondents endorsing a single psychotic item (Graham, 2000). Thus, the discriminant capacity of this scale is adversely affected by item diversity.

Greene (2000) discussed the literature that demonstrates the scale's inability to identify the criterion group from a normal group. There are also more incidents of false positives than was originally suggested. Friedman et al. (2001) recommend use of the Harris and Lingoes Subscales (see chap. 4) as aids to interpreting elevated *T*-scores. In general, elevated scales may suggest general paranoid features that include ideas of reference, grandiosity, persecutory ideation, excessive sensitivity, and rigid opinions. However, the subscales and other supplementary scales need to be reviewed for clarification.

Scale 7—Psychasthenia (*Pt*)

Although Scale 7 has relatively homogeneous item content, the criterion group on which it was based only included outpatients (McKinley & Hathaway, 1942). The term *psychasthenia* is an antiquated diagnosis that included those who were plagued with excessive doubt, worry, compulsions, obsessions, and fears. It is somewhat similar to the modern diagnosis of Obsessive–Compulsive Disorder (Graham, 2000). McKinley and Hathaway had trouble gathering the criterion group because the disorder rarely caused an individual to be hospitalized. Furthermore, outpatient subjects did not lend themselves to the in-depth screening that was available for inpatient subjects.

Only 10 of the 48 items are unique to the scale. Thus, this scale often becomes elevated with other Clinical scales. Scale 7 is highly correlated with and loads on

Factor *A* (Welsh, 1956) of the *MMPI–2*. Scale 7, like the Welsh's *A*, is considered a general gauge of overall distress and relates for this reason to most psychopathology scales (Friedman et al., 2001; Graham, 2000; Lachar, 1974). Duckworth and Anderson (1995) conceptualized the scale as measuring more long-term anxiety (trait anxiety) as opposed to situational stressors (state anxiety), but this conclusion is not well substantiated empirically.

High scorers (> T65) tend to be anxious and tense. They have a general feeling of distress and have trouble with decisions and self-esteem. Extreme elevations (> T90) indicate persons in acute crisis who may not be thinking clearly and require immediate interventions. Overall, Scale 7 was based on a small criterion group that was diagnosed with something that does not exist in contemporary nosology. Furthermore, the scale covaries highly with the other Clinical scales. The Welsh *A* scale may be a better logical alternative.

Scale 8—Schizophrenia (*Sc*)

The medical profession identified schizophrenia over 100 years ago. Nonetheless, better differential diagnoses have helped to classify those suffering from this debilitating illness. Thus, in the 1940s, Hathaway and McKinley's (Hathaway, 1956) criterion group consisted of heterogeneous patients who were determined then to meet to diagnostic criteria for schizophrenia. The original group members were all diagnosed as having schizophrenia, but they most likely included those with affective disorders with psychotic symptoms and schizoaffective disorder (Friedman et al., 2001). Clearly, someone in an acute psychotic phase of schizophrenia would be obvious to a trained clinician in a clinical interview. However, the scale's intention was to tap more subtle expressions of the disorder.

The scale consists of the largest number of items of any of the Clinical scales (78). Only 26 items are unique to this scale. Although the diagnosis of schizophrenia centers around specific criteria in the *DSM–IV–TR* (2000), item content coverage is diffuse. Graham (2000) used the broader criteria of a psychotic disorder and suggested that high scorers suffer from unusual thoughts, hallucinations, and delusions. However, Graham gave over 30 interpretive statements ranging from someone being stubborn and opinionated to someone being overtly psychotic. Duckworth and Anderson (1995) identified high scorers as having poor judgment and/or being under extreme situational stress. Furthermore, elevations can be seen in those who recently abused psychoactive substances or experienced a head trauma. Members of specific minority groups often produce elevated *T*-scores possibly due to the marginalization experienced in the current culture.

The original scale did not effectively discriminate persons who had schizophrenia from normals. Thus, the full raw score value of *K* was added. This correction helped to boost the scale's discriminative ability and reduced false positives (Friedman et al., 2001). Apparently, those suffering from schizophrenia were more likely to minimize their deviant behaviors. Thus, the correction by K served to separate the true schizophrenia group from normals. However, it is possible for defensive persons falsely to elevate Scale *8* while endorsing only a few or no psychotic items. Understanding *K*'s influence on Scale *8* is necessary before any predictions are made from the scale.

Those scoring in the extreme range (> T90) are probably not suffering from a psychotic disorder. As stated early, someone in a clearly acute phase would probably not require testing for diagnosis. Thus, the extreme range is most likely indicative of intense psychological turmoil (Butcher et al., 2001). High scorers (T65–T90) may be dealing with a psychotic disorder, but may also be persons who have intense feelings of being estranged from society and misunderstood by others. Thus, the special scales are required to make the appropriate interpretations. Greene (2000) described low scorers (< T45) as being conventional, realistic, and unimaginative.

Scale 9—Hypomania (*Ma*)

The manic mood is characterized by an expansive ego, loquaciousness, irritability or euphoria, reduced need for sleep, and flight of ideas (*DSM–IV–TR*, 2000). The term *hypomania* describes this mood but is less informative regarding duration and intensity. Someone in an acute manic episode would not likely sit for the administration of the *MMPI–2*. Likewise, mania and most hypomania would be clearly evident to the trained clinician in a clinical interview. McKinley and Hathaway (1944) constructed the criterion group from 24 patients suffering from mild to moderate mania. The diagnostic criteria for hypomania have become essential components in diagnosing variant forms of bipolar disorder, such as Bipolar Disorder, Type II, and its near relative, Cyclothymia.

Scale *9* consists of 46 items, with only 16 unique to this scale. Scale *8* shares the most with Scale *9* (11 items), and the remaining shared items are spread across the remaining Clinical and Validity scales. The items cover a variety and content that is not necessarily specific to hypomanic symptomology. Thus, elevated scores can suggest a myriad of things: impulsivity, narcissism, extraverted personality, expansive, and maniclike moods (Graham, 2000; Greene, 2000). The scale can be informative when used in combination with other scales. When Scale *9* is elevated, this suggests that the behavioral components of the paired scale are more likely to be exhibited. For example, if Scale *4* and Scale *9* are elevated in tandem, this may suggest that the respondent is at higher risk for violent and manipulative actions.

Bipolar disorder, in general, is diagnosed by history and not necessarily by mental status. Scores greater than T65 suggest an impulsive, energetic, and social individual that may exhibit irritability or amorality (Graham, 2000). Raskin and Novacek (1989) discussed this scale as measuring the component of narcissistic personality disorder. Lewak, Marks, and Nelson (1990) used the clinical concept of a *manic defense* found in psychodynamic nomenclature. The manic defense describes a defensive mechanism that activates persons in behavior and thought in order to avoid frustration and unhappiness of their current conditions. Scale 9 could offer some potential for recognizing these several constructs, but the multiplicity of item contents and potential meanings might only clutter the diagnostic picture. Thus, knowledge of the respondents' history, plus use of the special scales, are required to infer the meaning of an elevated score.

Scale 0—Social Introversion (Si)

Scale 0, like Scale 5, was developed later and not originally part of the Clinical scale canon (Butcher et al., 2001). The criterion used in selecting this group was not based on a clinical sample. Instead, a psychological test, the Minnesota T-S-E, was used as a criterion (Evans & McConnell, 1941). The scores were reported to discriminate high and low scorers on this scale. Thus, high scorers tended to withdraw from social engagements and activities. All subjects used were women, but Drake (1946) later normed the scale on males and found that men did not significantly differ in their responses from women.

Twenty-seven of the 69 items of Scale 0 are unique. Item content tends to fall into two main categories: maladjustment and social participation. Harris and Lingoes (1968) did not construct subscales for Scale 0. However, Ben-Porath, Hostetler, Butcher, and Graham (1989) developed 3 subscales after the MMPI–2 revision. These include Shyness/Self-Consciousness (Si1) and Social Avoidance (Si2). These two scales appear to sample approximately what their names suggest. The third scale is more related to Factor A than to specific interpersonal qualities and was not found to be useful in the current work. These two useful subscales arrange the items into content homogenous groups. Ward and Perry (1998) found that the three subscales accounted for most of the variance in Scale 0. Thus, Scale 0 includes the nonspecific variance of the third subscale that was found not to be useful.

High scorers (> T65) avoid others and can become uncomfortable in social situations (Butcher et al., 2001). Thus, they are pathologically introverted and may lack self-confidence. Greene (2000) suggested interpretation at low elevations (< T45) as describing those that are extroverted and outgoing. As with the other Clinical scales, the clinician needs to be aware of the content endorsed by the respondent before making interpretations. It is necessary, therefore, to use the special scales for convergent validity and especially the content subscales suggested by Ben-Porath et al. (1989).

CODETYPES

In order to increase diagnostic efficacy, researchers and clinicians have combined the Clinical scales into 2-point and 3-point configurations. However, if all 10 Clinical scales are used to form various combinations, there are 90 2-point codetype possibilities (i.e., if, e.g., 1-2 and 2-1 are treated differently) and 720 3-point codetype possibilities (Graham, 2000). Unfortunately, understanding all possible codetypes and their correlates does not increase precision. Instead, codetypes compound item overlaps and increase saturation with the Factor *A* (Welsh, 1956) or Demoralization (Tellegen et al., 2003) variance. Despite these misgivings, several codetypes have been found to have higher occurrences and strong external correlations, making them worth noting.

Extensive reviews of the codetype literature are available (Friedman et al., 2001; Greene, 2000). They should be consulted by those who desire a more expanded treatment. Those who plan to interpret codetypes should at a minimum become highly familiar with the composition and meanings of the component Clinical scales on which they are based in order to modify their impressions as needed. Likewise, the precautions mentioned earlier regarding item overlaps among their component scales and the compounding of saturation with Factor *A* should be taken into account. The codetypes reviewed offer an exceedingly abbreviated introduction to some commonly seen combinations.

Sample of 2-Point Codetypes

Scales 2–7. This pair of high points may indicate a significant affective disorder that is creating intense intrapsychic pain. The respondent is most likely in an agitated depressive state consumed with rumination of negative self thoughts (Friedman et al., 2001). They may be more driven with a need for success. They can be perfectionistic and rigid, but find little satisfaction in their own work or accomplishments. This pattern is often seen in the psychiatric setting (Greene, 2000).

Scales 4–6. Respondents scoring highest on these two scales may be dealing with a personality disorder. This may indicate narcissism, borderline, or antisocial traits. The respondents have little empathy for others and view the world as a dangerous and hostile place. They see that others are exploitative and manipulative, and this justifies their own behavior. There is some self-aggrandizement and externalizing of blame to others. If Scale *6* is very elevated, then this may indicate possibility of psychosis or paranoid delusions.

Sample of 3-Point Codetypes

Scales 1–2–3. These scales form the Neurotic Triad and can often elevate together (Greene, 2000). When Scales *1* and *3* are substantially higher than Scale *2*, the front of the profile resembles the letter *V*. Respondents with this scale configuration are seen to express conversionlike symptoms. They are under emotional duress, but find it difficult to express this anguish via verbal and psychological expression. Consequently, they develop physical symptoms in order to obtain desired care and nurturing for themselves. If the elevations are an inverted *V* (higher elevations on Scale *2*), then the respondent can be seen as depressed with a hysterical component (Friedman et al., 2001). They are unsuccessfully using denial and repression as defenses. Their depressive symptomology includes a heavy loading of physical symptoms and neuro-vegetative features (i.e., disturbances of sleep, appetite, etc.).

Scales 6–7–8.   This codetype is often seen with Scales *6* and *8* being substantially higher than Scale *7*. Thus, it was given the label *psychotic valley* (Graham, 2000). It is shaped like the 1–2–3 *V* but appears at the right-hand side of the profile. This configuration most likely indicates someone dealing with a significant psychotic disorder. These persons are most likely plagued with hallucinations and delusional thoughts. They tend to withdraw from others and view society as a threat. Diagnosis of schizophrenia, schizoaffective disorder, or an atypical psychotic disorder may be warranted.

CONCLUSIONS

The traditional Clinical scales remain cornerstones of *MMPI–2* interpretation. This paradigm was developed at the outset for *MMPI* and has persisted through the *MMPI–2* revision up to the present time. The Clinical scales were developed empirically using criterion groups to determine the items that belong within each scale. Items were chosen for the scale if they discriminated the criterion group from the normal group. The eight Clinical scales, plus *5* and *0*, helped establish the *MMPI* as one of the premiere objective personality measures.

Evidence accumulating through the years has shown problems that were only partly corrected by the *MMPI–2* revision (Butcher et al., 1989). Recent work on the Restructured Clinical (*RC*) scales has sought to address the unresolved problem of excessively high correlations among the Clinical scales that compromise their discriminant validity. The *RC* scales approached this empirical issue by removing the influence of Demoralization and eliminating all item overlaps (Tellegen et al., 2003). This important shift within the *MMPI/MMPI–2* paradigm seeks to preserve the focal meaning of the Clinical scales while correcting those features that have overburdened them with nonfocal variance. This reorientation is seen as hospitable to further innovation within the paradigm.

Comparing of *RC* and Clinical Scales

In order to examine the operation of the *RC* scales vis-à-vis the Clinical scales in the sample, a correlation matrix was obtained containing the eight *RC* and Clinical scales from each subset plus *A* and *RCd*. This was done in the *MMPI–2* subset of the database using non-*K*-corrected Clinical scale scores. *RCd* correlated at slightly higher levels with scales *RC1, RC2, 1, 2, 3, 4, 7*, and *8* than did *A*. The *A* scale's correlations were slightly higher than those of *RCd* with the remaining *RC* and Clinical scales. These findings suggest that further study using *RCd* and *A* as alternative means of removing Demoralization variance could possibly enhance the results already achieved by Tellegen et al. (2003).

Overall, correlational results within three subsets of the correlations were congruent with expectations based on the *RC* developers' findings. First, *RC1–RC4* and *RC6–RC9* had generally smaller intercorrelations among themselves than the Clinical scales *1–4* and *6–9* had among themselves. Second, correlations between the related pairs of *RC* and Clinical scales were high (.72–.84, median 76.5) for six of the eight comparisons. For two pairings, the correlations were lower: *RC3-3* (−.17) and *RC4-4* (.47).

For the preceding two pairings that fell below the levels anticipated, additional analyses were completed to identify how well the respective *RC* and Clinical scale versions performed in relation to other special scales. *RC3* related at significantly higher correlational levels than did Clinical scale *3* to *Cared for vs. Neglected, CYN, TSC/S, Trust, 3NA*, and *6N*. All correlations were in the expected directions and differences favored the *RC3* version overwhelmingly. *RC4* related more highly than did Clinical scale *4* to *Initiating vs. Guilt-Prone, ASP, W-AUT, Imp-B, Imp-T, MAC-R, ANG, W-HOS, TSC/R*, and *Re*. Correlations were all in the expected directions and *RC4*'s relations with these relevant scales far exceeded those for Clinical scale *4*. Thus, the low relations found between the *RC3-3* and *RC4-4* pairings did not reflect unfavorably on those *RC* scales. It was concluded that the *RC* scales added considerably greater clarity to empirical results than could be obtained with Clinical scales in this data set.

4

Synopsis of the Special Scales:
Sources and Interpretation

As *MMPI* use matured, the value of item content became more evident. Leary (1956, 1957) articulated the multilevel interpersonal method for diagnosis and this provided a theoretical foundation for valuing item content. The first two levels of Leary's method help to reconcile the interplay between the Clinical and Content scales (Friedman et al., 2001). Level I data are more objective in nature and yield information on how others see the individual (i.e., Clinical scales). This may or may not be commensurate with the way that individuals see themselves. Level II data remain subjective, exhibiting perspectives based on individual experience. This information reflects the individual's internal phenomena and subjective experience (i.e., Content scales).

Exclusive loyalty to using the original Clinical scales and ignoring item content can only capture one aspect of the diagnostic picture. The inclusion of Level II data, or item content, allows respondents to reflect on and express their inner experiences to the clinician. Furthermore, the heterogeneous item content of the Clinical scales can produce confusion in clinical interpretation.

Unfortunately, when the *MMPI–2* was released, many special scales were left for dead. Special scales that had a long history with the *MMPI* were simply discarded out of concern that they had become irrelevant with the revised version. However, there is evidence supporting the continued relevance of many of the almost forgotten special scales (Levitt & Gotts, 1995), as demonstrated by findings that appear in later chapters of the present report. Thus, the following is a review of both many *MMPI–2* special scales that are currently being used and many that have been resurrected by this present study.

HARRIS AND LINGOES SUBSCALES

One of the original attempts to capitalize on the multidimensionality of selected Clinical scales resulted in the Harris and Lingoes (1968) Subscales. Those authors attempted to formulate dimensionally homogeneous subscales from each of the Clinical scales by using their combined clinical judgment. There was no interrater reliability reported, thus a conference technique was most likely used. Thirty-one original subscales were created from six Clinical scales.

According to Harris and Lingoes (1968), Scales *1* and *7* did not submit readily to subclassification. Nonetheless, they were able to develop subscales with minimal overlap from Clinical scales *2, 3, 6,* and *9.* One exception to the relative absence of overlapping is that the subscale Brooding (*D5/2B*) is a subset of subscale Subjective Depression (*D1/2SD*). In the original *MMPI*, there were three composite scales, but the composite scales were not generally considered useful and were dropped from the *MMPI–2*. Thus, the Harris and Lingoes Subscales now total 28. Because few items from the original Clinical scales were lost, the Harris and Lingoes scales remained relatively unscathed.

The Harris and Lingoes Subscales are helpful in many different clinical venues and they are used to an unknown extent. According the *MMPI–2 Manual* (Butcher et al., 2001), these subscales should be interpreted cautiously and in the context of their parent scales due to the lack of research support for their independent use as well as some scales' relatively low reliability. Greene (2000) likewise pointed out that research is limited with these subscales. A study by Lingoes (1960) suggested only that factor analyzing the Harris and Lingoes scales results in at least 7 factors and possibly as many as 14. Greene (2000) observed regarding this that these factors might supply information otherwise unavailable through use of the standard Clinical scales.

Reliability and Validity of Harris–Lingoes Subscales

Recent studies on the reliability of interrater item assignments to subscales have produced mixed results. Miller and Streiner (1985) attempted to use judges to replicate the original Harris and Lingoes Subscales. The judges agreed consistently on Physical Malfunctioning (*D3/2PM*), Denial of Social Anxiety (*Hy1/3DSA*), Need for Affection (*Hy2/3NA*), Somatic Complaints (*Hy4/3SC*), Family Discord (*Pd1/4FD*), Naivete (*Pa3/6N*), Lack of Ego Mastery, Cognitive (*Sc3/8COG*), Bizarre Sensory Experiences (*Sc6/8BSE*), and Amorality (*Ma1/9AMO*). Furthermore, other studies have found many Harris and Lingoes Subscales with limited reliability (Davis, Wagner, & Patty, 1994; Kelch & Wagner, 1992; Wrobel, 1992). Unfortunately, the *MMPI–2 Manual* does not give reliability coefficients on the Harris and Lingoes scales. From the current research program reliability coefficients were more positive. The current study procedures are reviewed in chapter 6 and reliabilities are presented in Appendix B.

Validity studies have also been elusive on the Harris and Lingoes Subscales. Fortunately, in recent years, a few studies have examined the validity of scales often used in forensic evaluation. Specifically, Authority Problems (*Pd2/4AC*) appears to predict well psychopathy and antisocial behavior (Lilienfeld, 1999; Osberg & Poland, 2001). In fact, the data in these studies suggests that *4AC* captures the core of the psychopathic deviate and assesses the callousness, lack of empathy, and egocentricity associated with the antisocial personality.

In one study (Meloy & Gacono, 1995), the *4AC* scale correlated significantly ($r = .31$) with the *PCL-R* (Hare, 1991). The *PCL-R* is currently considered one of best measures to predict the presence of psychopathy (Monahan et al., 2000; Monahan et al., 2001). Although *4AC* was found to be unreliable in the present study of psychiatric inpatients, it is conceivably more reliable in an offender population, so further study is needed. Furthermore, the remaining Harris and Lingoes Subscales of the Psychopathic Deviate *Pd* Clinical scale help to differentiate between true antisocial personalities and other persons with antisocial traits. Familial Discord (*4FD*) was shown to be associated with family dysfunction (Bloomquist & Dossa, 1988). Osberg and Poland (2001) performed studies using the *MMPI–2* with a sample of prison inmates. In addition to the validity support for *4AC*, they also found support for Amorality (*9AMO*) and Self-Alienation (*4SA*) to be positive indicators of a criminal history.

Unfortunately, validity studies with the quality and specificity, as mentioned previously for the Psychopathic Deviate Clinical scale, have not been done on the remaining Harris and Lingoes Subscales. However, there has been an unpublished dissertation study on the criterion validity of the Harris and Lingoes scales (Calvin, 1975). It is riddled, however, with methodological problems, among which is that the sample consisted of psychiatric inpatients only. Thus, only limited inferences could be drawn from these findings. Regardless of these shortcomings, this study holds value when considered in the light of the limited studies available on the validity of the Harris and Lingoes Subscales.

Calvin set up seven criteria, some of which were clinically based such as diagnosis, the patients' attitudes toward their significant others as reported by those same significant others and by the patient, and the patients' views of their reasons for admission. Other procedures used by Calvin (1975) remained objective: the 30-item Nurse's Observation Scale for Inpatient Evaluation (*NOSIE*; Honigfeld & Klett, 1965) and the Gorham Brief Psychiatric Rating Scale (*GBPRS*; Overall & Gorham, 1962), which is based on the psychiatric interview. Neither the *NOSIE* nor the *GBPRS* is intended for research and, unfortunately, there were no interrater reliabilities reported for this investigation. Because the *NOSIE* has 30 items that were used individually by Calvin, there were 37 possible criterion measures relative to the Harris–Lingoes Subscales. The actual number per subscale varied from as many as 10 to as few as 2, but none provided a solidly objective standard. Calvin himself determined the criteria for each scale, another weakness of this investigation.

Calvin found that the Harris and Lingoes Subscales for Clinical scales *2, 6,* and *8* did rather well in relating to the same criterion measure as their respective Clinical scales. Thus, according to Calvin, very little was gained for the interpretation of a Clinical scale by using its Harris and Lingoes Subscales. However, the Harris and Lingoes Subscales *3NA, 3SC, 4FD, 4AC,* and *9IMP* were all significantly related to criteria to a greater extent than their respective Clinical scales and appear to offer more specific clinical information. Thus, Calvin's research, albeit limited in inferential rigor, is useful in that it suggests a degree of validity for some of the Harris and Lingoes Subscales.

Use of the Subscales Illustrated

The strength of the Harris and Lingoes Subscales remains in their ability to determine the cause of a significant elevation of a Clinical scale (Butcher et al., 2001; Graham, 2000; Greene, 2000), and it is this manner of interpretation that remains the most common way of utilizing these subscales. Because of the multidimensionality of the Clinical scales, a respondent may have, for example, an elevated score on Scale *3* without symptoms of dissociation, on Scale *4* without being antisocial, on Scale *6* without being paranoid, on Scale *8* without being psychotic, and on Scale *9* without being hypomanic. The subscales help the examiner determine whether such diagnoses may be warranted. This was the original intent of Harris and Lingoes (1968), that is, the subscales were to be used to assist with profile interpretation. On the other hand, the validity and reliability of the subscales for isolated use remain questionable. Thus, the *MMPI–2 Manual* (Butcher et al., 2001) encourages interpretation of the subscales only when the scores of both the subscale and its parent scale are above T64.

The following three cases are presented in order to demonstrate how the Harris and Lingoes Subscales are used. Although the cases were not randomly chosen, they are not atypical. Such cases constitute about 25% of all records, and an even higher percentage of records interpreted by the MDAC group using the Lushene's software (Lushene, O'Neil, & Dunn, 1974). Subscales in the MDAC archive were scored before revisions based on the current research, but they still usefully show conjoint use of subscales and the Clinical scales.

Sherry was a 28-year-old single, Caucasian female with a high school education. Her *K* was T60 and her *F* was T52. Her *MF* was markedly low at T30 and her *Pd* was T66. She obtained a single high scale peak on Scale *6* of T72. The Harris and Lingoes Subscales of Scale *6* indicated that this elevation was not due to manifest paranoid ideation, inasmuch as *6PI* was not seriously elevated. Also, Sherry endorsed no items on the Indiana Severe Reality Distortions scale (*I–RD*), which is composed of all of the delusion and hallucination items in the original *MMPI* pool. The other subscales indicate that the Scale *6* elevation was due primarily to the subject's view of herself as a moral, virtuous individual and one who tended to be somewhat naive (*6N*). The elevation of *6* was also a function of some tendency to be hypersensitive (*6P*). These attributes do not add up to a paranoid tendency in the classical sense, although they may suggest a predisposition to some unrealistic skewing of self-perceptions.

Kendra was a 22-year-old married, African-American, female, high school graduate who was referred by a physician for help relative to an elusive physical complaint. Her *F* at T63 was only moderately elevated and her *K* was T49. Her record was unremarkable, except for a 2-point code of *4-3*, with both scores under T75. The elevation on Scale *3*, however, required closer examination. The Harris and Lingoes Subscales of Scale *3* showed clearly that an important share of the elevation on that scale was due to *3LM*, Lassitude-Malaise. This subscale taps a group of physical symptoms frequently associated with anxiety and depression. On *3NA*, Need for Affection, the respondent endorsed 6 items with a score of only T46. This subscale is composed of the many items on Scale *3* associated with emotional immaturity, naivete, and attention seeking. Equally important, Kendra failed to endorse a single item on the Indiana Dissociative Symptoms scale (*I–DS*; see Indiana Rational Scales in this chapter). *I–DS* is composed of all the dissociative symptoms in the *MMPI–2* pool. Traditional interpretation of Scale *3* can be confusing because it is possible to have a respondent with health concerns and somatization without the naivete and emotional immaturity. It is with the Harris and Lingoes Subscales that one can make this differentiation.

Stephanie was a 24-year-old married, Caucasian female. She received the supposedly paradoxical *4-7* 2-point code. Thus, a thorough scrutiny of the subscales was necessary. It happens that she is socially anxious rather than socially poised. Subscale *4SI*, Social Imperturbability, is quite low, and this patient's score is within normal limits on *4SOA*, Social Alienation, a scale that measures the tendency to externalize blame, to feel put upon by society, and so on. Subscale *4AC*, Authority Conflict, is also within normal limits. Much of the elevation on Scale *4* is evidently a function of *4SA*, Self Alienation, a subscale composed of a series of depressionlike items that describe dissatisfaction with the self rather than the environment. The elevation of *4SA* is not at all congruent with the traditional interpretation of a high Scale *4*.

Levitt and Gotts (1995) concluded that the value and clinical utility of several Harris and Lingoes Subscales were evident from both research and clinical support. Furthermore, the current clinical research program has also provided support for the clinical utility of the Harris and Lingoes Subscales both in conjunction with and in some instances independent of the corresponding parent scales. Table 4.1 offers clinical interpretation of selected Harris and Lingoes (*H–L*) Subscales. Note that additional descriptions of these and the balance of the *H–L* subscales are found in Friedman et al. (2001) and Greene (2000).

WIGGINS CONTENT SCALES

Harris and Lingoes established subscales that were more homogeneous in content than were their six corresponding Clinical scales. On the other hand, Wiggins (1966) created a set of 13 Content scales based the entire *MMPI* item pool.

TABLE 4.1

Clinical Interpretation of Selected Harris and Lingoes Subscales

Subscale	Interpretation
2PR (D2)	High scorers claim to lack sufficient energy to carry on routine activities. They also report unexpressed anger. When other depression indices are high, a low score on this scale points to a suicide potential.
2MD (D4)	High scorers feel that they are beset by cognitive difficulties, including inability to reason clearly, to make decisions, or to think logically. Memory is also impaired, or so they report.
3DSA (Hy1)	Low scorers tend to be socially maladroit and anxious, shy, to embarrass easily, and are generally uncomfortable in social situations. This scale clusters with 4SI (Pd3) and 9IMP (Ma3). High scorers are socially comfortable. Respondents scoring above T70 may be reflecting denial.
3NA (Hy2)	High scorers seek favorable regard by others by adopting a Pollyanna attitude toward society. This scale has substantial cofluctuation with 6N.
4SI (Pd3)	See 3DSA.
4AC (Pd2)	High scorers are rebellious and have difficulty accepting standards of behavior that impose responsibilities and interfere with personal gratification. They may be unaware of their angry feelings and lack empathy toward others. Due to its unreliability, however, this scale is replaced by W-AUT (see Wiggins scales).
4FD (Pd1)	High scorers reject the family situation and report that it is affectionless, stressful, and lacking in emotional support.
4SOA (Pd4)	High scorers feel isolated, misunderstood, and put upon. They lack a viable social support system and tend to blame others for their problems. This scale cofluctuates with 8SOA, which is interpreted similarly. These respondents are also likely to score high on 4FD, making the claim that family members and intimates fail to provide support.
6P (Pa2)	High scorers regard themselves as hypersensitive. They believe that they can be emotionally injured more easily than others and they heal less quickly. They are accordingly identified here as socially vulnerable.
6N (Pa3)	High scorers claim to be moral and virtuous. These respondents appear naïve and perhaps too trusting. They seem to believe that people in general are benign and honest, which justifies their own moral outlook and behavior.
8SOA (Sc1)	See 4SOA. The two subscales cofluctuate markedly, despite minimal item overlap.
8COG (Sc3)	High scorers on this subscale admit to problems similar to those of the high scorer on 2MD: inability to reason, concentrate, and remember. However, they believe that their mental processes are not simply dulled; they have become threateningly strange. Thus, high scorers on 8COG tend to be more disturbed by their cognitive deficits than high scorers on 2MD. The two subscales frequently elevate as a pair.
8CON (Sc4)	High scorers on this subscale announce that they are so emotionally upset that they have lost motivation to behave in a constructive or productive fashion. This is often a consequence of cognitive problems that are reflected in high scorers on 2MD and/or 8COG. This subscale tends to cofluctuate with Work Attitude (WA) Scale and Work Interference (WRK).

(Continued)

TABLE 4.1

(Continued)

Subscale	Interpretation
9AMO (Ma1)	High scorers hold to the philosophy that a person is foolish not to take every possible advantage of all situations, usually—but not invariably—short of outright violation of the law. They tend to be somewhat selfish, cynical people who perceive life as an endless series of minor skirmishes in which the person who is not overburdened with scruples is usually victorious. They also believe that most other people share their views.
9PMA (Ma2)	This subscale is a measure of sensation-seeking. High scorers have a high optimal stimulation level, a strong "need to seek arousing sensations and experiences via stimulus novelty and complexity, risk taking and other varied sources of excitement" (Zuckerman, 1979). Thus, high scorers are persons who are driven from within to live on the edge. This subscale is most probably the explanation of why only Scale *9* of the *MMPI–2* Clinical Scales has consistent positive correlations with Zuckerman's Sensation Seeking Scale.
9IMP (Ma3)	See *3DSA*

Wiggins began his quest by building on the original 26 content categories established by Hathaway and McKinley (1940). Wiggins concluded that there were 13 distinct factors to the *MMPI* item content. His original sample consisted of nonpsychiatric college students. He later used both a psychiatric and nonpsychiatric general population to validate the scales.

Any statistical technique that employs samples is subject to error, especially a sample of college students only (Butcher, Graham, & Ben-Porath, 1995). Furthermore, there have been attempts, without much success, to create new scales by factor analysis of the *MMPI* item pool. However, Wiggins was able to avoid the many statistical and methodological pitfalls by employing two procedures in his method.

The first procedure is recognizable as expertise in decision making about item face validity. Wiggins preferred to conceptualize this process as an application of intuitive skills. Wiggins and a colleague examined each factor, identified items that did not appear to fit logically with the factor to which the original analysis had assigned them, and transferred these items to factors with which their content appeared more congruent. This helped to prevent premature, erroneous assignment of items to factors. He thereby avoided some of the sampling error related to assignment of items that had undercut the accuracy of previous factor analytic studies of the *MMPI*.

Wiggins also computed correlation coefficients between each item and each of the total factor scores. Those items that had coefficients below .30 or that correlated more highly with any other factor than the one to which they were assigned initially were removed.

Wiggins did not give the number of items that were manipulated as a function of clinical judgment, although the text suggests that the number was considerable.

More than 200 items were eliminated as a function of the content analysis. These methodological maneuvers may very well account for the substantial clinical success of the final scales developed by Wiggins. Fifteen scales resulted from the procedure described thus far. Two of these tentative scales lacked sufficient internal consistency even after the removal of noncontributing items. Wiggins decided to abandon them based on their lack of homogeneity. The remaining scales have all proven clinically useful.

It should be considered as a tribute to Wiggins' intuition and methodology that two of the more recent factor analyses of the original *MMPI* item pool (Foerstner, 1986; J. H. Johnson, Null, Butcher, & K. N. Johnson, 1984) emerged with approximately the same factors as did Wiggins two decades earlier.

With the revision of the *MMPI* to the *MMPI–2*, both Wiggins (Butcher, Graham, Williams, & Ben-Porath, 1990) and the *MMPI–2* revision team (Butcher et al., 1989) believed that the Wiggins scales were dead and unusable in the new version. However, this appears to be far from the truth. Kohutek (1992) used the Wiggins scales with the *MMPI–2* items on a sample of psychiatric individuals. Kohutek found that transposing the scales to the *MMPI–2* revisions did not statistically change the scores on the Wiggins Content Scales.

A study by Levitt, Browning, and Freeland (1992) helped clarify how much the Wiggins scales were affected by losses of items in the revision. The Wiggins scales had a median raw score difference of 0.64 for a psychiatric sample and 0.605 for a nonpsychiatric sample. Furthermore, the current clinical research program also demonstrates the statistical correlates and, in Appendix B, reports reliabilities of the Wiggins scales. The Wiggins scales have turned out to be hardier than was originally believed even in the face of item losses.

However, changes have occurred in the scales that require a critical look before they are simply used in the *MMPI–2*. Ten of the 13 Wiggins (1966) Content scales shrank in length as a result of the revision, but only Religious Fundamentalism (*REL*) was thoroughly decimated (Table 4.2). Aside from *REL*, the item loss percentages among the remaining 9 altered scales ranged from a low of 3.7% for Social Maladjustment (*W-SOC*) and Phobias (*W-PHO*) to a high of 32.1% for Poor Health (*W-HEA*). From the perspective of numbers of items lost, a total of 41 scored on the Wiggins scales became unavailable for use in *MMPI–2*. This amounts to an average of 4.1 items per scale for affected scales. Omitting *REL*, the average loss is 3.3 items per scale; for the affected plus intact scales, the average loss was 2.5 items per scale. The current study, described in chapter 5, furthered the evaluation of the changes and determined that, in addition to the *REL* scale, Feminine Interest (*FEM*) lacked reliability and is not clinically useful. The loss of *FEM*, however, does not appear to have resulted from the revision process. Thus, 11 Wiggins Content Scales remain. Levitt's (1990) analysis of the *MMPI* revision's impact on the Wiggins Content Scales is updated in Table 4.2.

The recovery of 11 Wiggins Content Scales brings with it a wealth of empirical studies on their validity and applicability (Boerger, 1975; Jarneke & Chambers,

TABLE 4.2

The Effects of the *MMPI–2* Revision on Numbers of Wiggins Items

Wiggins Content Scales		MMPI	MMPI–2	% Items Lost	Useful
W-AUT	(Authority Conflict)	20	20	0.0	YES
W-DEP	(Depression)	33	33	0.0	YES
W-FAM	(Family Conflicts)	16	16	0.0	YES
W-FEM	(Feminine Interests)	30	23	23.3	NO
W-HYP	(Hypomania)	25	23	8.0	YES
W-HOS	(Manifest Hostility)	27	25	7.4	YES
W-ORG	(Organic Symptoms)	36	32	11.1	YES
W-PHO	(Phobias)	27	26	3.7	YES
W-HEA	(Poor Health)	28	19	32.1	YES
W-MOR	(Poor Morale)	23	22	4.3	YES
W-PSY	(Psychoticism)	48	45	6.2	YES
W-REL	(Religious Fundamentalism)	12	1	91.7	NO
W-SOC	(Social Maladjustment)	27	26	3.7	YES

Sources: Levitt's (Copyright 1989 by Lawrence Erlbaum Associates) table, based on Lachar and Alexander (Copyright 1978 by the American Psychological Association) and Wiggins (Copyright 1966 by the American Psychological Association). Adapted with permission.

1977; Lachar & Alexander, 1978; Loper, Kammeier, & Hoffman, 1973; Mezzich, Damarin, & Erickson, 1974; Nichols, 1984, 1987; Payne & Wiggins, 1972; Taylor, Ptacek, Carithers, Griffin, & Coyne, 1972; Wiggins, Goldberg, & Applebaum, 1971; Woodward, Robinowitz, & Penk, 1980).

The remaining Wiggins Content Scales generally continue to relate to the original factors established by Wiggins and can be generalized to various populations (Greene, 2000). Changes to *W-HEA* are great enough to make it a different scale and thus an exception to the preceding general conclusion. Those changes are alluded to in the interpretations that appear in Table 4.3. The clinician can feel confident in using the Wiggins scales with *MMPI–2*. They can, at times, add both richness and convergent evidence when used in conjunction with the Tryon, Stein, and Chu (*TSC*) Cluster Scales and the *MMPI–2* Content Scales that are mentioned later.

Interpretations of the Wiggins scales have been proposed by Lachar and Alexander (1978) and Graham (1987), as well as by Wiggins himself (1966). Graham also suggested interpretations for low scores on each of the scales. However, the Wiggins scales, like most special scales, are unidirectional. Low scores usually have no practical significance.

Table 4.3 presents the interpretations for high scores suggested by Wiggins (1966) and Lachar and Alexander (1978). Their descriptions vary by scale in the amount of detail provided. Lachar and Alexander presented both detailed and terse summaries. The same was true of Wiggins. Often when one of them offered a more detailed account, the other would be notable for its brevity. Nevertheless, it will be obvious that the two sources agree substantially concerning interpreta-

TABLE 4.3
Interpretation of the Wiggins Content Scales

	Based on Wiggins (1966)	Based on Lachar & Alexander (1978)	Based on Levitt (1989)
Authority Conflict (W-AUT)	High W-AUT persons see life as a struggle for survival. They are sure that others cannot be trusted to treat them fairly. Instead they anticipate them to behave in a cold-hearted manner in order to extract gain for themselves at the expense of those who unfortunately become their prey. There is no limit to how far they will carry things to gain their objectives.	Endorsed item content reflects the expectation that people often will treat others in an exploitative manner. Responses imply disregard for social mores that regulate civil behavior. In patient groups these persons may push others to the limit. They use others. Their behavior may strain family relationships.	Wiggins' interpretation is extreme. It might apply to respondents who score above T70. For scores in the range T58-T69, the Lachar-Alexander interpretation is recommended. This scale is unchanged from its MMPI version.
Depression (W-DEP)	High W-DEP persons feel guilty and harbor many regrets. They feel that life is no fun for them any longer. Complaints include loss of concentration and absence of goals that motivate them. Self-concept is negative. They worry a great deal about the present and future. They experience feelings of social alienation. They are intropunitive and depressed.	High W-DEP persons admit to many of the symptoms that go with depression. These include reduced interest in their surroundings, negative outlook, harsh judgment of their personal shortcomings, and dwelling on problems. Among patients, self isolation, guilty feelings and reduced activity occur.	Wiggins states the case well, but some high W-DEP persons may simply be screaming loudly for help, not classically depressed. This MMPI scale remains unchanged.
Family Problems (W-FAM)	High W-FAM persons report having had an earlier home life that lacked affection. Parents were overly critical, picking on them over small things. They were easily provoked. MMPI items are not always clear regarding the context, but mostly refer to the family of origin and the childhood home life.	Responses suggest familial pathology. Both problems in the family of origin and the current family context are causes of concern. Among males, high W-FAM reports may signal a hyperactive style that is associated with substance abuse and other out of control behavior.	The Lachar-Alexander and Wiggins' interpretations of high W-FAM are unsupported by clinical experience for males; most high scorers are referring to their current home. This scale is preserved intact.

Hypomania (W-HYP)	High W-HYP persons are prone to being excited, tense and restless. Their energy may impart a sense of well-being.	High W-HYP persons say they relish a rapid paced lifestyle. Irritability or loose affect may also be present. Others view very high scorers as hyperactive and immature. They externalize blame and will misuse other people in selfish ways.	Wiggins' interpretation fits for scores T60–69. Above T70, the Lachar–Alexander applies, no matter who the respondent is. Two items were lost and two more cut in item analysis.
Manifest Hostility (W-HOS)	High W-HOS persons admit to sadistic feelings. They readily argue, try to outdo others and strive to get even if they feel they have been wronged. They have a low threshold for irritation and often behave in an ill-tempered manner. Their social behavior is excessively forceful.	High W-HOS persons admit to having poorly controlled feelings of anger and need to dominate others. They may act out on their anger and resentments. These traits may be linked among patients to violent and destructive behavior with an antisocial flavor.	W-HOS is an excellent measure of experienced anger but sadistic is a bit extreme. Two items were lost to the test revision and two more cut in item analysis.
Organic Symptoms (W-ORG)	High W-ORG persons report a variety of organic symptoms that involve possible central nervous system problems. Many of the complaints are specific, involving sensory and motor systems.	These persons' reports may have an organic origin or may relate to other underlying psychological factors. That is, some high scorers may have symptoms based on emotional conflicts.	W-ORG symptoms may indicate organic involvement or they may reflect a dissociative disorder. The scale itself does not distinguish. Item loss: 4.
Phobias (W-PHO)	High W-PHO persons report a vast array of aversions and fears that the literature identifies as phobias: e.g., being tightly enclosed, heights, and the dark.	Fears make these persons uncomfortable in many and varied contexts. They are seen by others as nervous, worried and phobic. They may isolate themselves and be depressed.	Almost half of the items in W-PHO do not refer to phobias directly. Scores as high as T60 may be obtained by non-phobic individuals. Lost: 1 item.
Poor Health (W-HEA)	High W-HEA persons are concerned about personal health and admit to a variety of gastrointestinal complaints centering around upset stomach and difficulty in elimination (this focus is cut in MMPI-2).	Multiple somatic complaints by high W-HEA scorers focus on the G-I system. They are focused on and worried about health. Some cardio-pulmonary signs may be reported.	Nine items were lost in the 1989 test revision, affecting this scale's interpretation. The Lachar-Alexander description is still generally applicable.

(Continued)

47

TABLE 4.3
(Continued)

	Based on Wiggins (1966)	Based on Lachar & Alexander (1978)	Based on Levitt (1989)
Poor Morale (*W-MOR*)	High *W-MOR* persons are low in self-confidence and fear that there is little hope that they can lead successful lives. They are overly influenced by what they believe others think and feel about them. *W-MOR*'s meaning overlaps that of *W-DEP* and *W-SOC*.	High scorers' responses show pervasive self-doubt. They dwell on past failures, blaming personal shortcomings. High *W-MOR* patients readily give up and withdraw when others' actions upset them. This happens often because of their hypersensitivity.	*W-MOR* is an index of self-image and self-esteem. Other depression indicators relate to it, and it correlates strongly with measures of negative self-concept. Only 1 item was lost to the test's revision.
Psychoticism (*W-PSY*)	High *W-PSY* persons report many typical psychotic-paranoid symptoms. They admit to disordered thinking and dissociative type experiences. Furthermore, they feel estranged from others and misunderstood by them.	Wiggins's description is followed. Lachar adds that patients cannot grasp why others act as they do, which adds to their suspicion and worry. Symptoms and adjustment may indicate psychosis is present.	Due to overlap of *W-PSY* and alienation scales, non-psychotic sociopathic individuals may obtain misleading high scores. Three items were lost to the test revision and 3 to item analysis.
Social Maladjustment (*W-SOC*)	High *W-SOC* persons are socially tense, easily embarrassed and inhibited socially. This makes them appear highly reserved. Low *W-SOC* persons are quite sociable and enjoy lively activity. This scale seems to cover an introversion-extraversion gamut.	Lachar concurs with Wiggins' high *W-SOC* description. Among patients, he adds, despair and suicidal ideation may appear, or defensive withdrawal may lead to reduced activity or to compulsive focusing of attention onto detail.	Wiggins' interpretation of low scores on *W-SOC* does not mesh with clinical experience. *W-SOC* is a one-tailed scale. Suicidal ideas are uncommon. Lost to revision: 1 item.

Sources: Levitt's (Copyright 1989 by Lawrence Erlbaum Associates) table, based on Lachar and Alexander (Copyright 1978 by the American Psychological Association). Wiggins (Copyright 1966 by the American Psychological Association). Adapted with permission.

tion. For each scale, some notes have been added that follow from extensive clinical application of these useful scales. Interpretation remains the same for these
scales when used with the *MMPI–2* items.

MMPI–2 CONTENT SCALES

Butcher, Graham, Williams, and Ben-Porath (1990) created the Content scales for
the *MMPI–2*. These became the first series of special scales developed exclusively from the *MMPI–2* item pool and not scale carryovers from the original
MMPI. However, they share striking resemblances to the Wiggins Content Scales
discussed in this chapter. Thus, the *MMPI–2* Content Scales share several similar
domains with the Wiggins scales and items substantially overlap.

Greene (1991) suggested that 10 *MMPI–2* scales are related by title to a specific Wiggins scale. According to Greene's computations, the range of item overlap among these pairs of scales is from 25% (*LSE* and *W-MOR*) to 83% (*FRS* and
W-PHO; *BIZ* and *W-PSY*). The mean item overlap computed from Greene's data
is 53.5%. In terms of correlations, every *MMPI–2* scale has a clear relative among
the Wiggins scales. This fact is clearly shown in Table 4.4. The data in the table
are based on the *MMPI–2* standardization sample (Butcher et al., 1990).

TABLE 4.4
Relationships of *MMPI–2* Content Scales and Selected Wiggins Content Scales

Reliability of MMPI–2 Content Scales		*Correlations of MMPI–2 Content Scales with Wiggins Content Scales*
T-R[a]	*Alpha*[b]	
.87/.90	.83/.82	*ANX* [*W-DEP* .83/.80] [*W-MOR* .77/.74]
.86/.81	.75/.72	*FRS* [*W-PHO* .92/.91]
.85/.83	.77/.74	*OBS* [*W-DEP* .75/.69] [*W-MOR* .79/.72]
.85/.87	.86/.85	*DEP* [*W-DEP* .91/.89] [*W-MOR* .80/.79]
.85/.81	.80/.76	*HEA* [*W-ORG* .84/.82] [*W-HEA* .81/.79]
.81/.78	.74/.73	*BIZ* [*W-PSY* .82/.84]
.82/.85	.73/.76	*ANG* [*W-HOS* .80/.79]
.89/.80	.85/.86	*CYN* [*W-AUT* .87/.84]
.87/.81	.75/.78	*ASP* [*W-AUT* .87/.88]
.79/.82	.68/.72	*TPA* [*W-HOS* .78/.80]
.86/.84	.83/.79	*LSE* [*W-DEP* .73/.70] [*W-MOR* .83/.79]
.90/.91	.84/.83	*SOD* [*W-SOC* .92/.92]
.83/.84	.77/.73	*FAM* [*W-FAM* .86/.82]
.91/.90	.84/.82	*WRK* [*W-DEP* .82/.79] [*W-MOR* .85/.82]
.88/.79	.80/.78	*TRT* [*W-DEP* .76/.75] [*W-MOR* .78/.75]

Note: Data based on Butcher et al. (1990). Female sample appears before slash, male after it.
[a]Test–retest.
[b]Cronbach's (1951) coefficient alpha.

All of the coefficients except one in Table 4.4 are at least .70, and more than one half are higher than .80. Obviously, this correspondence is due in large part to the substantial item overlap. However, other factors also play an important role as illustrated by rank-order correlations of only .53 between the item overlap in the scales analyzed by Greene (1991) and the respective gender-averaged correlation coefficients in Table 4.4.

The reliabilities of the *MMPI–2* Content Scales are also presented in Table 4.4 for contrast. It can readily be seen that *MMPI–2* and Wiggins Content Scale intercorrelations compare favorably with the reliabilities of the *MMPI–2* Content Scales. In fact, the scale intercorrelations are generally higher than the Cronbach (1951) alphas. Inferentially, the alphas offer a stronger measure of reliability than the test–retest coefficients due to sampling. Moreover, the alphas are based on the total normative sample—at least a thousand cases—whereas the test–retest coefficients were derived from only 111 female and 82 male subjects.

The *MMPI–2* Content Scales have been an excellent addition and provide more convergent information when using the cluster analysis approach. Scale definitions and interpretation are copyright protected and cannot be presented here. Users will have no difficulty accessing these in available sources, including Butcher et al. (2001), Friedman et al. (2001), Graham (2000), and Greene (2000). All provide guidance for interpreting the *MMPI–2* Content Scales.

TRYON, STEIN, AND CHU CLUSTER SCALES

In the 1960s, Tryon and his associates developed a mathematical method for creating independent scales from a large item pool using a special procedure known as cluster analysis, which is similar to factor analytic techniques (Chu, 1966; Stein, 1968; Tryon, 1966). This statistical technique was applied to 310 *MMPI* records representing 220 Veterans Administration Hospital inpatients and outpatients and 90 military officers matched with the patients for age and education. The analysis resulted in seven highly reliable clusters that can be considered to be scales for all practical purposes.

The Tryon, Stein, and Chu Cluster Scales (*TSC*) have made only rare appearances in research and little is known about their clinical usefulness from experimental data. Stein (1968) reported means on the seven scales for 20 male samples and 13 female samples, most of which had less than 75 subjects. He also reported intercorrelations with the Omnibus Personality Inventory (Heist & Yonge, 1968), the Edwards Personal Preference Schedule (Edwards, 1959), and the Strong Vocational Interest Blank, an earlier version of the Strong–Hansen–Campbell Interest Inventory (Hansen & Campbell, 1985). These samples were small and select: 50 University of California students studying abroad, 50 forestry students, and 50 "public counseling cases" at the University of California Counseling Center.

There was a handful of significant correlation coefficients, but their bearing on the validity of the various *TSC* scales remained unclear.

Boerger (1975) obtained *TSC* scale scores along with 18 other *MMPI* special scales scores from two samples comprised of 679 psychiatric inpatients. Sixty-three criterion variables were employed in an exploratory effort similar to the study of the Harris and Lingoes by Calvin (1975) previously described. Like Calvin, Boerger used the *NOSIE* (Honigfeld & Klett, 1965) and the *GBPRS* (Overall & Gorman, 1962) among his criterion measures.

Boerger analyzed his data by comparing mean scores for the highest scoring 25% of the sample on each scale with the remainder of the sample, and the lowest scoring 25% with the remainder of the sample. A rationale for this method was not clear and it appeared to have methodological difficulties. A bit less than 15% of all mean comparisons for the *TSC* scales were significant at the 10% level—appearing to be more a product of chance. Boerger's criterion, however, was significant in both samples; his reasoning was that $.10 \times .10 = .01$. A very much smaller number of comparisons reached Boeger's criterion. Because this was an inpatient group, *TSC/S, TSC/D,* and *TSC/A* did much better than *TSC/I, TSC/B,* and *TSC/R.* So there is a suggestion of some support for validity for the former threesome. But this consideration applies only to the *TSC* scales as measures of psychopathology. The Boerger data do not bear on the utility of the *TSC* scales as personality measures. Further research is clearly needed.

The Tryon, Stein, and Chu scales received insufficient attention in clinical circles ever to be established as useful *MMPI* scales. Unfamiliar methodology was one possible reason that they were not more widely adopted. Another plausible reason for their limited acceptance is that they arrived on the assessment scene at a time that the Wiggins scales were becoming widely accepted. For the *TSC* scales, it was an unfortunate fate of star-crossed timing. Since publication of *MMPI–2*, they have been in danger of being lost altogether before ever being tried. Whatever the reason may be for their neglect, there appears to be no research using the *TSC* scales with the *MMPI–2* item pool prior to the present study, although Levitt (1989) strongly favored them.

Unlike many of the *MMPI* special scales, the *TSC* scales were little affected by the test's revision. Three of the seven *TSC* scales—*TSC/D, TSC/I, TSC/S*—were unaffected by the revision. Only small numbers of items were lost (Levitt, 1990) from the remaining four scales (Table 4.5). The Autism scale (*TSC/A*) was most affected, with a loss of 13 % of its items. The remaining three scales each lost 5% or fewer of its items. Overall, only six *TSC* items were lost out of 191 (3.14% loss). By comparison, the overall *MMPI* lost 90 items plus the 16-second appearances of the *T-R* scale (18.73%). The survival rate for *TSC* items following the *MMPI* revision is, thus, a remarkable affirmation of the quality of the original scale construction process.

Clinically, all the *TSC* scales have been found to be useful measures. Although Levitt (1989) questioned the utility of the Autism (*TSC/A*) scale, the current study

TABLE 4.5
Effects of the *MMPI–2* Revision on the *TSC* Cluster Scales

TSC scale		MMPI	MMPI–2	% Items Lost
TSC/A	(Autism)	23	20	13.0
TSC/B	(Body Symptoms)	33	32	3.0
TSC/D	(Depression)	28	28	0.0
TSC/R	(Resentment)	19	18	5.3
TSC/I	(Social Introversion)	26	26	0.0
TSC/S	(Suspicion & Mistrust)	25	25	0.0
TSC/T	(Tension)	35	34	2.9

shows that it has clinical value in assessing disruptive thinking and as such contributes to the Cognitive Disorders cluster. Table 4.6 provides clinically based interpretations of these seven scales.

INDIANA RATIONAL SCALES

Levitt (1989) and a group of clinical psychologists at Indiana University Medical Center developed a group of scales using a rational process. The goal was to create scales that tapped areas that were not adequately covered by the clinical or special scales. Thus, they employed a technique of selecting items based on face validity and consensual expert decisions. This technique was not novel and had been used before (Ashton & Goldberg, 1973; Gynther, Burkhart, & Hovanitz, 1979; Jackson, 1975).

Seven scales were developed by means of expert judgments. Three judges determined the items for four of the scales. Only those items were included that were agreed on by all three judges: Severe Reality Distortions (*I-RD*; 18 items), Dissociative Symptoms (*I-DS*; 8 items), Obsessive–Compulsiveness (*I-OC*; 9 items), and Sex Problems (*I-SP*; 14 items).

A fourth judge was added for the creation of two additional scales: Self-Concept (*I-SC*; 14 items) and Dependency (*I-De*; 9 items). Only those items were included that were agreed on by three of the four judges. A seventh scale, Dominance (*I-Do*; 17 items), was developed independently by Levitt. Additional considerations were not recorded for why this specific method and sequence of scale development were used (Levitt, 1989).

The clinical psychologist item judges shared a common educational background as well as a common workplace, so the concepts used as scale titles were not defined. The only instruction was that every scale item should be manifestly face valid, requiring little or no inference to justify its inclusion in the scale. There were two special conditions. It was understood beforehand by the judges that only items dealing directly with hallucinations and delusions should be selected for *I-*

TABLE 4.6
Interpretations of the Tryon, Stein, and Chu Scales

TSC Scale	Interpretations
Autism (TSC/A)	A high score indicates a person who experiences strange thoughts, frequently slips into daydreams rather than engaging external reality, and if encountered in an inpatient setting is more likely than not to be diagnosed as having a thought processing disorder. In addition, these persons are prone to view their cognitive processes as inefficient and to make complaints regarding them. Derealization may be present. Low scorers deny these symptomatic expressions.
Body Symptoms (TSC/B)	High scorers are anxious about their physical health; they claim to have a variety of physical symptoms of the type commonly associated with anxiety and depression, such as pains, easy fatigability, feelings of weakness, and minor gastrointestinal complaints.
Depression (TSC/D)	High scorers are depressed, unhappy, brood a great deal, and feel under chronic tension. They lack energy and feel useless, incapable and guilty.
Resentment (TSC/R)	High scorers tend to express hostility in a typically adolescent fashion; they readily feel imposed on and denigrated and are likely to be impatient and irritable. These feelings differ from anger.
Social Introversion (TSC/I)	High scorers are shy, socially uncomfortable, easily embarrassed, and tend to withdraw when faced by stress, especially in situations involving interpersonal relations.
Suspicion & Mistrust (TSC/S)	High scorers are likely to be cynical and opportunistic and to mistrust the sincerity and benignity of the motivations of others. They may have a sociopathic orientation but are not considered paranoid in the classical sense unless other scales are elevated. Their mistrust suggests character defects rather than disordered thought. Low scorers tend to be naive and suggestible and are relatively easily manipulated.
Tension (TSC/T)	High scorers are anxiety-prone, claim to worry chronically, and tend to become tense easily. Elevation suggests a traitlike disposition toward various expressions of anxiety, including obsessions, panic attacks, and phobic concerns. They are at risk as well for comorbid depression.

RD. In selecting items for *I-De*, the judges began with the 54 items in the Dependency scale (*Dy*) (Navran, 1954).

Levitt (1989) did not publish reliability or validity studies on the scales. Instead, the psychologists using them accepted them as clinically useful. One study (Nash, Hulsey, Sexton, Harralson, & Lambert, 1993) used the *I-RD* scale in work on long-term effects of childhood sexual trauma. The researchers found that *I-RD* successfully differentiated among four groups of women who were grouped on the basis of sexual abuse versus nonabuse as children. The other prior research link for the Indiana Rational Scales is that *I-De* was based on the earlier established Dependency scale (Navran, 1954). Levitt affirmed, based on clinical experience, that these *MMPI* scales yielded valid clinical information.

The *MMPI–2* revision affected the various Indiana Rational Scales differently. Three were completely unaffected (*I-OC, I-De, I-SC*) by item losses. The Sex

Problems scale (*I-SP*), which was scored differently for each gender, was most affected, with losses of 33.3% of items for females to 35.7% for males. The remaining three affected Indiana scales lost between 6.2% and 12.5% of their items. Using the average items lost for the male and female versions of *I-SP*, a total of 8.5 items was lost from four scales, for an average item loss per scale of 2.1. After adding the three unaffected Indiana scales, the average item loss drops to 1.2 per scale.

This current clinical research program has retooled these scales and computed reliability coefficients (see chap. 6 and Appendix B). See, especially, changes to the *I-DS* scale. Two of the Indiana Rational Scales were determined to be unreliable (*I-De* and *I-SP*) and could not be salvaged. Because of their importance and the unavailability of comparable scales, replacements were developed. The five remaining Indiana Rational Scales are assessed in chapters 8 and 9 in terms of their contribution to clinical prediction equations. A more thorough assessment of these scales will require studies with different kinds of patients from other settings. Table 4.7 provides interpretation for the five surviving scales.

TABLE 4.7
Interpretations of the Indiana Rational Scales

Indiana Rational Scale	Interpretations
Severe Reality Distortions (*I-RD*)	High scorers are probably psychotic, especially when other indicators of psychosis are present (e.g., > T70 on *BIZ* and *W-PSY*). The individual is probably actively or most recently has experienced hallucinations or delusions.
Dissociative Symptoms (*I-DS*)	High scores may suggest the presence of a dissociative disorder. Hysteroid personalities are likely to have elevations of T60; individuals scoring at T70 or above are usually the victims of severe dissociative tendencies. When *I-RD* and other scales measuring psychotic traits are also elevated, the dissociative symptoms need to be evaluated as parts of a disordered thought complex.
Obsessive–Compulsiveness (*I-OC*)	High scorers on *I-OC* indicate severe obsessive–compulsive disorder, either as neurosis or as an aspect of a psychotic disorder. Individuals with obsessional traits or obsessive–compulsive personalities also elevate on this scale but can be differentiated by using other corroborative data sources.
Dominance (*I-Do*)	The items on this scale describe individuals who have strong views that they vigorously defend. They regard themselves as relatively independent of the views of others and are outspoken and self-confident. This is not equivalent to *DO* (Gough et al., 1951).
Poor Self-Concept (*I-SC*)	This scale measures the extent to which the individual has a negative self-image. Individuals scoring high on this scale are low in self-esteem and self-confidence, and regard themselves as relatively incapable and generally unattractive.

SCALES DEVELOPED BY THE CURRENT RESEARCH PROGRAM

A series of scales for identifying the personality disorders (*PDOs*) was developed and here is called the Indiana Personality Disorder Scales. These are treated at length in Levitt and Gotts (1995) and in chapter 6, to which the reader is referred. Two other new groups of scales, the Psychosocial Development Scales and the Critical Inquiry Scales (see Appendices A, B, and C), receive extensive attention in chapter 7. Their presentation there will suffice for understanding their design and initial validation, as well as how they are used and interpreted. A scale was developed (Appendix E) to measure Psychogenic Rage (*Rage*). Additional exposition is included for the Impulsivity Scales.

The Impulsivity Scales

The development and status of the Impulsivity Scales is covered in chapter 7. Further information on their clinical interpretations is provided in this section, together with a brief review of empirical support. There are three subscales consisting of items selected to measure different aspects or components of impulsivity. The sum of the three represents their composite potential. All correlations reported hereafter were significant beyond .001.

*Behavioral Impulsivity (***Imp-B***).* Imp-B includes two basic types of behaviorally oriented items that differ from one another in the life history segment to which they refer. One group of items refers to the past, including some misbehaviors that occurred in school during childhood as well as other past norm violating behaviors whose times and locations are less specified. A second basic type consists of items that report an inclination to act out in some manner. These items often suggest a strong impulse to action without stating whether the action took place or may take place at some future time. This scale correlates more strongly with Pd (.63) and PdK (.46) than does either of the other individual components. These individuals also are notable for seeking excitement and stimulation ($9PMA$, $r = .60$) and being low in social responsibility (Re, $r = -.78$). High scoring persons manifest antisocial traits. Low scoring persons are behaviorally inhibited.

*Ideational Impulsivity (***Imp-I***).* Imp-I items present expressions of attitudes and sentiments that are ill-considered or poorly thought out. Their endorsement reveals a predisposition to make snap judgments. That is, high scoring persons fail to reflect on what they are thinking before they blurt something out. This implies some deficiency in ego functioning wherein the executive editing capacity fails to assert itself. High scores occur in persons with thought process disorders (Sc, $r = .74$; ScK, $r = .59$; Pa, $r = .51$; $S+$, $r = .71$), ego inflation ($9EI$, $r = .66$), authority conflict (W-AUT, $r = .75$), hostility (Ho, $r = .85$), suspiciousness

(*TSC/S, r* = .75), and an attitude of social alienation (*So-Alien, r* = .74). Thus, psychotics and those with strong antisocial traits elevate on this scale. Low scores relate to the overcontrol and suppression scale *R* (*r* = −.42), thereby appearing with lower scores on all of the foregoing scales as well.

Affective Impulsivity (Imp-A). *Imp-A* is comprised of items indicating that strong, unexpected, or labile affect stimulates the person to act. This scale includes an element of loss of emotional control that catches the person off guard. Both anger (*ANG, r* = .78) and resentments (*TSC/R, r* = .79) figure prominently in triggering dyscontrol, with anxiety (*ANX, r* = .61) and depression (*2SD, r* = .54) playing lesser roles. Low scorers overcontrol hostile expression (*O-H, r* = −.69) but admit to being troubled by social anxiety (*Impert, r* = −.51). They exert considerable effort in maintaining themselves in a state of continual affective constriction.

Impulsivity Total (Imp-T). *Imp-T* represents the summation of behavioral, ideational, and affective expression or restriction of impulses. Although the items of the three subscales all fit well into the total scale, the three components relate to one another more moderately (*r* = .51–.60). Their partial independence from one another helps to explain the ways these varied aspects of impulse expression can relate differently to various external criteria. Thus, whereas *Imp-T* provides an overall estimate of suppression versus expression, it is important to consider the pattern of subscales. Extreme scores in either direction on any of the four scales indicate less satisfactory management of impulse life, whereas scores in the moderate range suggest more healthy ways of handling impulses.

OTHER VALUABLE SPECIAL SCALES

Among the surviving Harris and Lingoes Subscales, Wiggins Content Scales, Tryon, Stein, and Chu Cluster Scales, and Indiana Rational Scales, there are some 49 clinically proven measures covering a wide range of symptoms and traits. When the *MMPI–2* Content Scales are included, this increases the number to 64. The addition of the PDO and Impulsivity Scales further enlarges the array of special scales. This collection of scales greatly enhances the diagnostic capacity of the traditional Clinical scales. Furthermore, there are additional scales of proven utility, some kept and others bypassed in the *MMPI* revision, which can be invaluable to the clinician who uses special scales.

The Control Scale (*Cn*)

Some seriously emotionally disturbed individuals urgently require hospitalization. Others, whose symptoms appear to be serious, maintain themselves in the community, at least marginally. A perennial clinical problem involves telling one from the other in order to determine who does and who does not need more intensive treatment.

A *MMPI* approach to this problem was attempted by Cuadra (1956). Cuadra decided on a contrasting group approach, simple in conception, but tedious to carry out. The first step was to select 30 young, reasonably well-educated psychiatric patients who had voluntarily sought treatment and were tested within 15 days of admission. These "criterion abnormals" were then matched with a group of "criterion normals," which was Caudra's way of describing a group that was equally as disturbed, but for whom hospitalization had not been recommended. The two groups were essentially similar in age and education and were almost identical in scores on *MMPI* Clinical and Validity Scales. Cuadra had to sift through 4,000 records in order to obtain his criterion normals.

Cuadra's Control Scale (*Cn*) consisted of 32 items that had discriminated the two criterion groups best for both sexes plus an additional 18 items (total = 50), which did not differentiate the criterion groups as effectively but did discriminate them in the same direction for both sexes. There was little overlap in the total scale scores between Cuadra's criterion groups. The range of scores for the "normal" was from 27–45; for "abnormals" it was from 9–33. Only four scores in the normal group were below 30; only one of the abnormals was above 30.

Forty-one of the 50 items on *Cn* survived the *MMPI* revision. Of these items, 33 remained in the scale following the current item analysis (see chap. 6). This represents a major shift in the scale's composition. Moreover, in the current analysis, three items that Cuadra had originally keyed false were shown by both their correlations and content to belong with the true keyed items. The scale is changed in yet another respect. It originally displayed some balance of true versus false item keying. That is no longer true; about 85% of its items are now keyed true. Thus, it is no longer appropriate to interpret it in the original manner.

A validity question must be addressed: Can the scale be used any longer in accordance with its original intention? That is, should low scorers with serious psychopathology receive more intensive treatment, such as inpatient or partial hospitalization? Second, are high scorers (> T65) better able to subsist on a traditional outpatient basis? Because of its implications for therapeutics and allocation of limited mental health resources, it is important to obtain answers to these questions.

Most assuredly, the present database is less than ideal for the study of these questions. Nevertheless, the scale—whatever it now is—is revamped and ready to be tried out. One thing is known about it: Even after revised scoring, the 33-item *Cn* (*Cn-33*) still correlates .92 with the unrevised 41-item version of the *Cn* (*Cn-41*) scale that does not have the three item reversals. It maintains the same pattern of correlations with the five other prognosis scales and at somewhat higher levels in every case: *Cn-33* correlates from .55 to .70 with four of the scales and *Cn-41* correlates from .45 to .60. For the single prognosis scale that relates negatively to the other five, *Cn-33* correlates –.61, and *Cn-41* correlates –.49. These early results call for continued study of the scale. Some further study appears in chapter 10.

The Pepper and Strong Altruism Scale AKA Conventionality (5C)

In an unpublished report, Pepper and Strong (1958) proposed a five subscale breakdown of the *MMPI* Scale 5 (Masculinity–Femininity). The Pepper and Strong breakdown of Scale 5 resulted in the following subscales: Denial of Masculine Occupational Interest (*5DMO*), Feminine Occupational Interests (*5FOI*), Personal and Emotional Sensitivity (*5PES*), Sexual Identification (*5SI*), and Altruism (*5A*).

The Pepper and Strong scales appeared to have good face validity and seemed to compare well with other breakdowns of Scale 5 (Schuerger, Foerstner, Serkownek, & Ritz, 1987). Levitt (1989) reviewed these scales and concluded that *5DMO* and *5FOI* are encompassed by the Wiggins Feminine Interests Scale. *5PES* was redundant with the Harris and Lingoes Poignancy Scale (*6P*). Moreover, *5SI* was mislabeled and did not appear to be useful.

Apparently, no published research on the validity or reliability of the Pepper and Strong scales exists. However, clinical experience indicated to Levitt (1989) that the Altruism scale was the only independently useful Pepper and Strong scale. Individuals scoring high on the Pepper and Strong Altruism Scale endorse traditional American cultural values like honesty, candor, and fair play. They tend to be somewhat unsophisticated; scale scores have moderate positive correlations with *3NA* and *6N* and are also positively related to Lie scale scores. *Altruism* appears to be a misconception of what the scale measures, although no doubt high scorers would agree that generosity and selflessness are virtues. *Conventionality* appeared to be a more appropriate descriptor and label, thus *5C*. Fortunately, the *MMPI* revision did not delete any *5C* items. Thus, this scale is available in *MMPI–2*. It is studied in chapter 9. For interpretation, see Table 4.8.

Depression Subtle (D-S)

Due to variations in the wording of Clinical scale items, these can be broken down into obvious and subtle categories. In principle, an obvious item is one for which the significance of a true or false response should be manifest to most respondents. Few adults would have difficulty comprehending the meaning of endorsement of items like "I am a very happy person," or "I have seen some strange things in my lifetime." On the other hand, most respondents would not understand the assessment meaning of endorsing an item like "I would rather be certain than to guess what people might mean," or denying "I have thoughts that I prefer not to discuss."

TABLE 4.8

Interpretations of Other Valuable Special Scales

Scale Name	Tentative Interpretations
Control (*Cn*)	Low scorers with serious psychopathology should have more intensive treatment (inpatient or partial hospitalization); high scorers (> T65) are better able to subsist on a traditional outpatient basis. However, a high score does not necessarily rule out a "faking bad" response posture. Extensive revision requires a revalidation of the *Cn* scale (see chap. 10).
Conventionality (*SC*)	Individuals scoring high on the Pepper and Strong Altruism Scale endorse traditional American culture values like honesty, candor, and fair play. They tend to be somewhat unsophisticated, scale scores have mildly positive correlations with *3NA* and *6N* and may also positively relate to *L* scale scores in defensive records.
Depression-Subtle (*D-S*)	The Depression-Subtle (*D-S*) scale appears to measure anger suppression or denial of angry feelings and irritability. Even though the items derive from Scale 2, Depression, as a group they do not emphasize covert signs of depression. Because the scale so strongly suggests inhibited but socially acceptable behavior, it may in a few instances provide, as Levitt (1989) believed, an indirect indication of dysthymia. On the other hand, that interpretation would require evidence of a patent effort to conceal depression. Item analysis revisions to the scale (i.e., loss of items *5, 143, & 148*) have further attenuated the possible link to concealment of depression.
Dominance (*Do*)	This extensively revised scale emphasizes positive leadership qualities. High scores may equally emphasize self-confidence without a necessary implication of forcefulness.
Ego Strength (*Es*)	This much-revised scale may still measure the ability to achieve an integration of one's ego. Nevertheless, only low scores are used to infer ego weakness. Much further study is needed.
Extreme Suspiciousness (*S+*)	High scores on the *S+* are paranoid persons at some level. Not all are psychotic; some will be diagnosed as paranoid personality disorders. Obvious content permits exaggeration.
Hostility (*Ho*)	High scorers are prone to be cynical, irritable, angry, and resentful. They can be suspicious of other people's intentions and view the world with distrust. There is some indication that high *Ho* scorers are more likely to develop health problems.
Overcontrolled Hostility (*O-H*)	High scorers appear to have strong inhibitions against the expression of aggression and characteristically deny hostile feelings, usually obtaining low scores on such scales as *W-HOS*. They are considered to be quiet, passive, and unassuming. They are also given to aperiodic rage reactions in which they may or may not attack others or destroy property. A diagnosis of overcontrolled hostility is more supported when *W-AUT*, *W-HOS*, and *TSC/R* plus Impulsivity Scales are low.

(Continued)

TABLE 4.8
(Continued)

Scale Name	Tentative Interpretations
Paraphilia *(Pe)*	This scale measures respondent propensity to participate in a range of paraphilic behaviors. The tendencies that are tapped by the scale are in accordance with the regressive personalities and primitive sexual development of pedophiles, exhibitionists, and voyeurs. See new findings in chapter 6.
Work Attitude *(WA)*	Patients who score in the range T60–69 on *WA* are complaining that their daily life functioning is impaired to some degree but not enough to require hospitalization. Scores of T70 and above indicate that emotional disturbance is so intense that patients feel they cannot function productively. Hospitalization or medication may be requisite, depending on the level of *Cn*. Although revised, *WA*'s core meaning remains (chap. 10).

The original classification of *MMPI* items as obvious or subtle was the work of Wiener and Harmon (1946), later published under Wiener's (1948) name. Wiener and Harmon essentially used two methods of distinguishing items. All items on the *F* scale and on Scales *1, 7,* and *8* were automatically assigned to the obvious category on the grounds that they measured psychopathology, presumably directly, although this is not specifically stated. The remaining items on Scales *2, 3, 4, 6,* and *9* were categorized by the authors' "pooled judgments"; the procedure is not further detailed.

The Wiener and Harmon dichotomy for the scales has not held up well in research (Weed, Ben-Porath, & Butcher, 1990). Levitt (1989), based on his clinical experience, concurred with that judgment for all of the scales except Depression Subtle *(D-S)*, which he found to be a useful scale relative to dysthymia. The current clinical research program has found that *D-S* does in fact contribute to the empirical definition of depression but in a direction opposite to that suggested by Levitt (chap. 8). See Table 4.8 for interpretive guidance.

Dominance (*Do*)

Gough, McClosky, and Meehl (1951) developed a scale that they named Dominance *(Do)*. Their method first involved having students identify peers who exhibited influence over others and had strong leadership qualities. Then they examined *MMPI* records completed by those identified as having the most and least of the foregoing characteristics. Items that differentiated between these groups were designated as the *Do* scale. It has generated only a small amount of research.

A content analysis study of *Do* items that survived in *MMPI–2* was carried out in the current research program in view of the potentially differing meanings of *dominance*. A consensus of five judges using a focus group format suggested that an equally applicable name for the scale would be self-confidence. The name of the original scale was, however, retained. Item analysis resulted in several items being cut based on responses of this patient population. In chapter 9, it is compared with the *I-Do* scale in predictions of personality characteristics. See a tentative interpretation of the *Do* scale in Table 4.8.

Ego Strength Scale (*Es*)

Barron's (1953) Ego Strength (*Es*) Scale was developed by comparing the *MMPI* records of patients who, following psychotherapy, were improved with those from individuals who were unimproved. The *MMPI* was completed in a pretreatment/posttreatment design. Item responses that were identified reliably with improvement constituted the *Es* scale. The scale was so named because its items suggested that improved patients were also those whose answers showed they had a capacity for personal integration. This, Barron inferred, was a sign of underlying ego strength. Unfavorable reviews of the *Es* scale are sobering (Greene, 1991; Levitt, 1989), even though it has been used widely (Moreland & W. G. Dahlstrom, 1983).

Of the 52 remaining *MMPI–2* items that comprise the scale, only 37 remained after the present item analysis (chap. 6). Naturally, this raises questions regarding if and how much of the original meaning of the scale is still present in its revised form. This scale is studied in chapter 10 for its potential contribution to patient prognosis. A tentative interpretation is given in Table 4.8.

Extreme Suspiciousness (S+)

This is a relatively obscure scale and does not appear to be used in many of the well-known interpretive and survey texts for the *MMPI–2* (Friedman et al., 2001; Graham, 2000; Greene, 2000). Nonetheless, the Extreme Suspiciousness Scale (*S*+) provides the diagnostician with valuable information. A diagnosis involving patent paranoid ideation is made with reasonable confidence based on a high score on *S*+ (Endicott, Jortner, & Abramoff, 1969). About half of the 18 items on *S*+ are clear expressions of paranoid ideation. The remaining items express the hypersensitivity and excessive caution that are likely to underlie paranoid tendencies. High scorers on the *S*+ are paranoid persons at some level. Not all are psychotic; some will be diagnosed as paranoid personality disorders. Moreover, items are obvious and subject to willful misrepresentation. See chapter 8 for applications and Table 4.8 for interpretations.

The Cook and Medley Hostility Scale (*Ho*)

Ho was originally part of a group of 77 items chosen because they discriminated between school teachers scoring high and low on the Minnesota Teacher Attitude Inventory (Cook, Leeds, & Callis, 1951). Five clinical psychologists then selected the final 50-item version of *Ho* on the basis of "substantial agreement," which is not defined by Cook and Medley (1954). It was also not affected with the *MMPI* revision. However, four items were cut in item analysis (see chap. 6 & Appendix A).

   Ho is one of the few special scales that has been well represented in published research and it has given rise to some interesting findings. Jurjevich (1963) found that *Ho* did a better job of relating to the subscales of the Buss–Durkee Hostility-Guilt Index (Buss & Durkee, 1957) than five other item sets derived from the *MMPI*, including Scales *4* and *6*. McGee (1954) found that *Ho* had low but significant correlations with a word association test and a picture sorting test designed to measure hostility. Shaw and Grubb (1958) reported that underachieving male high school sophomores obtained a higher *Ho* score than did achievers. *Ho* also correlated .79 for females and .85 for males with the Hostility scale of the Guilford–Zimmerman Temperament Survey (Guilford & Zimmerman, 1949). However, Megargee and Mendelsohn (1962) reported that *Ho*, like 11 other *MMPI* measures related to hostility, failed to discriminate among three groups classified as extremely assaultive criminals, moderately assaultive criminals and nonassaultive criminals, and a group of noncriminals.

   Later on, *Ho* entered the health psychology field. Williams, Haney, Lee, Kong, Blumenthal, and Whalen (1980) found a significant relation between scores on *Ho* and the severity of coronary artery disease in a sample of more than 400 patients who underwent coronary angiography. In fact, *Ho* scores predicted the severity more efficiently than interview-based rating of Type A behavior. Smith and Frohm (1985), in a questionnaire study, reported that high *Ho* scorers were beset by the combination of a less satisfactory social support system and more frequent irritating events, making for what the authors characterized as "a distinctly negative psychosocial risk factor profile" (p. 514). Barefoot, Dahlstrom, and Williams (1983) and Shekelle, Gale, Ostfeld, and Paul (1983) reported that *Ho* was a predictor of the incidence of heart attacks and cardiac deaths over extended periods of time.

   Spielberger, Jacobs, Russell, and Crane (1983) found a significant correlation that averaged around .50 between *Ho* and the trait form of the State-Trait Anger Scale. A significant correlation was also reported between *Ho* and estimated potential for hostility based on interviews by Dembroski, MacDougall, Williams, Haney, and Blumenthal (1985).

   On the whole, the various field studies of *Ho* are strong testimony to its validity, but do not necessarily support the Cook and Medley choice of a scale designation. There is no supported theoretical framework that would make it possible to predict both that high school underachievers would be more hostile than achievers and that individuals who develop coronary artery disease would be more given to trait hostility than those who do not. See the section on somatic concerns in chapter 8.

A factor analysis of the *MMPI* pool (Costa, Zonderman, McCrae, & Williams, 1985) resulted in a Cynicism factor with 22 items in common with *Ho*. The cynicism content of *Ho* is so marked that Smith and Frohm (1985) suggested that the scale should be called Cynical Hostility. Thus, high scorers on *Ho* appear to be hostile, cynical, and at risk for health problems such as heart disease. See Table 4.8 for additional interpretive comments.

Overcontrolled Hostility Scale (*O-H*)

Several reasonably careful investigations arrived at the interesting conclusion that institutionalized criminals convicted of violent crimes tend to score lower on measures of aggression and higher on measures of control than do nonassaultive criminals and normal men (Blackburn, 1968; Megargee & Mendelsohn, 1962). This curious finding led Megargee (1966) to the conclusion that assaultive criminals come in two types: undercontrolled and overcontrolled. Accordingly, he set about devising a scale for the measurement of hostility in the overcontrolled person (Megargee, Cook, & Mendelsohn, 1967).

The 31 items of the earlier *O-H* scale are based on the *MMPI* records of four groups: extremely assaultive men convicted of murder, assault with a deadly weapon, and so on; moderately assaultive men convicted of no more than battery; criminals convicted for crimes other than violence; and normal men. Item analyses began with a 55-item scale that differentiated the assaultive from nonassaultive prisoners. However, there was considerable overlap between a group of violent criminals classified as overcontrolled and undercontrolled through expert judgment on the basis of examination of prison records.

Megargee et al. (1967) asserted that the scale measures simultaneously two different personality constructs that are usually thought of as separate: impulse control and hostile alienation. Thus, they believed that high scorers on *O-H* have serious conflict between strong aggressive impulses and perhaps strong inhibitions against the expression of aggression. The net consequence is that the hostile impulses are chronically restrained until they mount to a critical intensity, at which point the individual is likely to explode into a sudden act of extreme violence or perhaps psychosis.

Fortunately, the *O-H* scale has been subjected to a considerable amount of postdevelopment investigation. Most of the reported investigations support the validity of *O-H* in one way or another (Blackburn, 1972; deGroot & Adamson,

1973; Fredericksen, 1975; Haven, 1972; Lane & Kling, 1979, Megargee, 1969; Vanderbeck, 1973; White, 1970, 1975; White, McAdoo, & Megargee, 1973). Those investigations in which positive findings for validity were not obtained used questionable methodology: administering *O-H* in isolation instead of within the entire *MMPI* (Lester, Perdue, & Brookhart, 1974; Mallory & Walker, 1972; Rawlings, 1973) or using criterion groups that were contaminated by racial bias (Fisher, 1970).

O-H was developed with male prisoners and almost all of the subsequent work has tested male samples. The single investigation that included female murderers reported some evidence that *O-H* could also apply to women (Sutker & Allain, 1979). However, the evidence for validity is not strong and this is one of the few studies that did not support the ability of *O-H* to discriminate among male prisoners.

The clinical utility of *O-H* would be very restricted if it were applicable only to samples of incarcerated criminals. As it happens, the value of this interesting set of items ranges considerably beyond such limitations. Clinically, noncriminal male and female high scorers on *O-H* behave very much in accordance with the theoretical position of Megargee et al. (1967). They appear to have strong inhibitions against the expression of aggression and characteristically deny hostile feelings, usually obtaining low scores on such scales as *W-HOS*. They are considered to be quiet, passive, and unassuming. They are also given to aperiodic rage reactions in which they may or may not attack others or destroy property. They are rarely murderers. Diagnosing overcontrolled hostility is more supported when *W-AUT, W-HOS, TSC/R*, and the four Impulsivity scales are low (i.e., when indices of expressed hostility and impulse control are low), thereby indicating overcontrol of both kinds.

Three of the 31 items on the *O-H* scale were lost on the *MMPI* revision, leaving the *MMPI–2* with 28 items. These losses did not appear to damage the *O-H* scale. Major changes came out of the current item analysis, with 10 more item losses (*n* = 18) and the scoring direction for three other items switched (Appendix A). Chapter 9 examines the continued effectiveness of this revised scale. See Table 4.8 for preliminary interpretations.

Paraphilia/Pedophilia, Males (*Pe*)

The *Pe* scale, originally named Pedophilia scale (Toobert, Bartelme, & Jones, 1959), is discussed in some detail in chapter 6 as well as in Levitt and Gotts (1995). So it is examined only briefly here. By Levitt's (1989) assessment, in clinical practice, *Pe* has proven to be an outstandingly successful measuring instrument. Its ability to identify is not restricted to pedophiles. See important new findings regarding a modified version of *Pe* in chapter 6 and interpretation in Table 4.8.

Work Attitude (WA)

A significant aspect of emotional illness, which is sometimes neglected by diagnosticians, is the patient's subjective feeling of incapacity. Certainly there are multiple factors involved in individuals' belief that they have lost the ability to work productively in whatever setting. One of the most important is the subjective feeling that symptomatology is so overpowering that cognitive and intellectual capacities are stifled and motivation is undermined. The person feels disempowered.

The Work Attitude Scale (WA) (Tydlaska & Mengel, 1953) measures this feeling with reasonable accuracy. The scale was originally developed by contrasting groups of industrial employees who had received regular merit ratings of "satisfactory" over a 2-year period with a group of Air Force personnel, most of whom had gone AWOL or were disciplinary problems.

Fifty-eight items were selected by judges (not otherwise described) on the basis of estimated potential for distinguishing between the two groups. Items that dealt with sociopathic behavior, such as alcohol abuse and difficulties with authorities, were eliminated on the grounds that although they might very well discriminate the two groups, they would not be helpful for the purposes of the proposed scale.

MMPIs of the two groups were then examined. It was found that 37 of the 58 selected items discriminated at the 1% level. These became the Work Attitude Scale (WA). One of the 37 items was actually a T-R scale repeat, so 36 different items comprised the scale, of which 35 remain after the MMPI revision. The mean WA score for the group of Air Force personnel was 16.4, and for the industrial employees it was 7.0. All but one of the former had scores above 10, whereas nearly 80% of the latter had scores below 10.

The scale was subsequently cross-validated on college student samples (Tesseneer & Tydlaska, 1956). Faculty members at a small state college selected 26 male students with whom they were personally familiar and whom they identified as being outstanding examples of persons with good work attitudes. An equal number of students was selected by the faculty to represent those with poor work attitudes. The mean ages and IQs were essentially similar. The poor work attitude students were found to have a mean WA of 13.1 as compared to 7.3 for the good work attitude students. The former were also found to have more psychopathology in general as measured by the Clinical scales of the MMPI. Higher scores on the Clinical scales does not impeach the validity of WA. Instead, it may just as validly be interpreted as suggesting that one source of academic achievement difficulties is emotional upset.

Examination of 35 remaining WA items indicates that a plurality is found on DEP and TSC/D. Somewhat smaller groups are found in 2MD and 8CON. In fact, these are exactly the components that would be anticipated for this scale: dysphoric affect, interference with cognitive processes, and lack of motivation. Two additional items were removed based on item analysis (new $n = 33$) and one was rekeyed (see Appendix A).

The *WA* scale has been relatively neglected since the *MMPI–2* revision, but like many other scales, there remains strong potential for its use as a prognostic scale. Interestingly, it shares 12 items with the new *WRK* scale. One third of *WRK*'s items are new and 22 are carried over from *MMPI*. Thus, the overlapping 12 items represent 54.54% of the original 22 *MMPI* items. It is a curious fact that, with this high degree of similarity, a historical connection has not been established between the two scales. *WA* and *WRK* thus share a core of common meaning, but each offers unique perspectives on patient readiness to engage in productive activity. Chapter 10 further explores their contributions. Preliminary interpretation of *WA* is found in Table 4.8.

ADDITIONAL SCALES

Besides the scales that have been subjected to special study in the present research, other special scales are used in the analyses that appear in chapters 8–10 and in the interpretive materials of Appendices D and E. These include the *A* and *R* scales (Welsh, 1956); posttraumatic stress disorder scales *PK* (Keane, Malloy, & Fairbank, 1984) and *PS* (Schlenger & Kulka, 1987); addiction scales *MAC-R* (MacAndrew, 1965) and *APS* (Weed, Butcher, McKenna, & Ben-Porath, 1992); gender role scales *GM* and *GF* (Peterson & Dahlstrom, 1992); and the Validity, Clinical, and Content scales for *MMPI–2* (Butcher et al., 2001). Further information on the construction, content, and interpretation of these scales will be found in most of the following four sources: Butcher et al. (2001), Friedman et al. (2001), Graham (2000), and Greene (2000).

5

Overview and Results of a Clinical Research Program

From its beginning in 1986, the research reported here took place at a state-operated psychiatric hospital using clinical records generated in the ordinary course of admitting and treating patients. The research was initiated primarily for the purpose of improving patient diagnostic formulation and care. At the outset, plans included developing local norms that might better identify conditions and treatment needs.

A structured research protocol was not followed. That is to say, a uniform assessment battery was not adopted. Instead, each patient was assessed using those instruments judged most necessary and appropriate to answer immediate clinical questions. From 1986 onward, psychology staff seminars, individual training, supportive work review, and supervision were employed as means of assuring that assessments were conducted in a standardized manner. Eugene Levitt worked on a regular monthly schedule from 1986 to 1994 with the first author in efforts to maintain acceptable assessment performance by staff. They also jointly performed a number of quality checks on the archive described later.

The research database was to be complemented by use of the hospital's preexisting psychology assessment archive that is later described. Use of this piecemeal archive raised reliability and validity issues that had to be attacked rigorously if it were to be incorporated into the new database. Obviously, this kind of scientist-practitioner research calls for much patience because data accumulate slowly, and many patient records turn out to be less than might be hoped for due to the interfering influence of severe pathology. Nevertheless, with several hundred admissions per year, usable data did accumulate. Moreover, some of the preexisting archive eventually did meet standards for inclusion.

PATIENT POPULATION

During the period when data were being collected, the hospital received most of its admissions through the four community mental health centers that together with their satellite offices serve southeast Indiana. This region included counties extending along the Ohio River from parts of greater Louisville eastward to the Indiana suburbs of Cincinnati. It then reached northward beyond Columbus and Bloomington, stopping short of Indianapolis.

The region has smaller cities and towns dispersed throughout more sparsely settled rural areas. Agriculture and manufacturing, along with retail and service sectors, are southeast Indiana's principal forms of economic activity and employment. Persons of minority background accounted for about 15% of the region's population. These characteristics of the region also portray closely what amounts to a fairly descriptive profile of the backgrounds of patients whose clinical records were reviewed for inclusion in the research samples.

Only persons with severe and persistent forms of mental illness, chemical dependency, and developmental disability were eligible for admission to the subject hospital. Indiana's state-operated facility admission policies plus the effects of patient pathology on functional levels resulted in an inpatient group of mainly lower socioeconomic background whose work experience was primarily in low skill occupations. Diagnostically, the hospital population from which samples were drawn included persons with disorders of the foregoing types plus personality disorders and combinations thereof. Records of a few patients who were diagnosed with dementia, amnestic disorder, or subnormal intelligence were included in the database in order to examine effects of cognitive deficiencies on various kinds of psychological testing results. Finally, a small number of records were holdovers from outpatient services formerly offered by the hospital.

Adult males included in the main the study ($n = 943$) had a mean age of 33.30 years, with a range of 18–74. The corresponding sample of adult females ($n = 593$) averaged 37.25 years of age, with a range of 18–77. Adolescents who had completed an *MMPI* before the advent of *MMPI–A* were also studied, but those findings are not included in the present report. In addition to the types of patients already mentioned, the hospital performed forensic evaluations and treated persons who had completed serving a sentence but then required further services before their reentry into home communities. These too are in the sample.

CREATING A CLINICAL DATABASE

By 1986, when the present work started, approximately 14,000 patients' test records and reports had accumulated and were maintained as an archive by the hospital psychology department. Although the collection was loosely organized, it was securely stored by the department in a location distinctly separate from the rest of the patient medical records. In 1986–1987, the collection was systematically inventoried, organized, and cataloged for the first time. This was done in order to ready the archive to become part of a working database.

As attempts were made to draw an initial random sample of 700 cases for study, the archive's serious limitations soon became apparent. For example, many records were exceedingly brief, consisting of little more than the results of a clinical interview, perhaps some behavior ratings, and a synoptic psychological report. One long-standing practice that limited the usefulness of a vast number of *MMPI* protocols was that patients had been instructed to complete only the first 399 items. This permitted the examiner to score the basic scales, but it precluded the use of scales that incorporated items falling past that artificial stopping point.

As the initial reworking of the archive neared completion in early 1987, the decision was made that for a patient record to be included in the final database it must have a complete *MMPI* protocol (i.e., abbreviated administrations would not be useful). Records having in excess of 30 answers blank or that had been completed in a random or careless fashion were to be excluded. A student worker appointed for summer 1987 began the process of organizing satisfactory records as a separate part of the archive. Second, the summer student searched a card file in the medical records department for the assigned diagnoses of each patient having a complete *MMPI*. Patient diagnoses are discussed later in this chapter.

Identification numbers were assigned next to each acceptable case in a manner that later would support the retrieval of information while completely excluding any personal data that might compromise patient confidentiality. As time permitted, the summer student worker commenced hand scoring of the *MMPI*s using commercially available templates, plus locally devised templates for scales with no commercially published sources. About one half of the usable *MMPI*s had been completed with Form R and the rest with the Group Form, hence scoring templates were assembled for both. This began a laborious process that would continue for the next several summers with a succession of student workers.

By the time of the publication in 1989 of *MMPI-2*, creation of the hospital's *MMPI* database was well under way. Scoring and coding had advanced to the stage of beginning some data entry on the campus of Indiana University, Bloomington. Thus, an especially challenging task came along with the arrival of *MMPI-2*. The task was to ponder these questions: Was it possible to use data from both *MMPI* versions in a unifying way within the database? If so, then what strategies would be needed to increase the chances of a successful blending? If not, then would the effort already invested necessarily be lost? There were no immediate or apparent answers to these questions.

Years passed. By fall 1996, all scales had been scored for most of the sample and entered into a computerized database. Separate data files were kept of Group Form and Form R records. Eventually, all Form R records were converted by computer to Group Form format and the data files were merged.

Concurrently, psychology staff with their predoctoral interns had begun using *MMPI-2* and experimenting with ways to score scales that they had used with

MMPI but that had lost items to the test's revision. After 1999, use of *MMPI* was discontinued altogether. *MMPI–2* records began to accumulate and were computer stored. By late 2002, the database reported on here was essentially complete, with few records being entered thereafter. Now, for the first time, it became possible to experiment and seek answers to the questions first raised in 1989.

Transforming the Database

A series of methodology and inferential problems needed to be solved in the construction of the database in preparation for later analysis. This chapter section presents key considerations for the reliability and scale revision studies that were conducted. Other procedures preliminary to data analysis are treated in sufficient detail to guide those who may wish to consider ways for transforming *MMPI* data vis-à-vis *MMPI–2* and returning them to usefulness.

Item Wording Comparisons.   Work by Ben-Porath and Butcher (1989) on the effects of rewording 68 *MMPI* items that appear in *MMPI–2* effectively demonstrated that functional characteristics of those items were not compromised by the changes. Their findings support a conclusion that the converse was also likely true. That is, it implied that the 68 items answered in response to the original *MMPI* wording could be used in conjunction with the remaining *MMPI–2* items to form scales and that responses to earlier wording was still comparable.

Relative to the performance of those 68 specific items, the preceding conclusion affords a basis for including them during parallel item analyses of identical scales that are being scored from either version of the test. When these 68 altered items are combined with 392 items that entered *MMPI–2* unchanged, the two versions of the test share 460 items that may be construed as being interchangeable without detracting from scale performance. Consequently, there would be no detrimental effect on scales that use only items from this pool of 460. Items deleted during the test's revision would of course be excluded because they are unavailable in *MMPI–2*. The issue remained concerning how to integrate them with the 107 items new to the revised test.

Analysis Illustrated.   Following from the foregoing line of reasoning and the issue of comparing test versions, a solution gradually emerged to the dilemma of how the hospital's *MMPI* and *MMPI–2* patient sample databases might be studied jointly in complementary ways. The process is illustrated with the following hypothetical example:

> Suppose that an *MMPI–2* scale contains 17 items, 15 of which are also available in *MMPI*. Suppose further that there are two independent samples, one of which completed *MMPI* and the other *MMPI–2*. Item analyses are first completed for the 15-item scale in each sample. Next the 17-item version is item analyzed using the

MMPI–2 sample. Results of item analyses for the 15-item scales then are compared and contrasted between the two samples. If the analyses produce essentially similar results in both samples, then the inference is made that the sample completing the *MMPI* would likely have responded to the two unavailable *MMPI–2* items in a manner similar to the responses made by the sample that completed the *MMPI–2*.

If, as in the foregoing illustration, results are comparable for a shorter version of a scale whose items appear in both *MMPI* and *MMPI–2*, then the conditions would appear to support what amounts to modifying the *MMPI* scale score by an adjustment factor that compensates for the item(s) appearing only in *MMPI–2*. If this could be done accurately, then the *MMPI* scale would perform as a surrogate for its *MMPI–2* counterpart.

Making Scale Adjustments. Specifically with reference to the hospital database, if adjustments of this kind could be made to scales in the *MMPI* portion of the sample, then the 460 items that it shares with *MMPI–2* would become fully usable and would not be at risk of becoming potentially unusable or irrelevant. A further necessary piece of the solution would be to derive a method for adjusting an *MMPI* scale's mean to correspond to its *MMPI–2* successor.

Although adjusting a scale in the manner described may seem to depart from customary scale construction procedures, the practice of estimating a desired scale length is not new or without precedent. To cite just one example, a standard topic in psychometric theory concerns how the length of a test affects its reliability and finding ways to estimate the increase in reliability that would result from adding some specific number of items (Nunnally, 1967). That is, methods exist for estimating the reliability of a scale if its length changes.

A Bayesian Approach to Adjusting Means. The present question, however, is not how to estimate the reliability of a scale that has been lengthened. Rather, what is needed is a method for adjusting a scale's mean value to accommodate those specific items that are absent from the scale. The approach taken to these calculations in the present study was based on Bayesian reasoning (Morgan, 1968).

The line of reasoning proceeds from defining what is known regarding an *MMPI–2* scale in a normative sense. Thus, it begins with the known itemmetric values (*knowns*) of individual items (Butcher et al., 1989, Appendix G) that together add up to a scale's mean. The value of an item that is present in an *MMPI–2* scale, but absent from *MMPI*, is defined here as the proportion of persons in the normative (CX) sample who responded to it in the keyed direction.

It should now also be apparent that the sum of proportions for absent items equals the total value or weight associated with the absent items. Furthermore, it can be seen that the normative CX mean of the *MMPI–2* scale minus the CX weighted sum of absent items represents what the mean would be if those particular items were absent. Now if the first of these knowns (i.e., the sum of CX item weights) is assigned as the numerator of a ratio in which the denominator is the second of these knowns (i.e., the CX mean minus the sum of CX item weights), then the ratio fully expresses the relevant knowns derived from *MMPI–2* normative data.

A third known is the hospital sample's *MMPI* scale mean. Let it become the denominator of a second ratio whose numerator is yet to be determined. That is, the numerator is an unknown that is to be computed from what is known. The sample mean qualifies as the denominator for this second ratio because it, like the denominator of the CX ratio, is already missing or absent the items in question. In this sense, it entirely parallels the normative CX mean minus the sum for the unavailable item weights. The unknown numerator for the second ratio can now be defined as an estimate for what the weighted value of the absent items would have been if the *MMPI* patient sample had the opportunity to respond to them. Finally, the two ratios are operationally defined as proportional to one another, thereby leading to the following statement of equivalence:

$$Sample\ item\ wts = [(sample\ m) \times (norm\ CX\ item\ wts)]\ /$$
$$[(norm\ CX\ m) - (norm\ CX\ item\ wts)]$$

In order to estimate a properly adjusted *MMPI* sample mean (i.e., a mean no longer affected by absent items but comparable to an *MMPI–2* mean), it is necessary to add to it the estimated sample sum of missing weights (i.e., the value of the unknown that was solved). Adding these two values results in an estimate of what the *MMPI* sample mean would have been if the absent items had been available to be responded to by patients who completed *MMPI*. Note that this must be done separately for males and females, because their means differ.

Performing Individual Score Adjustments.   The preceding discussion of how *MMPI* means can be transformed leads readily into examining a method for adjusting the individual patient's score on an *MMPI* scale for which some of the items appear only in *MMPI–2*. Bayesian (Morgan, 1968) reasoning again underlies the approach taken. The necessary computations can, however, be considerably abbreviated, simplified, and patterned after the mean adjustment, as is demonstrated later, after the rationale for computation is presented.

The process starts with the case of a patient's score on an *MMPI* scale that requires adjustment for items present only in *MMPI–2*. The ratio for what is known normatively regarding the *MMPI–2* version of the corresponding scale remains unchanged from its earlier definition. Now the denominator of the second ratio is defined differently: Instead of being a sample mean, it is the raw score that an individual patient obtained on the *MMPI* scale. The unknown in the numerator is defined as the estimated weight or value of those items appearing in *MMPI–2* to which the patient had no opportunity to respond.

The logic of proportionality survives intact. That is, the patient's *MMPI* raw score was lowered by an amount proportional to the quantity by which the sample mean was lessened through the unavailability of the absent items. In parallel with this it is relevant to note that the *MMPI* mean for the scale can be none other than the mean of all the patient raw scores that comprise it.

Assume next that the absent items measure essentially the same core characteristic as do the remaining items of the scale. Observe that this assumption can be evaluated against the results of item analysis of the *MMPI–2* version of the scale. Because this is so, it follows that the single best predictor of what a given patient's responses might have been to the absent items is the sum of that patient's responses to those items that were answered in *MMPI*. This is, by definition, that person's raw score. The unknown numerator of the second ratio is accordingly defined as an estimator for the individual patient of the weight or value of those scale items that were absent from the *MMPI*. This unknown is calculated as before, after substituting the individual patient terms for the former patient sample terms, as follows:

$$Absent\ item\ wts = [(raw\ score) \times (norm\ CX\ item\ wts)]/$$
$$[(norm\ CX\ m) - (norm\ CX\ item\ wts)]$$

In order to arrive at the patient's estimated or adjusted score for the scale, the raw score and the estimated absent item weights are summed. This conceptual formula is helpful for understanding the process but less practical for computing. To arrive at a useful computing formula, a different norm CX ratio will be used than formerly. It is the ratio of an *MMPI–2* scale's CX mean divided by the same CX mean after it has been adjusted downward by subtracting from it the summed CX item weights of items absent from *MMPI*. In effect, this ratio expresses the proportional relation between the true CX mean (now a numerator) and CX mean after removal of combined the CX weights of all items absent from *MMPI* (in the denominator). If this expression is changed from a ratio by dividing its numerator by its denominator, then the result represents a factor by which the true mean is greater than the adjusted mean. An example will serve to clarify this:

**Suppose that an *MMPI–2* scale's mean is 30.0 and it contains
10 items that are not present in *MMPI*. Suppose next that
the sum of weights for those 10 items is 6.0. Then their ratio,
as defined previously, is:**
$$[30.0/(30.0 - 6.0)] = (30.0/24.0) = 1.25$$

This example expresses the actual relation that obtains between the missing items and the scale. This relation further indicates a proportional relation that applies as well to a sample scale's mean, such that its adjusted mean divided by the nonadjusted mean should also equal 1.25, within some error of estimate.

Recognize next that the arithmetic procedure is reversible. That is, if the nonadjusted mean were multiplied times 1.25, then it would provide an estimate of the adjusted mean. This is a useful term because it indicates by what amount the nonadjusted mean would need to be multiplied to provide an estimate of the true mean. This outcome is due to the fact that the relation represents a constancy for a particular partitioning of the scale within the normative sample. As long as the scale's norm remains unchanged, the relation is a constant. The term specifying the degree of this relation will now be identified as the *adjustment factor* for a particular scale. When the adjustment factor is applied by multiplication to an individual's *MMPI* raw score, the result is an estimate for that person's adjusted score. That is, it estimates what the person's *MMPI–2* raw score would have been. Omitted item responses are adjustable by a similar approach.

It will be evident that in the same way that each scale differs from all others in item composition and central tendency, separate adjustment factors are required for the purpose of estimating each different scale's adjusted mean and each adjusted patient score. By reflecting back on the fact that male and female CX itemmetric percentages most often differ for the identical items and their normative means usually differ as well, it will be clear that separate adjustment factors are required for each gender as well as for each scale.

Handling Missing Data.   As was earlier mentioned, records having more than 30 incomplete or doubly marked answers were excluded from the database as a matter of quality control. The question of missing data was revisited at the outset of data analysis. The actual numbers of missing items was quite small. The 923 adult males left an average of 1.92 answers blank, with the true mean falling between 1.69 and 2.15 (95% confidence interval) and an overall range of 0–29. For 593 adult females, the mean for blanks was 2.84, 2.47–3.22 was the 95% confidence interval, and the range was 0–27. Yet, even with these small numbers, when using casewise deletion for missing data during data analysis, unacceptably large numbers of cases are lost. In order to avoid this outcome, missing data were replaced expediently with item mean values for males and females separately before proceeding with analyses.

Coding Diagnoses

As diagnoses were retrieved from the medical records department for patients in the sample, they were transcribed to include both the standard *Diagnostic and Statistical Manual* (*DSM*) series numeric code (American Psychiatric Association, 1968, 1980, 1987, 1994, 2000) and the verbal descriptor that accompanied it. Diagnoses had been assigned to patients during time periods when each of the four referenced *DSM*s was then currently in use at the hospital. From this it will be apparent that the database included patients who had been admitted to the hospital from the 1960s onward. How these codes from different *DSM*s were made conformable to one another is described later.

A large percentage of patients in the sample had more than one admission to the hospital, and multiple diagnoses might be assigned during a single admission. This meant their card file entries could present an array of diagnoses with qualifiers for an individual patient for each admission. Examples included admitting diagnosis, provisional diagnosis, revised diagnosis, final diagnosis, and discharge diagnosis. Moreover, multiple possibilities occurred in a few cases on more than one admission. The diagnosis selected in these cases was the one assigned as a final diagnosis for the admission during which the *MMPI* was administered. Difficult decisions were noted and reviewed by the senior author.

Making codes conformable to one another from the various *DSM*s was accomplished in the following manners. In the first instance, an annotated comparison of *DSM–II* (1968) diagnoses was published as Appendix C in *DSM–III* (1980). This was used to make *DSM–II* diagnostic assignments congruent with those in *DSM–III*. In practice, however, the parallels were at times incomplete due to the major revisions of classification that had occurred with the publication of *DSM–III*. Thus, at times the comparison matches were not isomorphic. All problematic *DSM–II* diagnoses for individual patients were identified and listed for later study by the senior author. Later studies of these problem cases required obtaining the complete patient clinical file and reviewing it for specific diagnostic signs that would support more exact matches to *DSM–III*.

As was true for the *DSM–II* to *DSM–III* conversion, each succeeding *DSM* has included a diagnostic cross-reference listing. In general, *DSM–III* readily converted into *DSM–III–R* (1987) without requiring the same level of intensive review as had been needed for some of the *DSM–II* categories. *DSM–III–R* was adopted early in the study as the standard into which all diagnoses were converted up until the publication of *DSM–IV* (1994). With its availability, all diagnoses were transformed one final time and entered into the database.

A peculiarity was encountered in the documentation maintained by the medical records department for a specific and somewhat lengthy interval of time while *DSM–II* was in use. Several longtime employees were asked if they were aware of this quirk or remembered how it had transpired. No explanation was forthcoming. The peculiarity was that card file records created during this interval made no reference to diagnosis. Some of those diagnoses were later located by pulling the complete patient record file. Before that process could be completed, however, the medical records department underwent a major records removal project. Records of patients who had been discharged for more than 7 years were boxed and shipped to state archives. Cases that could not be reviewed prior to this event were lost to the study based on an established inclusion criterion that a diagnosis must be available for the patient's record to be a part of the study.

An initial data file was set up to store assignments in their exact diagnostic code formats. This process assured that all information was retained in a form that could later be retrieved and arranged into those combinations that might prove important and relevant for analysis. After all diagnoses were entered, tabulations were completed of the numbers of cases appearing in each category.

Based on the tabulation results, a second diagnostic data file was created in a mainly dichotomized format (i.e., condition present = *1*, not present = *0*) that lent itself to data analysis. Composite adjustment variables were also developed in the file that were used to identify relevant and nonrelevant comparison groups for particular diagnostic categories. This second data file was used in all studies that involved examining patients by diagnostic category.

Demographic Influences on Response Consistency

IQ. Of particular interest was a possible effect of intelligence on response consistency as measured by the *MMPI–2*'s *VRIN* scale. In preparation to study this relation, Verbal IQ scores were merged as a single variable from the records of patients who had completed any edition of the Wechsler Adult Intelligence Scale series (Wechsler, 1955, 1981, 1997). A total of 849 records had received a Wechsler Verbal IQ (*VIQ*) score. From the foregoing scores a second variable was generated and labeled *NewIQ*. This variable assigned each patient's *VIQ* to one of three categories: *1* = mildly mentally retarded (MR) (*n* = 54), *2* = borderline intelligence (*n* = 272), and *3* = normal range intelligence (*n* = 523). Males and females are combined in these counts.

It is important to recognize that the numbers of cases found in the three categories do not necessarily represent a proportional distribution of ranges of verbal intelligence in the composite *MMPI* sample of 1,516 adults. Because intelligence testing was performed on a nonroutine basis, those tested included an oversampling of individuals who were thought to need confirmatory testing to validate the impression that they functioned below the normal range. Normal range individuals were tested for other reasons, including to check for effects of substance abuse or alleged cerebral dysfunction, in preparation for adult education or GED completion, and as a part of vocational planning and referral.

Patients scoring in the normal range of verbal intelligence (code *3*) received a *VRIN* score average of T53.78. This differed from the mean score for patients who scored in the borderline range, who produced an average *VRIN* score of T59.04. A *t*-test comparison for these independent samples was significant beyond .000000, with $t = 5.19$. As might be anticipated, mild MR patients had an even higher *VRIN* average (M = T67.82). It differed reliably from that of the intellectually normal ($t = 7.24$, $p < .0000$).

As already seen, the mean *VRIN* scores of mildly MR patients fell within the range of scores considered somewhat inconsistent yet valid. Even so, their mean was more than 1.2 standard deviations below a level considered to be clearly invalid. This finding raised the following question: Are some persons with mild MR able to respond to *MMPI*-type items consistently or reliably? Should they be excluded automatically from testing without considering their level of literacy?

In an effort to explore these questions, the records of the 54 mild MR patients were studied in detail by considering also their Performance IQ (*PIQ*) scores as a potential predictor of response consistency. Because not all patients had been administered both verbal and performance portions of the Wechsler scale, the actual number of cases having the two scores was 589. A multiple linear regression equation was formed, treating *VRIN* as the dependent variable and *VIQ* and *PIQ* as independent variables. A multiple R of .34 was obtained for this prediction, resulting in an F ratio of 39.835 for the overall solution ($df = 2$, 586, $p < .0000$). The beta assigned by the equation to *VIQ* was significant ($t = -3.77$, $df = 586$, $p < .0002$). The beta for *PIQ* also contributed significantly to prediction of *VRIN* ($t = -2.87$, $df = 586$, $p < .005$).

These findings suggested that for the purpose of predicting patient ability to answer *MMPI*-type items reliably, *VIQ* by itself was not a sufficiently strong variable. It should be supplemented with *PIQ*. This conclusion led to a further review of the distribution of *VRIN* scores relative to the combined predictors *VIQ* and *PIQ*. Of the 54 mild MR patients, 24 received *VRIN* scores < T65 (valid), 14 had *VRIN* scores ranging from T65–T79 (somewhat inconsistent but still valid), and 16 scored at > T79 (invalid).

It is noteworthy that all mild MR cases with insufficient response consistency would have been excluded from further analysis on the basis of their *VRIN* scores alone. On the other hand, 38 of 54 valid mild MR responders (70.37%) would have been excluded invalidly and unnecessarily from further analysis if the decision to include/exclude were made solely on the basis of IQ.

One strong implication is that IQ is not a reliable indicator of ability to complete *MMPI*-type items. In fact, scatter plots made of the relation between *VRIN* and IQ revealed substantial numbers of outliers in all ability ranges: normal, borderline, and mild MR. Further, it is clear that a substantial majority of persons who are of borderline intellect can respond to *MMPI*-type items with an acceptable level of consistency if they possess the requisite literacy skills. As a result, patients who tested in the borderline and mild MR ranges were included in the sample based on functional literacy for the specific task of responding to *MMPI* items, as assessed by their *VRIN* scores. The decision was based on the same criterion used for the normal or gifted. Greene (2000, p. 29) took a similar perspective. See more on validity adjustments in chapter 6.

Gender. A second demographic variable studied was gender. Gender's relevance to data analysis centers on the issue of whether there are, in this sample, gender differences in ability to complete *MMPI*-type items reliably. It was already known from tabulations that some diagnoses were assigned infrequently to patients in this sample. The number of cases needed to permit analysis of low incidence diagnoses would, thus, require combining males and females. Hence, whether males and females respond with equal reliability to *MMPI*-type items has a bearing on whether or not they can be combined for analysis. Within the composite adult sample of males and females, the relation between gender and *VRIN* was zero order ($r = .01$, $df = 1,514$). It was concluded that males and females responded with similar consistency and could be combined for analysis.

    Age.   A final demographic variable that was explored as a preliminary to other data analysis was patient age. Within the adult sample, age was unrelated to *VRIN* ($r = -.01$). Older patients, who on average had fewer years of formal schooling, demonstrated as much capacity as younger patients to respond to *MMPI*-type items in a consistent manner. In order to further check this conclusion, patients from the 55 years and older group were compared with those from the 18 to 54 age group. The mean score for *VRIN* in the older group was T56.50, whereas in the younger group it was T55.06. With 1,514 degrees of freedom, $t = -1.12$, $p = .26$, this nonsignificant finding again supports the conclusion.

    In conclusion, measured intelligence variations, gender, and age were found to be unlikely to confound or invalidate findings during later statistical analyses within this adult sample. From this it was concluded that, in general, patient groups could be formed and merged on an as-needed basis for the purpose of analysis, without regard to these factors. For indepth discussion of demographics and *MMPI/MMPI–2*, see Greene (2000).

6

Renewing the Old:
Scale Recoveries and Losses

Now that many issues of methodology have been explored and settled, it is time to review findings relative to issues that bear on the reliability and validity of scales that are applied clinically in the content cluster approach.

DYNAMICS OF THE ITEM ANALYSES

Just before reviewing scale reliability results, it is instructive to illustrate the dynamics involved in the work performed when completing the evaluation of each scale. If all of a scale's items were present in *MMPI*, then the item analysis was completed in the larger database separately for males ($n = 1020$) and females ($n = 637$).

In order to accomplish reliability checks for scales also containing any of the 107 items found only in *MMPI–2*, item analyses were completed both in the *MMPI* database and in the smaller *MMPI–2* database (n's = 135 males, 21 females). The *MMPI–2* data were analyzed both for the full set of items and for the items that appear in both versions of the test. Then comparisons were made back and forth between the results for the items shared in both versions.

If the sets of results agreed for the shared items, then the methods described earlier were used to, in effect, adjust the *MMPI* sample's results for each scale by an amount proportionate to that contributed by the items appearing only in *MMPI–2*. Agreement was high between the male samples for all comparisons made. The female sample for *MMPI–2* provided somewhat less stable results because of its small size. This was compensated for by performing comparisons among the highly stable results for the 1,657 *MMPI* cases and the 135 male *MMPI–2* cases.

In any event, no large discrepancies were found in comparisons of the two female samples that could not be adjusted. Reliability coefficients would at times appear overly high in the smaller female sample. These were adjusted relative to the smaller male sample to correspond to the patterns and levels of similarity for alpha coefficients between males and females in the larger *MMPI* sample. Adjusting the scale mean values to fit CX norms was not dependent on sample characteristics. It was carried out as reported in the end notes for Appendix B. Finally, the scores of individual patients in the *MMPI* database were adjusted as described in chapter 5.

APPRAISING AVAILABLE SCALES

A literature search regarding scales to be used in the content cluster system revealed that nearly all of both recently constructed and the habitually used scales were judged to need no additional item analysis. Scales fitting this description are listed in Appendix A for ready reference.

Reliability Checks Needed

In contrast to the scales just mentioned, some that are used regularly in psychological practice were identified as in need of further study. Among those so identified were the Harris–Lingoes Subscales (1968). Obviously, there is hesitancy about modifying a scale that others find useful and rely on for their work. Yet, in the interest of objectivity, minor changes were made to several scales and more extensive changes were visited on others. So several scales used with confidence by Levitt (1989; Levitt & Gotts, 1995) did not escape change. Scale compositions resulting from the item analyses appear for all scales in Appendix A. Appendix B rounds out the information by citing the sources of scales and their internal consistency reliabilities for this population.

The scale versions signified by the item compositions reported in Appendix A are the same scale versions used throughout the present clinical analyses and descriptions of the hospital inpatient population. No harm comes to the traditional version of any scale, and no scale suffers irreversible damage from the changes introduced here. All scales remain as readily available as they were before this writing and can be reconstructed by using the annotations in Appendix A to restore them. Thinking alternatively about these changes, the traditional scorings combine with the new and revised scale versions covered here in ways that can enrich the options and possibilities for *MMPI-2* interpretation.

SCALES FOUND TO BE UNRELIABLE

A few scales were found to be clearly unreliable when item analyzed. Analyses of these scales with their original full *MMPI* complements of items and comparisons of them with the modified *MMPI-2* versions did not suggest that the unreliability was due primarily to item losses that occurred in the test revision, except in the instances of two scales. Next, the possibility was entertained that the unreliability might partly be a function of the inpatient samples used in the study. This, however, would be an unpalatable conclusion to accept, because the scales are expected to perform their intended measurement function with this type of patient population. If that was the reason for unreliability, then nothing was lost.

A third possibility was considered, namely, that the affected scales measure highly complex variables that are necessarily of low internal consistency. This is a possibility that would be seriously entertained if the scales in question were as complex as the basic Clinical scales. This explanation might also be considered for other scales developed by the method of criterion or comparison groups and whose composition eludes intuitive analysis. But because other scales were found to be reliable that deal with human characteristics as complex as those measured by the edited scales, it is difficult to support this line of reasoning. It is further germane to observe that when correlations were examined for some particular *MMPI–2* scale of interest between it and the two versions of another scale—the traditionally scored and the revised versions—in a head-to-head comparison, expected relations were nearly always a bit more clearly seen when the comparison was made with the revised version.

Unrepairable Scales

Two scales were irretrievably lost due to unreliability. One of these, the Assertiveness scale (Ohlson & Wilson, 1974), was developed by the empirical method of contrasting groups. It is possible that this scale fell victim primarily to item losses (14 of 55 lost) that occurred in the *MMPI–2* revision. It is difficult to assess this possibility by way of subjective judgment, because item inclusion was not based on intuitive assignment. The scale may instead have fallen victim to intervening cultural change in gender attitudes, expression, and stereotypes. Or, the unreliability may simply be due to the collapse of a scale whose validity was inherent only in the unique qualities of the samples used in its construction. The Wiggins (1966) Femininity scale was found likewise to be unreliable. No suitable substitute scale was found for either of these defective scales.

Scale Replacements

Satisfactory substitutes were identified to replace two unreliable Harris–Lingoes Subscales: (a) *3IA*, Inhibition of Aggression and (b) *4AC*, Authority Conflict/Problems. Two additional unreliable scales from the Indiana Rational Scales group (Levitt, 1989) either were extensively revised or recreated. Formerly they were called the Indiana Dependency (*I-De*) and Sexual Problems (*I-SP*) scales. Although *I-De* was not lost due to item cuts, *I-SP* was hurt by losing five key items. No similar revisions or replacements were made for scales outside this group.

Using the *MMPI* and *MMPI–2* databases, eventually studies were carried out for all of the scales used in the clinical analyses except for established scales noted in the legend at the front of Appendix A. Reliabilities for the scales generally fell into the moderately high to high range for longer scales and were somewhat lower for shorter scales, as can be seen by inspecting Appendix B. Note that all findings reported in either Appendix A or B are a direct result of these studies. Thus, an important additional step was to review the results against those from other investigators. In the process, results were compared with those from others' studies of scale composition. No problematic discrepancies were found in research reported.

VALIDITY ADJUSTMENTS: THE *AdjAll* VARIABLE

Validity adjustments were created to match standard score cutoffs that were recommended for five different indicators. Cutoffs for four of these appear in Butcher et al. (2001), with a fifth found in Levitt and Gotts (1995). Standard scores were needed before starting the adjustment process. Standard scores were obtained by calculating linear *T*-scores for each of the five scales.

The five Validity scales used were: *VRIN, TRIN, F, F_B,* and Mean Elevation (*ME*). Further information on *ME* appears later in this chapter and the appendices. Next the Validity scales' linear *T*-scores were each transformed to dichotomized variables. The cutoffs for *VRIN, TRIN,* and *F* were each set at T80; the cutoff for F_B was T110; and the cutoff for *ME* was T75. If a patient's score fell below a cutoff for any one of the five scales, then that record was assigned the code *1* in the dichotomized variable corresponding to the scale. If the *T*-score was above the cutoff, then a code of *0* was assigned.

Valid records were those having a code of *1* for all five variables. A *0* in any of the five coded variables resulted in the case being designated invalid. A single variable, Adjusts All (*AdjAll*), was generated from these. It was stored as a validity indicator for each adult case. A code of *1* in *AdjAll* signified a valid record. Of 923 adult males in the *MMPI* database, 637 received a code of *1* in *AdjAll*, whereas 286 were coded as invalid on one or more of the five indicators. Of 593 adult females, 383 were valid and 210 invalid. As a result, the total available sample of valid cases was 1,020—a number that by coincidence is the same as the original number of all males in the *MMPI* database.

AdjAll and Effects of Extreme True Responding

AdjAll effectively removes from analysis those records having out of bounds scores on the four traditional scales and *ME*, as noted earlier. There remained a lingering question about the possible effect on the validity of patient records of excessive True item responses. Records of this type are frequently encountered in the database. This issue can be framed by the question: Does *AdjAll* eliminate excessive True responding as a possible source of invalidity?

In order to answer this question, two sets of frequency distributions were examined for adult females and males. First, a distribution of the complete adult sample for each gender was made based on a variable containing counts of the total number of True responses made on each record. A decision rule was made that patients exceeding the 95th percentile on their gender's distribution for total number of True responses would be labeled at outliers.

Surprisingly, the 95th percentile rule resulted in an identical cutoff for both genders. Records having more than 371 True responses would fall above the set cutoff 5% of the time. After empirically setting the actual cutoff score, *AdjAll* was applied to the samples as a means of removing invalid cases. Revised distributions were then made for each gender minus their invalid cases. The two gender distributions were examined to determine the adjustment's effect on numbers of cases left that exceeded the cutoff. No female patients exceeded the cutoff, but one male patient did so (0.15%) by receiving a sum of 372 True responses.

AdjAll, based on these findings, appears effectively to remove nearly all validity problems that might be due to excessive True responding. Although applying a *TRIN* cutoff of T80 might be expected by itself to exert a comparable corrective effect, it did not have that result. Applying *TRIN* alone in the preceding analyses left 3.04% of females and 3.34% of males above the cutoff of 371 True responses. By examining components of *TRIN* in chapter 7, the *TRIN* scale's functioning may become clearer via a different response consistency analysis.

Considering the percentages of cases that eluded *TRIN*, it may be asked if the cutoff was inaccurately placed too low by tying it to the 95th female and male patient percentiles. This may be examined from the perspective of the estimated means and standard deviations for numbers of True responses given, on average, by the *MMPI–2* normative sample. Normal females had a mean of 220.12, with an estimated standard deviation of 40.01. So a raw score of 371 for True would fall 3.77 standard deviations above the mean of normals. Normal males had a mean for True responses of 211.71, with a standard deviation of 42.38 estimated. A raw score of 371 for a male patient would be 3.76 standard deviations above the normative mean. The cutoffs actually do not appear to be at fault. The conclusion from these checks is that *AdjAll* functions as a convenient and accurate way of making adjustments for invalid records.

UPDATING THE INDIANA RATIONAL SCALES

Origins of Indiana Rational Scales

Levitt (1989) and his colleagues at the IU Medical Center applied computer-based *MMPI* interpretive software that was developed by Lushene for use within the Veteran's Administration Medical Centers (Lushene et al., 1974). The IU group, which organized itself as the Multiphasic Data Analysis Corporation (MDAC), came to recognize that existing scales of that era did not touch on some areas that were clinically important to their work. The group, following Levitt's lead, decided to develop scales to cover the neglected areas.

Methods of Construction. In the process of developing new scales, the MDAC group resorted to the face validity technique, which Levitt (1989) acknowledged to be a rational rather than an empirical process. This method, he believed, had been demonstrated to be effective for item selection when constructing an inventory (Ashton & Goldberg, 1973; Gynther et al., 1979; Jackson, 1975). That is, items were assigned to scales solely on the basis of unanimous agreement for some scales and by consensus of three out of four expert judges for others. Six scales were developed by this method, and a seventh scale, Dominance, was developed independently by Levitt (1989).

Scales Assessed. Although the MDAC group had provided interpretation for many thousands of records, they seemingly remained consistent with their rational approach by not creating from them a database that might have been used to further validate the scales they created. By the time that he was preparing to write an account of the IU interpretive approach based on Lushene's work and the improvements that MDAC had created, there was hence no database. He desired to remedy the obvious absence of supporting data to buttress the valued MDAC accomplishments, and so quickly gathered data from an opportunity sample of 100 persons that he styled as the "Indiana Sample Data" (Levitt, 1989). What was lacking in empirical documentation, however, was at least partially offset by a wealth of insights regarding which scales usually covary with one another, what it means when an expected interscale relation is not present in a patient record, and other perspectives that had grown from interpreting thousands of *MMPI*s.

The Rational Scales. The seven scales developed through the foregoing processes were referred to collectively as the Indiana Rational Scales. They included measures for the following clinical constructs: Severe Reality Distortions (*I-RD*), Dissociative Symptoms (*I-DS*), Obsessive–Compulsiveness (*I-OC*), Sex Problems (*I-SP*), (Poor) Self-Concept (*I-SC*), Dependency (*I-De*), and Dominance (*I-Do*). Further perspectives on each of the scales were provided by Levitt (1989; Levitt & Gotts, 1995). Apparently, only *I-De* was developed by starting with items of an existing scale, Navran's Dependency (*Dy*) scale (1954).

Current Empirical Status of the MDAC Scales

Levitt made changes to the scales in the years from 1989 until the publication of a revised edition of his book (Levitt & Gotts, 1995). These alterations in scale composition were incorporated into the revised scales, and all appear in the same source. The present research involved analyzing all of the Indiana Rational Scales by empirical methods and reporting the results, with any changes reported in the present work. Levitt also offered suggestions for using various of the Harris–Lingoes scales in close combination with one another. Three of those suggestions and the products deriving from them were studied empirically in the present research program, with results presented later.

Severe Reality Distortions.   The MDAC *I-RD* scale lost a single item to the *MMPI–2* revision and none to item analysis. Internal consistencies are very satisfactory. None of its items are unique to it, with 16 of 17 items now appearing in the new content scale *BIZ* and the remaining item showing up in four other psychoticism measures. In terms of validity, *I-RD* and *BIZ* are correlated with other variables at similar levels of significance. *I-RD*, however, was developed before the publication of *MMPI–2*, and thus lacks four new *BIZ* items found there. Assessing its relevance, it was a unique scale when it was initially prepared, especially in its exclusive focus on the presence of delusions and hallucinations. *BIZ* now appears to be a stronger scale.

Dissociative Symptoms.   The measure of dissociative symptoms (*I-DS*) lost no items to the *MMPI–2* revision and instead gained two valuable additions during the present analysis. One half of its items (5) are found also in Bizarre Sensory Experiences (*8BSE*), and two each of these same five also appear in Wiggins Organic Symptoms (*W-ORG*) and the new critical inquiry scale for Neuropsychological Signs (*NeurPsy*). Thus, it shares some of its variance with behavior patterns that might point to cerebral dysfunction and/or psychoticism. Five of the remaining items are unique to *I-DS* in the sense that they appear in none of the other three scales just listed. For a scale of its length, it has moderately high alpha coefficients. Validity coefficients were computed between it and measures of psychoticism (*BIZ*, .76), anxiety (*ANX*, .60), and organic disorders (*ORG*, .72; *NeurPsy*, .73; *HEA*, .61). It captures as an *MMPI–2* scale supplement some of those dissociative features that are measured only in separate, much longer interview and questionnaire procedures. It is, accordingly, recommended as a screening scale for dissociation.

Obsessive–Compulsiveness.   The MDAC scale *I-OC* lost one item to the *MMPI–2* revision and none to item analysis. Its reliability coefficients are quite modest. Five of its eight items also appear in the new Content scale *OBS*. It still contains three items that are unique to it and stand up satisfactorily to both content and item analysis. It shows some balance between items suggesting obsessions and others pointing up compulsive behaviors. It thus offers a second scale to pair up with *OBS*. Its correlation with *OBS* is of course high ($r = .81$), with a 62.5% item overlap. Based on the *DSM–IV* view that obsessions are manifestations of anxiety, its correlations with anxiety spectrum scales are presented here:

Pt (.72), *Pt K*-corrected (.55), *ANX* (.62), *FRS* (.46), and *A* (.73). Appreciating further the occurrence of obsessive thinking in psychosis (American Psychiatric Association, 2000) now recognized in *DSM–IV–TR*, the following correlations may also be suggestive of *I-OC*'s validity: *Sc* (.71), *Sc K*-corrected (.59), *Pa* (.53), and *BIZ* (.66). Whereas *I-OC* filled an empty niche when it was developed, *MMPI–2* users now have the longer and more reliable *OBS* as well.

Self-Concept.   The (poor) Self-Concept scale's (*I-SC*) item composition is unchanged from 1995 to the present. Reliability coefficients are moderately high. When *I-SC* was developed, only the Wiggins Poor Morale (*W-MOR*) scale was available. Now the new *LSE* Content scale adds to the *MMPI–2*'s capability to measure this construct. Seven of *I-SC*'s 14 items also occur in *LSE* and six in *W-MOR*. Yet it has five items that do not appear in either of the other scales. These five unique items appear from both psychometric and content analysis perspectives to be appropriately assigned in a scale measuring this construct. In terms of validity, *I-SC* correlates more strongly than does *LSE* with the Harris–Lingoes Subscales *3LM* (.62 vs. .56) and *4SA* (.70 vs. .63) and the new Content scale *DEP* (.79 vs. .75). *W-MOR* has 13 items unique to it and correlates more strongly with *WRK, ANX, HEA*, and *OBS* than does either of the other scales. *LSE* has five unique items. Thus, although the three scales intercorrelate with one another around .80 to .83, each potentially offers insights into different aspects of depressed or damaged self-concept.

Dominance.   *I-Do* lost two items to the *MMPI–2* revision and an additional three to item analysis, reducing it from 17 to 12 items. Its reliabilities are quite modest. In view of this weak showing, it is important to recognize that it and the Dominance (*Do*) or Self-Confidence scale do not measure the same things—a reality attested to by the correlation between them of only .18 before and −.01 after both scales had items cut as a result of revisions to improve their internal consistencies. *I-Do* remains a stand-alone scale with no parallel. *I-Do* correlates negatively at low levels with all of the *MMPI–2* Clinical Scales, the highest being −.33 with *D*. It relates negatively to *R* (−.56) for both males and females, suggesting that persons who are high in this type of dominance "take ascendant roles in interpersonal relationships" (Graham, 1990, p. 146). In fact, among 1,020 males, *R* had its highest correlation with *I-Do*. But, among 637 females, *R* was their third highest correlation behind *Ma* and *MAC-R*, which both correlated negatively in the lower .60s.

A NEW DEPENDENCY SCALE (*Depnd*)

The remaining two MDAC or Indiana Rational Scales, *I-SP* and *I-De*, both proved to be unreliable. No *I-De* items were lost to the *MMPI–2* revision. This rational scale, thus, was an unreliable measure both in its original version when it contained 9 of those items and in its revised version of 10 items (Levitt, 1989; Levitt & Gotts, 1995).

In the search of items for a replacement scale, as during its original MDAC development, Navran's (1954) rationally derived *Dy* scale was once again checked closely for items that might be useful, bearing in mind all the while that dependency has more than one face and the different faces of dependency are not necessarily strongly correlated with one another (Bardwick, 1971; Kessler, 1966). Among Navran's original selection of 57 items, 25 were found that appeared to be promising. One outside item was added to these. When checked by item analysis, the resulting 26-item scale was highly internally consistent. It was named Dependency/Self-Doubt (*Depnd*) based on a substantial focus of the item content on low self-confidence that is viewed here as a dependency sign. It correlated in expected ways in a variety of comparisons: D (.56), K (−.70), *ANG* (−.72), *SOD* (.53), and with the new *DPND* personality disorder scale (.87).

TOWARD ASSESSING SEXUALITY/INTIMACY FAILURE (*Sexual*)

Damage Control and Repair

During the *MMPI–2* revision, the sexual problems (*I-SP*) scale lost five essential items (*MMPI* numbers T69, T470, T519, & T548; *F*430), all explicitly dealing with issues of sexuality. Replacement items were not found among the 107 new items. The scale, nevertheless, covered issues that are not otherwise treated by any extant scales, making its revitalization a worthy objective. In order to do this, the scale's focus was broadened from sexual problems alone to include also the wider issues of willingness to engage in self-disclosure, interpersonal openness, and other indications of a capacity for intimacy. Using this refocused objective for the scale, the 8 original items remaining were joined with 11 items representing the new content focus.

Reliability and Validity

The new scale had relatively high internal consistencies. It was named Sexuality/ Intimacy Failure (*Sexual*). The validity of this new scale was evaluated in terms of its correlations with the following scales: *GM* (females, −.49; males, −.61); *GF* (females, −.36; males, −.17). The greater impact of intimacy failure is seen in *GF* for females and *GM* for males. Patients who had higher intimacy failure scores were likely to experience greater social discomfort: *SOD* (females, .36; males, .43).

Possible SES Effect

Also of interest was the scale's relation to *MF* (females, −.18; males, .33). Thus, in this predominantly lower SES sample, females with stereotypically higher femininity (i.e., lower *MF*) and males with lower masculinity (i.e., higher *MF*) both scored higher in Sexuality/Intimacy Failure. It seems likely based on other evidence that with a better educated, middle class-oriented sample, different findings might be expected for males, with predictions for females being less clear (see Friedman et al., 2001, pp. 112–119).

VALIDATING SCALE COMBINATIONS

Levitt (1989; Levitt & Gotts, 1995) made a series of suggestions for ways that the information provided by *MMPI* scales might be combined. One of these involved examining the magnitude of the difference between *T*-scores of *I-De* and *I-Do*. This was foreclosed by the loss of *I-De* to unreliability. Whether or not the new scale *Depnd* would interface in this way with *I-Do* is the proper subject for another study, but that question goes beyond the present objective of formally evaluating suggestions originally developed by Levitt. More of his suggestions found in the foregoing sources are examined in this section.

Mean Elevation (*ME*) of the Profile

Levitt considered an early suggestion by Modlin (1947) that the scores of the nine Basic scales (i.e., excluding *Si*) should be combined as a rough index of psychopathology, and then he carried it in another direction. He proposed that standard scores from the eight Clinical scales be combined to form an overall index of the tendency to produce an elevated record. He reasoned that because a majority of clinical profiles can be characterized as either a high-point code or a high-point pair, overall elevation of scales is an unexpected event.

His proposed solution was implemented in what he called "the Human Computer Program" (Levitt & Gotts, 1995, Appendix V) in the Validity section of interpretation. This proposal was intuitively appealing and was supported by the clinical review of numerous patient profiles. However, no formal study had been conducted to determine the defensibility and limitations of this approach. Note that the decision rules advocated in the 1995 source included other combinations of elevation that are not pursued in the studies reported. Instead, the studies were limited to validating one index of mean elevation.

Reliability Approximation for ME.   In the present research, an internal consistency reliability was computed for the sum of the eight Clinical scales expressed as linear *T*-scores but before applying the *K*-corrections. Establishing no

K-correction would result in using Levitt's decision rule that records whose *ME* exceeded T70 would be interpreted as possibly usable but exaggerated. However, a different cutoff, T75, was used in the following analysis.

It was clearly understood before undertaking this analysis that, with the massive numbers of item overlaps among the scales, equal numbers of linear dependencies are created and lead to an invalid estimation of the alpha coefficient. The objective of the analysis hence was not to generate a precise estimate but instead to gain some crude notion of whether there would be any credible evidence to support the purported cohesiveness of the scales. If none were found, then this approach could be set aside and regarded as an interesting but unworkable one. This examination would further indicate the contribution of the various Clinical scales to the composite result—something not previously evaluated.

With the Clinical scales entered as items, an average interitem correlation was computed of .46 for females and .50 for males. The resulting coefficients for alpha were: females (.86) and males (.88). These coefficients are actually lower than might be anticipated, given the stabilities of the respective scales coupled with the large amount of item-specific variance shared among the scales. On the other hand, the evidence cited earlier regarding the characteristics of typical profiles would suggest that combining the scales in this manner does pose some challenge for the detection of cohesiveness.

Relations to Its Source Scales.   Correlations of the individual scales with the total score vary widely for adult males from a high of .83 each for *Pt* and *Sc* and a low of .32 for *Ma*. *Pa* was the next highest at .71, followed by *D* at .67, *Hs* at .65, *Pd* at .60, and *Hy* at .59. The highest and lowest correlations with the total score appear discontinuous to an extent from the rest. Partial similarity of correlations was seen, with some shifting emphases and lower levels of relationship for adult females: high for *Sc* (.81) and *Pt* (.79) and low for *Ma* (.24). *Pa* (.67) was next highest, followed by *Hs* (.66), *D* (.62), *Hy* (.57), and *Pd* (.54).

Prevalence Rates Found.   Checking on the effects of classifying patients by *ME*, patients scoring above the *ME* cutoff were compared with those below it. Prevalence rates were 72 (12.1%) adult females scoring above the cutoff and 521 below. Those below would be judged as not having overly elevated profiles. Dividing the adult males at the cutoff resulted in 787 valid cases and 136 (14.7%) with exaggerated profile elevations.

Validity of ME.   Validity checks were made by comparing correlations of *ME* with other dichotomized variables that together make up the *AdjAll* index. *ME* correlated for females and males, respectively, as follows: *F* (.47/.56), F_B (.56/.44), *VRIN* (.01/.01), *TRIN* (.11/.04). These findings show that *ME* primarily shares its variance with those patient response characteristics that also elevate *F* and F_B, while being essentially independent of the response consistency measures

VRIN and *TRIN*. These latter measures, thus, are seen to make their own independent contribution to identifying questionable *MMPI–2* records.

   Incremental Discrimination.   Next the incremental discrimination of invalid cases was examined by calculating the percentages of cases that would fall above the cutoff with *ME* added to *F* and F_B, as compared with the combinations of *F* and F_B only. Among adult female patients using *F* by itself, 26.31% of records are judged invalid. This increases to 30.52% by adding F_B and to 31.87% with the addition of *ME*. For adult males, *F* alone identified 22.21% of records as invalid. When *F* is combined with F_B, the total rises only fractionally to 22.32% and then to 28.17% when *ME* is joined with the other two.

   Conclusions.   The results show that *ME* adds to the discriminative power of the two most widely used indices of records that are invalid due to exaggerated reporting of psychopathology. This increment was especially important in the male sample. Interestingly, a combination of the eight scales has been used by others to assess general maladjustment (Graham, Barthlow, Stein, Ben-Porath, & McNulty, 2002). Based on the present study, it is recommended that *ME* not be used alone, but instead in combination with the other scales in the *AdjAll* correction variable as a way to detect invalid records.

Trustworthy/Trusting (*Trust*)

Another of Levitt's (1989) suggestions was that scores for the Harris–Lingoes Subscales *3NA* and *6N* be used in close coordination. To accomplish this, he recommended that their respective *T*-scores be added. The result would then be interpreted in combination with scores for *9AMO* and the *L* scale. The brief presentation here formalizes the process of combining *3NA* and *6N*, while saving the balance of Levitt's suggestion for treatment in the clinical interpretive parts of the present work.

   The Source Scales.   One change each was made to *3NA* and *6N* during item analysis. The two correlated positively (females, .73; males, .70) with one another before the scale revisions (see Appendix A). Their correlations rose (females, .79; males, .78) following the revisions. Furthermore, they share three of their items (unchanged by the revisions). These overlapping items alone are insufficient to account for the substantial correlations found.
   The prospect of adding the *T*-scores of the two scales presented some obvious drawbacks. Because the scales are not perfectly correlated, high or low scores on just one of the two scales could result in a score of fused *T*-scores that is much more representative of the one scale's than other's variance. In order to avoid this complication, the direct solution of combining the items into a single composite scale was adopted, with results described next.

Reliability and Meaning.   A total of 17 different items were available from the two scales. They were placed in a single pool and subjected to item analysis as a scale. The result was that all items fit satisfactorily and were retained. Reliability coefficients for internal consistency were moderately high (see Appendix B). The result supports Levitt's suggestion. At the same time, it demonstrates a greater cohesiveness among the items of the source scales than might have been suspected from a superficial consideration of their disparate origins as subscales of the *Hy* and *Pa* Clinical scales. The new scale was named Trustworthy/Trusting (*Trust*), an epithet that potentially reflects on what the high scoring respondent affirms about others and in turn implies about the self. In addition to the element of trust, the naïve component remains. Thus, extremely high scores in some instances may suggest the gullibility of the ingénue or, as Levitt (1989) originally suggested, in other instances may represent an assertion of personal virtue or act as a defensive declaration regarding personal integrity.

Validity.   As for the validity of the *Trust* scale, it can be inferred from the following series of correlational comparisons. Those with high scores on *Trust* report low levels of characteristics measured by these scales used with the data base: *CYN* (females, $-.90$; males, $-.89$); *TSC/S* (females, $-.84$; males, $-.83$); *Ho*, original (females, $-.85$; males, $-.85$); *Ho*, revised (females, $-.86$; males, $-.86$); *ANG* (females, $-.57$; males, $-.60$); *TSC/R* (females, $-.66$; males, $-.70$); *W-HOS* (females, $-.72$; males, $-.74$). Conversely, those who score low on *Trust* report being more suspicious, cynical, hostile, anger prone, and resentful than others.

Imperturbability (*Impert*)

Three Subscale Merger.   Another of Levitt's clinical observations about the covariation of the Harris–Lingoes Subscales led him to suggest that *3DSA*, *4SI*, and *9IMP* were measuring similar things and should be combined by adding their respective *T*-scores. He interpreted this composite as an index of social anxiety versus social comfort. This suggestion was not formally examined by quantitative analysis, so its status continued to depend until now on the empiricism of an informed intuition. It is subjected here to more formal analysis.

Available Items.   The *MMPI–2* revision kept the three scales intact. Item analysis also left *3DSA* unchanged. Substantial changes were made to *4SI* by the restoration to it of five of six items that were originally assigned by Harris and Lingoes from outside of *Pd* but are now usually omitted from *4SI*. A sixth item was tried, but was inappropriately placed and thus not used. Graham (1987) recommended retaining all of the Harris–Lingoes item assignments to the *Pd* subscales in order to assure their comparability with prior scoring and research, a practice that Levitt followed in his scoring of subscales. The composition of *9IMP* also was modified by the removal of three items that failed to mesh with the scale appropriately. Hence at the outset of the process of combining the three scales, substantial changes had already occurred that might affect the outcome. Nevertheless, the process was carried out.

Reliability. In their unmerged forms, the three subscales contained a total of 22 items, 15 of which were not redundant of one another. Two items were shared by all three subscales, two more by the subscale combinations *3DSA–4SI* and one by the pairing of *4SI–9IMP*, thereby accounting for the reduction of the pool's size by 7 items. In order to emphasize a previous point, it is noted that all 5 of the items added to *4SI* were included in the 15-item pool. Item analysis of these items resulted in the removal of one item that had been restored to *4SI*. The remaining 14 items comprise the new scale, Imperturbability (*Impert*).

Estimated reliability of the scale based on its internal consistency was moderately high. Its reliability slightly exceeded that of *3DSA* and strongly exceeded that of *9IMP*. It also slightly exceeded *4SI*, whose reliability would have been as low as that of *9IMP* if the five original Harris–Lingoes items had not been restored. Clearly, then, the new scale is more reliable than the summed scores of its three source scales. This composite scale might resolve Krishnamurthy, Archer, and Huddleston's (1995) unreliability concerns about the restricted upper limit standard score for the *3DSA* and *4SI* subscales.

Validity. A remaining question is whether *Impert* is any more valid than the source scales from whose items it was formed. This question was examined by correlational analysis. As Levitt reasoned, the combination of these scales should correlate inversely with measures of social maladjustment and social introversion. The three subscales plus *Impert* were compared to scales known to measure these criterial attributes: *SOD, Si1, TSC/I,* and *W-SOC.* For all comparisons made, the more reliable *Impert* produced larger correlations with the listed scales than did any one of the three Harris–Lingoes Subscales for both adult females and males. Accordingly, findings are reported here for *Impert*'s relation to the other scales: *SOD* (females, −.75; males, −.76), *Si1* (females, −.89; males, −.90), *TSC/I* (females, −.87; males, −.87), and *W-SOC* (females, −.81; males, −.82). This appears to have been a successful empirical translation of the original suggestion into a quantitatively supported scale that can be used with *MMPI–2* to measure imperturbability (high score) versus social anxiety (low score) (i.e., high *Impert* means denial of social anxiety).

Social Alienation (*SoAlien*)

Merging Scales. A final merging of items is derived from an observation that *4SOA* and *8SOA* cofluctuate even though they share only four of their items (Levitt, 1989). One of the shared items results from an add-back to *4SOA*. Levitt proceeded to interpret this combined pair of scales as representing an important part of the sociopathic individual's makeup. No changes were made to *8SOA* as a result of its item analysis. Both add-backs of Harris–Lingoes items and cuts based on item analysis resulted in a different item composition for *4SOA*. The two scales contained a nonredundant pool of 31 items after adjusting for their overlaps.

Reliability. The pool of 31 items was submitted to item analysis. All items survived the analysis, resulting in a new scale that is designated Social Alienation (*SoAlien*). Its alpha coefficients are high and slightly exceed those of both source scales.

Validity. Correlations were computed for *4SOA, 8SOA*, and *SoAlien* with a series of scales representing the sociopathic spectrum. *SoAlien* generally exhibited the strongest relation of the three with comparison scales. An exception occurred when the comparisons were made between *Pd* and *4SOA*, which had a relation that was slightly stronger than that between *Pd* and *SoAlien*. *SoAlien* was the scale most strongly related to the following pertinent scales: *ASP* (females, .55; males, .58), *W-AUT* (females, .54; males, .53), PDO *ANTI* (females, .58; males, .62), *8DI* (females, .73; males, .76), *Imp-B* (females, .61; males, .61), *Imp-I* (females, .75; males, .79), *Imp-A* (females, .51; males, .61), and *Imp-T* (females, .75; males, .79). Thus, patients scoring high on *SoAlien* were likely also to receive higher scores than others for all types of impulsivity, defective inhibition, authority conflict, and antisocial behavior and propensity.

RECOVERING THE PARAPHILIA/PEDOPHILIA SCALE (*PE*)

The Pedophilia scale (*Pe*) was empirically developed by comparing a group of offenders convicted of pedophilic acts with offenders not convicted of a sexual crime (Toobert et al., 1959). A comparable cross-validation study was also conducted. The scale had known validity for males only. During the *MMPI–2* revision, 6 of *Pe*'s 24 items (25%) were lost. The lost items' *MMPI* numbers were: T53, T95, T206, T490; F435, F556. Four of the items lost had appeared in the Wiggins Religious Fundamentalism (*W-REL*) scale. All but one of *W-REL*'s items were eliminated from *MMPI–2* as a part of the process of updating the test and removing items thought to be objectionable to respondents. Three more items were cut from *Pe* during item analysis, leaving only 15 of the original items.

Because the kind of content found in *W-REL* was no longer available in the *MMPI–2* item pool, it was not possible to locate items that were potentially comparable in content focus. For a scale that has been validated by the method of criterion group comparisons, the loss of 9 of its 24 items (37.5%) is a potentially devastating amount of change. Yet it was essential that it be salvaged if at all possible, because, as Levitt (1989) noted, this was a unique and subtle scale that had shown itself to be of considerable clinical value for assessing a wide range of the paraphilias (i.e., its value was not limited assessing pedophiles).

Search for Replacement Items

It was a given that the scale could not be returned to its original state, but perhaps enough of its original discriminative power remained that it could be returned to usefulness. Faced with this challenge, additional items were identified that might fit in with the scale's remaining items in ways that strengthen it. Six possible replacement items were selected after repeated reviews of the entire *MMPI-2* item pool in parallel with the still remaining items (see Appendix A). It was interesting in view of the prior validation methods that all of the items added were selected from among the 107 new items added during the *MMPI-2* revision. That is, none were original *MMPI* items that had been overlooked or discarded in the studies of Toobert et al. (1959).

Reliability Established

The resulting pool of 21 items and the surviving pool of 15 items were item analyzed separately. Both pools were analyzed for males in the *MMPI-2* database, and the pool of 15 was analyzed for males in the larger *MMPI* database. A relatively high coefficient alpha (.81) was found for the revised scale. The 15-item scale was also usable but was lower reliability (.72). These are respectable alphas for a scale whose content focus is as diverse as that of *Pe*. All items that were entered into the analyses were retained. In consideration of its broader applicability, the scale was renamed Paraphilia/Pedophilia, but the original short name, *Pe* (Toobert et al., 1959), was kept alive.

Validity Study Complications

A cutoff was set at T75 for *Pe*. Even so, attempts to validate the scale were limited by the many cases that exceeded the cutoff. The number of high *Pe* scoring records far exceeded the likely incidence of these disorders in this hospital population. As it turned out, this first roadblock to conducting a validity study was easily circumvented. This was possible because the vast majority of cases with high *Pe* scores occurred in invalid records that were purged when the correction variable *AdjAll* was applied to the records.

To gain an appreciation of the size of this effect, the following specifics are germane. Of 923 adult males in the larger sample, 173 received *Pe* scores greater than T74, but after application of *AdjAll*, only 38 valid cases remained (4.1% of the 923). The problem of many invalid high *Pe* scores was corrected, but with the result of a sizable sample attrition. It was, nevertheless, more realistic to arrive at an incidence of 38 cases who might be oriented to perform paraphilic acts than to consider that a total of 173 high *Pe* scorers fit this description.

The low incidence of valid *Pe* cases, however, posed a second problem. The problem was that there would be too few valid high *Pe* score cases to study in the smaller *MMPI–2* male sample, (i.e., 4.1% of the 135 males would leave only five cases). This meant that analyses would need to be carried out using the shorter, 15-item version of the *Pe* scale using the larger *MMPI* male sample in order to achieve a workable sample size.

Pe Continues Valid

As a consequence of the complications just presented, validity analyses were completed using the 15-item scale, for which sample size was adequate. In view of the item analysis findings, it was judged to be reliable enough for this purpose. Furthermore, it could be anticipated from a comparison of item analyses for the two versions that the findings would apply as well to the longer and more reliable 21-item scale. As previously noted, the 923 male *MMPI* database sample yielded 38 high scoring *Pe* records that also passed all validity tests of *AdjAll*. To review a final inclusion criterion, the 38 cases all had scored T75 or higher on the 15-item version of the *Pe* scale. Descriptively, the 38 high scoring records had a mean *Pe* of T81.5 with a standard deviation of 4.33, which were not overly elevated.

Comparisons were made of the 38 *Pe* positive records with 599 other valid adult male records whose *Pe* scores were less than T75. This comparison group's mean was T55.50, with a standard deviation of 10.05. A series of *MMPI–2* scales was selected for their possible relevance to the paraphilias (see Gebhard, Gagnon, Pomeroy, & Christenson, 1965) and used for comparing the groups with t tests for independent samples. Results of all comparisons were significant ($p < .001$, $df = 635$).

Means for the two groups are presented with the high *Pe* scorers appearing first each time: *GM*, T34.27/T44.27; *Sexual*, T66.77/T49.42; *SOD*, T60.66/T49.69; *Impert*, T35.90/T48.65; *Depnd*, T71.49/T54.42; *Sadist* tendencies, T58.77/T50.73; and *6P*, T65.15/T52.78. Variances of the two groups were compared for each of the preceding variables as a precaution in view of differing standard deviation for the two groups. All F ratios compared were nonsignificant and had associated probability levels ranging from .13 to .85.

The *Pe* scale clearly differentiated between paraphilia-oriented male patients and other non-paraphilia-oriented male patients for all of the comparisons made. When otherwise valid records were sorted based on *Pe* scores, the groups' means were separated by wide, easily discernible distances. The mean *T*-score distance between groups for the seven comparisons was 12.65 *T*-score points or 1.265 standard deviations. The comparison group's standard scores on these variables were all within 0.6 of a standard deviation or less from CX means calculated for the *MMPI–2* norm group. It was the high *Pe* scoring group that exhibited the larger mean departures from the normative means.

Characteristics of High *Pe* Males

The findings reported earlier suggest that male high *Pe* scorers whose test records are otherwise valid possess an extremely limited number of traditional masculine attributes, experience sexual/intimacy failure and difficulty being open to others, are prone to social discomfort and social anxiety, have high dependency and low self-confidence, may seek pleasure from inflicting psychological or other pain on others or having it inflicted on them or possibly both, and keenly feel vulnerable in interpersonal situations. The results give sufficient testimony to the survival of the scale's ability to detect paraphilias to commend it for continued study and use. Study is especially needed for the longer version of the *Pe* scale that could not be adequately evaluated using the hospital's available database.

UPDATING THE INDIANA PERSONALITY DISORDER (PDO) SCALES

Background

A series of Indiana *PDO* item lists was developed by Levitt and Gotts (1995) based on repeated searches through the full pool of original *MMPI* items. After an item list was compiled, items were merged randomly with those selected by Morey and his associates (Morey, Waugh, & Blashfield, 1985) in order to mask their respective origins. Only items appearing in both *MMPI* and *MMPI–2* were included in order that the list could be applied to either version of the test. This enlarged item pool was then subjected by a panel of eight clinical judges to a procedure of matching to *DSM–III–R*'s (APA, 1987) and Millon's (1987) criteria for each of the 11 *DSM*-listed personality disorders. A full account, with details of the rationale and methods used, appears in Levitt and Gotts (1995). They are referred to here as the Indiana Personality Disorder Scales.

The outcome of the item selection process was a series of item sets that corresponded to the combined criteria, but thereafter were limited to those disorders listed in *DSM–III–R*. The less definitive term *item sets* was used in the Levitt and Gotts (1995) book rather than *scales* in view of how the impending publication deadline foreclosed the possibility of including in the book results of item analyses and other ongoing work. That is, the standard meaning of a *scale* would not be met because of the restricted kinds of empirical information that could be included by the manuscript deadline.

Original Reliabilities

The findings that arrived too late for inclusion in the book indicated that the internal consistencies were generally acceptable for the original versions of the scales, with some apparent exceptions. The prior omission is amended by the inclusion here of the Cronbach alpha coefficients from analysis of the original item sets: Antisocial *PDO*, 24 items (.80); Paranoid *PDO*, 19 items (.84); Narcissistic *PDO*, 17 items (.78); Histrionic *PDO*, 15 items (.69); Borderline *PDO*, 29 items (.87); Passive–Aggressive *PDO*, 14 items (.79); Dependent *PDO*, 22 items (.76); Obsessive–Compulsive *PDO*, 16 items (.73); Avoidant *PDO*, 16 items (.80); Schizotypal *PDO*, 17 items (.81); Avoidant-schizotypal core (Core 1), 7 items (.59); and Avoidant-schizotypal-schizoid core (Core 2), 14 items (.83). All patient means differed from the corresponding CX equivalent means, with patient means suggesting a greater incidence among them of traits associated with the respective disorders. They now were scales.

PDO Scales Insufficient for Diagnosis

No matter whether they are conceived of as item sets or scales, the approach recommended by the authors for using them differed from approaches of their predecessors in the following essential respect. The scores were not recommended to be used to identify the personality disorders in isolation from other evidence. In practice, this meant that the obtained scores were not to be interpreted in the absence of supporting/corroborating findings from other specified *MMPI/MMPI–2* scales that appeared to be germane to the respective disorders. This led the authors to present a first approximation of lists of specific, related scales that they recommended reviewing in parallel with the personality disorder scores (Levitt & Gotts, 1995, pp. 85–86, 147–154). The lists would be revised and expanded based on experience with their use in applied diagnostic work.

The rationale underlying the previous recommendation is based on a view that the *PDO*s, as they are identified and differentiated from one another by the *DSM* and Millon criteria, represent complex compounds of personality features. Because they are compounds rather than simply mixtures, they present themselves more or less predictably as pervasive and enduring behavior patterns that affect the person's functioning. All of the scales used to make inferences about the *DSM* PDOs, including the scales presented here, are too brief to encompass and sample adequately the scope of each disorder.

If, for example, approximately 18 items are used to sample a *PDO* for which 9 criteria are specified, an average of two items would be available to represent each criterion. This is not adequate, especially when it is recognized that each criterion resembles a trait that in other psychological measurement contexts would be operationally defined by its own pool of many more items. The scales may be reliable, but the reliability of item sampling cannot be when so few items are available, on average, per criterion. It would, therefore, be more accurate to think of the available *PDO* scales as most useful as screening devices whose results require confirmation by a process of reviewing data that corroborate what the scale points to as needing to be checked further.

Scale Revisions and Reliabilities

Some of the original scales were not as reliable as would be needed for clinical use. Possibly this could be remedied by locating additional items that had been passed over in the original composite item. Now items would be considered if a majority of the original judges had agreed on their placement in a specific scale. This increased the number of available items and shifted more of the emphasis on decision making about item inclusions away from the judges to the item analysis process.

By the time this revision was started, a substantial part of the database had been computerized locally. Along with this, greater numbers and more diversity of patients in the sample opened the potential for stronger inferences to be made about item inclusion and exclusion. This enlargement of possibilities meant that instead of limiting the review to only those scales whose reliability was originally below levels desired, it would now be in order to run new item analyses for all of the scales. Items were added if they improved a scale's internal consistency. In the process, the reliabilities of the weakest scales improved, and for some the improvement was considerable, as can be examined by comparing the original reliabilities with those in Appendix B.

Evidence for Validity

The discriminative power of the revised scales was evaluated by examining separately samples of adult females ($n = 383$) and adult males ($n = 637$) from which all patients exceeding any of the validity scales limits were excluded. The variable *AdjAll* (see earlier discussion) was used to remove all invalid cases. Linear *T*-scores provided a comparison to normals in the CX sample. Mean scores for the patients were highest on the Borderline *PDO* scale (females, T60.09; males, T58.43). Both genders also scored slightly in excess of one half standard deviation higher than normals on Dependent *PDO* (females, T55.61; males, T55.15) and Obsessive–Compulsive *PDO* (females, T55.94; males, T55.04). Avoidant *PDO* tendencies were also prominent (females, T54.77; males, T55.47). Two additional scales pointed up significant departures from the means of normals for both genders: Histrionic *PDO* (females, T53.67; males, T55.20) and Schizotypal *PDO* (females, T53.82; males, T54.34). The largest mean difference between the genders was for the Antisocial *PDO* scale (females, T51.32; males, T55.96). For the remaining scales, female and male patients did not differ markedly from each other or from the means of normals.

Only one of the preceding mean variations (i.e., Borderline *PDO*) would be of possible clinical relevance if scores tightly clustered around their means. But that is not true of other *PDO*s. Of the 637 valid adult male cases, 152 (23.9%) received Antisocial *PDO* scores equal to or greater than T65, whereas 38 females out of 383 valid cases (9.9%) received scores in the same range. Moreover, mean scores on related scales for those patients with the elevated *PDO* scores were also elevated: *ASP* (females, T68.48; males, T66.72) and *Pd* (females, T66.81; males, T68.14).

Similar calculations were made for those scoring high on the Paranoid *PDO* scale. Of the valid female cases, 38 (7.3%) were at T65 or above; in the case of males, 107 (16.8%) had similarly elevated scores. Females who were above the cutoff had average scores on *Pa* of T66.81, and males had scores of T65.15. A scale measuring suspicious character traits was developed by Stein (1968) as a part of the Tryon, Stein, and Chu (TSC) Cluster Scales. Adult females with valid records and Paranoid *PDO* above the cutoff had a mean score on this scale of T67.69, and males meeting the same criteria had a mean score of T71.40.

Comparable studies with the other scales generally suggested that they too related in expected ways to criterion *MMPI–2* scales that are commonly included in clinical practice. Special mention is made here of the treatment of the Passive–Aggressive *PDO* that had been in all of the *DSM*s up through its 1989 edition, *DSM–III–R*. It became a *DSM–IV* "further study" scale. Downgrading its status in the current *DSM* unfortunately has not caused it to disappear from the patient population nor from the citizenry at large. Consequently, the practice here has been to continue to treat it as a listed disorder that is to be identified by Millon and *DSM* "further study" criteria. The view here, to rephrase the saying of a noted American humorist, is "word of its demise has been much exaggerated."

Recent Developments

Schizoid.   The method originally developed for identifying Schizoid *PDO* (*SCZD*) required conjoint use of multiple scales. This proved to be cumbersome. Alvin Jones, for example, found the procedure confusing (A. Jones, personal communication, April 17, 2002). An easier to use procedure was developed in the form of a single scale. This was comprised of items in the Morey et al. (1985) overlapping list plus the Levitt and Gotts (1995) item set that was referred to as the Avoidant-schizotypal-schizoid core, or more briefly, *Core 2*. Three of the Morey items (79, 157, and 405) were not retained because they correlated negatively with the scale scores for both females and males. Based on criteria for the disorder, these items should have correlated positively. Implications of this apparent discrepancy for the scale's validity are considered in chapter 9.

Cutoff Scores. Interpretation of *PDO* scales was anchored to the 85th percentile level within a reference patient sample in 1994. In order to offer a broader frame of reference that would be applicable in more and varied patient settings, cutoffs have been anchored to the CX norms. Patients who scored above the CX 85th percentile on any one of the 11 scales were now screened as positive for the disorder. If multiple scores exceeded this, clinical judgment was made of whether one of the disorders was primary, the patient had more than one *PDO*, or it was a case of a mixed or not otherwise specified (NOS) disorder.

There was a problem. At linear T70 (about 95th percentile), percentile levels for the 11 scales ranged from the 78th to the 97th for adult females and from 80th to 94th for adult males. Such variation results from differing properties of each scale's score distribution. Further, the scales were all at least moderately correlated with one another, resulting in many co-occurring elevations that needed to be differentiated from one another. Making clinical decisions about which score was primary, secondary, and so on, thus required greater commonality of meaning than was afforded by unadjusted linear *T*-scores. Changes were made.

Scale scores were statistically adjusted in the research sample by using the 85th percentile as a uniform screening cutoff for the *PDO* scales. Classification of *PDO*s in chapter 9 was conducted using these anchored cutoffs. Because these adjustments derive from a particular sample, persons using a fixed standard score cutoff are cautioned that they need to evaluate how similar variations affect the comparability of scores across the *PDO* scales within their own practice settings.

The PDO Sample. A *PDO* analysis sample was formed of only those adult cases whose scores were valid (earlier in this chapter see the use of the composite *AdjAll* variable). Patients with Axis I disorders also produced elevated scores on the *PDO* scales. Thus, all patients who were assigned psychotic, bipolar, depressive spectrum, or anxiety spectrum diagnoses during their admission were excluded from the *PDO* sample. Following these procedures, 586 valid adult patients with no major MI diagnosis remained in the sample.

A comparison group was formed within the *PDO* sample. Patients whose 11 *PDO* scale scores all fell at or below the 72nd percentile became a comparison group. There were 157 patients with scores below the cutoff on all 11 scales. An additional 80 patients fell between upper and lower cutoffs and were excluded from further analysis. There remained a valid sample of 349 *PDO* cases of which 66 were clinically classified as mixed disorders and 283 represented single *PDO*s. The number of singly classified cases varied from 57 for the Schizoid *PDO* to 13 for Passive–Aggressive *PDO*. Findings for the 11 scales appear in chapter 9.

Distress (Dist). Merging the *Core 2* scale into the new Schizoid *PDO* scale raised the question of whether the *Core 1* scale was of any further value or if its use should be discontinued. It was an index of distress that previously was used with *Core 2* plus other scores to identify the Schizoid disorder. It was renamed Distress (*Dist*) based on its known sensitivity to patient distress levels.

The question of keeping or dropping *Core 1* was decided by pairing it in a series of regression equations separately with each of three *PDO* scales: *BORD*, *DPND*, and *AVDT*. These three were chosen because each is associated in the patient sample with considerable distress, as seen in their correlations with *Core 1*: *BORD*, .69; *DPND*, .70; *AVDT*, .76. Thus, patients classified as having any of these three disorders might be experiencing high to very high to extreme distress. The classification alone would not reflect the severity of their distress.

When *BORD* and *Dist* were used jointly to predict depressive symptoms as measured by *DEP*, the combination worked far better than either did alone. *Core 1*'s contribution was valued at $t = 7.69$, $df = 583$, $p < .0000$. Next, *Core 1* was paired with *DPND* to predict dependency (*Depnd*), and a highly significant result was again obtained ($t = 10.06$, $df = 583$, $p < .0000$). In the third instance, *Core 1* and *AVDT* were used to predict social discomfort (*SOD*). The addition of *Core 1* to *AVDT* increased the efficiency of *AVDT* alone (*Core 1*'s $t = 7.97$, $df = 583$, $p < .0000$). Based on these results, the *Core 1* was retained as *Dist*.

REVIEW AND PREVIEW

Chapter 6 has reviewed verifications, refinements, rescue operations, and replacements made for the scales used by Levitt and Gotts (1995). Levitt's (1989) observations for combining the scores of various scales were also carried out. This report brings the account for all of those up to the present by documenting their current status. This clinical research program has also developed new scales for use with *MMPI–2*. Their development is the subject matter of chapter 7. Sufficient detail is provided there to verify the extent to which the new scales are reliable and of probable clinical value. The reporting of methods will usually be sufficient to support replication efforts.

New Developments for *MMPI–2*

The tradition of identifying particular *MMPI* and *MMPI–2* items as critical extends at least as far back as a list developed by Hellman (Grayson, 1951). Items expressing serious pathology appeared together in a single list, without regard to the type of pathology that they might indicate. The intent was that symptomatic responses were to be taken seriously and followed up during interviews with either the patient or a knowledgeable informant (W. G. Dahlstrom & Welsh, 1960, Appendix G).

CRITICAL INQUIRY PROCEDURE & RELATED SCALES

Features of Contemporary Critical Item Lists

Current lists developed for use with *MMPI–2* are less general than this early list in the sense that they now contain items divided into multiple specific categories. Item lists for these scales appear in each of three major sources (Butcher et al., 2001, Appendix D; Friedman et al., 2001, Appendix A, Table A.6; Greene, 2000, Appendix B, Table B.12). Two useful critiques of the critical item approach and related lists, each completed from a quite different perspective, are available elsewhere (Friedman et al., 2001; Greene, 2000).

Rationale

Completing an *MMPI–2* extends to the respondent an unusually wide-ranging opportunity for reflection and self-examination. When the respondent happens to be a patient, the test record also creates an occasion for examiner and patient to engage in further communication about presenting problems, desired outcomes of treatment, and related issues. Thus, apart from the issue of any potential role that critical items might play in the unraveling of pathology or estimation of the validity of the record, reviewing selected answers together after the test is completed can be directed toward therapeutic goals and further can contribute to a more focused therapeutic alliance.

Individual critical items may be answered in the keyed direction for quite diverse reasons by different patients. This occurs as a result of the variability of meaning that items hold for individuals. That is not to say that items are not sufficiently intelligible or their meaning is an elusive quality. Much of the variability arises from the subjective aspect of self-examination rather than from qualities of the items. The meaning derived depends on the patient's internal anchoring points and on the subjective probabilities against which an item is read and judged. Of course, the testing situation also prompts some level of awareness that the product of that examination will also receive the attention or perhaps even close scrutiny of others. For these reasons, a particular critical item response may indicate much or little. Only discussion of it by the patient may lead to clarification of the meaning.

Even so, the examiner may or may not learn by inquiring whether a critical item response has much or little meaning. On the other hand, the examiner who does not inquire most assuredly will not learn about the patient's meaning. From another perspective, failure to learn what the patient actually meant of necessity will not pose an inferential problem. This is so because the many scales and abundant strategies available for analyzing *MMPI–2* tend, on average, to offset uncertainty associated with responses to individual items.

Accurately interpreting an individual's test record is undeniably a prime responsibility of the examiner. It is not the only responsibility, however. When certain high profile critical item responses are made, the examiner's duty may be to provide the patient with a communication forum regarding the answers given. For example, if the response alludes to a potential danger or harm to self or others, it could be construed as negligent not to bring up the subject of how the patient intends the answer to be understood. The clarification can then be made a part of the clinical record. Ethics concerns can also be triggered in such instances. From a liability perspective as well, it may be prudent to bring certain responses to light. The upshot of this is that there are implied duties for the examiner when a patient makes critical responses, and as a result there are inherent risks if their importance appears to be ignored or neglected.

Design for Critical Inquiry

Whenever the subject comes up concerning whether or not to inquire into critical patient responses, it generates concerns and discussion about the pragmatics of investing professional time in an activity that may offer only an indefinite and limited payoff. It is, therefore, essential that the scope of any proposed inquiry be of a manageable size. Controlling the amount of effort and time consumed in the process is achieved by having a defined procedure or protocol that guides the examiner as well as sets clear boundaries for the process.

Desiring to have such a procedure for use with *MMPI* prompted the senior author, who then worked at another hospital, in 1983 to undertake developing one for local use. From the outset, the intent was not simply to develop another set of critical items. The name *Critical Inquiry* was chosen as a way of emphasizing that the focus was on how the process of inquiry was conducted. Nevertheless, because this marked a new beginning, selecting items to represent the patient issues that were critical in that particular hospital population would become a necessary part of the activity. By 1984, the procedure was designed and an *MMPI* inquiry instrument was ready. No thought was given at the time to its potential applicability to other settings or its dissemination beyond that hospital.

Revisions were made to fit another hospital setting when the author changed affiliation in 1986. Then *MMPI–2* was published. This introduced new critical items that greatly increased the test's relevance to clinical questions at the new hospital. The inquiry instrument was completely updated. Thereafter, the procedure was refined progressively through the 1990s as it was taught to and used by staff and a succession of predoctoral psychology intern classes. The clinical instrument and procedure that appear as Appendix C eventually reached their present form.

The Instrument Developed

The preeminent objective of this effort was always to have a procedure of critical inquiry that would be of practical value in daily inpatient practice. This aspect was validated principally through clinical experience and the consensus of staff who used it with patients of varied diagnoses.

The instrument reviews answers to 90 items. Brief descriptors identify for each item possible symptoms that the response may suggest. Of the 90 items, 84 are keyed either True or False. Inquiry is conducted for these only if a patient's answer to any of the 84 matches the key. Six items are inquired irrespective of the patient's answer, based on the repeated clinical finding that personal interpretation plays an unusually large role in how they are answered, and they all potentially deal with a single diagnostic focus: hypomanic symptoms or their bipolar opposites. It further has been found clinically during use of the procedure that patients spontaneously comment on linkages among the various answers being discussed. This often results in a patient simply stating that the response currently being inquired about was given based on the same life experiences or circumstances as those previously discussed in connection with an earlier item inquiry. In this way, the patient defines the thematic linkages.

Scales Emerging from Critical Inquiry

Besides judging their local value, specific studies were done to check the psychometric properties of groups of the items. Clusters of the 90 items that offered promise as scales were formed and evaluated within the *MMPI* and *MMPI–2* databases. The outcome of these efforts was the series designated as Critical Inquiry Scales, for which item composition appears in Appendix A. Of the scales in that group, only the one identified as Sado-Masochistic Signs (*Sadist*) uses items that are not part of the Critical Inquiry Worksheet.

All of the Critical Inquiry Scales were found to have acceptable internal consistencies (Appendix B). Scores were computed from the patient database, and their raw score means were compared with the CX equivalents that appear in Appendix B. In all comparisons for both males and females, clinically meaningful differences were found between the patient groups and normals, as can be seen by comparing the means in Appendix B with the following female patient/male patient means: Neuropsychological Signs, 4.54/3.98; Addictive Activities, 2.09/5.36; Suicide Subtle, 3.19/3.39; Suicide Obvious, 0.66/0.75; Suicide Total, 3.85/4.14; Panic, 7.41/6.39; and Sado-Masochistic Signs, 4.04/5.01. No scale was constructed from the inquiry items that measure antisocial, hypomanic, or psychotic/delusional symptoms, because established scales of known quality were already available for each.

Effort to Administer

Examiner burden was also evaluated for the Critical Inquiry Worksheet. For the sum of all the 84 items that are inquired only if answered in keeping with the key, the following patient means were obtained: females, 22.05; males, 24.80. These means compare to the corresponding sums across the 84 items, using CX norms of 8.65 and 9.24, respectively, attesting to the overall discriminating power of the item aggregate.

After adding to each of the patient means above the six items that are inquired irrespective of answer, on average with an inpatient population, the examiner can expect to inquire about 28 items for females and from 30 to 31 items for males. In practice, however, these average numbers of item inquiries get reduced by patient identified thematic linkages of the sort mentioned earlier. That ordinarily shortens the length of the inquiry. In view of the known average numbers of items to be inquired when using the procedure outlined in Appendix C, the critical inquiry phase of the psychological examination is judged not to cause an excessive burden in terms of either effort or time. These items are useful only if inquired, although the Critical Inquiry Scales may still be scored.

Recommendation

A final word is in order for those who may consider adopting the critical inquiry procedure in Appendix C. Because the 90 specific items used for inquiry were selected based on patient care issues in a specific hospital, they may not cover the most salient issues in the user's clinical setting. The types of patients encountered in the local practice setting should be reviewed carefully when evaluating whether or not these particular 90 *MMPI–2* items will be needed for inquiry. Nothing precludes modifying the item set. There are other well-constructed alternative item sets that may recommend themselves from the perspective of optimizing the match of inquiry items to local patient characteristics and the needs of the clinical service (Butcher et al., 2001; Friedman et al., 2001; Greene, 2000).

PSYCHOSOCIAL DEVELOPMENT SCALES

Origins of Positive Attribute Scales

A small number of currently available *MMPI–2* scales appear to measure positive attributes when scores are average to modestly elevated. Examples include *K*-correction (*K*) (Meehl & Hathaway, 1946), Wiggins (1959) Social Desirability (*Sd*), Edwards (1957) Social Desirability (*So*), Social Responsibility (*Re*) (Gough, McClosky, & Meehl, 1952), Dominance (*Do*) (Gough et al., 1951), Gender-Role Masculine (*GM*) (Peterson & W. G. Dahlstrom, 1992), Ego Strength (*Es*) (Barron, 1953), and Superlative (*S*) (Butcher & Han, 1995). Gender-Role Feminine (*GF*) is not included in this group because of Peterson and W. G. Dahlstrom's (1992) finding that spouses of both genders who scored higher on the scale were more negatively rated by their marital partners. Group averages for all of these scales are higher among normals and lower in patient samples. In contrast to these scales, most successful *MMPI–2* scales were developed to measure psychopathology.

It can be readily verified by inspection that the foregoing more positive trait scales achieve their result generally by scoring groups of items in a direction opposite to the direction that the same items are usually scored when they appear in psychopathology-oriented scales. That is, the identical items are employed in both kinds of scales. The difference, however, is not simply a result of switching the direction of scoring. Rather, positive attribute scales are constructed much as are psychopathology scales. At times, the method is the comparison of groups, one of which is identified as possessing a greater amount of the positive trait. At other times, they are derived by rational scale construction methods. Combinations of these methods may be used as well at different stages of a scale's construction.

Untapped Potentials

Large numbers of the 460 items shared by *MMPI* and *MMPI–2* appear in one or another of the positive attribute scales referenced earlier. Even so, the manifold possible combinations into which these 460 items could be grouped to form positive attribute scales has hardly begun to be explored to the extent that has been done for psychopathology scales. Furthermore, some of the 460 shared items do not appear in any of the positive attribute scales, creating more possibilities for new scale formation. Only two of the scales listed, *GM* and *S*, were developed following publication of *MMPI–2*. Thus, relatively fewer of the 107 items that appear only in *MMPI–2* have as yet been similarly assigned. By actual count, only 16 of the 107 new items appear in either *GM* or *S* scales.

Toward Measuring Psychosocial Development

The aforementioned facts suggested that the 567-item pool well might contain sufficient material to support an effort to develop an interlinked series of scales that could capture aspects of psychosocial development, as this was conceptualized by Erikson (1963). Repeated searches for prior activities directed toward this end uncovered no precedents or leads in the literature. This could have been a warning sign that there may have been prior abandoned attempts that went unreported. It is also possible that the literature's silence simply meant this had not been tried. Jumping far ahead in the story for a brief moment, it ultimately turned out that 140 *MMPI–2* items could be assigned to one or another of six scales of psychosocial development. Of the 140, 38 were found in the 107-item pool that is present only in *MMPI–2*. Thus, if a similar unrecorded effort did occur in the past, then it would have been hindered by the unavailability of these items.

In order to trace the more remote origins of this work, a very brief digression will refer to some former applications of Erikson's work in other quite different contexts. Specifically, our interest in applying the Eriksonian psychosocial theory to other areas commenced years earlier with the design and validation of an interview for measuring parental generativity (Gotts, 1983, 1989), and with the construction of Eriksonian rating scales (Gotts, 1989) used to rescore Cohen and Weil's (1975) child assessment instrument, the Tasks of Emotional Development Test (*TED*). These and other experiences led to an enduring interest in applying Erikson's theory in what others would perhaps regard as unlikely and untested arenas.

This commitment to testing the limits of a theory has resulted now in what may seem to some to be the incongruity of deriving positive psychosocial measures from the premier instrument used to measure psychopathology. Any incongruity on this count is, however, in the mind of the beholder. The theory of psychosocial development presents a dark side. It sees development in terms of the individual engaging a succession of unavoidable challenges, the outcomes of which may be enriching or disastrous. It was not the product of studying a sample of normal individuals. It was, in many senses, a recasting of the human condition, psychopathology and all, into a normative framework. From these focused beginnings, the present work has evolved.

Erikson's Psychosocial Development Formulations

Erikson (1963) adopted a lifespan developmental perspective in his theory of normative psychosocial crises. The series of eight lifespan eras commences in infancy and extends through the process of aging and end of life issues. In his "Eight Ages of Man" presentation, he characterized the periods as follows: trust vs. mistrust; autonomy vs. shame and doubt; initiative vs. guilt; industry vs. inferiority; identity vs. role confusion; intimacy vs. isolation; generativity vs. stagnation; and ego integrity vs. despair.

This brief review clarifies for those who are less familiar with Erikson that the crises are not limited to unipolar outcome possibilities. Ego enriching and ego diminishing outcomes are always in play. One will outweigh the other. Each successive life cycle era presents a new challenge to the individual that requires rebalancing and restabilizing the accomplishments that were gained in prior crises at the same time that the new era's challenges are being actively engaged.

Trust, for example, is not a static asset and mistrust is not an unchanging liability. Instead, the two define a tension between two poles. Continuing this example, the meaning of a favorable outcome for the trust–mistrust crisis is one that tilts more strongly toward trust and, through the later succession of life crises, comes once again into a balance favoring trust more than mistrust.

In the last of these respects, Erikson's theory posits an empirical quality of normative crises that is found also in the *MMPI–2* positive attribute scales cited earlier. In both the crises and the positive attribute scales, the human condition does not typically produce such massive reserves of coping strength that they expel from the psyche all of the dark possibilities. Thus, persons who describe themselves as having infinite amounts of positive attributes appear either to be in denial or otherwise out of touch with reality. Based on the same parallelism, it could be anticipated that scales constructed for the psychosocial crises would have positive implications if scores were average to moderately elevated but that highly elevated scores would imply unrealistic self-appraisal.

Searching for Psychosocial Indicator Items

The present scale construction challenge was to discover whether *MMPI–2* might contain items to represent aspects of each of the eight crises and, further, whether they were present in sufficient numbers to support formation of reliable scales. The search for psychosocial indicators required repeated hunting forays through the 567 items of *MMPI–2* for those that might capture some criterial aspect of one or another of the eight Eriksonian developmental crises. Lists of item numbers of possible inclusions were compiled for each of the eight crises. A benchmark for item inclusion was a scale measuring a specific crisis would need to include those items whose content centers on the defining features of the normative developmental challenge. That is, an item should have an explicitly identifiable linkage to the processes and outcomes of the specific crisis scale to which it is assigned. When all possibilities seemed to have been written down in the preceding manner, cross comparisons were made among the eight lists to eliminate item overlaps.

Following a similar guideline to that used for inclusion, the exclusion rule was that an item would be retained in that single list for which it provided a best fit to the defining criteria of a particular normative developmental crisis. Setting this restriction would later support study of the relations among the measures of the crises without the risk of having findings that were simply artifacts of shared items. Up to this point, all selections were based on clinical judgment.

Avoiding Psychopathology Intrusions

Erikson identified relations between particular serious forms of psychopathology and the failure of persons to resolve adequately the challenges of the various developmental crises. This suggested that the scales should not include items that operationally preestablish or predetermine the relations in question between serious pathology and developmental failures. This called for exclusion of items that made obvious reference to the primary pathology itself. If items expressing major pathology figured heavily in a scale's composition, then that fact would in effect create an artificial relation via scale construction. Any relation later found when using one of the scales might be no more than an artifact of a kind of empirical circular thinking.

After all eight lists of items has been compiled and cross-checked, each of six potential scales was scored in the *MMPI–2* database. This was possible after sufficient items were identified for each of the first six crises to undertake this next step. Although some items were found that related to the seventh and eighth of the normative crises, there were too few of them to use further in scale construction.

Reliabilities of Tentative Scales and Later Scale Refinements

Internal consistencies were calculated for each of the tentative scales. Alpha coefficients were acceptable for five of the scales and lower than desired for the scale representing identity vs. role confusion. The six scored item sets were viewed now as the first drafts of potential scales and were merged with a file of all 567 raw item responses.

The next step was undertaken for the purpose of refining and enhancing earlier selections that relied on intuitive judgment only. In this step, correlations were computed between each tentative scale and all raw responses for each record. Correlations were used in two ways, as discussed later.

First, tentative item placements were evaluated by considering whether an item already assigned to a scale correlated more highly with it than it did with any of the five remaining scales. Items not meeting this criterion would be reassigned to the scale with which they correlated most strongly—but only provided that a review of item characteristics sufficiently corresponded to essential features of the crisis that the other scale was designed to measure.

Second, additional items were found that previously were overlooked and that appeared to belong with one of the scales. An item was added to one of the tentative scales, but again only if it properly fit the normative crisis. Many items that could have been added at this stage were not because they would have served only to confound the relation between a psychosocial development scale and a severe form of psychopathology. In this connection, see the earlier discussion on why this type of confounding was to be avoided.

The refined item sets were scored and alpha coefficients again computed. All scales had improved, with the problematic identity vs. role confusion scale reaching a more acceptable and less modest level. Correlations between refined scales and raw item responses were obtained one additional time, leading now to a few minor adjustments.

A final version of each scale was scored in *MMPI–2*. A shorter version of each scale was also scored in the larger database using the items that appear in *MMPI*. Internal consistencies were now computed again in both the *MMPI–2* and *MMPI* databases. The coefficients were compared back and forth between the two databases and males and females as discussed earlier in another context. Alpha coefficients, normative means, and standard deviations for six psychosocial scales that resulted from the preceding processes appear in Appendix B. Scale compositions are presented in Appendix A.

Assessment of Resulting Scales

The resulting scales were judged to be reasonable approximations to the constructs provided by their theoretical roots and to be sufficiently reliable to be subjected to validity checks. It is true, however, that the item pool did not lend itself to extensive sampling of some facets of the underlying constructs. For this reason, the resulting scales were assigned names that resemble Erikson's labels for the crises but that differ enough from them not to be construed literally as either capturing or exhausting the full scope of original meanings. The resulting names assigned, in developmental sequence, for the six bipolar scales are:

Feels Cared for/Loved vs. Neglected/Disliked (*Cared for vs. Neglected*)

Autonomous/Self-Possessed vs. Self-Doubting/Shamed (*Autonomous vs. Doubting*)

Initiating/Pursuing vs. Regretful/Guilt-Prone (*Initiating vs. Guilt-Prone*)

Industrious/Capable vs. Inadequate/Inferior (*Industrious vs. Inadequate*)

Life-Goal Oriented/Ego Identity Secure vs. Directionless/Confused (*Ego Identified vs. Confused*)

Socially-Committed/Involved vs. Disengaged/Lonely (*Involved vs. Disengaged*)

Validating the Psychosocial Scales

A few of the validation checks made for these scales will be reported in some detail, but many that led to congruent findings are summarized only briefly. The validation checks followed three strategies. One was to study how much their items overlap the Superlative (*S*) scale and its five subscales (Butcher & Han, 1995), the newest and most prominent of positive attribute scales and, further, to check correlations among them. The second was to check the relation of each Psychosocial scale with each of the *MMPI–2* Content Scales (Butcher et al., 2001) relative to the issue of the linkages between developmental failure and more severe forms of psychopathology. For these first two kinds of studies, scales were adjusted for item overlaps that could possibly interfere with assessing the degree of relation that was present independently of them.

A third strategy was to send the item lists to a small number of practicing psychologist colleagues who use *MMPI–2*, requesting that they help identify what were simply referred to as six reliable *factors*, each of which was known to point to "a positive form of self-concept or self-presentation" for which the high end meant more of the positive quality and the low end meant the opposite. Item numbers appeared as six lists on a single page in columns labeled *A* through *F*. The order of their placement from left to right was the exact reverse of their Eriksonian task sequence. That is, the first (*A*) list was the items representing Socially Committed/Involved vs. Disengaged/Lonely. The purpose of this third strategy was to evaluate how obvious versus subtle the scales might prove to be when they were judged by more psychologically sophisticated respondents.

Item Correspondences with Superlative Scale

Of the 50 items in the Superlative scale (Butcher & Han, 1995), 16 (32.0% of its total) also appear among the 140 items of *MMPI–2* that were assigned to Psychosocial Development Scales (11.4% of the total). Eight of the 16 overlaps are found in subscale *S1*, Beliefs in Human Goodness; four in *S2*, Serenity; none in *S3*, Contentment with Life; one in *S4*, Patience and Denial of Irritability and Anger; and two in *S5*, Denial of Moral Flaws. One item from *S* (184) that does not appear in any subscale is the final of the 16 overlaps.

Cared for vs. Neglected shares its four overlaps (20% of its total) with *S1* only. Autonomy vs. Doubting does not overlap with any *S* items. Initiating vs. Guilt-Prone has the four remaining overlaps found in *S1* plus both of those from *S5* and one each from *S2* and *S4*, making its eight-item overlap (27.6% of its total) the largest and most diversified for any of the psychosocial scales. Industrious vs. Inadequate shares its single overlap with S2. Ego Identified vs. Confused contains the one unassigned item, 184, with its only other overlap being with *S2*. Involved vs. Disengaged has its single overlap with *S2*.

It is apparent from a review of the patterns of overlap that *S1* and *S2* of the *S* subscales and the Psychosocial scales Cared for vs. Neglected and Initiating vs. Guilt-Prone together account for most of the overlaps in either direction. In the case of *S2*, its four overlaps are dispersed across four different Psychosocial scales, whereas *S1* divides its overlapping items evenly between the Psychosocial scales that account for the most overlaps from the other side. Thus, there seems to be no overall correspondence between *S*'s subscales and the six Psychosocial scales.

Shared Meanings Between Superlative and Psychosocial Scales

What can be stated with some confidence is that the Psychosocial scales as a group share some of the qualities embodied in the Serenity and Beliefs in Human Goodness subscales of *S*. Describing the overlapping relations from the other direction suggests that the Superlative scale captures a recognizable bit of the meanings inherent in the Eriksonian constructs of *trust* and *initiative*. This is next examined from a correlational perspective instead of from item overlap.

Correlations were computed among the Psychosocial scales and *S* with its subscales, after these were adjusted to remove the effects of item overlaps. Note that for all of the following relations, degrees of freedom is 154 and $p < .001$. *S*'s strongest relation was with Initiating vs. Guilt-Prone ($r = .69$). *S1* related most strongly to Cared for vs. Neglected ($r = .56$). *S2* related almost equally to Industrious vs. Inadequate ($r = .61$) and Autonomous vs. Doubting ($r = .59$). *S3* related at somewhat similar levels to all six psychosocial scales (from $r = .45-.53$). *S4*, like other scales in the group, had its strongest relation with Initiating vs. Guilt-Prone ($r = .57$). *S5* is an exception to all of the preceding comparisons, with its relations to all Psychosocial scales ranging only from a correlation of .30 down to .09 and probability levels falling correspondingly.

Relationships with New Content Scales

A second strategy was to examine relations among *MMPI–2* Content and Psychosocial Scales as evidence of the latter group's capacity to reveal linkages between severe forms of psychopathology and problems arising during the various normative developmental crises. All of the following findings remained significant ($p <$ .001) after adjustment for item overlaps. Cared for vs. Neglected was associated negatively with all *MMPI-2* Content Scales (typical r's greater than $-.50$ on up to $-.66$), with lower than the foregoing but still significant associations found for *SOD, FRS,* and *HEA.* Autonomous vs. Doubting had markedly strong associations with *ANX, DEP, WRK,* and *TRT,* all showing correlations from $-.68$ to $-.73$. Initiating vs. Guilt-Prone's strongest showings were with *TPA, ANG,* and *OBS* (r $= -.64--.70$). Industrious vs. Inadequate's strongest correlation was with *ANX* (around $-.70$). Ego Identified vs. Confused had particularly prominent linkages to *DEP, TRT,* and *ANX* ($r = -.59--.66$). Involved vs. Disengaged correlated most clearly with *DEP, TRT,* and *ANX* ($r = -.60--.73$).

Interestingly, *BIZ,* which is notable by its absence from the preceding high-lighted relations, had its strongest correlation ($r = -.64$) with Cared for vs. Neglected. Within the Eriksonian framework, it would be predicted that this most severe form of psychopathology, which includes expressions of ego fragmentation and decompensation, is likely associated with problems that originate very early in development. Another Content scale that is not mentioned, *CYN,* relates most strongly to Cared for vs. Neglected and Initiating vs. Guilt-Prone ($r = -.58--.59$). *ASP* links up most strongly with Initiating vs. Guilt-Prone and secondarily with Cared for vs. Neglected ($r = -.54--.64$). *LSE* comes in for its strongest readings with Autonomous vs. Doubting and Involved vs. Disengaged ($r = -.55--.63$). *FRS* and *HEA* have generally lower associations than the other new Content scales with all of the Psychosocial scales, their highest being with Autonomous vs. Doubting ($r = -.49--.54$).

Although the foregoing findings appear to invite the formulation of a variety of hypotheses regarding the etiology of disorders for which the new Content scales offer symptomatic expression, it is premature to go much beyond acknowledging here that those possibilities exist. This word of caution is needed, because the findings derive from one inpatient population only. Comparative studies with more varied samples will be needed before testing predictions based on Erikson's clinical observations about the origins of specific psychopathologies.

Obviousness-Subtlety of the Scales

The third strategy for examining the Psychosocial scales sought to clarify the extent to which their content might be obvious vs. subtle. It offers a strong test of whether the specific thrust or focus of each scale would likely be detected by a psychologically sophisticated person. Based on the reviews of the six item lists by a small number of psychologists, the answer would appear to be that, without having prior knowledge or access to the construction rationale, it is unlikely that more than a few sophisticated respondents would grasp fully the sense in which the items and scales relate to one another as a series.

Considered from another perspective, perhaps the fact that generally the psychologist reviewers failed to fathom the extent of what the scales might be sampling tells less than it would seem on the surface of things. It is not necessary, for example, to recognize specifically what the Superlative (*S*) scale measures in order to produce a score that turns out to be unrealistically high from the perspective of what most people are like. Rather, based on *S*'s mean item probability of over .50, a less insightful form of responding achieves the same end if the respondent simply picks obviously positive attributes. This seems even truer for the Psychosocial scales, with a mean item probability around .75.

It is possible using the hospital databases to consider whether this kind of event occurred in patient responses to the Psychosocial scales, as compared with other positive attribute scales. To do this, percentages were calculated of patients receiving scores equal to or greater than T65 for the Psychosocial scales and the positive attribute scales listed earlier. Instead of removing from the database cases that would be purged by applying the variable *AdjAll* (see chap. 6), they were retained in this analysis in order to keep available any cases with excessively high scores on selected validity scales.

With the cutoff established for scores equal to or exceeding T65 in the following comparisons, those above that level might suggest possible inflation of the respondents' positive attributes. Among adult males and females, none (0.0%) received scores that reached or exceeded T65 on four of the Psychosocial scales. Thereby, none seemed to exaggerate being Cared for, Autonomous, Industrious, or Involved. No male, but some female, patients (0.5%) exceeded this for Ego Identified; no patients did with *AdjAll* applied. Both males (1.2%) and females (1.7%) went above the limit for Initiating. Overall, the patient sample did not exhibit tendencies to describe themselves in overly positive ways as measured by these scales. Production of less favorable self-reports is to be expected on average from the kinds of patients whose scores are in the hospital database.

Comparative results for most of the other positive attribute scales revealed a similar trend: *So* (females, 0.5%; males, 0.9%), *Do* (females, 0.7%; males, 0.0%), *GM* (females, 1.5%; males, 0.3%), *S* (females, 0.0%; males, 2.2%), and *Es* (females, 2.4%; males, 2.6%). Excessively high scores were uncommon in this hospitalized population. Nevertheless, results for other scales of this group attest to the reality that overstating positive attributes does occur among these psychiatric inpatients. Patients more often equaled or exceeded T65 for the remaining scales of this group: *Re* (females, 5.6%; males, 1.1%), *K* (females, 5.7%; males, 4.6%), and *Sd* (females, 20.1%; males, 17.7%). The large divergences among them were a curiosity.

It is reassuring for the purpose of interpreting high scores of several of the foregoing scales to realize how unlikely patients were to present themselves as possessing positive attributes in quantities that either they or most other people are not likely to exhibit. For other positive scales, it is more than a little puzzling and unnerving to see the swollen percentages of patients whose scores exceeded the T65 cutoff.

Further calculations were made for two additional scales that were not listed earlier but are also known to be subject to positive inflation. These also show that exaggeration of positive qualities occurs among these kinds of patients. The scales with respective percentages for females and males follow: Other Deception (*ODecp*) (females, 19.1%; males, 14.7%) (Nichols & Greene, 1991) and Over-controlled Hostility (*O-H*) (females, 8.1%; males, 8.1%) (Megargee et al., 1967). Combining them with those above increases to 16 the group of positive attribute scales that produce considerably varying percentages of patients who fall above T64. These differences are analyzed further later.

Analyzing Differential Rates

The preceding observations regarding obvious versus subtle qualities of scales are strengthened by recasting them in another guise. Christian, Burkhart, and Gynther (1978) developed ratings for each of the 566 *MMPI* items. They are reproduced in the itemmetric appendix for *MMPI–2* (Butcher et al., 2001) for the items retained in the test's revised edition. In preparation for analyses, these ratings were summed for all 16 scales listed in the preceding section. Most items in the 16 scales had ratings available. A small number were missing ratings for some items. A correction accommodated this difference: Sums were converted next by dividing each by the number of item ratings that were available.

The Original Rating Study. The original ratings were bidirectional, with judgments being made using a 5-point rating scale that varied from Very obvious at the one end to Very subtle at the other. The scale's midpoint was defined as being neither obvious nor subtle. Note, hence, that scale means that were calculated in the present study were actually of ratings for the bipolar dimension: obviousness versus subtlety. For simplicity, the results may be referred to here as *mean obviousness ratings*.

What They Measured. The ratings produced by Christian et al. (1978) covered one important aspect of obviousness by having each item judged from the perspective of whether it indicated a psychological problem. This was done by three groups of judges who were identified by the authors as naïve relative to psychopathology. Judges completed ratings in a design that resulted in separate composite ratings for each item when answer keyed True and when answer keyed False. Mean obviousness ratings accordingly were prepared for both True and False answers to be used in the present study.

Gender Neutrality of the Ratings.   The original obviousness ratings
were found to be highly similar for both female and male judges. Christian et al.
(1978) consequently decided to combine and publish the ratings made by the
composite of all judges, regardless of gender. If their ratings were to be used to
study the positive attribute scales further, then these latter variables would need to
be merged across gender as well. Thus, with reference to findings reported earlier,
adjustments were made that produced for each of the scales: (a) mean gender-
neutralized item proportions (*MProp*) for normals and (b) mean gender-
neutralized percentages of patients with scores that exceeded T64 (*%>T64*).

Obviousness Linked to Desirability.   Christian and his associates
found and discussed a correlation of −.78 between their obviousness ratings for
items keyed True and a published set of item desirability ratings. Desirability ratings were not available for study relative to items keyed False. The general direction of their interpretation tended to assign particular importance to a linkage
between obvious psychopathology and low social desirability ratings. That is,
there was the implication in their discussion that respondents may behave as they
do as a function of their tendency toward making socially desirable self-
attributions. This conception emphasized the tendency to approach a positive.

New Obviousness Variables Created.   In order to study this implication as well as alternative ones, the newly combined ratings were reformatted in a
number of ways and stored as variables alongside the item proportions (*MProp*)
of normals and percentages greater than T64 (*%>T64*) among patients. The newly
formed variables were percentage of items in a scale keyed False (*%KeyF*), the
mean rating for items per the scale's key (*M%Key*), the mean rating for items directly opposite the key (*M%Opp*), percentages of items obvious and subtle per
key (*Key%Obv* and *Key%Sutl*), percentages of items obvious and subtle opposite
to key (*Opp%Obv* and *Opp%Sutl*), percentage of items for which the keyed direction proved to be more subtle than did the opposite direction (*Key<Opp*), and percentage of items for which the direction opposite the key was more subtle
(*Opp<Key*). In a world of simplistic reality, only obvious and subtle items exist.
The world of item responding is not ordered by this dichotomy, as demonstrated
by the widely ranging item ratings (Christian et al., 1978).

Redefining Differences.   Note that Christian et al. (1978) identified all
departures from the rating scale midpoint as being either obvious or subtle. A different procedure was followed in forming the preceding indexes: *Key%Obv*,
Key%Sutl, *Opp%Obv*, and *Opp%Sutl*. A rating was only counted as obvious if it
fell at or beyond a point halfway between Obvious and Neither. In terms of their
5-point scale, only ratings greater than 3.49 were considered obvious. Similarly, a
rating was identified as subtle only when it was less than 2.51. The variables

Key<Opp and *Opp<Key* were counted when the difference between them exceeded 0.99 on Christian's rating scale.

New Empirical Relationships.

With the 16 scales assigned values for each the 12 variables, correlations were computed. Relations of the other variables to the percentages of patients with standard scores exceeding T64 (*%>T64*) was of particular interest. With 14 degrees of freedom, the following correlations are all highly significant (*p* < .01) between *%>T64* and other variables: mean item proportion (*MProp*) answered per key by normals (–.81), *M%Opp* (–.70), *Opp%Stl* (.83), and *%KeyF* (–.63). A linear regression equation was solved with *%>T64* as the dependent variable and the other four variables as predictors. The *%KeyF* was noncontributory to the solution and was removed. The three remaining variables all received significant betas in the solution: *MProp* (*p* < .001), *Opp%Stl* (*p* < .001), and *M%Opp* (*p* = .002). The multiple correlation for the equation (*R* = .95) was very highly significant (*F* = 39.995, *df* = 3, 12, *p* < .0000).

The Christian et al. (1978) finding of a correlation of –.78 between ratings of obviousness and desirability probably resulted from the same processes that produce the relation between *%>T64* and *MProp* (–.81). That is to say, desirability is a potential candidate for both findings. Other processes appear to be at work as well and are seen in the individual *%>T64*'s correlations with *M%Opp* and *Opp%Stl*. This latter possibility is illustrated further by the low correlation between *MProp* and *M%Key* (*r* = –.25, *p* = n.s.) as compared with the strong correlation between *MProp* and *M%Opp* (*r* = .74, *p* < .01).

A Syncretism of Item Valences.

The foregoing findings suggest perhaps that a second process affects the outcome not by inclining responses toward the socially desirable but instead away from socially undesirable self-attributions. The sharing of variance that is seen in the regression equation between these vying forces suggests a new formulation: There is a syncretism at work between approach and avoidance valences that are associated with each particular item. From this it follows that there is a syncretistic averaging of these opposing valences whenever groups of items are combined to form scales.

How Naïve Respondents Receive Inflated Scores.

Returning now to the beginning of this exploration, it appears that responses to the items of positive attribute scales are influenced by the conjoint operation of aspects of obviousness–subtlety and desirability–undesirability. Moreover, within and across scales, these forces operate in multiple combinations that as yet have not been successfully charted. The many ways that these work together are equally unknown to both naïve and sophisticated persons. As was stated earlier, an unsophisticated person need not be aware of what a scale is measuring in order to produce a score that seemingly exaggerates pathology or asserts its absence. Strong item cues of obviousness or desirability prove to be unnecessary. Modest cues of item valences in one direction in combination with weak cues of valences in another direction may be enough to result in positive attribute scale scores that appear inflated.

The Role of Subjective Characteristics. Obviously, there is more at work than item characteristics. The responder's contribution must be factored in. It is a source of both true and error variance in the result. Thus, items and scales differ in another respect. They differ in the valences that they present relative to respondents' subjective and highly personal inclinations to approach versus avoid expressing answers that inhere in an item's possibilities. Herein resides an item's potential to reveal something personal. Moreover, approaching positive self-attributions versus avoiding negative ones does not likely occur for the same subjective reasons, and it does not require equivalent valences across respondents. Prior extensive attempts have been made to understand how item probabilities (A. L. Edwards, 1957) and obviousness (Christian et al., 1978) affect item responses. More study is needed of the role of individual approach and avoidance tendencies as influences that interact with item characteristics.

DIFFERENTIATING COMPONENTS OF IMPULSIVITY

A Need to Assess Impulsivity

In 1984, at which time the senior author was affiliated with another hospital, the need arose to assess and better understand patient impulse control lapses that were associated with several high profile incidents of acting out. Possible *MMPI* scales were sought in W. G. Dahlstrom and Welsh (1960) in a chapter on the assessment of emotional control. There a scale for assessing Impulsivity (*Im*) was described briefly as a subset of items from a scale appearing in the California Psychological Inventory (Gough, 1957). The list of 21 items found in *MMPI* was reviewed and found to contain at least 7 items that appeared promising, along with others that would not contribute to the objective for which the scale was needed.

Referring now to their *MMPI–2* item numbers, the following items seemed to have potential: True: 37, 85, 145, 150, 389; False: 83, 100. Other items in the *Im* scale did not appear to lend themselves to the immediate objective. Examples are True: 31, 32, 53, 86, 225, 316, and 456, and an item lost in the *MMPI* revision, 545. Additional extensive searching at the time failed to turn up other scales for consideration.

As a next step, all items in *MMPI* were reviewed three times, and on each pass the numbers of items that might be suitable were written down. After this, other members of that hospital's psychology staff were asked to review the item list, in terms of their experience with the hospital population and the recent patient acting out problems, and to decide if any of those items should be considered for inclusion in an impulsivity scale to be scored using the *MMPI* record.

Impulsivity Components

When a final pool of 52 items had been selected, additional content analysis was carried out in order to determine if there might be clusters of items that could form subscales. The analysis suggested that items were worded in ways that introduced the possibility for patients to report on three different aspects of or tendencies toward impulsivity. These were identified as *behavioral, ideational/attitudinal*, and *affective*.

Items assigned to the behavioral group were those containing declarations of action potentials or past actions that occurred hastily or were inappropriately controlled ($n = 19$). Items fell into the ideational cluster if they expressed ideas, attitudes, and perspectives that implied limited reflection or forethought ($n = 20$). The affective set consisted of those items presenting expressions of sudden, episodic emotional arousal that tended to catch the respondent off guard and to test or overwhelm the person's self-control ($n = 13$). All 52 items were assigned exclusively to one or another of the subscales for further study.

It could be inferred from the item wordings that the three item types would permit a patient completing the *MMPI* to express experiences of impulsive tendency that had appeared in any of three differing styles or manifestations. Single styles or combinations of these could be expressed. The three styles or manifestations, respectively, suggested the following forms of impulsivity: acting out tendencies, egocentric and need-based thinking, and emotional dyscontrol. Hand scoring templates were made for the resulting three subscales.

Initial Study

The background work was completed by mid-1985. The *MMPI* protocols of 50 female and 50 male discharged inpatients who had attended a substance abuse treatment program were randomly selected now from the departmental collection by a psychometrist who maintained these records. These were scored, and the three resulting subscales plus a total impulsivity score across all 52 items were checked for internal consistency using the coefficient alpha. The alphas were within acceptable limits to support further study of the four scales. All items correlated positively with their respective scales and with the impulsivity total. Items having relatively lower correlations with the scores for their respective item sets were retained rather than removed at this time in view of the limited variety of patient characteristics represented in the sample.

Normative itemmetric data based on the original Minnesota sample were listed for 50 of the 52 items (W. G. Dahlstrom & Welsh, 1960). Using methods described earlier in the chapter, mean response probabilities for the two unlisted items were estimated by making proportional comparisons of probabilities between two data sets: (a) the patient sample's responses to the 50 listed items and the two without norms and (b) Minnesota norms for the 50 items. Estimated item probabilities/proportions for the two unlisted items were combined with the Minnesota norms for the 50 items, resulting in adjusted normative means for each of the four scales.

Because the procedures for estimating unknown standard deviations had not been developed by 1985, sample standard deviations were substituted in combination with the normative means in formulas used to compute estimated linear T-scores for each of the 100 patients for the four scales. The means for these approximated patient T-scores were on the order of two standard deviations higher than the means (i.e., around T70) calculated from the Minnesota norms.

In an attempt to evaluate the validity of the Impulsivity scales, possible indications of patient impulsivity that might be found in patient hospital records were listed and summarized on a one-page worksheet. Hospital records were then reviewed for the 100 patient sample. Findings from the review were recorded on a separate worksheet for each patient as a means of documenting possibly relevant behavior or administrative actions taken during the hospital stay.

This initial review turned out to be of limited worth for checking validity. This was at least in part due to the lack of standardized and systematic documentation of the events of interest. This is not atypical of clinical record keeping in this type of setting. The single outcome that could be inferred from the study was that patients who were more impulsive, as suggested by higher scores on these scales, were likely to relapse and be readmitted to a treatment program after a shorter time interval than was true for those who scored lower. This single finding was made possible by a specific administrative practice of courts in the hospital's catchment area: All persons arrested a third time for a substance related offense, including public intoxication, were sent as mandatory admissions to a treatment program without regard to judicial discretion. These events thus created the sole datum of relevance to the initial validity study of the scales.

Later Validation Work

After the Impulsivity scales were placed in service at the present hospital in 1986, validity studies resumed. Particular interest centered on the relation of these scales to Overcontrolled Hostility ($O\text{-}H$) (Megargee et al., 1967), Pd, Re, and, after the appearance of $MMPI\text{--}2$, to the new Content scales ASP, TPA, ANG, and CYN. Minor adjustments were made to the Impulsivity scales following the $MMPI$ revision, through which 51 of the 52 items survived. One item lost from Behavioral Impulsivity ($Imp\text{-}B$) was replaced by a new $MMPI\text{--}2$ item. New item analyses with the more diverse sample in the hospital database led to dropping one item and reassigning another. The revised scale compositions and resulting reliabilities are those reported in the appendices.

After adjustments were made to remove all item overlaps, $O\text{-}H$ regularly varied inversely with all four of the Impulsivity scales (females, $r = -38\text{--}.50$; males, $r = -.43\text{--}.54$). The corresponding relations were significantly higher with the revised *O-H* (see Appendix A) that is used in the present study (females, $r =$ $-.61--.76$; males, $r = -.62--.78$). Each subscale was related at about the same level with *O-H* (i.e., mostly r's in the mid- to lower .60's) with a strong combinatory effect for the three being apparent in the much higher level of Impulsivity Total (*Imp-T*) (females, $r = -.76$; males, $r = -.78$).

Clinical experience added to the impression of the usefulness of the Impulsivity scales. In patients identified with intermittent explosive disorder, *O-H* would usually be high, indicating overly rigid control of expression that would periodically break down and fail. These cases also always had extremely low scores on the impulsivity scales, which gave the same signal of exaggerated controls. At other times, *O-H* failed to provide a clear indication, whereas the Impulsivity scales still functioned as predictors of impulse breakthrough.

Other important validity evidence came from examining the relation of impulsivity to the other scales noted earlier. Female results appear in parentheses followed by those for males. *Pd* and the Impulsivity scales were correlated positively at very highly significant levels ($r = .47–.66$; $r = .58–.73$). *Pd*'s strongest subscale relation for both genders was with Affective Impulsivity (*Imp-A*) (.60/.64), whereas again all three subscales contributed additively to the relation with *Imp-T* (.66/.73). Impulsivity and *Re* were negatively related also at very highly significant levels ($-.44--.70$; $-.45--.66$), with Ideational Impulsivity (*Imp-I*) yielding the strongest subscale results ($-.66$; $-.61$).

For all comparisons with the four listed Content scales, *Imp-I* registered a larger degree of relation than did *Imp-B* or *Imp-A* The Content scales' relations with *Imp-I* were: *ANG* (.57/.63), *TPA* (.64/.65), *ASP* (.64/.64), and *CYN* (.70/.64). These are impressively high for *ASP* and *CYN* in view of the actual results being attenuated by removals from *Imp-I* when considering that four of its overlaps with *CYN* and five with *ASP* were sidelined before correlations were computed. The corresponding relations for the overlapping scales ranged higher: *CYN* (.81/.76) and *ASP* (.78/.78). Removal of overlaps in fact so attenuated the relation between *Imp-A* and *ANG* that it dropped from (.77/.76) to (.55/.55), thereby losing its spot as having the strongest relation to *ANG* to the *Imp-I* subscale, which had no overlaps with *ANG*. This brief overview of findings for the Impulsivity scales validates their place within the content cluster interpretive approach, in which they will later be shown to play prominently.

RESPONSE CONSISTENCY MEASURES

Comparing *F* and F_B

Work on new measures of response consistency began with observations regarding a series of incomplete parallelisms of the *F* and F_B scales as indicators, respectively, of the test-taker's response attentiveness or attitude between the two halves of *MMPI–2*. Notice was taken of an overlapping zone in the sequence of item presentation shared by those scales. That is, examining the item sequence 281–361, 14 of *F*'s 60 items (23.3%) appeared, as did 12 of F_B's 40 items (30.0%).

A Possible Inferential Problem

This does not present a problem for the use of *F* to decide how valid responses to the clinical scales may be. Neither does it detract from F_B's role in drawing inferences about possible exaggeration in responding to the new content and other supplementary scales. Nor does it interfere with the use of *Fp*, *VRIN*, and *TRIN* conjointly with the infrequency scales. It does, however, raise a cautionary note regarding the suggestion that comparison of *F* and F_B provides information about how well the respondent's attention and cooperation have held up over the course of taking the test (Butcher et al., 2001).

Following the initial observations about a zone of item sequence overlap, additional examinations were carried out. A second comparison simply tabulated the percentages of items keyed True/False. It turns out that 68.33% of *F*'s items are keyed with True as the infrequent response, whereas 92.5% of F_B's items are keyed True. A tendency for inpatients to give a larger percentage of True responses will accordingly elevate the latter scale to a greater extent than the former.

The foregoing prediction is illustrated by comparing itemmetric CX norms for True responses across all 567 test items to those in the present database. Mean True for CX norm females is 220.12, and for the database adult females it is 256.98. The mean CX norm value of True for males is 211.71, and for database adult males it is 271.11. Before removing from the adult samples those patients who obtained excessively high scores on the two preceding infrequency scales, their mean standard scores were compared for *F* and F_B. These means for females were T68.44 for *F* and T76.52 for F_B. Males for the respective scales had mean scores of T67.07 and T71.75.

These differences in standard score level are associated with individual tendencies to answer True, as shown by correlations between counts of the number of True answers in each record and scores for *F* and F_B, with coefficients shown in that order: adult females .63 and .69; adult males .66 and .72. This lends supports to the assertion that F_B's larger percentage of items keyed True is associated with greater numbers of True responses.

Further *F*–F_B Differences

Another focus of comparison for *F* and F_B was to learn what the typical percentages of response of normals are relative to each scale's answer key. The published data for *MMPI–2* offer two paths to an identical answer to this question. The solution by a longer method sums per answer key the CX norms for the items of each scale and then divides by the number of items. This solution, except for the possible introduction of rounding errors, produces the result that is obtained if the normative mean for the scale is divided by the number of items in it. Normal females responded according to the key for the items of F an average of 6.10% of the time, whereas for F_B their average was 4.85%. For the norming group of males, the two corresponding percentages were 7.55 and 4.65. From these figures, it becomes immediately apparent that the average F_B keyed response is a less likely occurrence.

This kind of finding simply means that the F_B items are lower incidence or less commonly occurring events than those in the F scale. An outcome of the type seen for F_B results from inherent properties of the item pool itself at the level of item wording and content. That is to say, the items of F_B necessarily differ from those of F by way of including wording and content that generate greater constraints against endorsing the keyed answer. See the discussion earlier in this chapter of item characteristics. The constraints may appear in individual F and F_B item wordings as differences in content characteristics, such as the intensity, severity, or frequency of the behavior; whether the statement refers to a past or present or contemplated or perennial frame of reference; the acceptability or desirability of the behavior; and so on. In short, like most items, these inherently display polarity, and the items of F_B are more highly polarized on average than those of F. The two item pools thus differ in innumerable and unlisted ways.

A Different Approach to Response Consistency

The foregoing discussion points up the lines of evidence that led to rethinking how measurement methods might be used to create a stronger form of comparison between items appearing in the first and second halves of *MMPI-2*. The new approach does not compete with the use of F or F_B as measures of infrequent responding. Those scales stand on their proven merit. The new approach was initiated instead to prepare a product that would assess with clarity and a fully balanced parallelism whether a patient's manner of responding differs between the first and second halves of the test.

Criteria for Item Pairs

The process commenced with setting an arbitrary line of demarcation between items numbered 283 and 284 as marking off the halves of the test. Items were to be drawn in matching pairs that appeared, respectively, in the two halves. The *MMPI-2* Content Scales would be the sources of all items. Criteria were set for each item pair as follows: the pair must come from the same Content scale, both be keyed as True or as False (i.e., keyed the same), be located each in a different half of the test, and generate as nearly as could be matched identical percentages of agreement or endorsement. Gender differences in percentages of agreement with the key would be allowed if they were relatively small and so long as the item percentages balanced or matched between items of a pair within each gender. Finally, if an item appeared in more than one Content scale, it could be included only one time in the new measure.

Item Pairs Selected

Using these criteria and several iterations of sifting possible items, 43 pairs were selected. They could come from any of the Content scales that would yield item pairs meeting all seven specifications. Items were keyed to be scored in a positive direction. That is, items were scored in the direction that reflected more favorably or desirably on the respondent. This is the direction that items were answered most often by normals in the CX samples. The pairs were then separated into two item sets, with one appearing in each half of the test.

Overall, CX norms were computed for each item set. Item means were found to be almost identical for both genders between the two sets that represent the two test halves. Estimated CX standard deviations also were nearly identical for the two halves within genders, and those for males were larger than for females (Appendix B). Internal consistency coefficients for the two sets were high. Scales found in the two halves were named Response Consistency 1st Half (*RCon1*) and Response Consistency 2nd Half (*RCon2*). Each of the scales had a high alpha coefficient.

Patient Data for Consistency

These scales were evaluated for mean response tendencies in the hospital *MMPI–2* database. Compared to the CX norms, females in the hospital sample produced less self-favorable raw score means for *RCon1* of 25.00 and for *RCon2* of 27.10. A parallel comparison for male patients with CX male norms revealed less self-favorable means also: *RCon1* 26.68, *RCon2* 27.53. Three of the four raw score means were more than one standard deviation lower than CX norms, with one (*RCon2* for males) being 0.94 standard deviation lower.

The large *MMPI* database contained 27 of the 43 items found in each half of *MMPI–2*. Exact CX itemmetric values were summed for the 27 items available in and the 16 items absent from each of *RCon1* and *RCon2* in *MMPI*. These sums were worked through a sequence of formulas separately for each gender and scale resulting in a series of four gender-by-scale proportional adjustment factors. Raw scores for sums of the 27 available items were then multiplied by the factors, resulting in 43-item version facsimile scores. Means calculated from these scores approximate within a small error of estimate the patient means for the longer versions of the two scales. Thus, they offer a more stable estimate of mean differences between patients and normals than do means of the small *MMPI–2* sample.

Female patient adjusted means estimated from *MMPI* for *RCon1* and *RCon2* are 27.53 each. The corresponding means for male patients were *27.43* and *28.13*. Their resemblance to the *MMPI–2* values can be inspected by referring to norms in Appendix B. Once again, the patient means tend to hover around one standard deviation, more or less, below those of the normals.

After transformation to standard scores, *RCon1* and *RCon2* from a patient sample can be compared to one another. Standard score differences as great as one standard deviation (i.e., a *T*-score difference of 10 points) are cause for concern that a patient's test-taking behavior reliably differs between the two halves of the test. Differences of two standard deviations (20 *T*-score points) between *RCon1* and *RCon2* were extremely rare. Although score differences of T10 occurred often enough to challenge records acceptable after applying *VRIN* and *TRIN*, those differing by 15 *T*-score points dropped slightly after applying them.

Patient Inconsistency Prevalence Rates

The adjusted, transformed *MMPI* database was large enough to provide estimates of prevalences for differences as large as those just discussed. Adult female and male samples were first adjusted to exclude all invalid records. Based on current interpretive practice, the exclusions made by *AdjAll* would presumably have eliminated most questionable records. *RCon2* was greater than *RCon1* by as much as one standard deviation in the female sample of 383 valid cases 7.31% of the time, but exceeded it by two standard deviations only 0.26% of the time. Deviations could also occur in the direction of *RCon1* being larger than *RCon2*. Departures in this direction of as much as one standard deviation occurred 5.22% of the time, with two standard deviation differences found present for 0.78% of the records. Combining rates of discrepancy in the two directions, as many as 12.53% of female records fell beyond one standard deviation and 1.04% of these exceeded two standard deviations.

The same procedures were followed for the adult male sample of 637 valid cases. A slightly larger percentage of male *RCon2* scores exceeded *RCon1* by as much as 10 *T*-score points: 8.79%. Only 0.157% of these differences surpassed two standard deviations. In the instance of records for which *RCon1* was larger than *RCon2*, 3.92% of male patients fell beyond the one standard deviation level and none beyond two standard deviations. Male patients had a combined 12.71% prevalence for differences of 10 *T*-score points between the two halves of the test in either direction, with only 0.157% being more than 20 *T*-score points different.

Interpreting the Inconsistency Scores

Notably, both genders had higher prevalence rates for discrepancies in the direction of $RCon2 > RCon1$. To review an important related point about the way that these scales are keyed, a higher standard score signals either a more positive or a less negative self-presentation. This aspect of patient test-taking behavior asserts itself across a diverse sample of contents (i.e., the items cut across most of the Content scales). For this reason, the finding that $RCon2 > RCon1$ means that patients more frequently produced questionably elevated positive self-descriptions over the second half of the test compared with the first half, even in the context of closely matched samples of content. This may be viewed in light of the earlier discussion of the avoidance side of item responding as an example of the effect of extreme item polarity. That is, the highly polarized, lower frequency behaviors of F_B are avoided by endorsing their opposites. The result is more favorable scores. Finding a discrepancy between $RCon1$ and $RCon2$ in a test record provides the examiner an additional interpretable bit of information.

Using the 10 T-score point difference between $RCon1$ and $RCon2$ in either direction was suggested earlier as a necessary benchmark for when to engage in follow-up investigation. In this connection, tentative prevalences from a diverse inpatient sample of otherwise valid records are restated for comparison. Adult females and males had prevalences of 12.53% and 12.71%, respectively, for records with a T10 difference in either direction. Because $RCon1$ and $RCon2$ fall into distinctive zones of the response sequence, they provide an additional tool for assessing the consistency of patient behavior over the course of the test. Moreover, because differences are conveniently calibrated in terms of standard scores and can occur as either $RCon1 > RCon2$ or $RCon2 > RCon1$, they lend themselves to further focused inquiry. If these scores are found not to differ from one another, then the examiner is assured regarding the sequential consistency of the test record. Both otherwise valid and invalid records can be compared in this way, because consistency within an invalid record may also be interpretable.

Other Response Consistency Scales

The items in the two scales just discussed were susceptible of being assembled in other combinations that make them more comparable in application to *VRIN* and *TRIN* and partly parallel to those in meaning. The first method of combining items is to follow the same positive keying as before, with this one difference: One point is given for each pair for which both are answered in the keyed direction. A second method reverses the preceding one, assigning one point for each time both items of a pair are answered in a direction opposite to the key (i.e., if the key is T–T for the pair, then F–F answers for the pair receive one point). A third combining method is to assign one point for each time the members of a pair are answered in different directions (i.e., T–F or F–T). Three additional scales were scored by these methods.

The first two were highly reliable. The third scale was of fairly modest reliability, but reliable enough for a scale of its type, as is explained later.

Note that items are no longer scored individually—only in pairs. The first method of scoring pairs creates a scale that is named Self-Enhancing (*RCon+*). The second method of scoring pairs results in a scale called Self-Effacing/Down-hearted (*RCon–*). These two scales can, respectively, be used to infer whether or not the response pattern displays an elevation in either of these respects. When the former score is considerably elevated, it may suggest that the respondent is exaggerating positive qualities. Excessive elevation of the latter scale may mean that the respondent is self-presenting in a negative light for secondary gain, is begging for help, or is a very demoralized individual. The third scoring method produces a scale called Self-Inconsistent (*RIncon*). The relatively modest alpha for this scale results from opposing/conflicted tendencies. Scales of this type are inherently complex and hence of lesser internal consistency.

Deriving CX equivalent norms for these three scales involved applications of probability theory. Each pair of items has a probability associated with its true and its false directions. These are presented in the itemmetric table (Butcher et al., 2001) as percentages. When those are converted to proportions, the probabilities of true answers to each item of a pair are multiplied to obtain the likelihood that they will occur together. The same is done for the combination of false answers to both items of a pair. Two possible combinations must be obtained for pairs answered in a mixed way: one by multiplying the true probability of the first item by the false probability of the second, another by multiplying the false probability of the first item by the true probability of the second, and finally by using the additive rule for combining the two results (i.e., the mixed answer combination has two part probabilities that, when added, equal its probability).

The preceding procedures were applied to all 43 item pairs for all of their possible combinations. Each pair now had three probabilities associated with it based on the calculations already outlined. Then all probabilities for each gender and for each pair's three probabilities were combined. This was not done, however, by adding True–True probabilities with True–True and False–False with False–False. They were instead combined by summing them according to the scoring keys for *RCon+* and *RCon–*. All probabilities for mixed answers were, on the other hand, combined directly without requiring a specific scoring key. The end products of these many calculations are the normative means appearing in Appendix B for *RCon+, RCon–*, and *RIncon*.

EXPLORING *TRIN*'S COMPOSITION

The design of *VRIN* is fairly open and direct, having an underlying template resembling the older Carelessness scale (Greene, 1978). The design of *TRIN* is more indirect, based on scorings and calculations that are not presented independently but only in combination. The user may, thus, have questions about such issues as how well *TRIN*'s part scores might perform by themselves as stand alones or how much each part actually contributes to the overall discrimination provided by the scale. It may be informative at the outset to approach the analysis of such questioning by an indirect process. The indirect process shifts attention away from *TRIN* for the present and redirects it to the manner of construction of two hypothetical scales.

Comparing Imaginary Scales

This will be done by returning to the earlier discussion of the item pairs used in the new response consistency measures. Suppose that the same available probabilities from *RCon+* and *RCon–* were combined in two ways different than before. For example, probabilities for all True–True pairings and all False–False pairings could be summed across the 43 pairs without regard to the keys used for form *RCon+* and *RCon–*.

In order to infuse this hypothetical example with some tangibility and place it within easier grasp, sums were calculated as suggested of all True–True pairings. This was done without reference to a key and based solely on the probabilities previously calculated for all pairs. If this is carried out, then the hypothetical example takes on the semblance of a hypothetical scale. It would, in fact, generate the following means for the sum of all True–True response pairs: 7.63 for females and 7.89 for males. If the same were done for all False–False pairings, then it would stand for a second scale whose means would be 23.13 for females and 22.91 for males.

The preceding means may be compared with the real sums of *RCon+* and *RCon–*. The calculated means are actual, but the examples are not scales. Their alphas are unknown and their real-world correlates remain unstudied. Yet, they represent possible scales that would, if expressed in standard score form, have potential to identify excessive pairings of either specified type. That is, they can reveal either surplus True–True or False–False answering that violates the rules of probability relative to the CX norms.

Returning now to *TRIN*, it is a scale that measures response sameness when there should be none by drawing attention to the substrate of logical versus illogical responding to item pairs. In this regard, it does not differ from *VRIN*, although they differ in other respects. The two hypothetical scales might even complement *TRIN* through measuring, as they seem to do, response sameness when there should be none, by focusing on a different substrate (i.e., the substrate of probable vs. improbable responding to item pairs).

Out of the preceding discussion of hypothetical scales, a perspective emerges about True–True and False–False responding. It is that they can be differentiated from each other and, thus, can be measured separately rather than merged as they are in *TRIN*. The analysis now turns back toward its starting point by partitioning

TRIN into components that correspond to the hypothetical scales for the purpose of finding what can be learned about them.

Partitioning *TRIN*

The partitioning made of *TRIN* simply scores the item pairs keyed True, sums those that match the key, and stores these as *TRIN* True (*TR-T*). It performs parallel operations for the item pairs keyed as false, storing that score as *TRIN* False (*TR-F*). Rather than subtracting *TR-F* from *TR-T*, they are added to each other to form *TRIN* Sum (*TR-S*). These are the three scales for which alpha coefficients are reported in Appendix B. Those show that *TR-T* is modestly reliable, *TR-F* is unreliable, and when these two are summed, the composite *TR-S* reflects in its very low reliability the effects of diluting the more reliable *TR-T* component by adding to it the unreliable *TR-F* component. Normative means were calculated in the same manner as was reported for the new scales *RCon+* and *RCon–*.

Findings for *TRIN* Components

The three *TRIN* components together with *TRIN* scored as recommended by Butcher et al. (2001) were then compared correlationally with each other in samples of adult females and adult males both before and after removing invalid records by applying *AdjAll*. Before removal of invalid records, *TRIN*'s highest correlation was with *TR-T* (females, .75; males, .73) and its lowest with *TR-F* (females, .06; males, .14). *TR-S* was intermediate (females, .72; males, .71), primarily being influenced by *TR-T*. After removal of invalid records, *TRIN*'s relation with the component variables changes dramatically: *TR-T* dropped (females, .33; males, .43), *TR-F* increased (females, .37; males, .37), and *TR-S* now increased (females, .51; males, .56).

The correlations calculated prior to removal of invalid records are germane to the issue of what aspect of *TRIN* is of greatest salience relative to detection of inconsistent responding. The answer unquestionably is *TR-T*, with the *TR-F* component appearing to contribute little to the process. The overall set of findings may be interpreted in the following manner. Performing as it is designed to, *TRIN* primarily asserts its discriminatory function when inconsistent records are present. *TR-T*, the main component contributing to that part of *TRIN*'s variance that identifies response inconsistency, drops in its importance to *TRIN* after removal of the variance associated with the invalid cases. Now the relation of *TR-F* to *TRIN* increases relative to the residual, nondiscriminatory variance of *TRIN* simply due to *TR-F*'s part–whole contribution to the calculation of *TRIN*. These relations are obscured when the components are combined arithmetically to form *TRIN*.

Returning to the hypothetical scales presented earlier, the same lines of scale development can also be envisioned for the components of *TRIN*. That is, its item pairs could be scored by assigning one point for each pair of true responses and done similarly again for all pairs of false responses, without regard to the pairs of items on which they occur. This would result in two new scales.

Suppose this were done. How would they perform? First, they would be *TRIN* derivatives but not *TRIN* components. That is, they would bear no direct relation to *TRIN*, nor could it be reconstructed from them without resorting back to the original item pairs. Further, they would not function in the same manner as would the hypothetical scales derived from the Response Consistency pairs. The Response Consistency hypothetical scales would retain their underlying probable versus improbable empirical linkages. By contrast, if the scales just suggested were constructed in a similar manner using *TRIN* item pairs, the relations among the pairs would undergo degradation of some of their logical versus illogical empirical linkages. The point of this is that logical–illogical linkages of pairs are powerful but less flexible, whereas probabilistic links are less powerful but far more flexible. In any event, the actual components of *TRIN* have now been unmasked and made accessible for further examination and clinical application.

FORMATION OF THE CONTENT CLUSTERS

How the clusters were formed traces back to the clustering arrived at by Levitt and Gotts (1995). Clusters have been progressively refined since that time. All of the scales that are specifically highlighted in the appendices of this book were merged with the newer scales featured in Butcher et al. (1989, 2001), together with occasional stray scales of interest that popped up in the process of literature reviews or by being imported by an enterprising psychology intern.

Setting Limits on Scale Inclusion

The body of scales could, of course, grow infinitely. Limits must be set and then respected except for good cause. These perspectives have guided the inclusion of scales: scales that are supported by empirical evidence and are appealing for their clinical relevance. The foregoing were coupled with the practical limits of manageability, size, and assimilability. On the latter grounds, some acceptable scales have been set aside for the present and omitted without mention, explanation, or apology. Once the body of scales was settled on, gaps needed to be filled. Some of these gaps were closed by acquisitions, but others were covered by local research and development.

Interrelations Among Scales

Interrelations were examined by computing correlations among all scales that made it into the final collection. For any scales that had been modified by item analysis or other methods, the revised versions were used in the foregoing study.

Separate correlation matrices that were prepared by gender consistently demonstrated highly similar results for both males and females. So the reader will know that gender differences are absent unless they are singled out for mention and interpretive comments.

The Cluster Formation Process

Efforts were next directed to aggregating into groups those scales that were most strongly correlated with one another and whose external correlations with scales of other clusters were weaker. A second requirement for inclusion was that a scale would be interpretively useful if placed in a particular cluster. Using these approaches, most scales were easily situated. Some scales were more challenging to place. An example is a scale that measures autistic and disruptive thought processes, the *TSC* Autism scale (*TSC/A*) (Stein, 1968). The scale related strongly to more than one cluster. Eventually, its placement in a single cluster was made based on the confluence of multiple considerations. A small number of scales, on the other hand, needed for clinical reasons to appear in more than one place. Final decisions about where a more difficult to place scale would go relied on clinical judgment, sometimes swayed to no small degree by hunches about what would best suit a variety of users. These confessions will confirm the authors' recognition that there is no single correct solution to some issues that arise when forming content clusters.

Divergences of *MMPI–2* and *DSM*

MMPI–2 users will be familiar with the fact that it does not provide a tight match to the *DSM* series. Appendix D examines the match. Many scales measuring important qualities do not correspond to specific diagnostic categories of the *DSM*. There are many *DSM* codes for which *MMPI–2* items and scales provide limited to sparse information. For these reasons, matching the content clusters to DSM categories would call for a procrustean remedy. This is not attempted. It would have spelled violence both for *MMPI–2* scales and the *DSM*, each of which points to its own truth. A cluster solution that draws its insights primarily from *MMPI–2* needs to follow where that leads. That was the course taken to forming clusters. The results are briefly summarized next.

The 18 content clusters formed (see listing in chap. 1) correspond at times to no specific *DSM* category (e.g., I, Validity, and XVIII, Prognosis). One of the clusters receives mention only among the *DSM*'s so-called *V-code* conditions. These are conditions that arise as focuses of clinical attention but are not classified as mental disorders as such (e.g., Cluster XIII, Family Relationship Issues). The Psychosocial Development Scales intersect all clusters and belong to none. Some conditions arising from psychosocial issues appear, nevertheless, among the V-codes. Several clusters run parallel to broad *DSM* categories (Examples: II, Depressive Spectrum Conditions, and IV, Thought Process Disorders). Cluster X, Behavior Controls & Norms Violations, pertains to multiple *DSM* categories. Only XVII, the Personality Disorders, achieves a closer match to *DSM*.

REVIEW AND PREVIEW OF UPCOMING CHAPTERS

Chapter 7 brought to completion a series of three chapters that recounted how the clinical research program was carried out and with what results. The present chapter has reviewed those new scales that were developed for use with *MMPI–2*. New scales were designed and subjected to initial validity analysis for Critical Inquiry, Psychosocial Development, Components of Impulsivity, and Response Consistency. After that, the process of forming the content clusters was introduced along with explanation of their use in the diagnostic process.

Attention turns next in a series of three chapters to clinical applications of the newly created scales and those that were improved. That is, chapters 8–10 explore what is known clinically in terms of the psychosocial framework at its intersections with the content clusters. Limitations of the *DSM* approach vis-à-vis the use of *MMPI–2* content clusters are illustrated in these next three chapters and more explicitly exposed in Appendix D.

8

The *DSM* and Axis I Conditions

Scores on the six scales of psychosocial development represent outcomes of a sequential series of normative crises (Erikson, 1963) that occur during the years from infancy through early adulthood. The scales, however, do not examine those significant life events from a developmental perspective but instead as they exhibit themselves in adult respondents' attitudes, beliefs, and value statements. Thus, they measure in the adult the persisting dynamics of earlier gains and losses that cast shadows resembling residues of the normative crisis resolutions.

Neither the earlier outcomes nor their residues are static entities. They at all times are experienced as the balancing of dynamic forces that mirror the contrasting poles of each crisis. The balances are challenged continuously by ordinary vicissitudes of life circumstances that test the stability and resiliency of prior crisis resolutions. In these roles, the outcomes and residues repeatedly impress themselves in varied guises on the adult psyche and generate reactions.

ENGAGING THE PSYCHOSOCIAL CRISES

Consider next the processes whereby the outcomes and residues become parts of the individual's intra-psychic assets and liabilities. During earlier development, the phased appearance of each new normative crisis presents a qualitatively different kind of challenge. When a new crisis arrives, on the one hand, it entices the individual to strain toward the more mature prerogatives of the next stage by mastering its functional modalities. On the other hand, it discourages regressive clinging to the resolutions of prior phases.

To the extent that respondents engage each emerging crisis as a gift of both challenges and opportunities for growth, they acquire coping resources. Furthermore, despite misgivings to the contrary, the prior resolutions are not actually abandoned. Instead, they are transformed and integrated into the new ways of interacting in spheres of both external and internal reality. Moreover, as the individual continues to engage reality by using the established modalities, the residues of earlier resolutions appear and reappear with regularity and thereby remain accessible to self-examination and self-disclosure. It is these recurring events and the feelings that accompany them that the Psychosocial scales enable the respondent to communicate. The following interpretations of the scales emanate from these understandings of the psychosocial dynamisms that remain at work.

Feels Cared for/Loved vs. Neglected/Disliked

The Cared For.   Highly Cared for persons say that they feel treated fairly and considerately by others. This outlook appears to have its roots in their families of origin. A more internal locus of control is suggested by readiness to accept personal responsibility for life circumstances rather than attributing them to external forces beyond their control. This perspective on life events has aptly been traced to feelings of personal efficacy (Piaget, 1972) and efficacy has been shown to eventuate in a sense of personal causation (De Charms, 1968).

Accordingly, those who feel Cared for see others as more likely to be supportive, kind, sympathetic, and caring. In keeping with this, they describe themselves as highly open and nonguarded in interpersonal contacts. They further believe that the people they encounter are predictable and act out of cordial motives nearly all of the time.

These outlooks are associated with an inner certainty that others are likely to behave in a forthright and honest manner. That is, people are what they seem on the surface to be, without concealed motives and hidden designs. High scorers affirm that they try to treat others in keeping with these beliefs.

Based on a pervasive view of others as basically good, extremely high scorers imply that they are abundantly trusting. Thus, at times, they may disregard obvious reality to the point of displaying a naïve, Pollyannaish attitude of unbounded optimism. They prefer the company of those who have a compatible outlook and consider those who reject their optimism to be cynics. Although this outlook may sometimes lead to them being exploited by others, it tends to preclude catastrophic reactions to these events.

In its more exaggerated forms, this presentation will often cease to signify positive attributes. Instead, it may mask a predisposition to delusional disorder or massive denial, such as is occasionally seen in *la belle indifference* with conversion disorder or anorexia nervosa. That is, there are psychopathologies associated with excessively high scores on the Cared for vs. Neglected scale. Although these elevated scores were absent from the current inpatient sample, clinical experience offers interpretive suggestions. The following are examples of conditions that may be present in persons with extremely high scores: delusional disorder with grandiose features and a sense of entitlement, histrionic denial and exaggeration, self-enhancement for the purpose of concealing character flaws. Persons who present themselves as incredibly cared for and loved thereby alert the examiner of the need to consider these and other possibilities.

By definition, more modest elevations were seen in patients with average Cared for scores (T50–T64). Looking beyond this overall response level to their pattern of answer choices, they answered a mean of 65.9% of the scale's items in keeping with the positive direction of the bidirectional key. Thus, scores typically fell well below the maximum possible by 34.1%. Their rate of positive answer choice endorsements compared with an average of 45.1% answered in a positive direction by those who felt neglected, as described later. Average scorers expressed considerably less mistrust, suspicion, and cynicism than did patients who felt neglected. They were less guarded interpersonally and did not have prominent ideas of reference. But, unlike those with very high scores, they did admit to viewing others' motives and intentions with some caution and justifiable suspicion at times. In these regards, they took a more balanced and realistic view of themselves. No patient scores exceeded T64.

The Neglected.   When reminiscing about early life events, there are patients who feel neglected or treated as second rate or even actively disliked and rejected. Those scoring extremely low on this scale, for example, will recount childhood memories of deprivations, abuse, and other harsh treatment by their families. Feeling externally cut off or assaulted, these persons externalize blame for life's disappointments and troubles. They feel adrift in an uncaring world of people who, they believe, are devoid of human kindness or fellow feeling. Benjamin (1993) traced paranoid attitudes to similar origins.

Individuals view others as being energized and propelled by selfish motives to gain an advantage at their expense. Thus, they anticipate that others will conceal their intentions by dissimulation, even while they keep claiming that they are "trying to be helpful" or "to do what is best." Worse yet, they expect to experience loss or to be harmed at the hands of others. In keeping with their uncertainty about what others may be concocting, they relate to them in a wary, guarded manner as the only safe course of action.

For some of these patients, the profound lack of confidence in the predictability of interpersonal relations primarily affects their reality testing. Hence, their suspicions can be painfully intense, engendering ideas of reference. Persons who they think have opposed or harmed them become objects of their fear, resentment, and sometimes hatred. In a kind of virtual reality, those persons become opponents or enemies. The neglected obsess about their perceived injuries and how to neutralize the harm or even scores. Their obsessing may lead them to seek retribution by making accusations, legal action, or overt physical harm. Yet, an item average (45.1%) suggested patients felt somewhat cared for.

Some of the neglected and disliked follow another course, dwelling in an abyss of hopelessness and dysphoria. Obtaining a detailed life history for such individuals will often reveal significant depression during childhood. It is a kind of depression that is markedly notable for the degree of anhedonia that is present. This will have been manifested during early childhood by rapidly shifting play interests and an inability to settle down to any one thing. The school record will confirm that the depressive process continued to affect their learning. It is further informative simply to ask these persons what they liked to do when they were children and what they liked about school. Their interests and sources of gratifying experience appear to have been severely constricted.

Herein lies a puzzle. Why does one Neglected/Disliked patient externalize blame and adopt a counterattack mode while another retreats into resignation and despair? The source of these differences seems to be early temperamental dispositions that incline them along differing life courses. Thomas and Chess (1977) showed how active and passive forms of behavior disorders commence and persist from dispositions that are reliably seen in infancy. Uncovering the contribution of temperament to the expression of pathology adds to understanding the patient. The basic *MMPI-2 Si* scale and its cluster mates are useful in this regard. More importantly, knowing about this will suggest that the clinician use different therapeutic approaches with patients who present with actively versus passively expressed disorders.

Autonomous/Self-Possessed vs. Self-Doubting/Shamed

Autonomous. Persons receiving highly Autonomous scores report that their families treat them as adults by respecting their individuality. They claim also that they and family members always function in positive ways with each other. They see themselves as upright persons who maintain satisfactory self-control across a variety of ordinary and stressful situations. They believe in accepting personal responsibility for their actions.

These persons compare themselves favorably to others. They claim to be socially at ease, as well as to feel in balance, for the most part, both mentally or physically. Further, they state that they act decisively and are assertive in interpersonal contexts. They are tranquil and ready for what comes next. The qualities that they assert regarding themselves, if actually present, make them comparable in ways to a master of the martial arts who is also a master of self.

In this manner, the grandiosity of feeling excessively cared for in the prior life stage can be reinforced by a grandiose sense of personal mastery or control. That is, excessive autonomous feeling can turn toward willful insistence on having one's own way. This leads to defending determinedly the decisions and choices one makes as being necessarily right and good. How could things be otherwise when the overly autonomous individual is the one making those choices! Thus, a surplus of self-assurance may manifest itself by rigid insistence that "My way is the right way" or by the unwavering demand, "Be reasonable and do what I say."

Because the overly autonomous person is also convinced of being upright personally, there is the risk of inflexibility of conscience that often extends to the actions of others. These same excesses lead in some persons to an obsessive–compulsive rigidity directed toward the goal of keeping everything under personal control.

For the foregoing reasons, moderately elevated scores on this scale are more likely to represent true positive attributes, whereas excessively high scores raise doubt concerning their accuracy. The average scoring patient answered a mean of 70.6% of the items in a positive direction, significantly below (29.4%) the maximum that might be claimed. Unlike those who might attain very high Autonomous scores, they admitted to having self-doubts and feelings of shame. Compared with the Doubting scale (see later), they reported less shyness, shame, and sensitivity to criticism. No patient scores exceeded T62 on this scale.

Doubting.   Persons scoring toward the low end of this scale report that their families have intruded into their personal affairs and left them conflicted over their status as adults. Often they are troubled by unfinished childhood business and entertain regressive fantasies. Their locuses of responsibility and control are decidedly external. They do not do; they are done to. Jealousy and strife within their families are commonplace.

They view themselves as evil, damaged goods. This expresses itself in ongoing intropunitiveness that reinforces a core of shame. Affective presentation will confirm this impression. Psychologically, they may feel like lepers or pariahs. This makes them uncomfortable being in the limelight or at the center of attention. Being in such situations leaves them panicked that others are fully cognizant and contemptuous of their shameful state of being. They feel hatred toward those who expose them to shame or even those who witness their painful embarrassment.

In order to escape from interpersonal situations where they feel outmatched, intimidated, or looked down on, many self-doubting persons submit readily to others' wishes. As a result, they may appear compliant and agreeable when in the immediate presence of those whom they view as their betters. But, that impression is a misleading one. The reality is that they may be seething inside. Once out of hearing, they often express the passive–aggressive resentments that they have held in check while in the presence of those who impose on them.

Some of the shamed frustrate the wishes of others by acting as if they do not understand or are incapable of doing what is asked of them. It will at times be suspected that—when they say they "forgot" what they were told to do, or when they have spoiled something they were asked to care for or failed to start a job on time—they in fact may have acted deliberately in order to discourage others from making further requests of them. Claiming incapacity or disability as a reason for failure is a more extreme version of the same (Dreikurs, 1957). Because the shame-oriented person feels indecisive, awkward, and profoundly self-doubting, it requires little self-deception to plead incapacity.

Patients in this hospital sample's lowest scoring group, on average, did not provide self-attributions that were as negative as the preceding description. In fact, they answered a mean of 52.2% of the scale's *MMPI–2* items in a positive direction, even though their standard scores (T35 and below) appeared extreme when compared to those of normals. Only 1.12% of patients had scores that were three standard deviations below the mean (T20 and below). This suggests that extremely low, as well as high, scores may be of questionable validity.

Initiating/Pursuing vs. Regretful/Guilt-Prone

Initiating.   The initiators have learned those skills of planning and anticipating that enable them to pursue goals actively while remaining within socially acceptable bounds. Being active and doing things are major goals and sources of satisfaction. The capacity to observe boundaries while thus engaged leaves them free, they say, from guilt, regrets, and the need to apologize.

They have tried out a variety of roles and learned to fit into them and to own them. This process of role adoption has enlarged their capacity for appreciating others' viewpoints and understanding the reasons for them acting as they do. They, consequently, report that their interpersonal relations are guided by a sense of mutuality. Strong emotions and resentments are so well controlled that they do not disrupt relationships.

Socially conforming behavior is the norm for them. These individuals so strongly identify with social norms that they respond automatically to test items, denying that they have violated or would ever violate behavior norms. Nevertheless, they may engage in egocentrically motivated pursuits without recognizing that they have strayed beyond the bounds of some norm until a misstep draws this to their attention. This occurs when they become greatly absorbed in their pursuits and regard their actions at the time in light of an immediately appealing goal. When an infraction is brought to their attention, they express surprise and assert that they did not know that they were doing wrong. These persons report having acceptable behavior during their school years and deny a history of antisocial actions. Overall, they exhibit the conventional morality of obedience (Piaget, 1967) and respond to test items accordingly.

They have abundant energy, enthusiasm, and curiosity, and they enjoy interpersonal competition. These forces together create their immense potential for pursuing whatever fascinates them. Herein also hides the danger of their focusing on pursuits of the moment. They fail at times to recognize that a boundary has been breached. Some adult antisocial behaviors that result in legal charges appear to begin innocently enough with energetic pursuits after one pleasure or another. All of this happens without apparent norm violating intent. Again, the following are typical reactions when initiators are brought to task: (a) "I'm sorry. I didn't think I was intoxicated." (b) "We were only playing around. I didn't mean to hurt anyone." (c) "I thought it was okay to go in there. There wasn't a sign or any-thing." The pattern of denial that asserts itself in extremely high scores that the Initiators receive on this scale again marks their behavior when they become en-snared in some misadventure.

Patients with valid records received high scores 0.93% of the time, and no pa-tients with invalid records had scores in this range. All of the elevated scores fell between T65 and T69, so none was extremely high. The genders were about evenly represented among high scorers. About one half of the group had various psychotic diagnoses, with the rest being of diverse classifications. Patients with scores of average elevation showed both more of a balance between acceptance of the norms and recognition of their personal shortcomings relative to them. They, for example, admitted to intrusive, egocentric actions that would not be acknowl-edged by those with extremely high Initiating scores. They also confessed more readily to feeling guilt about their indiscretions. They responded, on average, to *MMPI–2* items at a rate below that of extreme Initiators (63.4% positive). On the other hand, they differed considerably from the low scorers who responded in more self-depreciating ways to items (only 45.3% positive). In particular, average scoring Initiators reported significantly less misbehavior as children and fewer antisocial behaviors and attitudes than did low scorers.

Guilt-Prone.   For persons receiving extremely low scores on this scale, life seems to abound with opportunities to engage in questionable, out of bounds, or frankly dangerous actions. They have taken part from childhood onward in a vari-ety of norm violating behaviors. These include using other people. They partici-pate in many of them with awareness of what they are doing rather than stumbling into them innocently. Knowing right from wrong does not deter them. Even though they are cognizant of the unacceptability of their actions, they continue to focus on immediate gratification to the exclusion of anticipating the consequences of their intrusive behaviors.

They differ from the initiators in how they handle the aftermath of such events. Some dwell on their regrets. Others make excuses or lie in an effort to deflect blame onto someone else. Still others simply reject the consequences and react angrily toward those who catch them or express disapproval. Depending on the individual's emotional disposition, either anxiety develops when they must face consequences or wariness occurs in anticipation of reprisal from those whom they have wronged.

Those who react angrily to being caught engage in determinedly active forms of opposition. Those who do this turn with the passing years in ever more norm violating directions. These developments underlie antisocial behavior patterns from an early age wherein immediate rewards are sought by deviant actions. Some of the guilt-prone act in more passive–aggressive ways. Only 0.56% of the patients responded with extremely low scores (< 3 SDs). A somewhat higher rate reasonably may be expected among convicted felons.

Industrious/Capable vs. Inadequate/Inferior

Industrious. High scorers on this scale find their lives interesting and engrossing. For some, their pattern of strong involvement in productive activities began in childhood in the guise of a favorable outlook on school and by way of their participation in extracurricular events and youth organizations. Others identified more with hands-on work and found ways to earn spending money or to help their families with chores. Their prior positive life accomplishments have resulted in exceptional confidence in their ability to succeed in the present and the future.

Industrious persons' energy, attentional focus, and positive mood toward productive activity are associated with regular participation in employment. They express enjoyment in being busy. They persist in the face of adversity and proceed to do whatever needs to be done to finish a job. They derive from work the assurance that they are useful members of their community. This assurance that their contribution is valued is a source of both confidence and satisfaction.

Overcommitment to productivity often means that individuals curtail social involvement and neglect family life and leisure. The workaholic pattern then eventuates in health risks, constriction of interpersonal ties, and emotional vulnerability to the effects of economic cycles on employment or advancement. Patients with average Industrious scores responded to 66.9% of items in this way. With their balanced outlook, they had reduced emphasis on success, energy resources, and personal capability. None of the patient sample scored above T58 on this scale. Compared to the Inadequate feeling (see later), they reported that they had more energy, were better able to work, expected to achieve greater success, and experienced greater enjoyment of life.

Inadequate. As they were growing up, the Inadequate feeling found that they did not easily accommodate to school routines. Many concluded that formal learning was a pursuit for which they were ill equipped. Their memories of school days are remarkably negative, and they may defensively denigrate school as irrelevant. For others, the poor school experience has led to a palpable sense of personal inadequacy. Self-confidence is correspondingly impaired unless they have been so fortunate as to find alternative avenues to satisfaction in productive work. Even then, feelings of dissatisfaction linger beneath an exterior of successful employment.

The inadequate have low personal expectations for their success in new ventures, and they give up when they meet adversity. They consider so little of their abilities that they readily defer to others' opinions and leadership. Many have uneven employment records with frequent job changes, absenteeism, and substandard job performance despite apparently adequate ability. Fundamentally, they are disappointed with themselves and struggle with an abiding conviction that they are less capable than others.

Compared with the preceding description of the inadequate, low scoring patients overall responded to items of this scale in less self-depreciating ways, with 51.4% of their responses being somewhat positive. A notable subgroup of them (6.52%), however, scored three or more standard deviations below the national norm (T20 or below). Among the six Psychosocial scales, Industrious vs. Inadequate produced the largest percentage of patients with extremely low scores. Using Erikson's (1963) terms, this subgroup's inferiority feelings are profound and rival those for mistrust, shame, and guilt.

Life-Goal Oriented/Ego Identity Secure
vs. Directionless/Confused

Ego Identified.   High scorers claim that they firmly grasp attainable life goals. Even when confronted with life's many uncertainties, they have faith that they can reach out and take hold of a future that has meaning for them. These individuals actively pursue their goals through identification with a career path and the expression of their sexuality. Life outcomes are influenced, they believe, by their choices and actions. This perspective resembles what Maslow (1968) and others believed to be the essence of self-actualizing persons—an apparently uncommon breed and not expected to be present among these inpatients.

Whereas family and friends are important to them, they distinguish and maintain their own boundaries. They regard themselves confidently, believing they are capable of handling whatever life sends in their direction. They, thus, exude an optimism about the future and their capacity to be ready for it.

Among valid adult patient records none fell into the high scoring group (T65 and above). That is, no scores were extremely high, ranging well below T70. All the higher scores were produced by females. Interestingly, none of the records rejected as invalid scored above T60 on this scale. Patients whose scores were average responded to 70.2% of the items in a direction favorable to themselves. Unlike maximum scores, they admitted to being influenced by others more than they cared to be, not always being able to meet life's demands, and having some personal defects or deficiencies. Yet, as compared to low scorers, they experienced less conflict over career choice, were better able to plan their life course, felt greater positive self-regard, and could envision a future. Once again, the moderately elevated scores are more credible unless those subjects being tested are recognizable as highly gifted persons or individuals who display a grandiose outlook.

Confused.   Low scorers cannot apprehend with any certainty a future for themselves. Choices and opportunities that come their way seem enigmatic, confusing, unclear, without meaning, and/or unattainable. Unbounded indecisiveness precludes planning and setting realistic goals.

Their career and sexual identities may remain murky and conflicted. When they attempt to resolve these ambiguities, they do so as persons whose fate is controlled by the external forces of family disagreement and pressure, what they believe to be unmanageable personal flaws, life's imponderables, and chance. These people feel put upon and harassed by life circumstances. They are ill at ease with themselves and may obsess over the burden that they have become for others. A distinctly defined ego identity eludes them. As a result, they must navigate life without compass or chart. Only 1.49% of patients in this sample scored three or more standard deviations (T20) below the normative mean for this scale. Extremely low scores seem likely to represent a form of intentional exaggeration of misery and feelings of inferiority more than a state of confusion.

Socially Committed/Involved vs. Disengaged/Lonely

Involved. High scorers on this scale identify themselves as extremely engaged with other people. They enjoy their involvement and believe that other people reciprocate their positive feelings. They say that they mingle comfortably and easily in all social situations. Their sense of belonging socially is strong.

They deny having interpersonal conflict with family and other intimates. Their view of married life is comparably idyllic. It corresponds to the idealized state referred to as *marital bliss*. These individuals claim that, for them, this is a continuous rather than a temporary or occasional condition. They report abundant affection, happiness, companionship, and satisfaction as being the norm for them.

The involved practice exceptionally honest, open communication and are likely, they say, to tell others explicitly what they are thinking and feeling, even when this might prompt unpleasant feelings in others. In fact, they report no hesitancy about letting others know their innermost thoughts. They further affirm that they seek out opportunities to communicate with others rather than waiting for them to initiate conversation.

This group's stated ways of relating to others may appeal to a few kindred spirits, however it likely conveys different impressions to others. The incredibly open communication that they claim would often generate hurt feelings, interpersonal conflict, and a tendency for others to distance themselves from them. The force of their direct style may convey histrionic sensationalism, gross insensitivity, or possibly sadistic intent. It follows that their belief that nearly all people respond to them positively appears to be a serious misapprehension. Such a belief could only be sustained by denial or some other reality distorting strategy.

Average scoring patients in the hospital sample answered a mean of 71.4% of this scale's items in this manner. None of the valid adult sample scored above T60 on the Involved vs. Disengaged scale. Compared with maximum possible scores, they typically did not claim that it was easy for them to converse with new acquaintances or to mingle at social gatherings. They further did not claim to reveal their inner thoughts and feelings as freely. They did, however, generally report that others liked them. Compared with the disengaged (see later), who answered only 48.8% of the items in the involved direction, the average scoring patients reported engaging in some open communication and relating more comfortably with others.

Disengaged.   The disengaged are those with fairly minimal scores on this scale. They present a pitiable picture of themselves as both socially isolated and painfully wishing not to be that way. Consequently, these individuals feel unlikable, bereft of companionship, and deeply lonely. It is difficult, if not impossible, for them to modify their situation inasmuch as they believe that they are not capable of making friends.

They experience significant interpersonal conflicts with family and those few persons with whom they have tried to experience closeness. Comparable feelings permeate their perspective on romantic alliances and marriage. Their own bitterness about their affectional deprivation may appear in the form of cynical pronouncements that overgeneralize their personal frustration as if it were the condition of all people.

They are exceedingly reticent about opening themselves up to scrutiny by others. Blocked and censored communications are the norm for them. They will go out of their way to avoid communicating with others. Their active avoidance keeps them disengaged. Moreover, they communicate by their nonverbal behavior that they have no desire to relate. This is not the case, but others reasonably conclude that they are disliked and are being avoided. The low rate for such powerful feelings of isolation can be judged from the fact that only 1.12% of valid adult patient records received scores as much as three standard deviations below the mean (T20) on the Involved vs. Disengaged scale. Markedly low scores, hence, are suspect as giving evidence of a disposition to fake bad. Such cases should be subjected to close examination.

PSYCHOSOCIAL SCALES, CONTENT CLUSTERS, AND AXIS I CONDITIONS

Studying *DSM* Axis I Linkages

Weak DSM–MMPI–2 Linkages.   The construction of the *DSM* dichotomized categories is covered in chapter 5. Initial examination of relations among the diagnoses and *MMPI–2* scales produced only a limited number of significant results. The diagnoses related with any consistency to *MMPI–2* scales in a sparse number of content areas. Others have encountered similar challenges when seeking to find direct, clear-cut correspondences between psychiatric diagnoses and *MMPI/MMPI–2* (Franklin, Strong, & Greene, 2002; Pancoast, Archer, & Gordon, 1988; Wetzler, Khadivi, & Moser, 1998).

Although it would have been useful to treat the diagnoses as one class of crite-rion variables, this was obviated except for a narrowly restricted set of findings. A similar conclusion was reached when the diagnoses were examined in relation to a smaller sample of *Rorschach* records ($n = 54$) that were coded using the Compre-hensive System (Exner, 1993, 2000; Weiner, 1998). Then a third comparison was made of *MMPI-2* scales and *Rorschach* codes in the same small sample. Once more, only a small number of significant findings emerged that were not system-atically aligned with one another. Based on the foregoing, major emphasis is given in the analyses here to content clusters instead of psychiatric diagnoses. See Appendix D for more on *DSM*, and chapter 11 on *Rorschach* ties.

For all analyses performed by the broad *DSM*-related content clusters in this chapter, the Psychosocial scale scores were partitioned into ranges based on de-parture from T50 by plus or minus 1.5 standard deviations. Scores in the midrange were further divided at T50. This resulted in the following classifications: Very low T35 and below, Low T36–49, Average T50–64, and High T65 and above. These groupings were stored as six categorical variables in which the following respective codes were assigned: *1, 2, 3,* and *4*.

The inpatient cases who received high scores (Code *4*) were either completely absent from the sample or there were too few of them to support separate analy-ses. On the other hand, those inpatients with very low scores were numerous enough to form groups for analyses.

Overall Level of Psychosocial Difficulties. A principal components factor analysis was performed for the 1,020 valid cases in order to examine the structure of the six Psychosocial scales in their standard score form. A single ex-tracted factor accounted for 54.3% of the total variance. All of the scales corre-lated with the factor .65 to .83. The high unity of their structure meant they could be combined in various ways for the analyses that appear in this chapter.

Information from the six Psychosocial scales was combined for use in subse-quent analyses as follows. First, a separate dichotomized variable was created for each of the six Psychosocial scales. In each variable, very low scores were identi-fied by a code (*1*) and higher scores (i.e., *2, 3,* and *4*) by a different code (*0*). Sec-ond, the six scales were merged into a composite variable that represented an overall level of psychosocial difficulty reported by each patient. That is, if a pa-tient reported a difficulty (Code *1*) on only one of the scales, then a score of *1* was assigned and so on up to a maximum of six.

AdjAll had identified 1,020 valid adult cases. Of these, 537 were valid cases of males and females combined who had reported a problem (i.e., had a very low score) on one or more of the scales and 483 valid cases who had no ($n = 0$) identi-fied psychosocial problems. The distribution of 537 cases formed a data pyramid: 6 difficulties identified ($n = 4$), 5 ($n = 26$), 4 ($n = 44$), 3 ($n = 87$), 2 ($n = 130$), and 1 ($n = 246$).

Data Configurations for Analysis. The foregoing patients were then assembled into two configurations suitable for data analysis. In the first configuration, patients having no identified psychosocial problems were compared with the aggregate of all those who identified one or more problems. These analyses compared the presence versus absence of psychosocial difficulties across the content clusters.

In a second configuration, patients with a single psychosocial problem ($n = 246$) were compared with a combined grouping of patients who reported having three or more psychosocial problems ($n = 161$). These analyses explored the question of whether or not a larger loading of psychosocial difficulties results in greater problems in various Axis I areas that are represented by the content clusters.

Analyses of Presence vs. Absence of Difficulties

Thought Process Disorders. A multiple regression analysis compared patients who reported psychosocial difficulties with those who did not report these. Because of many item overlaps among *MMPI–2* scales that appear for the psychotic spectrum and other content clusters (i.e., many unavoidable linear dependencies are present), a preliminary analysis was performed of each content cluster as a means of identifying and selecting for a final analysis only those scales that appeared to contain somewhat independent pools of variance. Predictor variables entered into this preliminary solution were *Sc*, *ScK*-corrected (*ScK*), *BIZ*, *I-RD*, *8BSE*, *W-PSY*, *I-DS*, *Pa*, *S+*, and *6PI*. For ease of reference, a listing of all abbreviated scale names appears after the Preface.

Five of the scales survived preliminary inspection and were entered into an actual regression equation. It produced a multiple R of .65, accounting for 42.47% of the variance, $F(5, 1014) = 149.70, p < .0000$. Betas were assigned to these surviving, statistically significant variables: *Sc* (1.02), *ScK* (–.35), *8BSE* (–.17), *S+* (.08), and *6P* (–.10). Patients with no reported psychosocial difficulties had means on the predictors ranging from T47.75 (*Sc*) to T53.86 (*6PI*). Those reporting psychosocial difficulties had predictor means ranging from T59.05 (*ScK*) to T62.28 (*6PI*). Thus, the groups differed by about one standard deviation for this content cluster. The conjoint functioning of *Sc* and *ScK* are notable findings, and incremental contributions appeared for other variables. The contribution of *Sc* to the solution, in effect, is moderated by the corrected *ScK* when both versions of the scale are used, and the resulting R is greater than when only one of the versions is used.

Depressive Spectrum Conditions. The preliminary list of scales for depressive conditions included: *D*, *TSC/D*, *DEP*, *W-DEP*, *2SD*, *2B*, *2PR*, *3LM*, *8EA*, and *D-S*. Although all of the scales reliably separated the two groups, the preliminary equation quickly eliminated duplication and narrowed the list to two scales. The equation that resulted from entering them accounted for 44.15% of the variance ($R = .66$) and produced $F(2, 1017) = 402.05, p < .0000$. The two surviving scales both contributed at highly reliable levels to the solution with the following assigned betas: TSC/D (.58) and D-S (−.17). Means for the psychosocial difficulties group and no difficulties were, respectively: TSC/D T65.56 and T48.51; D-S T45.83 and T54.51. The differences between the means for two nonselected scales, for example, D and DEP were T10.75 and T15.05, respectively, compared with TSC/D's T17.05 difference.

Anxiety Spectrum Conditions. The content cluster scales—Pt, PtK-corrected (PtK), TSC/T, ANX, $Panic$, A, PK, PS, and $4SA$—were evaluated in a preliminary analysis. This led to a final selection of four predictors. A multiple R (.69) found by the regression solution explained 48.25% of the variance, $F(4, 1015) = 236.57, p < .0000$. Each of the four predictors contributed significantly to the solution, resulting in the following betas: Pt (.39), PtK (−.10), $4SA$ (.15), A (.27). Scale means for the no psychosocial difficulties group ranged from T46.50 (Pt) to T53.37 ($4SA$) and for the group with difficulties from T61.24 (PtK) to T68.64 ($4SA$). All differences between the groups exceeded one standard deviation. It is notable to observe again the conjoint functioning of a clinical scale in its uncorrected (Pt) and corrected (PtK) forms. The placement of $4SA$ in the anxiety cluster was also strongly supported.

Obsessions and Phobias. The four scales—OBS, I-OC, FRS, and W-PHO—are parts of the anxiety cluster but were singled out for separate analysis because they are treated separately in the DSM series. I-OC, whose original value has been absorbed by OBS, was not included in the prediction equation. The three scales that were entered each contributed reliably and together produced a multiple R of .56 for a multiple R squared variance of .31 and $F(3, 1016) = 154.75, p < .0000$. Betas associated with each scale were: OBS (.49), FRS (−.18), and W-PHO (.27). Means on these scales for the difficulties versus no difficulties groups were, respectively: OBS T59.38 and T46.79, FRS T56.09 and T50.82, and W-PHO T56.39 and T49.41.

Cognitive Disorders. These disorders were clearly differentiated from intellect by first comparing the two psychosocial groups' IQ scores. The groups differed on none of the three indexes (Verbal, Performance, Full Scale). Scales checked in a preliminary analysis of this cluster were: $2MD$, $8COG$, TSC/A, $8BSE$, $NeurPsy$, W-ORG, I-DS, and Inconsistency ($RConPr$). Four scales were kept in the final analysis. The regression solution yielded a multiple R of .66 that equated to 43.71% of the variance and resulted in $F(4, 1015) = 197.02, p < .0000$. Each of the following scales reliably entered the solution, with the following betas: $2MD$ (.44), $8COG$ (−.13), TSC/A (.33), and $RConPr$ (.14). Means of the no difficulties group ranged from T44.86 (*RConPr*) to T47.91 (*8COG*). Those for the difficulties group went from T55.74 (*RConPr*) to T63.80 (*2MD*).

Somatic Concerns. This cluster provided nine scales for preliminary inspection: *Hs, HsK*-corrected (*HsK*), *HEA, TSC/B, W-HEA, 2PM, 3SC, TPA*, and *Ho*. Five of these were retained by regression analysis. A multiple *R* of .60 explained about 36% of the variance. The betas attached to the successful predictors were: *Hs* (.71), *HsK* (−.60), *HEA* (.20), *TSC/B* (.28), *2PM* (.10), *Ho* (.13), and *TPA* (.10). The overall prediction equation produced an $F(7, 1012) = 80.78, p < .0000$. Means for the difficulties group ranged from a low of T56.66 (*TPA*) to T61.98 (*2PM*) and for no difficulties from T45.14 (*TPA*) to T54.24 (*2PM*). The two groups differed greatly on all scales in the cluster, and the listed four were found to operate more independently of others. The *Hs* and *HsK* forms complemented one another, and other scales added validly to the solution. Contributions of *Ho* and *TPA* are in keeping with prior research (see chap. 4).

Stimulus Seeking and Drive. The scales in the short list for this cluster have some bearing on bipolar disorders in addition to their characterological implications. The preliminary list consisted of *Ma, MaK*-corrected (*MaK*), *W-HYP, 9PMA, 9EI*, and *2PR*. The three successful entries had the following betas: *Ma* (1.52), *MaK* (−1.42), and *2PR* (.37). The amount of variance determined by these three was 37.42%, $R = .61, F(3, 1016) = 202.47, p < .0000$. Means for the no difficulties versus difficulties groups, respectively, were T50.34 and T56.17 (*Ma*), T51.30 and T54.95 (*MaK*), and T44.15 and T60.22 (*2PR*). The complementarity of *Ma* and *MaK* in the prediction of psychosocial difficulties is noted.

Substance Dependency. The Critical Inquiry Addictive Activities (AA) scale was not employed in this analysis because it could only be scored fully in *MMPI-2*. Two *MMPI-2* scales for predicting chemical dependency are included in the Behavior Controls cluster but are treated separately here in order to fit the *DSM* Axis I category. These are *MAC-R* and *APS*. Surprisingly, the more popular of these scales barely differentiated the two groups, with the mean for *MAC-R* being T61.26 in the psychosocial difficulties group and T59.31 for the no difficulties group ($t = 2.59, df = 1018, p < .01$).

With *APS* as the solitary scale left, groups were compared by *t* test rather than regression. Whereas *APS* differentiated the groups ($t = 10.18, df = 1018, p < .0000$), the means were unexpectedly low: no difficulties (T45.16) and psychosocial difficulties (T52.83). The low means for *APS* did not result from the *MMPI*-to-*MMPI-2* score estimation process. This was verified by a finding of comparably low scores in the *MMPI-2* sample that was scored directly without resorting to estimation. In view of the known high rate of substance abuse in this sample, these very average mean values are difficult to interpret or reconcile. Thus *MAC-R* and *APS* were not useful for identifying both group differences and their actual levels of substance dependency. Nevertheless, based on substantial evidence of the *MAC-R*'s value relative to a variety of the chemical dependencies (Lachar, Berman, Grisell, & Schoof, 1976; Levitt & Gotts, 1995), it is retained as a core scale in the database.

Analyses of Differing Psychosocial Difficulty Levels

The analyses reported in this section are based on the second data configuration. In these, valid adult patients who reported a single psychosocial difficulty ($n = 246$) are compared to those who reported three or more ($n = 161$). As in the preceding analyses, preliminary checks were made of all scales in each cluster, after which final regression analyses were performed. The reports omit the preliminary listing and all begin with the final regression analysis.

Thought Process Disorders. Six scales entered the final analysis. The multiple R was .72 and total variance explained was 52.14%. All six of the final scales related significantly to the criterion. Their betas were: *Sc* (.86), *ScK* (−.35), *BIZ* (−.29), *8BSE* (−.17), *W-PSY* (.30), and *S+* (.21). The overall solution was highly significant: $F(6, 400) = 72.62, p < .0000$. The means for one versus multiple psychosocial difficulties ranged from T53.30 (*S+*) to T56.87 (*8BSE*) for the former and from T64.20 (*ScK*) to 69.54 (*Sc*) for the latter. All differences between the two groups were around one standard deviation. The two groups differed on all of the variables in the content cluster.

Depressive Spectrum Conditions. The solution for this equation used four scales, with the following betas: *TSC/D* (.17), *W-DEP* (.32), *2PR* (.13), and *D-S* (−.38). All were significant. The multiple R was .67 for a variance total of 44.74%: $F(4, 402) = 81.37, p < .0000$. Means for those with a single difficulty were *TSC/D* T59.74, *W-DEP* T59.26, *2PR* T53.69, and *D-S* T49.10. The corresponding means for those with multiple difficulties were: T73.96, T72.84, T56.01, and T40.41. Whereas all of the variables in the depressive cluster reliably differentiated between the groups, only those in the equation were sources of more independent variation.

Anxiety Spectrum Conditions. A large multiple R (.70) resulted from the solution to this equation: $F(5, 401) = 79.18, p < .0000$. The solution expressed 49.68% of the variance. These were the scales that reliably remained in the regression equation plus their respective betas: *PtK* (−.12), *TSC/T* (.26), *ANX* (−.44), *A* (.49), and *PK* (.44). Means for one difficulty ranged from T57.12 (*A*) to T59.26 (*ANX*); those for multiple difficulties went from T65.38 (*PtK*) to T72.67 (*PK*).

Obsessions and Phobias. A smaller amount of variance was captured by the scales in this part of the anxiety cluster (29.26%) based on a multiple R of .54. The result, nevertheless, was highly reliable: $F(3, 403) = 55.56, p < .0000$. The *I-*

OC scale's share of variance was totally provided by *OBS* (beta .42). Two other reliable scales and their shares were: *FRS* (−.21) and *W-PHO* (.38). Means of the two groups were all clearly spaced apart from each other: One difficulty versus multiple difficulties (*OBS* T55.50 vs. T65.65; *FRS* T53.25 vs. T60.03; *W-PHO* T53.08 vs. T60.03).

Cognitive Disorders. IQs were again checked and no differences were present between the two groups. Only two scales reliably distinguished the groups from one another: *2MD* (beta .19), whose means were for one difficulty T59.34 and for multiple difficulties T69.13; and *TSC/A* (beta .48), whose means were for one difficulty T53.17 and for multiple difficulties T64.85. The two groups differed: $F(2, 404) = 97.89$, $p < .0000$, $R = .57$, R squared .33.

Somatic Concerns. The scales *Hs* (beta .73), *HsK* (beta −.69), *HEA* (beta −.36), *TSC/B* (beta .41), and *Ho* (beta .37) together predicted 37.40% of the difference between the two groups ($R = .61$). Their respective means for one and multiple difficulty groups were: *Hs* T58.24 and T62.65; *HsK* T56.06 and T54.93; *HEA* T57.73 and T62.13; *TSC/B* T57.77 and T63.53; and *Ho* T54.40 and T67.94. The overall result was significant: $F(5, 401) = 47.91$, $p < .0000$.

Stimulus Seeking and Drive. Four scales from this content cluster contributed to predicting the psychosocial score. They and their betas were: *Ma* (1.96), *MaK* (−1.88), *2PR* (.31), and *9EI* (.17). Note that *9EI*, which fits here, was not a reliable indicator of the difference reported earlier between the no difficulties group and those who reported having psychosocial difficulties. The present solution produced a multiple *R* of .62 and a matching variance of 39.02%, with an *F* ratio $(4, 402) = 64.31$, $p < .0000$. The single psychosocial difficulty group was contrasted with the multiple difficulties group, revealing the following means, respectively: *Ma* T54.11 vs. T60.45; *MaK* T53.58 vs. T58.19; *2PR* T54.73 vs. T68.11; and *9EI* T52.57 vs. T61.45.

Substance Dependency. In the final comparison of this configuration, once again, *MAC-R* failed to aid in prediction of psychosocial difficulties. At the same time, *APS* offered a low efficiency prediction ($t = 2.81$, $df = 405$, $p < .01$). The means of the two groups for *APS*, however, were out of line with the known high incidence of substance dependency in the hospital sample. Thus, neither of the scales offered a reliable means of estimating levels of psychosocial difficulties.

CONCLUSIONS

In chapter 7, the six Psychosocial scales were compared with other positive attribute scales in order to illustrate both how they resemble and differ from those that are most widely used. Second, they were analyzed relative to the new *MMPI–2*

Content Scales. Each individual Psychosocial scale was shown in those studies to exhibit reliable and meaningful relationships. The present chapter began by extending those studies of individual scales. After that, it raised their analysis to another level by examining the larger issue of how psychosocial difficulties relate to Axis I disorders. The way this was accomplished is summarized briefly.

Patients Reporting Psychosocial vs. No Psychosocial Difficulties

Analyses were performed of patient reported psychosocial difficulties with data arranged in two configurations. In the first of these configurations, valid adult patient records were divided into one group who reported no psychosocial difficulties and a second group who reported having one or more psychosocial difficulties. That is, the latter group received very low scores ($< T36$) on one or more of the six scales that were constructed to represent aspects of life crises first identified by Erikson (1963). The two groups were then compared by regression analyses in which the predictor variables were *MMPI–2* scales organized into content clusters that correspond broadly to approximated *DSM* Axis I categories.

The prediction equations effectively differentiated between the two groups by drawing in separate analyses on content cluster scales that represented thought process disorders (i.e., the psychoses), depressive spectrum conditions, anxiety spectrum conditions, obsessions and phobias, nonintellective cognitive disorders, somatic concerns, and stimulus seeking and drive (i.e., bipolarlike manifestations). Substance dependency scales failed to identify the groups meaningfully.

The findings demonstrate that patients who report psychosocial difficulties differ significantly from those who do not in multiple ways relative to Axis I conditions. It may reasonably be hoped that future studies with these scales will increase understanding of the etiology of various major psychiatric disorders that may have their origins in failure to gain those life skills that arise from more successful and balanced resolution of each of the psychosocial crises.

Single Versus Multiple Psychosocial Difficulties

The subset of valid adult records for patients who had reported one or more psychosocial difficulties was further examined with the data configured a second way. The sample was now partitioned into two new groupings: those who had reported a psychosocial difficulty on only one of the scales, and those who had reported three or more (i.e., up to six possible) psychosocial difficulties.

Regression analyses were again carried out. The content clusters representing Axis I disorders again reliably differentiated the groups—this time for patients reporting single versus multiple psychosocial difficulties. It is important further to note that the most predictive cluster scales tended to reemerge in both series of regression analyses. On a more cautionary note, it can be seen by inspecting the two sets of findings that scales that were useful in one prediction context were not equally effective in the other and sometimes even dropped out.

Contributions of the Clinical Scales

The traditional Clinical scales were included in the content clusters along with other scales and entered in all preliminary prediction equations. Six Clinical scales (*Hs, D, Pa, Pt, Sc, Ma*) were entered into prediction equations with the content clusters to which they belonged respectively. All except *D* contributed to the regression solutions. In all instances, other scales added incrementally to prediction results. Implications for future prediction refinement can be gained from the foregoing and also from the manner in which clinical scales in *K*-corrected and noncorrected forms interacted with one another in ways that increased the total variance extracted.

The failure of *D* to contribute to the solution for the Depressive Spectrum cluster raises the question of why it failed to do so when *Hs, Pa, Pt, Sc,* and *Ma* all contributed to predicting psychosocial difficulties. One possibility is that the *D* scale is more complex than are the other four scales. If that is the reason, then it is not likely an artifact of the scale's construction but instead a result of the complexity of the depressive syndrome itself. The degree of this disorder's complexity is evident in the *DSM–IV* alternative criteria that apply to it: mood is either depressed or person is anhedonic; weight is either up or down; insomnia or hypersomnia is present; there is reduced ability to concentrate or indecision. Combinations of these varying criteria along with others result in multiple possible clinical pictures, all of which have one name: *depressive disorders*.

The two configurations used in analyses were designed to answer specific questions, as noted earlier. A third configuration was used in regression analyses but was omitted from the preceding reporting for the first two. Its purpose was simply to estimate the maximum *R* obtainable. It is mentioned briefly here. It compared those with no psychosocial difficulties to those who had three or more. Of course, this resulted in larger mean group differences on all relevant scales. For these comparisons, multiple *R*'s accordingly were larger (range = .67–82, *M* = 75.14, median 72) than for no difficulties vs. difficulties (range = .56–.69, *M* = 63.29, median 65) and one vs. multiple difficulties (range = .54–.72, *M* = 63.29, median 62). Substance dependency prediction remained very weak, with only *APS* relating to psychosocial difficulties.

Other Conclusions

In keeping with Erikson's (1963) conception of normative life crises, these findings support the conclusion that psychosocial difficulties exist and in measurable quantity. Hence, both the presence of psychosocial difficulty and a greater loading of psychosocial difficulties appear to be associated with increased proneness to major psychiatric disorders.

Extreme psychosocial scores, whether high or low, were found to be unusual events that call for additional examination of the *MMPI-2* record's validity—at least insofar as regards these six scales. Highly elevated scores suggest possible exaggeration of one's positive attributes. These rarely appeared in valid patient records and never exceeded T70. Even among invalid records, high scores were scarce. Scores falling three or more standard deviations below the mean (i.e., T20 and below) were also unusual even in this population. These findings favor interpreting only psychosocial scores that do not fall outside of these boundaries. Those outside the limits will be seen usually as invalid.

Finding that extreme scores are questionable and that more modestly elevated or depressed scores are more interpretable also corresponds to the expectations based on Erikson (1963). That is, psychosocial coping resources are unlikely to be altogether absent, no matter how unfavorable a person's adjustment may appear to be. This was demonstrated when valid but very low scoring patient records were found, on average, to include positive self-attributions ranging from 45.1% to 54.6% to items on these six scales. Likewise, overwhelming levels of psychosocial coping resources are unlikely to be found in ordinary humans. Perhaps this occurs, but it is rarely expected even among those identified as highly favored, self-actualizing persons (Maslow, 1968). This patient sample provided no opportunity to evaluate the valid upper limits of positive responding. Study of those limits must be left for others who work with very different populations.

PREVIEW OF CHAPTER 9

Chapter 8 completed an initial tour through the Axis I disorders. Chapter 9 turns attention to the Axis II traits and disorders. Previously well-studied traits (e.g., social maladjustment) are explored using the scales of related content clusters while following the same data configuration designs that were used for Axis I in this chapter. Different approaches are taken to the analysis of the Axis II-listed personality disorders by focusing on both the general descriptions and specified criteria that appear in *DSM-IV*.

9

Clusters, Personality Traits, and Disorders

This chapter first uses the two data configurations that were introduced in chapter 8 to explore a series of content clusters that encompass major personality trait complexes. Each cluster has a vital bearing on criteria that define personality traits and the *DSM* Axis II designated disorders. What is known about them provides substantive material that is needed in order to implement the current approach to diagnosing the personality disorders (*PDO*s). The second half of the chapter examines the individual *PDO*s.

THE SOCIAL MALADJUSTMENT AND SOCIAL ANXIETY CLUSTER

Social Maladjustment/Introversion Scales

Dimensions of maladjustment can be identified relative to special areas of the person's functioning: marital, school, work, and so on. The present focus, however, is not on specific areas of functioning, but rather on maladjustment from its most global perspective. Four *MMPI–2* scales offer this global view: *SOD*, *TSC/I*, *W-SOC*, and *Si*. The *Si* scale is the most multifaceted.

These four scales equally may be seen to measure introversion. There can be no firm line of demarcation between social maladjustment and introversion in the popular, mass culture of contemporary America. It is a culture that values popularity, public persona, celebrity, and extraversion. Their opposites are not affirmed. Thus, social maladjustment and introversion share a common core of connotative meaning. The public perception thereby becomes the intrapsychic reality. So persons who by disposition exhibit a shrinking style of social behavior will often come to believe that their persona is unacceptable and that they are maladjusted.

It is apparent when examining the foregoing scales that they measure similar qualities. *SOD, TSC/I,* and *W-SOC* all correlate .90 to .91 with *Si* in the sample of 1,516 valid cases. This occurs because a majority of the items in each scale also are in *Si.* On the other hand, two thirds of *Si*'s items either appear in none of the other three scales or in only one of them. *SOD* has 5 items that are unique to it (20.83%) among the four scales. Relative to *SOD* and *W-SOC,* the *TSC/I* scale has 6 unique items (23.08%), but only 4 are unique relative to *Si* (15.38%). *W-SOC* has 5 items (19.23%) unique from *SOD* and *TSC/I* and 3 unique from *Si* (11.54%).

Although the numbers of nonoverlapping items are small for all of the scales except *Si,* their presence allows for nuances of scale meaning. *TSC/I*'s unique items place greater emphasis on maladjustment; those of *W-SOC* on unwelcome social reticence; and those of *SOD* on a preference for solitude. Therefore, despite their similarities, all four scales were entered into a preliminary prediction equation along with *Si1, Si2,* and Imperturbability (*Impert*). *Impert* is a scale that measures denial of social anxiety by merging items from *3DSA, 4SI,* and *9IMP.*

No Psychosocial Difficulties vs. Difficulties

All of the previously listed scales, except *W-SOC,* reliably remained in the final regression solution. Betas assigned to the scales were *Si* (.40), *SOD* (.39), *TSC/I* (.69), *Si1* (−1.00), *Si2* (−.44), and *Impert* (−.35). The multiple *R* of .57 resolved 32.36% of the variance for the two groups: $F(6, 1013) = 80.77, p < .0000.$ Means for the difficulties vs. none groups, respectively, were: *Si* (T47.56 vs. T57.89), *SOD* (T45.92 vs. T54.40), *TSC/I* (T44.99 vs. T58.86), *Si1* (T46.58 vs. T55.35), *Si2* (T47.01 vs. T51.83), and *Impert* (T53.33 vs. T43.02). Those with psychosocial difficulties were higher on all maladjustment/introversion scales and lower on imperturbability/denial of social anxiety, but they were not markedly more socially avoidant. Maladjustment/introversion remains an intermingled construct in the regression solution.

Single vs. Multiple Psychosocial Difficulties

The preliminary equation for this analysis included the same scales as did the preceding one. The reliable scales with their betas and respective means for multiple vs. single difficulties were: *Si* (.29) (T53.56 vs. T63.52); *TSC/I* (.46) (T53.10 vs. T66.70); *Si1* (−.56) (T51.32 vs. T60.69); *Si2* (−.13) (T49.53 vs. T55.11); and *Impert* (−.45) (T47.82 vs. T37.03). The overall solution produced $R = .54, 29.22\%$ of variance accounted for, and $F(5, 401) = 33.11, p < .0000.$ Compared with the solution for difficulties vs. none, this one assigned more emphasis to maladjustment as seen by both *W-SOC* and *SOD* disappearing from the solution.

SOCIAL VULNERABILITY AND ALIENATION

Feelings of social vulnerability and alienation are often close companions of social anxiety and maladjustment. This small cluster contains *6P* and *So-Alien*, a scale comprised of items from *4SOA*, as expanded, and *8SOA* (see Appendixes A and B). The solutions for both of the data analysis configurations selected the same two variables: *6P* and *So-Alien*.

For the no psychosocial difficulties vs. difficulties equation, a multiple R of .56 resulted in a determination of 31.62% of the variance, $F(2, 1017) = 235.18, p < .0000$. Beta for *6P* was .17 and the respective means were T48.15 vs. T57.73; for *So-Alien*, beta was .45 with means of T49.59 vs. T61.96.

For the single vs. multiple psychosocial difficulties solution, a multiple R of .66 led to 43.2% of the variance being determined, $F(2, 404) = 153.71, p < .0000$. Beta for *6P* was .16 with respective means of T53.56 vs. T63.69; for *So-Alien*, beta was .56 with means of T56.48 vs. T70.09. Those with no difficulties in the first comparison, and those with a single difficulty in the second, both expressed less feelings of vulnerability and less social alienation than did their respective comparison groups.

ANGER, HOSTILITY, SUSPICION, CYNICISM, RESENTMENT

Scales that were entered into the preliminary equation for this personality trait complex were *ANG, W-HOS, TSC/R, O-H, TPA, CYN, HO, TSC/S, Sadist*. Four of these were retained in the comparison of no psychosocial difficulties vs. psychosocial difficulties. These with their betas and means for the two groups were: *TSC/R* (.30) (T46.37 vs. T60.24); *O-H* (−.19) (T54.56 vs. T40.65); *CYN* (−.15) (T50.47 vs. T57.72); and *Ho* (.28) (T47.64 vs. T59.43). These mean differences in combination produced a variance resolution of 34.78% and a multiple R of .59, $F(4, 1015) = 135.30, p < .0000$.

A different combination of scales was required to predict how those with a single difficulty might differ from those with multiple difficulties. *O-H* was now absent and five scales entered the equation. Those with their betas and means for the respective groups were: *ANG* (−.22) (T51.47 vs. T58.91); *TSC/R* (.52) (T54.68 vs. T67.80); *CYN* (−.24) (T54.53 vs. T63.34); *Ho* (.32) (T54.40 vs. T67.94); and *TSC/S* (.28) (T55.81 vs. T69.18). The regression equation produced a multiple R of .64, $F(5, 401) = 57.00, p < .0000$ and accounted for 41.54% of group differences.

In the first of the two analyses, those with no reported psychosocial difficulties were low on resentments, cynicism, and hostility and were overcontrolling of hostile expression. Compared with patients who reported multiple difficulties, those with a single psychosocial difficulty expressed less anger, resentment, cynicism, hostility, and suspiciousness. The multiple difficulty patients' scores were from 1.3 to 1.9 standard deviations above CX norms for four of the scales but not for *ANG*.

VIRTUE AND MORALITY

The scales entered in the preliminary analysis were *Hy, 3NA, 6N, Trust, 9AMO, L*, and *5C*, based on observations made by Levitt (1989). Four of the six scales were accepted in the equation that compared patients with no psychosocial difficulties to those who reported difficulties. The betas and means of the two respective groups for the reliable scales were: *Hy* (.32) (T54.77 vs. T56.64); *3NA* (−.45) (T53.34 vs. T45.06); *9AMO* (.08), (T47.71 vs. T52.45); and *L* (−.15) (T60.62 vs. T53.68). The solution explained 25.67% of the variance for the two groups, with a multiple *R* of .51, $F(4, 1015) = 87.63$, $p < .0000$. Although some support was given to this composite, the relation found is a modest one.

When those with a single difficulty were compared to those with multiple difficulties, a different combination of four scales was needed to predict membership in the two groups. Now the effective scales, with their betas and respective means, were: *Hy* (.13) (T57.63 vs. T53.81); *3NA* (−.36) (T48.73 vs. T39.08); *6N* (−.15) (T47.85 vs. T38.68); and *L* (−.16) (T55.90 vs. T50.07). The solution associated 25.53% of the variance with group membership, with a multiple *R* of .51, $F(4, 402) = 34.46$, $p < .0000$.

As in the result for the first of the two comparisons, the relation is modest. Although *Hy* was not included in Levitt's original observation, the relations in both sets of comparisons were even less impressive when it was left out of the equations. It is concluded that the issue of virtue, although not irrelevant, was somewhat less salient psychosocially in this patient population than were the other issues already reviewed.

BEHAVIOR CONTROLS AND NORMS VIOLATIONS

The opposing side of the Virtue and Morality cluster appears in the current cluster. Scales for the behavior controls part of this cluster are any combination of the three individual components *Imp-B, Imp-I, Imp-A*, or the total *Imp-T, 8DI, 9EI, R*, and *Re*. Although *3IA* is unreliable, it was also given an opportunity to appear in the equation. Scales for the norms violations part of the cluster are *Pd, PdK, ASP, W-AUT, MAC-R*, and *APS*. The unreliable *4AC* was given a trial here.

The no psychosocial difficulties vs. difficulties groups were differentiated by a weighted combination of the following scales, whose betas and respective means were: *Pd* (1.19) (T56.65 vs. T65.62); *PdK* (−.91) (T58.47 vs. T62.86); *MAC-R* (−.19) (T59.31 vs. T61.25); *Imp-T* (.12) (T47.20 vs. T59.74); and *8DI* (.12) (T48.87 vs. T58.53). This group of scales differentiated the groups with a multiple R of .62, 38.56% of the variance resolved, and $F(5, 1014) = 127.26, p < .0000$.

A comparison was also made of patients with a single psychosocial difficulty versus those with multiple difficulties. The same five scales plus one additional scale, *9EI*, successfully separated these groups. The betas and respective means for the effective scales were: *Pd* (1.13) (T63.32 vs. T69.84); *PdK* (−.99) (T62.05 vs. T64.72); *MAC-R* (−.21) (T61.19 vs. T62.89); *Imp-T* (.16) (T55.15 vs. T67.05); *8DI* (.14) (T54.60 vs. T64.45); and *9EI* (.14) (T53.57 vs. T61.45). With a multiple R of .63, 40.26% of the intergroup variance was explained with $F(6, 400) = 44.93$, $p < .0000$.

Patients with psychosocial difficulties showed, on average, more antisocial tendencies, were undercontrolled with defects of inhibition, and were slightly more likely to have an alcohol or other substance problem. Those patients who reported multiple psychosocial difficulties compared less favorably with those who reported a single difficulty in these respects. They had slightly more antisocial traits and substance abuse problems; were considerably more impulsive with defective inhibition; and expressed greater ego expansiveness. The two unreliable Harris–Lingoes Subscales *3IA* and *4AC*, scored in the usual manner, failed to contribute useful variance beyond what was available from the other scales in the Behavior Controls & Norms Violations regression equations.

GENDER AND SEXUALITY

This cluster was represented by the following scales: *Mf, GM, GF,* and *Sexual* intimacy failure. All four were accepted as reliable in the regression equation that compared patients with no psychosocial difficulties with those who reported difficulties. Betas and means for these respective groups were: *Mf* (.07) (T44.11 vs. T47.86); *GM* (.27) (T49.13 vs. T40.06); *GF* (.08) (T46.66 vs. T45.97); and *Sexual* (.34) (T45.44 vs. T55.76). The overall regression equation resulted in a multiple R of .54, accounting for 29.06% of the variance, and $F(4, 1015) = 103.94, p < .0000$.

Patients with a single vs. multiple psychosocial difficulties were distinguished from one another by three of the four scales. Those scales with their betas and respective means for single vs. multiple difficulties were: *GM* (−.27) (T43.84 vs. T36.24); *GF* (−.14) (T47.11 vs. T44.17); and *Sexual* (.39) (T51.05 vs. T62.14). The composite difference between the two groups, based on these three scales, accounted for 32.11% of the variance with a multiple R of .57, $F(3, 403) = 63.54, p < .0000$.

In both group comparisons, patients who had more psychosocial difficulties had significantly fewer of the favorable gender qualities of either males or females and reported markedly more signs of sexuality and intimacy failure. All of the correlations among the scales in these two analyses were highly similar when computed separately by gender. This also was the case for their correlations with dichotomized variables that represented the group classifications. Hence female and male samples were merged. For this reason, the conclusions stated here hold for each gender as well as for the merged samples.

SELF-ESTEEM

The cluster scales that were available for preliminary analysis were *LSE, W-MOR, I-SC, 5C*, and *So*. Three scales highlighted differences between patients who had reported no psychosocial difficulties with those who had difficulties. Those scales with their betas and means for the respective groups were: *W-MOR* (.24) (T48.57 vs. T63.25); *I-SC* (.15) (T49.09 vs. T61.79); and *So* (−.25) (T52.21 vs. T37.50). All three scales are comprised of obvious item content. A satisfactory solution was obtained with multiple $R = .58$, total variance between groups 33.43%, $F(3, 1016) = 170.10$, $p < .0000$.

Both *W-MOR* and *So* from the prior list, along with *5C*, determined the solution to the equation that compared patients with a single difficulty to those who reported multiple difficulties. Respective group means and betas for the three scales were: *W-MOR* (.43) (T58.07 vs. 70.26); *So* (−.20) (T42.84 vs. T30.57); and *5C* (−.23) (T49.85 vs. T42.65). The two groups were clearly separated by the three predictor scales: $R = .68$, variance accounted for of 46.79%, $F(3, 403) = 118.13$, $p < .0000$.

Patients with reported psychosocial difficulties differed from those who reported none by reporting poorer morale, low self-esteem, and by attributing fewer obviously socially desirable qualities to themselves. Next, comparing those who reported multiple difficulties with those signifying a single difficulty, the multiple difficulties patients had much poorer morale, attributed an exceedingly low number of socially desirable qualities to themselves, and were lower in conventionality.

DEPENDENCY–DOMINANCE

These are the scales available for this cluster: *Do, I-Do, Depnd*, and *Re*. The unreliable *I-De* scale was subjected to an additional check by its inclusion with the other listed scales in order to find how it might perform in this more restricted context. The scales that determined the distance between patients with no psychosocial difficulties and those with difficulties, with their respective means and betas, were: *Do* (−.25) (T47.54 vs. T35.22); *Re* (.10) (T49.01 vs. T41.80); and *Depnd* (.37) (T47.23 vs. T62.53). This combination of scales explained 28.16% of the between-groups variance with $R = .53$, $F(3, 1016) = 132.74$, $p < .0000$.

A comparison was also made of patients who reported a single difficulty versus those with multiple psychosocial difficulties. The same three scales as those accepted in the preceding analysis were useful in differentiating the present groups. The new betas and respective means for single vs. multiple difficulties groups were: *Do* (−.22) (T39.88 vs. T29.16); *Re* (−.13) (T44.36 vs. T38.04); and *Depnd* (.41) (T56.72 vs. T70.26). The solution received a multiple $R = .62$, explained 38.56% of intergroup variance, and was highly significant: $F(3, 403) = 84.294$, $p < .0000$.

Patients with no reported psychosocial difficulties represented themselves, on average, as being similar to CX norms (i.e., near the 50th percentile) in being socially responsible, having some influence and leadership qualities, and not being burdened with low self-confidence due to dependency needs. Their counterparts who reported difficulties presented themselves as having less desirable qualities in all of those same respects. Patients who reported a single difficulty portrayed themselves on the three scales as having fewer desirable qualities than did those who were at the average of CX norms, whereas those with multiple problems described themselves in strikingly negative terms on those same scales. Based on the regression solutions, it would be as reasonable to think of this cluster in terms of high self-confidence and social responsibility vs. low self-confidence.

FAMILY RELATIONSHIP ISSUES

Four scales were available in this cluster: *FAM, W-FAM*, and two variants of *4FD*. One variant of the scale is designated *4FD-1*, the other *4FD-2*. The version called *4FD-1* contains the widely used form of that scale after removal of item 214. Restoration in the second version of Harris and Lingoes items 190 and 455 results in the scale designated *4FD-2*.

A regression equation comparing those with no psychosocial difficulties and those who reported difficulties selected three of the scales. Those scales with their betas and respective means for no difficulties vs. difficulties groups were: *FAM* (.25) (T51.44 vs. T60.56); *W-FAM* (.28) (T51.72 vs. T60.63); and *4FD-2* (−.18) (T51.37 vs. T57.88). These scales resolved only 13.6% of the intergroup variance, $R = .37$, $F(3, 1016) = 53.51$, $p < .0000$.

For the comparison of patients with a single vs. multiple difficulties, there was no unique regression solution. However, the scale *FAM* alone distinguished between the groups, $t = 8.88$, $df = 405$, $p < .0000$. The means were: single T56.42 and multiple T66.98. Simply stated, these analyses together indicated that patients with psychosocial difficulties report more family problems and these problems are magnified when a greater number of those difficulties are present.

DSM-LINKED PERSONALITY DISORDERS (*PDO*s)

Chapter 6 prepared the stage for examining these diagnostic groups. Briefly stated, the valid records of adult patients who scored at the 85th percentile on any *PDO* scale were compared with those of 157 valid adult patients who scored at or below 72nd percentile on all 11 scales. Comparisons were made using *t* tests for independent samples. The scales analyzed for each disorder were selected for their potential relevance to *DSM–IV* classification criteria. In the presentations that follow, when abbreviated reference is made to a scale it appears in capital letters (e.g., for Antisocial: *ANTI*) and when a classified patient group is referenced only the first letter is capitalized (e.g., Anti).

Adjusting upper and lower cutoffs to the specified percentile levels resulted in minor changes in means for the *PDO*s. If these were reported here, they could be a potential source of confusion. For example, persons trying to replicate any of these findings could find it more difficult to do so. Thus, although the specified cutoffs were used to classify cases, mean *T*-scores that are reported in the following accounts were computed in the usual unadjusted manner. That is, they are based on the CX means and estimated standard deviations reported in Appendix B for the *PDO*s. Means for other scales were unaffected because they were not adjusted to match percentile levels.

Mixed *PDO*s

Mixed *PDO*s present a potential source of confusion for classifying cases in view of their high ranging means on each of the *PDO* scales. These are as high as T69.90 for the BORD scale to a low of T57.63 for SCZD. All of the Mixed *PDO* means, however, were lower by 1.00 to 1.95 standard deviations than the means of the classified *PDO*s, when comparisons were made of their respective paired values (all *p*s < .000). There was a single exception to this finding. The mean NARC scale values for the Narc *PDO* T67.69 and Mixed *PDO* T60.83 differed by only 0.69 of a standard deviation.

It can be inferred from the relative means of the Mixed group across the 11 *PDO* scales that they on average reported, in descending order, high levels of borderline traits; intermediate levels of histrionic, passive–aggressive, antisocial and avoidant; and lower levels of dependent, obsessive–compulsive, paranoid, narcissistic, schizotypal, and schizoid traits.

Antisocial (*Anti*) *PDO*

On the *ANTI PDO* scale, the comparison (Comp) group had a mean score of T48.14 vs. the Anti (*n* = 33) patient group's T77.25. None of the other classified patient groups had a mean greater than the Passive–Aggressive (Paag) *PDO* group's T63.47 on the scale (i.e., a 1.38 *SD* separation). It is, nevertheless, important to differentiate the Anti group from Paag patients, because they have some similar scale elevations. The Anti group also differs from Paag patients by having significantly higher elevations on *ASP, 9AMO,* and *W-AUT.*

Scales used to contrast the Anti and Comp samples and their respective means were *ASP* (T70.28 & T47.85), *9AMO* (T63.32 & T45.80), *W-AUT* (T67.22 & T48.67), *Imp-B* (T68.45 & T50.92), *Imp-T* (T67.41 & T44.64), *Re* (T31.82 & T48.84), *CYN* (T63.26 & T48.27), *Ho* (T63.27 & T44.07), *TSC/S* (T63.53 & T46.71), *Sadist* (T58.44 & T44.98), *O-H* (T41.29 & T56.94), *Trust* (T38.28 & T55.87), *Cared for vs. Neglected* (T41.04 & T53.87), and *Initiating vs. Guilt-Prone* (T36.31 & T52.90).

All contrasting pairs of means differed by more than one standard deviation with a minimum value for $t > 7.5$ and $p < .000$ for all pairs. The scores on the selected scales for the Anti group corresponded to *DSM* criteria of norm violating behavior, impulsivity, irritability, recklessness, irresponsibility, callousness, and deceitfulness as evidenced by suspicion and mistrust.

Paranoid *(Prnd) PDO*

Patients classified as Prnd *PDO* ($n = 16$) contrast with the Comp group by being more suspicious (means)—*TSC/S* (T68.39 & T46.71) and *S+* (T67.13 & T47.29); mistrusting of others—*Cared for vs. Neglected* (T34.75 & T53.87); concerned with hidden meanings—*6PI* (T80.59 & T50.48); alienated and feeling put upon by others—*SoAlien* (T65.83 & T47.20); and resentful and prone to hold grudges—*TSC/R* (T60.03 & T43.29). Results of all of the preceding contrasts were highly significant (all $ts > 8.00$ and $ps < .000$).

Prnd patients received a mean *PRND PDO* scale of T72.96, whereas the Comp patients had a mean of T44.76. Their mean for *PRND* clearly differed from groups of patients classified as Anti, Bord, and Narc. It, however, exceeded the mean of Sczy patients by a less distinguishing amount (T72.96 vs. T65.50; 0.75 *SD*). Sczy differed from Prnd patients by obtaining higher scores on *BIZ, I-RD,* and *SCZY* scales. Moreover, during clinical contact, they present behaviorally as being distinct from one another.

Narcissistic *(Narc) PDO*

The total sample yielded 16 patients classified as Narc. Their mean classification score of T67.69 clearly separated them from the Comp group's mean of T42.16. Some challenges were encountered, however, when trying to differentiate them from Anti, Prnd, and Obcp patients. Narc patients differed from the Anti group by having less elevation on scales like *W-AUT, ASP,* and *9AMO,* and Anti patients were 1.68 standard deviations higher than Narc on the ANTI scale. The Prnd dif-

fered from Narc by having distinctly higher scores on *S+* and *6PI*, in addition to a
mean that was higher than the Narc group's by 1.66 standard deviations on
PRND. Finally, Narc and Obcp patients clearly differed from one another on their
respective classification scales, NARC and OBCP, by over 1.47 standard deviations for each comparison.

In evaluating Narc patients, it is more difficult to link specific *MMPI–2* scales
up with the individual *DSM* criteria. A more general match is achieved by recognizing the underlying burden of narcissistic pain, humiliation, and rage that may
not be as publicly exhibited by these patients. With this caveat in mind, Narc and
Comp groups were contrasted on the following scales: *ANG, W-HOS, TSC/R, Ho,
CYN, Sadist, Imp-I, W-AUT, 6P, SoAlien, Sexual*, and *Cared for vs. Neglected*.
The Narc group expressed more anger, hostility, resentment, cynicism, callousness, authority conflict, impulsive thinking, social vulnerability, alienation, intimacy failure, and feelings of not having their needs met. Group differences were
statistically reliable ($p < .000$) for all 12 scales.

Histrionic (*Hist*) PDO

DSM criteria for the Hist disorder generally are of a kind that would require direct
interaction with the patient before they could be reliably identified. Moreover, it is
implausible that a Hist patient would have both the insight and openness to make
self-reference statements that correspond directly to the eight *DSM* listed criteria.
As in the case for the Narc disorder, however, *MMPI–2* scales can tap into relevant subjective feelings, attitudes, and dispositions that do relate to the explicated
criteria.

The *HIST* scale did succeed in separating 21 Hist patients, for example, from
both Narc and Obcp patients by in excess of 1.7 standard deviations in each instance (both *ps* < .000). Hist patients were markedly higher than the Obcp patients
on *W-HYP* and *8EA*, but lower than they on *TSC/S* and *I-OC*. They were more
than one standard deviation above the Narc group on *Imp-A* and *W-HYP*.

Relative to the Comp group, Hists more often expressed mild dysphoria of
both depressive and anxious types (e.g., on *DEP* and *ANX*), greater dependency
needs (*Depnd*), poor morale (*W-MOR*), proneness to anger and resentment (*ANG
& TSC/R*), emotional lability (*Imp-A*), and need for stimulation (*W-HYP*), all at
probabilities of less than .000. Together these scores do afford hints as to the Hist
patient's abundant emotionality and interpersonal neediness.

Borderline (*Bord*) PDO

Not surprisingly, a substantial number of Bord ($n = 32$) patients were identified
within this sample. Their mean on the BORD scale clearly sets them apart from
the Hist group, as it does also for Prnd, Avdt, Paag, Bord, Depnd, and Szty—the

groups that, like Bord, display increased emotional disturbance. For this reason, they are also high on the *Dist* scale.

In the basic analysis of contrasts with the Comp patients, the Bord group expressed very high levels of depression and anxiety (*DEP & ANX*); moderate levels of cognitive disturbance (*2MD, 8COG, TSC/A, W-ORG*), angry feelings (*ANG, TSC/R, Ho*), impulsivity (*Imp-B, Imp-A*), excitement seeking (*W-HYP*), social vulnerability, and alienation (*6P & SoAlien*); and very low sense of industry (*Industrious vs. Inadequate*). All of these differences between Bord and Comp groups were highly significant ($p < .000$) and capture the flavor of the *DSM*'s general description of the borderline disorder.

Passive–Aggressive (*Paag*) PDO

Patients classified as Paag ($n = 13$) were the least frequently encountered in this hospitalized group, although the passive–aggressive trait was moderately present in the Mixed disorders. Thus, this interpersonal style occurred more often in combination with other traits than as an isolated pattern in this patient sample. A method for distinguishing Paag from Anti and Bord was discussed earlier. Paag patients differed from Dpnd patients by reporting less depression (*D, TSC/D, 2SD*) and social maladjustment (*SOD, TSC/I*); and more interpersonal forcefulness (*I-Do*), obsessionality (*I-OC*), hostility (*W-HOS*), ego inflation (*9EI*), and regrets and guilt (*Initiating vs. Guilt-Prone*).

Contrasting with the Comp group, Paag patients reported symptoms of depressed mood (*DEP, W-DEP, 2PR*), dependency (*Depnd*), low morale (*W-MOR*), tension and panic symptoms (*TSC/T, ANX, Panic*), remorse (*4SA*), obsessions (*OBS*), hostility and resentments (*W-HOS, TSC/R*), impulsivity (*Imp-T*), inflated sense of entitlement (*9EI*), authority problems (*W-AUT*), social alienation (*SoAlien*), problems with intimacy (*Sexual*), and issues with all six of the Psychosocial scales. For all of these contrasts, Paag differed significantly from Comp ($p < .000$). When used together with the *PAAG* scale, these scales were judged to cover most of the criterial characteristics for this disorder.

Dependent (*Dpnd*) PDO

Benchmarks for differentiating Dpnd *PDOs* ($n = 22$) from the Paag *PDO* were reviewed earlier. The Dpnd group contrasted relative to the Comp group with an exceedingly high mean *DPND* score (T82.30 vs. T46.20 for Comp). It was well separated from the remaining *PDOs* by this same scale.

Dpnd's distinctives when compared with the Comp group's included most of the *DSM* criterial issues. These were their dependency, low self-confidence, and poor morale (*Depnd, Do, W-MOR, LSE*); reduced energy and motivation to act independently (*2PR & 8CON*); experienced psychosocial deficiencies in the areas of industry, identity, autonomy, and intimacy in particular (all Psychosocial scales); social anxiety, maladjustment, and discomfort (*Impert, TSC/I, SOD*); high levels of both depression and anxiety complaints, with the former exceeding the latter (i.e., *TSC/D & DEP > ANX & TSC/T*); and interpersonal dissatisfactions and resentments more prominent than anger and hostility (*SoAlien & TSC/R > ANG & W-HOS*). All listed scales differentiated the Dpnd from the Comp group at highly significant levels ($p < .000$).

Obsessive–Compulsive (*Obcp*) PDO

For some comparisons, the Obcp patients ($n = 28$) resembled the Narc, Hist, and Dpnd groups. Earlier discussions of all three provided distinctives that set the Obcp apart from those disorders that score similarly to it on some clusters. The *OBCP* scale's mean for the Obcp group (T73.79) clearly set it apart from the Comp group (T46.46).

Obcp patient scores for scales in the major affective and mental illness clusters were noteworthy for being lower than is true for most other *PDO*s, even though those same scores were reliably higher than those of the Comp group. Their scores for obsessiveness were moderately elevated (*OBS* T62.37 & *I-OC* T61.60), phobias were even lower (*FRS* T58.81 & *W-PHO* T57.26), and they denied intrusive and disruptive ideation (*TSC/A* T53.77). Nevertheless, their focus on rules and order left them feeling guilty (*4SA* T64.07), with morale and self-esteem somewhat affected (*W-MOR* T60.36), and perhaps a tendency to be overly critical of themselves relative to their work accomplishments (*Industrious vs. Inadequate* T36.82).

Their emphasis on tightly guarding their impulses (*Imp-B, Imp-I*, & *Imp-A* all < T56.50) resulted in their average scores on these scales being lower than those for any other listed *PDO* group except for patients classified as Sczd. There was one cluster, however, that seemed less suppressed by their style. That is, their underlying feelings of dissatisfaction with others' imperfections burdened them with resentments, cynicism, hostility, and suspicions (*TSC/R* T60.44, *CYN* T61.35, *Ho* T60.82, *TSC/S* T66.00), but with only limited direct expression of anger or mean-spirited action (*ANG* T56.23, *Sadist* T52.33). In all of the foregoing respects, nevertheless, their average scores differed at highly significant levels from those of the Comp group ($p < .000$), with the exception of *Imp-B*, for which the difference was smaller ($p = .006$).

Avoidant (*Avdt*) PDO

Patients displaying an Avdt style ($n = 23$) resemble in ways those who are classified at Bord. The Bord patients surpassed the Avdt patients by 1.38 standard deviations on the *BORD* scale, but the Avdt patients exceeded Bord patients by only

0.82 standard deviations on the *AVDT* scale. Two other scales were highly useful for differentiating between these two groups: *ANG* and *TSC/R*, on both of which Bord patients scored significantly higher ($p < .000$). This finding relates to the intense and inappropriate anger criterion in *DSM* for the Bord *PDO*. Bords also differ from Avdts on the *PS* scale, which is an indication of their susceptibility to strong and undifferentiated episodes of intense feeling and personal instability.

It was further necessary to separate Avdt and Sczy patients, because their cluster profiles resembled one another in a number of respects. Drawing a contrast between these groups was easily accomplished first by using the *AVDT* and *SCZY* scales, on which they differed, respectively, by 1.75 and 2.10 standard deviations. Avdt patients also expressed stronger feelings of trust (*Cared for vs. Neglected* higher and *6PI* lower) and fewer psychotic thought patterns (*BIZ*) but simultaneously greater social unease (*TSC/I, W-SOC*) than did Sczy patients (all *ps* < .000). Other discriminations between Avdt *PDO*s and the remaining *PDO*s were easily accomplished.

In contrast with the Comp group, Avdt patients expressed far greater ill ease in social situations (*Si, SOD, TSC/I, W-SOC*), interpersonal vulnerability and alienation from others (*6P, SoAlien*), and self-recrimination (*4SA*); reported especially impaired functioning in the areas of autonomy, intimacy, and industry (Psychosocial scales) and interference with work performance (*WRK, WA*); lacked self-confidence and suffered with low self-esteem (*Do, LSE, W-MOR*); were subject to anxious and depressed moods (*ANX, TSC/T, DEP, W-DEP*); and offered more somatic complaints (*HEA, TSC/B, W-ORG*). This profile encompasses *DSM* criteria and associated conditions for this *PDO*. All listed Avdt differences from the Comp group were highly significant ($p < .000$).

Schizotypal (*Sczy*) PDO

Patients classified as Sczy ($n = 22$) could readily be differentiated by their mean score on the *SCZY* scale from those classified as Bord, Avdt, and Sczd. Although the *SCZY* scale did not as definitively separate the Sczy from the Prnd group, as was noted earlier, the Sczy patients' greater elevation on *BIZ* and *I-RD* made it possible to distinguish them from Prnd patients. Nevertheless, these two *PDO* groups overall produced similar *MMPI–2* cluster profiles.

In comparison with the Comp group, Sczy patients exhibited ideas of reference (*I-RD* T67.98 vs. T48.86), perceptual distortions and unusual somatic experiences (*8BSE* T67.51 vs. T50.48), and extreme suspicions and mistrust (*S+* T69.85 vs. T47.29; *Cared for vs. Neglected* T36.07 vs. T53.87); reported limited interpersonal engagement (*SoAlien* T68.37 vs. T47.20), intimacy failure (*Sexual* T57.15 vs. T43.23), little desire for affection (*3NA* T42.31 vs. T55.74), and lack of satisfactory interactions with family (*FAM* T65.07 vs. T49.80); and admission of social anxiety (*Impert* T44.48 vs. T54.35). Sczy differed from the Comp group on all of the listed scales (all *ps* < .000).

Additional criteria for this *DSM* disorder that are likely to be more accessible through face-to-face contact with the patient than by way of self-report are odd behavior and appearance, peculiar thinking and speech, and magical thinking. Individual items do, nevertheless, provide some clues regarding these expressive behavior variants.

Schizoid (*Sczd*) *PDO*

Division Into Subgroups. See chapter 6 for an introduction to recent changes made to the *SCZD* scale. As noted there, those changes still left unsettled questions about the scale's validity. For the present analysis, an additional partitioning of the Sczd (*n* = 57) patients was carried out. Each case that was classified as Sczd was examined individually in order to determine, in comparison to CX norms, what percentage of *MMPI* items were answered True. Records with fewer True responses would fall below 100% of the normative average and those with more would be above 100%. See Appendix B for CX true response norms.

A natural break was found in their True response percentage distribution between 105% and 108%. This break also happened to correspond approximately to the median. A division was then made of the Sczd sample, leaving 27 below and 30 above the natural break. Those cases that fell below the break were designated *LoTSczd*. Their percentages of True responses ranged from 73% to 105% of the normative group, with 21 of the 27 cases (77.78%) being at or below 100% True. Cases falling above the break ranged from 108% to 161% of the normative group. They were called *HiTSczd*. By these definitions, LoTSczd, on average, made fewer True responses than normals and HiTScd responded True to *MMPI* items more often than normals.

Following reclassification into the two subgroups, comparisons were made of their responses to the scales within the content clusters, including the *PDO* scales. The two subgroups were indistinguishable when their means were compared on the *SCZD* scale (LoTSczd, T75.30; HiTSczd T77.59, a nonsignificant difference). The HiTSczd group, however, had significantly higher scores on all of the remaining *PDO* scales ($p < .000$) except for the *DPND* scale. Their means for all *PDO* scales exceeded T53, whereas those of the LoTSczd were all below T50, except for the *SCZD* scale itself. The mean difference between the Hi and Lo groups for the other 10 *PDO* scales was 1.19 standard deviations.

HiTSczd and LoTSczd Differences. The HiTSczd group's highest means as well as its greatest mean differences from the LoTSczd group were on the *OBCP* scale (T60.80 vs. T44.44) and the *NARC* scale (T54.89 vs. T41.59). These findings provided another means for separating the two groups. The HiTSczd group's elevated scores on the *PDO* scales plus their overall slightly elevated cluster profile made it clear that they were not Sczd *PDO*s. That part of the sample was set aside for future study and is not further examined here.

Problems With Three Criterial Items. The LoTSczd group could now be reexamined relative to the problematic items *79, 157*, and *405* mentioned in chapter 6. Those items were keyed True in the Morey et al. (1985) overlapping schizoid scale. However, they correlated negatively in the full patient sample with the total scale score. Because the content of those items relates directly to *DSM* criteria, the negative correlations brought into question whether the present *SCZD* scale actually measures the schizoid *PDO*.

In order to evaluate this problematic finding, the percentages of the LoTSczd group who responded True to those specific items were compared with the overall percentages of other valid adults answering True to the same items. One-tail exact probability tests were performed for 27 LoTSczd versus 993 other valid adult records. Their respective percentages True for the items were: item *79* (51.85% vs. 31.42%), *157* (59.26% vs. 42.70%), *405* (88.89% vs. 69.31%).

LoTSczd Redesignated Sczd Group. In each instance, the LoTSczd patients answered True to the three items by wider margins than did all other adults with valid records (all three *p*s < .05). It is further to be noted that these patients were already classified as LoTSczd as a result of their overall lower rate of making True responses. Thus, they seemingly responded True to these three items in opposition to their demonstrated inclination to favor responding False relative to the normative CX sample. By doing so, they signified indifference to the opinions that others have of them (Items *79 & 157, DSM* Criterion *6*) and possibly flattened affect (Item *405*, Criterion *7*). With the issue of the three criterial items somewhat resolved, the LoTSczd group will be referred to provisionally as the *Sczd* patients.

The Sczd (*n* = 27) group was next contrasted with the Comp group in order to determine whether its pattern of *MMPI* scores matched criteria for the Sczd *PDO*. The overall content cluster profile of the Sczd was low and subject to only minor variations. So this group differed on few scales from the Comp group of patients who were at/below percentile 72 on all 11 *PDO* scales. This may be a result of the blandness, low affectivity, and detached nature of these individuals.

They did not report experiencing depression (*DEP* T51.90), anxiety (*ANX* T48.58), anger (*ANG* T44.29), and emotional distress (*Dist* T45.54). They denied: social anxiety and discomfort (*Impert* T52.05, *SOD* T53.18), interpersonal vulnerability (*6P* T46.70), feelings of social alienation (*SoAlien* T46.70), and being interested in excitement or social stimulation (*9PMA* T41.13, *W-HYP* T43.08). On both a measure of sexual intimacy (*Sexual* T42.60) and one of social intimacy (*Involved vs. Disengaged* T47.73), their low scores may well indicate a disinterest in social engagement.

LOOKING AHEAD

Attention in chapter 10 is directed at identifying prognostic signs that indicate how likely the patient is to benefit from psychotherapy, whether inpatient care is needed, resources that the patients bring to therapy, and barriers that need to be overcome for patients to make effective use of therapy. The scales featured can play a useful role within a managed care environment by assisting to set realistic expectations for patient progress. They also provide tools for more rational, as opposed to arbitrary, allocation of therapy resources. Chapter 10 also identifies scales that are of practical value in the management of risks that are common to all mental health services.

10

Prognosis and Risk Assessment Scales

Scales used for prognosis were identified by Levitt and Gotts (1995) as *8Con, Cn,* and *WA; 4AC* and *W-AUT;* the sum of *3DSA, 4SI,* and *9IMP;* and *TSC/S* and *S+.* The status of some scales has changed since that writing. One item of *8Con* was reversed during item analysis (Appendix A), but its meaning remained stable. As mentioned in chapter 4, *Cn* was revised extensively and needed to be revalidated. *WA* was also revised, but was judged to have retained its meaning (see chap. 4). The *4AC* scale was lost to unreliability, whereas *W-AUT* was unchanged. A new scale, *Impert,* was formed from the items of *3DSA, 4SI,* and *9IMP* (see chap. 6) and replaces their sum. Neither *TSC/S* nor *S+* was changed during item analysis.

Additional scales were selected to complement those prognosis scales that remained. The *L–F–K* triad was added as an index of receptivity to therapy. From the *MMPI–2* Content Scales, *TRT* and *WRK* were selected as obvious prognosis candidates. Regarding the latter of these additions, chapter 4 discusses some essential characteristics shared by *WRK* and *WA.* This is due, in part, to item overlap. The *Es* scale was omitted intentionally by Levitt (1989) as being of less value in his work setting and being contraindicated by much research. It was reexamined here as a much revised scale (chap. 4 & Appendix A) and is further evaluated in the present chapter. The new Psychosocial scales were included for their potential to identify broad areas of patient strength and difficulty.

Risk assessment draws on the *Critical Inquiry Worksheet* (Appendix C) that identifies behaviors that are dangerous to self or others. The search for risk factors is strengthened by use of Critical Inquiry Scales whose development was presented in chapter 7. There are the *Sadist* scale, three suicide risk scales (*Suic-S, Suic-O,* and *Suic-T*), *Panic,* and *AA.* General health also requires attention.

Panic is included because overwhelming emotional arousal exacerbates suicide risk (Weissman, Klerman, Markowitz, & Ouelette, 1989). Likewise, substance abuse is a known risk potentiating factor for suicide (Fremouw, de Perczel,
& Ellis, 1990), so the *AA* Critical Inquiry scale was included. Because empirical
linkages exist between impulsivity and both suicidal and aggressive acts (Polvi,
1997), the Impulsivity scales were added: *Imp-B, Imp-I, Imp-A,* and *Imp-T*.

EVALUATING THE CONTROL (*Cn*) SCALE

Considering Cuadra's (1956) method of scale construction, it was first thought
that it could not likely be validated in the present sample. Nevertheless, an attempt
was made to do so. Of the 1,020 valid adult cases, 236 (23.14%) had *Cn* scores
that exceeded Levitt's suggested T65 cutoff (Levitt & Gotts, 1995). A cutoff of
T70 also yielded an unbelievable number of positive *Cn* cases ($n = 117$, 11.47%).
Clearly, a T65 cutoff was not usable.

Finally, a T75 cutoff was used to select 52 cases (5.10%) of hospitalized patients who, perhaps by Cuadra's logic, could have done as well if they were
treated as outpatients. Compared with patients whose scores ranged from T65 to
T74, those above T75 evidenced greater pathology on all scales of the depression,
anxiety, psychoticism, and social maladjustment clusters (all $ps < .01$). Moreover,
the above T75 group scored as having more difficulties, as expressed in Eriksonian terminology (Erikson, 1963), with *trust, autonomy, initiative* and *identity*
(all $ps < .01$), and *intimacy* ($p < .05$). Eriksonian terms are used sometimes hereafter as a shorthand method of referencing the Psychosocial scales. These findings
did not support using the much revised *Cn* scale to assign persons to outpatient
services.

CUTOFFS FOR OTHER CORE PROGNOSIS SCALES

Similar procedures were followed for the other core prognosis scales: *Es, 8Con,
TRT, WRK,* and *WA*. That is, distributions were studied for each scale, cutoffs
were established, and the resulting high score patients were compared with those
who scored immediately below them in the distribution. None of the comparisons
of Psychosocial scale scores reported below were made between the very low
scoring patients and those above the cutoffs, all of which findings were highly
significant ($p < .000$). High scoring and comparison cutoffs appear later.

On all five of the preceding scales, compared with those patients who scored
just a little lower than they, high scoring patients received psychosocial scores
that supported use of the scales for prognosis. The level of support varied from
scale to scale. For high *Es* scorers only, autonomy scores were higher ($p < .05$).
Note that high scores on *Es* predict a more favorable outcome.

High scores on the remaining four core scales predict poorer outcomes. Lower psychosocial scores signify support for their use. Those high on *8Con* were lower on autonomy and industry (both $p < .000$) and identity ($p < .05$). High *TRT* scorers were lower on trust ($p < .05$) and on autonomy, identity, and intimacy (each $p < .000$). Trust, identity, and intimacy means were all lower ($p < .05$) for those who scored above the cutoff for *WRK*. *WA* high scorers were also lower on three scales: autonomy, industry, and identity (all $p < .05$).

The respective cutoffs set for the scales of the high and comparison groups were: *Es* T65 vs. T60–T64, *8Con* and *TRT* T80 vs. T70–T79, and *WRK* and *WA* T75 vs. T70–T74. The varying cutoff score placements across scales were made in order to accommodate differences in scale properties. Note further that the cutoff was set to include fewer *Es* high scores in this hospitalized sample in recognition of their substantial likely lower average level of ego resources. Cutoffs for the remaining four scales subsumed greater numbers of cases as a way of recognizing the sample's abundance of psychopathology. Using comparison groups that scored only slightly lower on the respective scales than did the high scorers enhances greatly the significance of the group differences reported earlier.

COMBINING *L–F–K* AND CORE SCALES

Factor Analytic Studies

Solution for Combined Scales. A principal components factor analysis was done of the scales: *L, F, K, Es, 8Con, TRT, WRK,* and *WA,* to which the *Cn* scale was added for additional study. The two-factor solution was rotated to varimax normalized solution. The first extracted factor (eigenvalue 4.23 accounting for 47.01% of the variance) included *TRT, 8Con, WRK, WA, F,* and *Es. Es* related negatively ($-.76$) to the factor, whereas the remaining scales related positively (*F* .68, *TRT* & *8Con* .80, *WRK* .81, and *WA* .86). *K* ($-.52$) had a secondary loading that was not resolved by rotation. *L* was unrelated ($-.03$) and *Cn* only minimally related (.41) to this rotated factor. This factor was identified as a predictor of unsuccessful versus successful outcomes and appears free of fake bad tendency.

In the same analysis, a second extracted factor (eigenvalue 2.47, 27.42% variance) was primarily defined by the scales *L* ($-.91$), *Cn* (.81), and *K* ($-.68$). That this factor was strongly defined by *L* suggested an element of exaggerated self-report. That interpretation could apply equally to the negative loading of *K*. The appearance of *Cn* in the factor further separated it from the five core prognosis scales by associating extreme elevation of its scores with exaggeration.

Solutions With Scale Removals. The same factor extraction procedure was used with the foregoing scales after removal of *Cn*. Its removal resulted in a single factor solution (eigenvalue 4.96, 62.06% variance). Now *K*'s loading on this factor increased from $-.52$ to $-.78$, whereas F's loading declined slightly from .68 to .63. L's loading of only $-.47$ indicated that the element of exaggeration did not fit well in the factor, and with Cn gone no second factor was detected.

A third factor extraction was carried out as before with the same scales after removal of the nonfitting L. Its eigenvalue of 4.77 accounted for 68.19% of the available variance. The F scale's loading remained below a critical .70 level, thereby showing that less than one half of its variance was associated with the factor.

Thus, in a fourth factor analysis, F was also omitted. Now all six of the remaining scales loaded on the factor (eigenvalue 4.42, 73.61% of total variance), and their relations with it accounted for from 60.72 to 86.52 of the individual scale variances. Because a question may arise about the inclusion of the closely correlated scales WRK and WA, a fifth and final factor run was completed with WA omitted. Its removal left the solution essentially unchanged, and hence WA was retained. The final conclusion was that the combined six scales defined the core prognosis factor, with higher scores predicting poorer outcomes. K and Es related negatively to other scales as expressed in the following formula:

$$\text{Prognosis} = (.865)(WRK) + (.859)(WA) - (.734)(Es)$$
$$+ (.698)(8Con) + (.653)(TRT) - (.606)(K)$$

PROGNOSIS SCALES AND PSYCHOSOCIAL MODALITIES

Relations were examined between the six core prognosis scales and the Psychosocial scales by using the former to predict each of the latter. Slightly differing regression prediction equations provided best fits for each Psychosocial scale. In five of the six equations, more than one half of each scale's variance was accounted for by the prognosis scales. Specific resolved variance amounts for Eriksonian modalities were: trust (53.71%), autonomy (59.24%), initiative (54.56%), industry (53.67%), identity (43.05%), and intimacy (51.27%).

A less sizable prediction for identity perhaps resulted from use of the *MMPI* sample's shorter version of the Ego Identified vs. Confused scale. The *MMPI* scale contains only 52% of the *MMPI–2* scale's 25 items and is less internally consistent than the latter version. On the other hand, 43.05% of its variance is not an insignificant amount: $F(4, 1015) = 191.79$, $p < .0000$.

Possible Influence of L on Psychosocial Scale Elevations

Before leaving this series of regression equations, one additional question was addressed by entering the L scale in combination with each final set of scales selected by the six respective equations. The question pertained to the possibility that higher scores on the Psychosocial scales might have resulted to some appreciable extent from patients responding to the *MMPI* items in intentionally self-enhancing ways.

Adding L increased the variance accounted for with only one of the five Psychosocial scales. This occurred for Initiating vs. Guilt-Prone. This scale's resolved variance increased from 54.56% to 59.06% (i.e., a 4.50% increase). Moreover, although L correlates with the other five Psychosocial scales at low levels (r = .26–.33), it relates to the Initiating vs. Guilt-Prone scale at a higher level (r = .54). Thus, interpretation of initiative level needs to be checked for possible self-enhancement in terms of reduced admission of guilt-proneness. Concurrent elevation of L will alert the examiner to this possibility.

Using Individual Psychosocial Scales for Prognosis

The patient who produces low scores on all or nearly all of the Psychosocial scales is likely to be in distress and may be thoroughly demoralized. The symptom complex becomes an overpowering focus of attention and a force that immobilizes the individual in ways suggested by the items of *8Con*. For such persons, providing immediate relief from the most troubling target symptoms will likely serve as a short-term therapeutic goal. This will be done in conjunction with supportive measures. Getting beyond this level of engagement is vital.

Once the patient is able to focus on goals other than symptom relief, a review of the profile of Psychosocial scales will suggest possible areas of coping strength that can be further explored. Clarification with the patient of strengths often will suggest strategies for further skill development and will increase hope. For example, if trust appears to be a strength or at least not to be a difficulty, then therapeutic communication can revolve around ways to apply this capacity to deal realistically with current life issues and relationships.

In connection with the suggestion that patient strengths be explored, the following facts support this as a workable plan of action. Of 1,020 valid inpatient adults, only 4 (0.39%) received very low scores on all six Psychosocial scales. Almost one half (47.35%) had very low scores on none of those scales. Overall, 947 patients (92.84%) had three or fewer very low scores.

Moreover, inpatients often scored at or above the normative group's 50th percentile on individual scales of this group. In fact, nearly three fourths of all patients scored at that level on one or more of the Psychosocial scales: 749 (73.43%). That is to say, about three out of four patients reported one or more strengths that could be built on in therapy.

Of the 271 patients who had no average or higher scores, only 4 had all low scores. Thus, 267 of the 271 had one or more scales that were higher than very low. Taking this approach excludes very few patients. Nearly all bring to the therapeutic context one or more workable areas of psychosocial coping capacity to be affirmed and used. Thus, searching for and valuing positive attributes does offer an alternative perspective on patients and therapy.

L–F–K: A MINIATURE PROFILE

L, *F*, and *K* are more than Validity scales. The shape of the *L–F–K* profile affords useful prognostic insights into the patient's receptivity and capacity to benefit from psychotherapy. The current understanding of these scales closely resembles that presented by Butcher (1990), although this chapter draws less from his book than from information presented in a series of his workshops and verified by personal clinical experience.

Usually some small elevation of *F* within the triad is necessary as a source of discomfort from which the patient desires relief. If that elevation occurs along with an average to slightly above average *K* score, then the patient is judged to have some personal resources that may be directed toward effecting change. In *MMPI–2* records with these *F* and *K* characteristics, a slightly lower *L* can be a positive sign of capacity for realistic self-examination.

High *F* along with low *L* and *K* were common miniature profiles in this patient sample. They were strongly associated with high distress and limited resources for engaging in forms of therapy that require active participation and acceptance of responsibility for follow-through. When *F* is high, *K* is low, and *L* is somewhat elevated, this pattern often suggests, in addition to the foregoing, a naïve and unrealistic outlook.

F is subject to other varied influences. Situational stress can increase this score (Friedman et al., 2001). Persons with disorganizing thought disorders receive high scores. High *F* can appear as a plea for help or an attempt to insure that desired services will be offered (Levitt & Gotts, 1995). It is elevated by some patients who feel incapable and want others to take care of them. That is, it is a sign of felt helplessness for patients whose neediness is overwhelming. Poor comprehension and carelessness in responding may be reasons for some patients receiving high scores. Consequently, varied situations and circumstances can and do result in unrealistically elevated *F* scores.

Then, too, elevations of *F* may occur in connection with more obvious secondary gain motives related to personal injury litigation, workmen's compensation, and legal charges. Whether *F* and other particular scales will be elevated in these secondary gain cases is not, however, fully predictable. This is the case because patients approach the *MMPI–2* with different subjective notions of what symptom reports will most impress others. Succinct guidelines for using other scales to narrow the many possibilities appear in Butcher et al. (2001).

High *K* along with somewhat less elevated *L* and low *F* communicates, "I'm fine. I don't have the problems that others think I do. I don't need the kind of help that you have to offer." Such individuals are not receptive to others' attempts to engage them in therapeutic work. When a similar pattern occurs but L is higher than K, then the patient is further likely to be an unusually unsophisticated person who is defensive either by style or in the face of other issues that are prompting a self-enhancing form of cover-up.

It would be misleading to couch the preceding K and L guidelines in terms of specific, invariant score levels. Higher socioeconomic status (SES), educational level, and cultural sophistication all tend to favor mild to moderate elevation of K and very average to low scores on L. Very high K scores are defensive signs for many respondents. The lower the person's education and SES are, the more this is true. These scores must, hence, be weighed in terms of the patient's general background and life experiences. Further discussion of the influence of patient background on these scores appears in Butcher (1990) and Friedman et al. (2001).

RAPPORT: SOCIAL ANXIETY, AUTHORITY PROBLEMS, SUSPICION

The issues considered here were all presented in Levitt and Gotts (1995) and will likely be intuitively grasped with little difficulty by clinicians who will appreciate their impact on developing rapport. They are covered briefly but sufficiently to link them to *MMPI–2* scales that are used to identify them.

Social Anxiety

Patients who are high in social anxiety experience the process of entering therapy differently than do others. For them it is a challenge to become comfortable with anyone new. A new therapist often appears to be a repeat of the usual interpersonal barrier.

The social imperturbability scale, *Impert*, does a good job of picking up on this issue. High scores on the scale represent low social anxiety; low scores signal strong difficulty warming up to others. Those who are high in social anxiety correspond behaviorally to the *DSM* descriptors of Social Phobia whether or not they meet all criteria for this diagnosis. *LSE*, *W-MOR*, *I-SC*, and *6P* will usually be elevated along with low scores on *Impert*. Mood disorders and self-medicating via substance abuse are frequent comorbid conditions.

These persons have low self-esteem, anticipate rejection, and are overly sensitive to real or imagined criticism or negative evaluation. These sensitivities clearly present to the therapist a prescription for the kinds of behaviors to avoid. The therapist must adjust the pace of treatment to their slow start-up. Therapist warmth is important, but an overly solicitous or seductive style may be experienced by them as a social rush routine. Moreover, it is not enough to be nonjudgmental and accepting. Rather, these attitudes must be communicated—

often over and over. They can become good therapy candidates once their initial reticence subsides.

Authority Problems

Persons with authority problems have personal history to overcome. They view many formally defined relationships as offenses against their sense of freedom. The therapy relationship may or may not be perceived as offensive to them. Much depends on the circumstances surrounding their intake. If they have been referred by someone in authority, then the feelings associated with this seeming assault on their autonomy may quickly transfer to the therapist. The therapist needs to recognize and defuse those feelings whenever they exist. The therapy will not go well if the therapist has a more formal, reserved style or tries to exercise what the patient views as illegitimate extensions of control or authority. Therapists must decide if they can be effective in treating these patients.

The *W-AUT* scale by itself is able to identify patients who have this as an issue. Elevation on the scale will usually be accompanied by elevations on a number of other scales. These include *CYN, TSC/R, TSC/S,* and *W-HOS,* among others. Other scales should be examined closely in the Behavior Controls and Norms Violations cluster and the Social Vulnerability and Alienation cluster in order to obtain an overall sense of how to approach this patient.

Suspiciousness

Suspicious persons hold deeply ingrained expectancies that others will not prove worthy of their trust. These individuals believe that others dislike them and wish to bring them harm and mischief. *DSM* descriptions of the Paranoid *PDO* and also of the Delusional Disorder cover the essential characteristics of persons affected by this trait. It is a given that these persons are difficult to relate to. Their autonomy needs and sensitivities closely resemble those just discussed. They do not usually fare well in therapy unless they have already come to understand and feel distressed by the interpersonal problems that their suspicions create. Even then, the therapist's approach must be specifically devised to counteract their moves to control, blame, attack, or withdraw (Benjamin, 1993).

Suspicious patients are recognized by elevations of their scores on *TSC/S, S+,* and *6PI.* They are expected to have low scores on *3NA* and *6N* and on their composite, *Trust.* The Cared for vs. Neglected scale should also be low. Persons with Delusional Disorder, however, will not necessarily be recognizable by many of these signs. Some have developed a persona with which they confront the hostile world by presenting themselves as seeming opposites of these. It is their delusions that set them apart. Their distorted ideas may not be immediately apparent, except to their intimates, if they are not otherwise grossly impaired.

RISK ASSESSMENT

Suicidality

Whether the patient is seen as an outpatient or on inpatient services, review of suicide risk indicators is essential. *MMPI–2* items and scales help in the process, but they must be supplemented with information from reliable sources on past plans or attempts. Patients will sometimes minimize the significance of prior attempts by explaining that they were "only trying to get (someone's) attention." Other explanations may be similarly offered. Prior attempts, nevertheless, must not be dismissed so easily. Although so-called *suicide gestures* may not involve intent to die, they do lead to unanticipated outcomes of permanent loss of function and sometimes death.

Despondency. Suicide risk can be thought of as arising from three sources: despondency, disordered thinking, and impulsivity. Despondency is invariably reflected in scales of the Depressive Spectrum Conditions cluster (e.g., *D, DEP, 2SD, TSC/D, 8EA,3LM, 2PR*). The *Suic-S* scale selects from the larger depressive item pool those items likely to capture some aspect of actual risk. Consequently, the *Suic-S* and *Suic-O* scales correlated well with one another ($r = .72$) even though they have no item overlaps. Moreover, the six individual items of the *Suic-O* scale correlated well with *Suic-S* ($rs = .37–.60$; mean $r = .49$). All of the items in these two scales are suggested for critical inquiry (Appendix C). These scores are combined in *Suic-T*, whose elevation indicates both despondency and more explicit expressions of suicidal risk.

Despondency and Patient Energy Level. As depressed patients improve, their energy may rebound and *2PR* scores drop. These signal a potentially increased suicide risk (Klerman, 1982; Levitt & Gotts, 1995; Levitt, Lubin, & Brooks, 1983; Pokorny, 1968). Clinical lore supports this view and recommends heightened vigilance to risk.

The foregoing view is intuitively appealing and thus deserves additional formal analysis in view of revisions to *2PR*. Both the much revised (Appendix A) and original versions of *2PR* were studied in relation to one another and to the Impulsivity scales and the Suicide Risk scales. The revised scale is called *2PR-Rev* here for comparative purposes but in Appendixes A and B is simply *2PR*.

In the *MMPI–2* sample, *2PR* and *2PR-Rev* correlated negatively with one another ($r = -.24$, $df = 152$, $p < .01$). In every comparison of these two scales with the remaining scales, *2PR-Rev* correlated at higher levels with all scales than did the original *2PR*. Relations between *2PR* and the Impulsivity and Suicide Risk scales were negative and significant only at the .05 probability level for *Imp-B*, *Suic-S*, and *Suic-T*, with none reaching the .01 level. *2PR-Rev* related negatively to all seven of the subject scales at probabilities well beyond .000. Examples of these strong associations are seen with *Imp-T* ($r = -.64$) and *Suic-T* ($r = -.63$).

Whereas the original *2PR* would have added little if anything to the prediction of suicide risk, the *2PR-Rev* scale should prove valuable in assessing such risk. Thus, the traditional interpretation was correct, whereas the original scale failed to capture the essence of the construct—at least as regards the present use of low psychomotor retardation as a warning sign of an energized patient.

Disordered Thinking. Suicide risk increases to the extent that the person's executive processes of rational thought and judgment are impaired. Impairment can result from the comorbid occurrence of a thought disorder. Thought Process Disorder cluster scales will draw the examiner's attention to this possibility (e.g., *Sc, Pa, BIZ, I-RD*). Cognitive impairment can have a similar effect. Scales in the Cognitive Disorders cluster that may suggest this are: *VRIN, 8COG, NeurPsy, 2MD, I-DS, TSC/A*, and *8BSE*. Items for critical inquiry in Appendix C further examine specific signs of cognitive impairment.

Impulsivity. The presence of excessive impulsivity is gauged by review of the scales *Imp-B, Imp-I, Imp-A*, and *Imp-T*. In the *MMPI–2* sample, impulsive thought related more strongly to *Suic-S* ($r = .55$) than did either behavioral ($r = .39$) or affective impulsivity ($r = .49$). Total impulsivity related at an only slightly higher level to *Suic-S* ($r = .58$) than did impulsive thinking. Panic disorder and panic attacks (*Panic* scale) generate an overpowering sense of immediacy and dyscontrol. The resulting undifferentiated state of arousal greatly stimulates impulsive thinking and action beyond their usual baselines.

Aggression

Danger to others is a second area for required workup during risk assessment. As is true of suicidal risk, obtaining a reliable past history is essential in the assessment of dangerousness to others. Also as in suicide risk, disordered thinking and impulsivity may be important sources of the behavior. Whereas panic does not typically lead to aggression, when it does the attacks tend to be vicious and heedless of consequences. The previously listed scales should be reviewed as may be needed.

The *Sadist* scale can be helpful if the history suggests cruelty and callousness. Scales in the Anger, Hostility, Suspicion, Cynicism, Resentment cluster are informative if a sadistic tendency is not found. Of these, it is especially useful to examine *ANG, W-HOS, TSC/R, O-H*, and *Ho*. Instrumental aggression, unlike the types already considered, is directed toward accomplishing a specific intended result. It is seen in the *DSM*-listed conditions: Conduct Disorder, Adult Antisocial Behavior, and Antisocial Personality Disorder. Thus, this kind of aggression is associated with the antisocial scales of the Behavior Controls & Norms Violations and the Personality Disorders clusters: *Pd, ASP, ANTI*, and *W-AUT*.

Chemical Dependency

The chemical dependencies exert far-reaching effects. They all create alterations of inhibitory and cognitive processes. Some also produce affective changes. These changes collectively loosen and undermine the usual regulators of behavior. Thus, the addictions are associated with increased risk for suicidal and aggressive actions. The dependencies, moreover, promote a behavior shift in the direction of the addicted person doing whatever is necessary to possess and use desired substances of abuse. This may result in their engaging in a variety of illegal behaviors over and above neglect of work, family, financial responsibilities, and personal health.

For all of the foregoing reasons, chemical dependency is a third type of risk factor that must be assessed. It compounds the other risk factors and creates additional risks that are unique to it. In addition to the *MAC-R* and the Critical Inquiry *AA* scales, other background needs to be checked, if at all possible by using multiple reliable informants. Background checks should include contacts with law enforcement agencies, medical contacts, prior treatment programs and history of compliance with treatment, and effects on work and family life.

Health Status

A fourth and final area for risk assessment is the patient's general health. The standard of care calls for a review of health history at a minimum, in addition to the other risk issues already covered. This will ordinarily be obtained by medical and nursing staff in multidisciplinary settings. If a concurrent medical workup is not a part of patient intake, then considerable responsibility devolves on the psychologist to obtain that history.

MMPI–2 in Health Screening. Fortunately, *MMPI–2* offers scales that at least screen the patient's self-reported general health. Those appearing in the Somatic Concerns cluster are *Hs, HEA, TSC/B, W-HEA, W-ORG, 2PM, 3SC,* and *TPA*. A pattern of elevations indicates that further investigation or medical referral is required. It is required because otherwise the psychologist may be disregarding warning signs that the *MMPI–2* has raised. The following paragraph details those "further investigation" duties that may not be immediately apparent or familiar to the practicing psychologist.

The psychologist who conducts further inquiry in order to decide whether to make a medical referral should review the following: family health history and reasons for deaths of close relatives; any history of being abused; hospitalizations or emergency room visits; chronic and acute illnesses; significant injuries whether or not medically treated; pending medical care; locations, types, severity, and frequency of pain and what remedies have given relief; prescription and over-the-counter preparations taken together with the reasons for their use and results obtained; nutritional supplements used; chronic problems or recent changes involving body weight, appetite, elimination habits, energy level, fatigue, sleep, mental clarity, and memory; and at least a brief review of all major somatic systems.

Much of the review can be organized into a locally devised inventory that is given to the patient for completion before the actual inquiry. If this kind and level of inquiry fall outside of the psychologist's ordinary practice, then the offer of a medical referral would be an expected standard of care.

CONCLUSIONS AND ADVICE

It is duly noted here that the *Cn* scale was not found to be useful. Second, after discounting *Cn*, it was found that six *MMPI–2* scales functioned together as a composite index of patient prognosis. The scales comprising the index are hence referred to as *core prognosis* scales. The core scales were then shown to predict about 50% of the variance of each of the new Psychosocial scales. Patients with more favorable prognosis were those whose self-reports also suggested that they possessed greater psychosocial coping capacities.

A finding for one core prognosis scale deserves special comment. Despite misgivings about the value of the *Es* scale that are abundant in the literature (Levitt, 1989), in the current application the revised *Es* scale made a significant contribution to defining the prognosis core. Regression analysis assigned to the *Es* scale a minus beta that identified it along with *K* as relating negatively to poor prognosis as defined by positive betas for *WRK, WA, 8Con,* and *TRT*. This finding must be regarded as support for Barron's (1953) naming of it: *ego strength*. Certainly a low score still could, as Levitt suggested, be identified as *ego weakness*. See chapter 4 for the earlier interpretation of *Es*'s meaning.

Another current finding that merits emphasis came from study of the revised *2PR* scale. This substantially modified scale now has a small negative correlation with the widely used *H–L* version (Harris & Lingoes, 1968). In the current application, the revised scale functioned better than did the original as an index of variations in patient energy level as this relates to detection of suicide risk. The original *H–L* scale delivered only a nonsignificant finding.

Prognosis and risk management information can and should be obtained routinely beginning with a review of the *MMPI–2* scales discussed in this section. The goals of prognosis are to make better treatment decisions and resource allocations in order to optimize patient outcomes. Risk management aims to prevent the occurrence of untoward events. Consultation should be arranged with other knowledgeable clinicians and, in some instances, legal counsel in order to review and validate the treating clinician's judgment in difficult and ambiguous situations. Adequate clinical documentation of clinician risk management efforts is also a means of demonstrating prudent management of risk.

11

Conjoint *MMPI–2* and *Rorschach* Interpretation

In the first edition of *The Clinical Application of MMPI Special Scales*, Levitt (1989) featured a chapter on coordinated use of the *MMPI* and *Rorschach*. Surprisingly, he made just a passing reference there in a footnote to his volume on the *Rorschach* (Levitt, 1980a). That book remains notable for Levitt's perceptive collating of interpretations made by seven major *Rorschach* systems that preceded Exner's (1993) Comprehensive System (*CS*). After collating the systems' treatments of 13 structural and three content variables, he identified a common interpretive core for each variable (Levitt, 1980a, Appendix 3).

Those understandings guided his case presentations in both the first and second editions of that work (Levitt, 1989; Levitt & Gotts, 1995). Whereas Exner's work was mentioned only in passing in the first edition, Levitt specifically directed readers of the second edition and in the 1980 *Rorschach* primer to take guidance from Exner (1993). He further profited from Exner's treatment of content perseveration, contamination, and the three-way partitioning of vista. He also discussed the interpretability of the *CS Rorschach* indices as being dependent on the total number of responses (*R*) given in a record.

AN ERA OF ASSESSMENT ADVANCES

It is important to recognize there have been significant milestones in assessment practice in recent decades. Consequently, the approach to conjoint *MMPI–Rorschach* interpretation used by Levitt (1989; Levitt & Gotts, 1995) now requires further updating. Those ongoing developments include, after a gradual start (Webb et al., 1993), ultimate widespread adoption of *MMPI–2*; ascendance of the

Comprehensive System over prior popular *Rorschach* systems (Piotroski, Sherry, & Keller, 1985); and a growing body of research on the *Rorschach* that positions it on a surer scientific footing.

Regarding this the growing body of research, it will prove useful for the reader to review two related series of papers organized by Meyer (1999b, 2001) and published together in *Psychological Assessment*. As the 13 presentations arranged by Meyer demonstrate, the *Rorschach* and its use remain matters of considerable contention. Yet, this controversy plus the ascendancy of the *CS* have resulted in greatly increased methodological sophistication and refinement.

Advances are recognizable in interrater reliability (McDowell & Acklin, 1996; Meyer et al., 2002; Viglione & Taylor, 2003); temporal stability (Gronnerod, 2003); study of effect sizes (Rosenthal, Hiller, Bornstein, Berry, & Brunell-Neuleib, 2001); comparative analysis of *Rorschach* and *MMPI* relative to reliability, stability, and validity (Parker, Hanson, & Hunsley, 1988); knowledge about effects of malingering (Schretlen, 1988, 1997) and defensiveness in records (Ganellen, 1994); and synthesis of knowledge (Exner, 1993; Weiner, 1998, 2001).

Progress in the foregoing areas is not universally acknowledged, especially as regards the *Rorschach*'s capacity to detect psychopathology or to support the formulation of diagnoses (Dawes, 1999; Wood & Lilienfeld, 1999; Wood, Lilienfeld, Nezworski, & Garb, 2001; Zalewski & Archer, 1991).

Based on their research, some have concluded that *Rorschach* and *MMPI-2/MMPI–A* probably do not measure the same things and their similarly named constructs do not reference the same external realities (Archer, 1996; Archer & Krishnamurthy, 1993a, 1993b, 1999; Blais, Hilsenroth, Castlebury, Fowler, & Baity, 2001). Others have attributed the *Rorschach* and *MMPI*'s seeming unrelatedness to differences in test interaction or response styles that can yield findings of comparability when subjected to more refined analysis (Lindgren & Carlsson, 2002; Meyer, 1999a; Meyer, Riethmiller, Brooks, Benoit, & Handler, 2000; Viglione, 1996).

Some findings suggest that *MMPI* and *Rorschach* relate to different external criteria (Blais et al., 2001; Caron & Archer, 1997; Ganellen, 1996; Hiller, Rosenthal, Bornstein, Berry, & Brunell-Neuleib, 1999). The *Rorschach*, for example, has demonstrated particular relevance to demonstrating the benefits of longer term psychotherapy (Weiner & Exner, 1991); clarifying characteristics of pedophiles (Bridges, Wilson, & Gacono, 1998); differentiating subtypes of sexual offenders (Gacono, Meloy, & Bridges, 2000); and identifying individuals who terminate psychotherapy prematurely (Hilsenroth, Handler, Toman, & Padawer, 1995).

In view of *MMPI* and *Rorschach*'s known empirical differences, Weiner (1993) suggested that there are distinct advantages to using them in a complementary manner. He further offered six guidelines for optimizing use of the *Rorschach* (Weiner, 2000) that appear applicable to case presentations. Those include incorporating both idiographic and nomothetic perspectives, pointing up strengths as well as weaknesses, and focusing interpretation on personality processes. Meyer (1996) and Stricker and Gold (1999) favored using the two instruments in ways that recognize the strengths of each for deriving a more complete picture of personality. This places the burden of integrating the parts (Lovitt, 1993) during the process of conceptualizing the individual case (Acklin, 1993; Viglione, 1999) squarely on the examiner. These perspectives provide a person-centered direction to the case presentations that follow.

CASE PRESENTATIONS

The two presentations made here were drawn from the *MMPI-2* database and were restricted to patients who completed a *Rorschach* that was administered and scored within the *CS* framework (Exner, 1993, 2000; Weiner, 1998). *Rorschach* composite scores and indexes were obtained using *RIAP-4 Plus* software (Exner, Weiner, & PAR Staff, 2001). Two *CS* qualified clinical psychologists independently scored the records and entered them into *RIAP-4 Plus*. Results subsequently were compared and discussed. Coding differences were reconciled by joint review with reference to primary reference sources.

Details of patient background were altered or omitted to prevent possible identification of individual patients. Only cases that produced valid or at least borderline *MMPI-2* records and *Rorschachs* with 17 responses minimum were considered. This was done in order to avoid the obvious situation of a clearly invalid *MMPI-2* or a defensive *Rorschach* that must somehow be bolstered or replaced by other patient data. The current cases illustrate both the possibilities (Joanna) and challenges (Patrick) of joint instrument use.

Joanna

Clinical Interview: Background.   Joanna is a married mother of two. She is a mid-30s Caucasian who grew up in a large urban center. She is a high school graduate whose employment has been in office work in which she also needed to engage the public. Despite the presence of mild clinical depression, her demeanor, seductive dress and grooming, readiness to talk about herself, and comfortable social interactions suggested the presence of histrionic traits. This impression was further reinforced by her confession of recent indiscreet relationships involving males whom she had known before her marriage.

Joanna grew up in a disorganized family of lower socioeconomic background and recalled deprivation and flagrant emotional and sexual abuse that she and her siblings experienced over their childhood years. With the passage of time, she has become alienated from her family of origin, viewing herself as different. This is not a wholly uncomfortable *different*; rather, she rejects what they are like and seldom contacts them to visit. Her alienation means, however, that she cannot turn to parents or siblings for emotional support. She has been in an unrewarding marriage for over 10 years with a man who provides steady financial support but whom she describes as disinterested in her emotional needs. Joanna enjoys and is devoted to her two elementary school age children. She worries about what would become of them now that she can no longer function and is in treatment.

Reason for Admission to Treatment. Joanna recently was the victim of a brutal assault by a male companion from her past. She realizes that it was his intention to kill her. She survived. At the time of intake, he was incarcerated and awaiting trial. The assault caused significant physical injuries, including cerebral impairment about which she voices a variety of specific cognitive complaints. Neuropsychological evaluation confirmed a number of infrequently encountered difficulties. Functional losses prevent her from returning to employment and make it impossible for her to engage in her customary avocations. She bears no visible scarring. Before treatment, she became homebound as a result of her injuries and due to posttraumatic symptoms, including flashbacks and fears that the perpetrator would find and harm her and her children. Joanna reports that her inability to function at her prior level is the primary factor feeding her depression. She expresses responsibility for meeting with him and "causing" what happened. Guilt is likely a factor in her depression.

Adequacy of Assessment Data. Note that all scale abbreviations appear in front of the book. *MMPI–2* scores appearing here are linear T except for the *RC* scales (Tellegen et al., 2003), which are uniform T or any raw scores (*RS*). Both the *MMPI–2* and *Rorschach* are valid for interpretation [L 62; F 75; K 43; F_B 58; *ME* 68; *VRIN* 52; *TRIN* 58; $RCon1$ vs. $RCon2$ = (T20 – T22); *Rorschach R* = 25]. Note that ($RCon1 - RCon2$) produced a smaller estimate of inconsistency across the halves of the *MMPI–2* than did ($F - F_B$) and matches *VRIN* and *TRIN*.

Failed Codetype Match. Her *MMPI–2* profile yields a *4-3* code (*Pd* 79; *Hy* 77), suggesting that she may have a chronic anger problem. Approximately equal elevations of these two might indicate both strong impulses to express the anger and to regulate its expression—a difficult balancing act. Further inspection of her *MMPI–2* special scales and *Rorschach* indices does not support the *4-3* codetype interpretation (i.e., *ANG* 36, *O-H* only 52, and *Rorschach S* = 1). See more *4-3* discussion later. The new *RC* scale profile (Tellegen et al., 2003) produces a spike *RC6* (RS14, T99), which also does not fit her (e.g., *S+* 62, *6PI* 57, *TSC/S* 59), and the *Rorschach* Hypervigilance Index (*HVI*) is not significant.

Of the *Hy* subscales, only *3SC* is elevated (81). This is certainly an understandable circumstance in view of her recent injuries. By contrast, the *Pd* subscales are elevated: *4SOA* 76, *4FD* 74, *4SA* 68, *4SI* 65. Together these might suggest instead that she produced a spike *4*, with the elevated *3* being an artifact of her somatic complaints. Certainly Joanna's early history could explain an antisocial inclination, and she further expresses in interview the social and family alienation that especially have raised her *Pd* score. But a spike *4* does not fit her well (e.g., *ASP* 52, *AUT* 49, *Imp-B* 50, *Re* 65, *9AMO* 45), and the substance abuse scales are low (*MAC-R* 45, *APS* 52). It is concluded that the spike *4* results from social alienation and family difficulties. Moreover, *FAM* at 81 supports this view.

Somatic Issues Confirmed. In connection with the earlier observation regarding *3SC*, the entire Somatic Concerns cluster is affected (*HEA* 76, *Hs* 67, *TSC/B* 73, *ORG* 92), as is the Cognitive Disorders cluster (*NeurPsy* 83, *8BSE* 90, *8COG* 67, *2MD* 66, *I-DS* 65). Along with these elevations, her 2 *Anatomy* responses and 10 *Morbids* on the *Rorschach* reinforce the view that she has unfavorable views of her body and its functioning. In the same context, her T42 on Autonomous vs. Doubting could possibly represent a psychosocial modality that may have been incremented downward. Without baseline data, this possibility cannot be evaluated further. In any event, a somatically concerned, cognitively disordered picture based on actual life events can be appreciated as a significant part of her current clinical picture.

Depression Present. Turning next to the content clusters as a new starting point, her second highest Content scale after *HEA* is *DEP* (68). Examining the remaining scales of the Depressive Spectrum Conditions cluster reveals elevation: *D* 66, *2SD* 67, *4SA* 68, *2MD* 66, *2B* 68. It is noteworthy that *8EA* (49), *3LM* (59), and *2PR* (46), which normally correlate closely with this cluster, do not in this case. Thus, she has not withdrawn from life nor become wholly disaffected, and her energy level is sufficient to create concerns regarding suicide risk (*Suic-S* 64), although she did not endorse *Suic-O* items and *Panic* is low (T55). Depression and suicide risk are manifested by positive scores on major *Rorschach* indexes: *DEPI* (RS 7) and *S-CON* (RS 9). A second piece of the current clinical picture is, thus, depression accompanied by suicide risk in the apparent absence of suicidal thoughts or plans. Nevertheless, Joanna has recently placed herself in harm's way and states that she would not try to flee if her attacker were to get free and come after her. Thus, she reveals a capacity to behave intropunitively while using a passive style.

PTSD. Although the possibility of a posttraumatic stress disorder was suggested by specific complaints during interview, the scales that purportedly detect this in some populations fail to confirm: *PK* 60, *PS* 57. This may be the case because she does not report overall demoralization (*RCd* 61, *A* 59) or complain of anxiety (*ANX* 56) or phobic concerns (*FRS* 46) or anger and hostility (*ANG* 36, *W-HOS* 38, *TSC/R* 48, *Ho* 55). These all tend to feed together with depression into the undifferentiated states that appear to elevate *PK* and *PS* scale scores. Her problems are more sharply focused. Thus, the failure of her posttraumatic symptoms to register on *PK* and *PS* should not lead to dismissing or discounting them. On the contrary, the *Rorschach* identifies this woman as currently being in a high state of distress that is the result of circumstances in her present life situation (m = 5) and that has increased her psychological complexity (Blends = 9, 6 of which are shading and color-shading blends).

Diagnostic Conclusions. The foregoing perspectives provided sufficient information to assign to Joanna the following diagnoses: Major Depression, single episode, mild to moderate severity even when adequately medicated; Posttraumatic stress disorder; Cognitive disorder, NOS. Although histrionic traits were observed and found in the assessment data, no diagnosis was assigned due to the presence of Axis I conditions. A gradual improvement was noted over several months, and this patient was eventually able to return to work, although some cognitive deficits remained at the time of last contact.

Transition Between Cases

The foregoing composite *MMPI–2–Rorschach* record offers many valuable additional perspectives on this woman's personality. It is necessary at this point, however, to leave her story in the interest of examining another case in order to illustrate a different result from conjoint use of the *MMPI–2* content cluster approach and *Rorschach*. The following record provides a less informative composite due to limitations of the records produced for both instruments. The reader will need to look closely to decide what the formal assessments actually added to what was available from the clinical interview. Records of this second type are, nevertheless, among more satisfactory ones in some inpatient settings.

Patrick

Clinical Interview: Background. Patrick reports a difficult childhood due to family poverty, an abusive father, an invalid mother, and disappointment with his younger siblings and their actions. He avoids contact with his family of origin. He dropped out of high school and later obtained a GED. Many years ago, he tried to take his life when his first marriage ended. He has adult children from that marriage. He has spent most of his working career steadily employed by others. Later in his working career, he started and operated a small business. He again attempted suicide when that venture failed. He and his current wife have been married a dozen years and have no children. They live in extremely substandard housing.

Patrick's health began to decline about 10 years ago and has become much worse in the past 2 years. He is now in his mid-50s. He is an unemployed, disabled Caucasian who is deeply in debt due in part to medical bills and the past failure of a business. He is treated for several chronic health conditions that leave him confined to his home, and thus far he has been denied disability benefits. He also reports having specific memory difficulties. Medical and neuropsychological exams support many of his claims. His wife is a factory worker whose insurance does not cover all of his medical expenses.

Circumstances Leading to Treatment.

The accumulated weight of life circumstances have left Patrick chronically, clinically depressed. He is affected by shame over his financial dependence on his wife; worry over his health, with a realistic fear that he is approaching a chronic state of bedfast invalidism as his mother did before her death; social isolation from nearly all contacts except his wife; concern about problems of one of his adult children; and despair that things will never improve. Patrick feels helpless and hopeless. A moderate degree of depression with suicidal thoughts brings him into treatment at this time.

When seen during initial contact, Patrick presents with a flattened, sad expression and speals in a monotone. Motor activity is somewhat slowed. Suicidal ideation is present. No signs of mood-incongruent thinking are present. Occasionally, he expresses magical beliefs that cannot be accounted for by his cultural background. His thinking is also marked by a tendency to overgeneralize from limited experience. Overgeneralization interacts with his pessimistic outlook to produce more negative cognitions. He reports recent episodes of emotional lability with uncontrolled sobbing. He also clearly articulates his perspective that everything in his life is out of control. Critical Inquiry of *MMPI–2* item responses yields similar themes and details.

Quality of the Assessment Record.

This patient produced generally valid records for both instruments [L 52, F 67, K 35, F_B 92, ME 75, *VRIN* 65, *TRIN* 72, *RCon1* vs. *RCon 2* = (T30 – T40); *Rorschach R* = 27], but with overreporting of psychopathology on the *MMPI–2* and possibly during interview as well. The overreporting was judged to have resulted from his pessimistic outlook. Some would classify the *MMPI–2* as borderline. It is actually typical of the better quality records in this inpatient setting. The third inconsistency measure (*RCon1* vs. *RCon2*) reveals a discrepancy between the first and second half of the test of 10 standard score points (T10), which falls well below the F vs. F_B difference.

Too Many Scales Elevated.

Patrick's *MMPI–2* does not offer a distinct codetype due to the similar degree of elevation for five Clinical scales (*1, 2, 3, 7, 8*) that all fall in the lower-80 to mid-80 standard score range. Next, the new *RC* scales were consulted to see if they might reduce the number of the uninformative scale elevations among the five Clinical scales. A clear elevation of two scales then emerged—one from among the prior five (*RC1* 86) and a new one (*RC6* 100). Now no other *RC* scale exceeded 72. The clarity gained by using the *RC* scales seems at first illusory, however, because it brings to the foreground a scale (*RC6*) that was not among the original five elevated Clinical scales. Clinical scale 6, moreover, has always been a maverick relative to how it was validated within the *MMPI* criterion groups framework (Friedman et al., 2001; Greene, 2000). These considerations necessarily raised the question: Should this interloper *RC6* finding be considered when *RC* scales have been so little studied?

What of RC Scale Combinations?   In reply to the rhetorical question just posed, the fact is that no normative information has been published to support the application of existing codetypes to the *RC* scores. Tellegen et al. (2003) stated instead that they are not interpretable on this basis. Thus, even though both Friedman et al. (2001) and Greene (2000) offered interpretations for the *6-1* codetype, it is unknown whether those characteristics apply to the combination: *RC6-RC1*. After weighing the known facts and unknowns, deciding to use the content cluster approach appeared to be a better course of action. That was done.

Confirmation for RC1.   The confirmation of Scale *1*'s elevation by *RC1* provided a straightforward option of singling it out for further study using the clusters. Clusters relating to Scale *1* accordingly were examined. This resulted in the following cluster arrays for Somatic Concerns (*HEA* 89, *Hs* 81, *ORG* 100, *TSC/B* 84, *3SC* 91, *2PM* 73) and Cognitive Disorders (*NeurPsy* 94, *2MD* 91, *8COG* 84, *8BSE* 100, *I-DS* 94). These scales, all of which are comprised of obvious items, fairly uniformly support a high somatic concerns interpretation. This does little more, however, than affirm what was already evident from interview and medical and psychiatric history for this patient. Finally, the *Rorschach* (*An* = 2) indicates the presence of somatic preoccupation, although not to an impressive or overwhelming degree.

Borderline MMPI–2 Rehabilitated.   What initially appeared to be a profile of multiple elevations has, with the help of *RC1*, become simplified to a spike *1*. That much is judged to be a value added result. Having now resolved a stalemate posed by this high profile *MMPI–2* record (*ME* = 75 with 5 competing Clinical scales), it is considered somewhat rehabilitated. It will be subjected to additional analysis. It can be hoped that further analysis leads to more informative findings that were not already obtained during to clinical interview.

Depression Analyzed.   Clinical concerns dictated that the presenting problem of depression with suicidal risk and history of suicide attempts should next be explored. The Depressive Spectrum cluster provided the following scales for that purpose: *DEP* 82, *D* 81, *2SD* 85, *2PR* 54, *2MD* 91, *2B* 79, *3LM* 88, *4SA* 72, *8EA* 66. Relative to the suicide risk aspect of this, he received the following *MMPI–2* scores: *Suic-S* 95, *Suic-O* 65, *Suic-T* 91, *Panic* 81. Also during Critical Inquiry to Item 524, Patrick revealed that during one prior suicide attempt he overdosed on a medication. He told no one about it, and it was previously unknown to his community caregivers. *Rorschach* findings are next reviewed.

Patrick's *Rorschach* record failed to confirm the presence of either depression or suicide risk by way of the *DEPI* and *S-CON* indexes. Each index failed by the absence of a single criterion condition to attain significance. Thus, even though he gave 27 responses, his High Lambda Style record (*L* 1.70) led to his omitting details of his experience that contribute importantly to detecting the presence of depression and suicide risk. Importantly, the absence of a positive finding for *S-CON* must not be misconstrued as evidence that suicide risk is absent (Exner, 1993). Interview and *MMPI–2* findings are, therefore, viewed as sufficient to assert that he is clinically depressed and poses a suicide risk.

Vulnerabilities. It is further possible next to consider what the two assessment instruments may tell about personality features that diminish coping efforts and increase suicidal risk. Each of these represents a potential area for behavioral intervention. Patrick has fewer coping resources than others (5 of 6 Psychosocial scales 1.1 to 3.0 *SD*s below normal, *Es* 4; *Rorschach EA* 6). Self-esteem is low (*LSE* 83, *So* 8; *Rorschach MOR* 4, Egocentricity Index 0.19). He obsesses about his problems and resists challenges to his pessimistic outlook (*OBS* 73; *Rorschach MOR* 4, *a:p* = 6:2). He exerts below average control of impulses and emotional expression (*Imp-B* 61, *Imp-A* 61, *Panic* 81; *Rorschach FC:CF* + *C* = 0:2). He focuses his attention in too restricted a manner after which he examines it haphazardly (*Rorschach*: Information Processing weaknesses).

Potential Assets. Interventions will more likely succeed if they can be linked to Patrick's strengths. Strengths seen in the *MMPI–2* include signs suggesting potential for rapport: only minimally suspicious (*6PI* 58, *TSC/S* 58, *S*+ 53), not particularly high in authority conflict (*AUT* 60), and not socially anxious (*3DSA* 51, *4SI* 52, *9IMP* 41).

All of the following additional potential assets are suggested by his *Rorschach* record. He displays sufficient reality testing ability to judge accurately his experiences (Mediation). Further, he can think and reason logically without distortion (Ideation). He is very willing to process emotional experiences (Affect). He is capable of and willing to engage in introspection (Self-Perception). He shows interest in interpersonal contact and is willing to interact in a constructive, give-and-take manner (Interpersonal Perception). Admittedly, the *Rorschach* also identifies impediments to his exercising each of these listed strengths. Nevertheless, the potential is present for him to gain skill and facility in using them to improve his functioning.

Diagnostic Conclusions. Patrick had Major Depression that episodically reappeared in times of special stress. There were interepisode periods when symptoms of major depression were absent. His suicide risk was elevated at the time of treatment. Based on his life history and self-effacing *MMPI–2* responses (e.g., Psychosocial scales low, *LSE* 83, *So* 8, *RCon+* 28, *RCon–* 81), it further seemed likely that Dysthymia of an early onset was present. Neuropsychological testing supported a diagnosis of Amnestic Disorder, NOS, mild. He had several Axis III conditions that were not a focus of the present review but are acknowledged to be among the major stressors that made him feel hopeless and helpless. Thus, no somatization diagnosis was assigned. A few months following treatment, Patrick was ruled disabled. With back payment of benefits, he was able to retire debts and to move with his wife out of the area. Further contact was lost at that point.

REFLECTIONS ON CASE STUDIES

Joanna and Patrick were both cooperative and reasonably informative during clinical interview. Background data essentially corroborated their accounts. Neuropsychological and medical findings further supported their complaints. Joanna's *MMPI–2* and *Rorschach* not only were valid; each offered a wealth of material. Patrick's *MMPI–2* was usable, but affected by overreporting. His valid *Rorschach* signaled a High Lambda Style, which, it is suspected, reduced its capacity to uncover more fully some of his personality characteristics. For each patient there were areas of agreement between the two instruments, but each provided perspectives that were unavailable from the other.

Other patient composite records are less satisfactory than those reviewed. At times, either the *MMPI–2* or the *Rorschach* will be patently invalid (Lovitt, 1993). Interpretations based on the one usable instrument will then need to be fleshed out and substantiated by other data sources. Interpretations from either *MMPI–2* or the *Rorschach* that are clearly contradicted by personal history, medical findings, and systematic observational data seldom deserve inclusion in the psychologist's report. In the inpatient setting with severely and chronically mentally ill persons, results of a formal assessment will at times prove to yield little useful information. Under those circumstances, frank acknowledgment is refreshing and required.

REASONABLE NONCORRELATIONS

Interpretation of variables within the *Rorschach* Comprehensive System is a complex process (Exner, 1993; Weiner, 1998). Multiple decision rules and steps are necessary parts of interpreting what a protocol reveals (Exner, 2000). Consequently, the meanings assigned to identical patient raw scores will not necessarily be identical. Rather, the interpretive meaning attributed to a particular score often results from its confluence with multiple other scores. Actually, a similar process of analyzing scores in their individual contexts operates in *MMPI–2* interpretation as well and is illustrated by the foregoing case studies.

It is true that the scores obtained for both instruments have nomothetic roots. They are like genotypes, in a sense, whose realized phenotypes veer away idiographically due to response style and contextual forces. The previous case study reviews offer glimpses into how contextual analysis is conducted during assessment. The end result of testing is simply scores. Scores have no meaning until it is attributed. Assessment by contrast involves analysis of scores for their contextual meaning. The ways these two instruments are used idiographically in assessment do not become irrational unless their nomothetic anchors are disdained and abandoned.

Direct *MMPI–2* and *Rorschach* score comparisons are appropriate if done for nomothetic purposes. Interpretation of the outcomes of direct and simple score comparisons indeed suggests they are basically uncorrelated (e.g., Archer & Krishnamurthy, 1999). A rational conclusion to this is that they probably measure different things (Archer, 1997). It is not rational to conclude from the absence of correlational congruity that one instrument or the other is producing incorrect information. The relative worth of information captured by either instrument must be evaluated by appropriate research methods within a framework that is contextually sensitive, appraisal focused, and informed by both idiographic and nomothetic processes.

IMPLICATIONS FOR CHAPTER 12

The preceding perspectives provide a necessary lead-in to chapter 12. In it *MMPI–2* score interpretation guidelines are offered relative to *DSM* Axis I and II conditions. Interpretations make use of the full range of scales covered in the present research. This approach provides broad coverage but allows only limited opportunity for presentation of contextual considerations. In this sense, chapter 12 tilts more toward the nomothetic.

Thus, use of chapter 12 invites further judicious contextual investigation by the clinician. That process consists of comparing the various *MMPI–2* scores with one another and with other data sources. The interpretive leads presented in chapter 12, consequently, are not offered as cookbook or formulary pieces. They serve to provide transitional, tentative perspectives only. The clinician's work involves using such leads in the process of searching the entire patient record for patterns, order, and interpretive meaning.

Interpreting the Individual
MMPI–2 Record

When undertaking interpretation of the individual *MMPI–2*, the examiner should be familiar with the literature on how demographic factors can influence the record. Greene (2000) provided an exhaustive and incisive analysis of research on the effects of age, gender, educational level, occupation, income, marital status, race, and ethnicity. He further used the Caldwell and *MMPI–2* normative data sets to illustrate variations. His review is an invaluable resource.

Of the foregoing factors, the single most important is education. Two studies were found that appeared after Greene (2000) wrote his review. Neither of these alters the conclusions reached there, although they do incorporate some of Greene's recommendations for improved study design (Arbisi, Ben-Porath, & McNulty, 2002; Hall, Bansal, & Lopez, 1999). Although many poorly designed studies suggest otherwise, race and ethnicity appear to have minimal to modest but inconsistent effects when scores are adjusted for validity and educational level. See chapter 2 for discussion of how education may affect Validity scales.

CONTEXT

A second major interpretive consideration is the context in which the evaluation takes place. The spectrum of contextual effects stretches from blatant defensiveness on one end to outright malingering on the other. More routinely, the examiner sees varying degrees of self-enhancement and the magnification of psychopathology that fall between these two extremes. The Validity scales plus careful review of background are the primary tools for untangling these motives.

Persons who are being evaluated in child custody, employment, and pre-sentencing or probation contexts, for example, are expected to understand that the situation calls for presenting themselves in as positive a light as possible. That is normal unless they miscalculate the situational demand as a mandate to fabricate or exaggerate virtues and personality assets.

On the other hand, evaluations relating to personal injury suits, workmen's compensation, and determination of competency to stand trial naturally invite self-presentation that favors an outcome desired by the examinee. Likewise, patients who want to be sure their problems are taken seriously and they are admitted to treatment have reason to be convincing. Some distortion in these contexts is to be expected. Inclinations to overstate, nevertheless, raise the question of the extent to which the examinee's answers provide valid information.

What review of the foregoing contexts makes clear is that the issue is not simply one of whether a response set is present. A response set is very likely present if the motive can be identified. The real issue to be addressed is a quantitative one relating to the strength of the response set. That is, is the set strong enough to distort excessively the examinee's actual status? The full array of *MMPI–2* scales needs to be employed to answer this.

ASSESSING THE VALIDITY OF THE RECORD

Response Completeness and Consistency

A clinical record with no more than 15 unanswered or dually answered items is likely usable. Nevertheless, immediate follow-up should be used to have the patient try again to answer omitted items. So long as items are not omitted in a concentrated pattern from a particular scale or scales, up to 30 omitted items may be tolerated. If more than 30 items are missing, then the patient either has not engaged in the requested effort or has been careless or is too disturbed to complete the test or is uncooperative. Such a record is likely invalid.

VRIN and *TRIN* need to be below T80 or the record is too inconsistent to be useful. When these scales are both below T65, the respondent has completed the test in a consistent fashion. On the scale designated *RIncon*, inferences about consistency derive from probability theory rather than from the semantic, logical links that underlie *VRIN* and *TRIN*. Scores on *RIncon* that equal or exceed T70 suggest that another kind of inconsistent responding may have compromised the record. After *AdjAll* correction, *RIncon* scores of T70 or above occur in from 4% to 7% of patient records.

Inconsistency may also occur in the guise of the patient changing response style or approach over the course of completing this lengthy inventory. A difference of T10 between *RCon1* and *RCon2* in either direction is one sign that response style may have changed between the first and second half of the test. A difference of T10 needs to be investigated. Differences as great at T15 indicate marked inconsistency.

A difference between F and F_B of more than T20 may also suggest that the two halves of the test have been approached differently. But a difference of T20 or more may instead suggest a personality difference. Patients with F greater than F_B by T20 or more differ from those with F_B greater than F by T20 by scoring significantly higher on Psychosocial scales, K, So, Do, Es, $Trust$, GM (for both genders), $5C$, $Impert$, and $O-H$. Moreover, those who are T20 higher on F_B than F report reliably more depression, anxiety, dependency, social discomfort and impulsivity, and they register poorer scores on the prognosis scales. Thus, when these scales differ by T20 or more, the patterning of elevations for listed scales and clusters needs to be inspected to determine if this results from a response style or from personality characteristics.

Self-Enhancement, Defensiveness

For a patient with 12 or more years of schooling of middle social class background whose assessment context favors a self-enhancing motive, the record is likely to be free of positive distortion if L, K, Do, So, $ODecp$, S, $RCon+$, and the Psychosocial scales are mostly below T65 (see also section on Coping Attributes later). In the same situation for a patient with less education and a lower SES background, positive distortion is likely absent if these scores are below T60. To the degree that scores exceed these suggested levels for each type of patient, score veridicality becomes increasingly doubtful. If the record does suggest a self-enhancing tendency, then the particular pattern of elevations for the listed scales will often prove informative. Subscales for S also may be useful in this analysis.

In addition to the foregoing signs of self-enhancement, $O-H$ is elevated; the average of Si, SOC, TSC/I, and $W-SOC$ does not exceed T60, whereas the average of $3DSA$, $4SI$, $9IMP$, and $Impert$ will typically surpass T50; summed True responses usually will be fewer than 220 for females and 212 for males; and psychopathology indicators will be overly low. If the patient appears too perfect, then the picture should be examined closely to see if it is too perfect to be true.

Self-Derogation, Discouragement

Although F and F_B cutoffs were set at T80 for the present research, for individual clinical applications these levels are too low and would result in rejecting records as invalid that validly indicate high levels of disturbance. The interpretive guidelines in Butcher et al. (2001) for F and F_B in various settings should be followed, as should their recommendations for using Fp whenever it is suspected that psychopathology is being exaggerated.

In addition to receiving below average scores on the self-enhancing scales, a number of other scales readily identify those who present themselves are disheartened and of low morale: *ME, RCd, RCon–, Dist, W-MOR, LSE,* and *I-SC.* Low scores on *RCon1, RCon2,* and *RCon+* reliably complement the pattern of self-derogation. The shape and elevation of the *L–F–K* validity profile will be relevant. When this overall impression is created, it needs to be accompanied, for example, by some subjective depression (*2SD*), anergia (*2PR*), waning motivation (*8Con*), brooding (*2B*), and similar signs of downheartedness to be credible.

Comparing the *MMPI–2* record to that of other individuals of similar circumstances often will suggest whether reporting is in line with expectations or suffers from overreporting. If exaggeration is a specific issue to be addressed by the assessment, then corroborating evidence will be needed from observation of affective tone and demeanor, reports of typical behavior in varied settings, and recent adaptive history. Exaggeration is likely present if these are not congruent.

COPING ATTRIBUTES

Whereas the *MMPI–2* is used primarily to assess psychopathology, this can be balanced by appraisal with the *MMPI–2* of assets as well. The discussion of positive attributes scales in chapter 7 provides an introduction to this neglected perspective. Giving attention to the Psychosocial Development Scales can afford insights into an array of essential coping skills.

Psychosocial Development Scales

Specific interpretive guidance will be found in chapter 8 for each of the six scales in this series, so those are not repeated here in detail. Cutoffs based on the present research consistently showed that patients scored around one standard deviation lower than the normative *MMPI–2* sample, with the scale for Industrious vs. Inadequate producing the lowest mean scores of all.

As a caution, only the Industrious vs. Inadequate scale is balanced for True–False responding. Patients who score substantially below the rounded mean values for *True* (i.e., females, 220; males, 212) have marked an inordinate number of items False and thereby may have produced invalidly high scores on five of these scales. In that event, the one balanced scale would stand out as lower than the other five.

Scores exceeding T64 generally suggest defensive underreporting. Only the Initiating vs. Guilt-Prone scale produced scores in this range among patients. Examination of the high scorers' records made clear that they did not possess even adequate coping skills in this regard. Scores above T64 on any of the six scales should be regarded as probable signs of underreporting. However, these may be accurate if adults who are known to be high functioning produce scores in the T65 to T74 range. Scores of T75 and above may indicate a grandiosely oriented or narcissistic style of defensiveness.

Average to high average scores (T50–T64) on any of the Psychosocial scales suggest the presence of positive coping capacity relative to the respective issues. Low average scores (T36–T49) are a normal range for many patients and are usually signs of realistic self-report. Low scores (T20–T35) indicate unusual coping deficits. Scores in this range may occur with some frequency in records that exaggerate psychopathology. Scores below T20 are exceedingly rare even among the seriously and persistently mentally ill and will offer a robust sign of exaggerated psychopathology.

Other Scales for Coping Attributes

The Superlative Self-Presentation scale (Butcher & Han, 1995) was developed and validated as a way of detecting self-enhancing defensiveness. Butcher et al. (2001) provided score range guidelines for its interpretation. In the present *MMPI–2* database, a somewhat lower cutoff was needed. Patients in this sample who scored above T65 on *S* were identified clearly as exaggerating virtues and omitting mention of their known psychopathology.

The cutoff for this inpatient sample matches that also established for the Psychosocial scales. When interpreting *S* and its subscales for inpatients similar to those studied here, score ranges used for the Psychosocial scales are recommended pending further study. Those guidelines will support use of these well-designed scales for studying personality coping assets, as well as those uses for which they were originally intended.

Another important coping asset is the capacity to manage impulses in a constructive manner. This means expressing needs, urges, and drives without either overcontrolling or undercontrolling. Thus, it is a sign of psychological balance in this regard when *Imp-B, Imp-I, Imp-A, O-H*, and *R* fall close to the normative CX mean (i.e., approximately T45–T55). Large departures from this range in either direction are associated with adaptive difficulties. Scores on additional scales may be interpreted as favorable when they are in the average to high average range (i.e., T50 to T60 or T65, depending on patient background). These include *K, So, Re, Es*, and *Do*.

MMPI–2 INTERPRETIVE SEARCH PROCEDURES

For many clinicians, high point Clinical scales and codetypes will be the starting points of the search for classifications and descriptions that fit the patient. Even when the result of the initial search seems clear, it needs to be tested against its component parts. Depending on clinician experience and preference, the components used may be combinations of subscales, the Restructured Clinical scales, Content scales, supplemental scales or, as are illustrated here, content clusters.

No matter what specific route the clinician follows after the initial search, the important thing is that the initial match not be the stopping point. Retesting the initial match matters because many initial matches will not prove out. When matches are subjected to a kind of idiographic cross-validation process by means of comparison with other scales, the quality of the assessment product increases. Interpretations that settle for untested initial matches are a lot like getting stuck with first impressions that are formed when first meeting a person. Some limits of initial matches are illustrated by the case studies presented in chapter 11.

Here is what some experienced *MMPI* users have observed about the risks of interpretations based on unwavering classification rules. Graham (1987) listed 44 interpretive statements that could be assigned to a high score on Scale *4* and 16 statements based on a low score. Many statements might apply, but some would be likely to fall off target. As Clopton (1979) observed, persons who endorse very different item subsets of a scale can receive identical scores.

Wiggins (1966) used his array of 13 Content scales to produce an extended example of the potential folly of ignoring collateral content. In the example, he displayed two hypothetical patients with totally identical *MMPI* profiles whose content scores were all different (mean difference 6.77 raw score points per scale). The potential result of retesting initial classifications is, hence, achieving homogeneity of interpretive variance by reconciling as many aspects of the record as possible.

AXIS I AND ALLIED CONDITIONS

Affective and Arousal Disorders

When supported by other data sources, *MMPI–2* scales are capable of identifying major depression, dysthymia, and aspects of bipolar conditions; anxiety, panic, phobias, obsessions, and social phobia; and anger regulation disorders. It is necessary in each instance to factor in the corroborative information that assists to confirm the classification.

Major Depression.   *MMPI–2* Scale *2* (*D*) includes the full range of major depressive symptoms but may elevate because of discouragement and poor morale. Of the *H–L* subscales, *2SD* (T65) best indicates the mood component for *DSM–IV* criteria A(1) and A(2). This latter criterion also links to elevation of *8EA*. These aspects need to be supplemented with data regarding the relatively pervasive and continuous presence of these symptoms. It is further necessary to establish when the episode commenced in order to meet the duration criterion.

Specific inquiry is required for the vegetative signs covered by Criteria A(3) and A(4), unless health status has been surveyed (see chap. 10). Criteria A(5) and A(6) are covered by *3LM* and *2PR* (both T65), with further information on agitation coming from elevations of the anxiety scales, *ANX, TSC/T*, and *Panic* (all T65), and confirmed by observation. The combination of depression and anxiety is the basis for agitated depression, and the physiological reactivity captured by the *Panic* scale taps into its overactive autonomic substrate.

Criterion A(7) is well covered by *LSE, W-MOR, I-SC, 2B*, and *4SA* (M = T62). The *2MD* and *TSC/A* (both T60) scales are particularly suited to making inference about Criterion A(8). Criterion A(9) is examined by referring to *Suic-S, Suic-O*, and *Suic-T* (T60 for *Suic-O*; T65 for the other two), along with use of the Critical Inquiry items that have been endorsed. History is an important adjunctive information source on suicide potential as well as the long-term course of the illness (i.e., single episode or recurrent, precipitating stressors and degree of improvement usually attained). See also chapter 10 for appraisal of suicide risk.

At least five of the foregoing nine criteria must be met for clear diagnosis. An atypical depression (NOS) may be present if fewer criteria are met. If psychotic symptoms accompany the episode, then *BIZ, 8BSE*, and *I-RD* (T60) should be elevated. Note that the overall patterning of depressive symptoms is more likely to be atypical among younger and elderly persons.

In addition to the criteria, major depression is expected to be accompanied by marked elevations of *DEP, TSC/D*, and *W-DEP* (all T65), whereas *D-S* (T42) should be well below average. Often somatic concerns will also elevate, with *2PM* and *3LM* (both T60) being the most likely scales to do so. The Psychosocial scales that are used to make inferences about autonomy, industry, and identity are likely to be low (under T40). Finally, Dependent, Avoidant, and Borderline *PDOs* often give strong depressive presentations (all T65) and are prone to mood disorders.

Dysthymic Disorder.   Dysthymia may be described by analogy as a bit less disturbed sibling of major depression. Many persons with dysthymia will in time develop the more severe disorder. Instead of nearly all the time, persons with this disorder are depressed most of the time. Very specific time criteria must be met for this diagnosis. These need to be obtained from reliable life history sources.

Two of the following major depression criteria reviewed earlier must be met to the extent noted in *DSM–IV*: 1, 3, 4, 6, 7, and 8. The methods of detection listed are appropriate here as well. It is expected that most dysthymics will at all times produce at least somewhat elevated scores on *2SD, 2MD, 2PR, LSE, W-MOR*, and *I-SC* (all T60) and low scores on *Do, K*, and *So* (all T40), whether or not they otherwise fully meet *DSM–IV* criteria 1, 5, 6, 7, and 8. Their Psychosocial scales will be correspondingly affected (under T40). This constant undertone of depression contrasts with that of those nondysthymics who have major depression only. During good interepisode periods of remission, they can be relatively free of these markers. If at times symptoms resemble dysthymia but with cycling features of hypomania, then the possibility of cyclothymia should be investigated.

Bipolar Disorder. *MMPI–2* gives clear signals regarding the depressive phase of this disorder, using the scales listed earlier, but is less sensitive to the hypomanic phase. These scales may suggest the presence of a hypomanic phase: elevations on *Ma* and *9EI* (both T60) when accompanied by low *2PR* (T42). Although *9PMA* and *W-HYP* would appear by their titles to be well positioned to detect hypomanic tendencies, they do not prove out to do so. Core items for this group (122, 226, 242, 267, 330, 366, and 529) are included in the Critical Inquiry procedure and are suggested for discussion irrespective of whether they are answered True or False. Only two of these appear in *9PMA*, whereas *W-HYP* contains all but one of the Critical Inquiry items (i.e., 529). Scales measuring psychosis should not be elevated.

Considerable corroborative information is needed regarding the shift from baseline to the hypomanic state and its duration as well as to confirm Criteria B(2), (6), and (7). The remaining criteria from B will usually be observable during clinical interview. Manic episodes, of course, will not require confirmation by psychological testing. Due to the risk of unreliable self-perception during the episode, it is necessary independently to confirm details of the change of state. As to the many subclassifications of bipolar disorder, reliable history is a primary data source recommended using patient interview, clinic records, and informants.

Generalized Anxiety Disorder. The following scales are expected to elevate for this disorder: *Pt, TSC/T, ANX, A, PK, PS, 4SA* (all T65). *Panic* may also be comparably elevated. These are too strongly intercorrelated to suggest any single scale as being more useful than the others for identifying this disorder. Patient interview presentation should be congruent. In order to better focus treatment, electromyographic and skin conductance monitoring can be useful in quantitative analysis of the roles that musculoskeletal and autonomic tension play for the individual patient.

Anxiety Spectrum scales should be elevated at a higher mean level than are the scales for the Depressive Spectrum cluster. Further, scales signifying phobic concerns (*FRS, W-PHO*) and obsessions (*OBS, I-OC*) should also be at levels clearly below the mean for anxiety scales. Social phobia (see criteria later) must not compete as a diagnosis. These *MMPI–2* exclusionary checks are needed in order to rule out other disorders as possibly primary.

Panic Attacks and Disorder. The examining psychologist will find that panic attacks are usually reliably reported by patients during initial contact. The *MMPI–2 Panic* (T65) scale will give a confirming signal. Critical Inquiry items are available for follow-up. If the attacks are associated with other disorders, then it will usually be possible to identify the predispositions and cues that need to be incorporated into treatment. In any event, essential information about the antecedents of attacks will be needed, and these are not highly likely to emerge from test results any more readily than from interview.

Some patients readily state symptoms of their panic attacks but are at a loss to identify internal or external events that precede them. In these cases, the clinician can instruct the patient to collect and record data about whatever immediately precedes an attack. Some patients are not able to follow through on this approach. An alternate procedure is to arrange in advance for an immediately available clinical telephone contact whenever an attack occurs, in order to permit timely interview. Continuous monitoring of skin conductance and heart rate during initial interview and ongoing therapy contacts can also capture otherwise elusive linkages between internal events and psychophysiological reactivity.

The interplay of panic attacks in substance abuse, depressive, anxiety, psychotic, and medical disorders needs to be considered in the overall evaluation. Panic attacks may be added as a qualifying remark for these other disorders. If it is to be identified as a stand-alone condition, then this can be as Panic Disorder either with or without agoraphobia. Agoraphobia will present like a mixture of anxiety disorder with phobic concerns and possible obsessiveness. *MMPI–2* cannot be relied on to distinguish it from these other patterns. Instead, detailed behavioral interviewing is needed to uncover data needed for effective treatment.

Social Phobia.   Subthreshold social anxiety is a common condition in the nonpatient population. Only when it interferes with important life functions or causes significant subjective distress is it considered a diagnosable disorder. Persons with this disorder often are able to identify biologically close relatives who also have had this or allied conditions. They describe themselves with high scores on *TSC/I* (T65); and *Si, SOD,* and *W-SOC* (*M* = T60); and with low scores on *Impert, 3DSA, 4SI,* and *9IMP* (*M* = T40). Feelings of social alienation may well be expressed (*SoAlien, 4SOA, 8SOA; M* = T65). They report shyness, social sensitivity, and avoidance of some social situations (*Si1, 6P, Si2; M* = T60).

Life history may suggest that the foregoing characteristics preceded clear manifestations of the phobia. A possible antecedent is unresolved childhood shyness of the slow to warm up type described by Thomas and Chess (1977) that progresses into Avoidant *PDO*. Thus, whether or not they are Avoidant *PDO*s, the *AVDT* scale likely will be above average (T65) and scores on the Autonomous vs. Doubting and the Involved vs. Disengaged Psychosocial scales will be low (under T40). Slight, noninterpretable elevation will also occur on the *W-PHO* scale, because it includes items relating to social phobia.

Other Specific Phobias.   Two scales will quickly reveal persons who have phobic concerns: *FRS* and *W-PHO* (T60). If phobias are the focus of clinical attention, then review of the individual items endorsed on these two scales will be the usual follow-up. After the target phobias are identified by the *MMPI-2* scales, behavioral interviewing will be needed to appraise and hierarchically arrange cues according to their relative salience and evocative strength.

Obsessions and Obsessive–Compulsive Disorder.

MMPI-2 scales for detecting obsessions are *OBS* and *I-OC* (both T60). Interview must be used to evaluate the extent to which the obsessions meet *DSM–IV* criteria. There is no comparable scale for compulsions. Lacking such a scale, the psychologist will find adequate guidance in the *DSM–IV* compulsions criteria to fill in this gap during clinical interview. Because *Pt* relates to the underlying character of the obsessive–compulsive (Friedman et al., 2001), its score will be elevated. Yet, due to *Pt*'s global scope, it is not determinative of this disorder. Notably, application of the *K*-correction to *Pt* significantly reduces its relation to *OBS, I-OC,* and the *OBCP PDO* scale, thereby confirming its saturation with global distress.

Posttraumatic Stress Disorder (PTSD).

MMPI-2 scales for this disorder, *PK* and *PS* like *Pt* and the *A* factor, cover a broad range of symptoms. Thus they correlate in the present database very highly with *A* (.88–.91), and, following *K*-correction, they still relate strongly to *Sc* (.79–.80) and *Pt* (.78–.81). They both also relate to *Pa* and *D* in the .60s. These extensive linkages to diverse forms of psychopathology may be appropriate for scales designed to single out persons who have experienced catastrophic forms of trauma. *PK* and *PS* unquestionably tap the distress of PTSD, but fail to provide information regarding specific *DSM–IV* criteria. Thus, *PK* and *PS* are viewed here primarily as useful in screening patients for PTSD. A positive screening result makes it necessary to explore all of the criterial aspects of the disorder by using the specific *DSM* guidelines. A PTSD diagnosis should not be made based solely on elevations of either or both of these scales.

Anger Dysregulation: Intermittent Explosive Disorder.

The Intermittent Explosive Disorder appears to be strangely placed in *DSM–IV–TR* in a catch-all category: "Impulse-Control Disorders Not Elsewhere Classified." In recognition of its connection to basic affective processes, it seems reasonable to treat it here instead. This is a disorder with a relatively distinctive pattern and a limited set of specific *DSM* criteria. It purports to reference "discrete episodes" but without specifying the time intervals that separate them. *DSM* characterizes the disorder as being rare. It is, nevertheless, likely to be encountered by psychologists both in inpatient and outpatient settings and in forensic work.

The disorder is not suspected until a dangerous episodic anger outburst occurs. When it does, it is unexpected and disproportionate to the precipitating circumstances. Further, to those who are familiar with the way the person usually behaves, the action seems to be very much out of character. A considerable body of research with the *MMPI-2 O-H* scale dispels some of the seeming mystery of why the behavior occurs. It is because the person customarily inhibits expression of anger, holding it inside. This defense against a powerful emotion is inherently unstable. As resentments accumulate, tension builds and at some point the anger can no longer be restrained. Some minor event triggers an episode of dyscontrol.

Persons with this disorder produce below average scores on *ANG, W-HOS, TSC/R*, and *Ho*, usually averaging T40 or lower. Concurrently, *O-H* will be elevated (around T65), signaling that low scores on the several anger spectrum scales indicate overcontrol rather than a placid disposition. Overcontrol may be more broadly exercised to include diverse expressions of impulses, needs, and drives. In this case, the four Impulsivity scales will also register exceptionally low scores (i.e., averaging under T45). All of the overcontrol scales are potentially subject to defensive underreporting by persons who believe they will viewed in an unfavorable light if they admit having any impulse life.

Anger Dysregulation: Psychogenic Rage.   When the pattern of anger outbursts is nonepisodic and is subject to being evoked on nearly any occasion, a different disorder needs to be considered. Based on clinical experience treating a number of these individuals, it is proposed that they be viewed as a group that is distinct from the Intermittent Explosive Disorder. The name *Psychogenic Rage* is proposed in Appendix E to describe the essence of the syndrome. It is not recognized in either the psychological or psychiatric literature and, accordingly, is absent from the *DSM* series. Thus, Appendix E should be reviewed closely before applying the suggestions offered here for its recognition.

Patients with psychogenic rage will most commonly see a psychologist following their arrest for battery, disorderly conduct, or destruction of property. Some referrals are made in the context of domestic problems involving physical abuse (i.e., battery of spouse or offspring). During initial workup, the behaviors will often be attributed to alcohol or other substance abuse. Further investigation, however, reveals that the behaviors are present during periods of abstinence. These are angry, tense persons who react violently to minimal provocations. They may or may not meet criteria for a personality disorder. In any event, a personality disorder does not encompass the dyscontrol and violence present.

Their readiness to anger, resentments, and grudges show up on a number of *MMPI–2* scales (*ANG, W-HOS, TSC/R, Ho*), averaging over T65. Resources for modulation of drives and impulses are weak: *O-H* under T40 and *Imp-A, Imp-I, Imp-B*, and *Imp-T* average above T65. These findings are strongly suggestive but not definitive. Others will produce a similar pattern across these scales but do not exhibit rages. Others who score similarly may be quarrelsome, verbally vicious, vindictive, threatening, and so on—but with the difference that they seldom lose control totally while dissolving into states of rage with distressing regularity.

Existing scales are useful but fail to capture the intensity of emotion, internal instability, and rapid loss of control. Psychogenic Rage (*Rage*) is an experimental *MMPI–2* scale that was designed to measure this disorder (Appendix E). Pending further study, it is suitable for screening and must be cross-validated idiographically by confirmation of the behavioral pattern. Psychophysiological monitoring is further recommended for confirming the psychogenic initiation of rage episodes and their susceptibility to interruption by behavioral intervention.

Thought Processing Disorders

Use of *MMPI–2* to identify thought disorders is supported by a number of validated scales. In the active phases of these illnesses, symptomatic expression is obvious and readily accessible to observation, conversation, and in cooperative patients, to formal clinical interview. Specific symptoms to identify are described in *DSM–IV–TR*. During acute episodes, administration of formal tests is difficult, resulting in mostly unsatisfactory and questionable records. Testing is more meaningful after the patient is initially stabilized.

Schizophrenia. Persons with this disorder score above T65 on *Sc, BIZ, I-RD, W-PSY, 8BSE, Pa, S+,* and *6PI.* However, persons with substance dependence disorders, Cluster A personality disorders, and organic mental disorders often obtain similar scores on several of these scales. Using the mental status examination in combination with *MMPI–2* usually suffices for sorting out the possibilities. If paranoid symptoms are more prominent, then *Pa, S+,* and *6PI* will be a bit higher and *8BSE* a bit lower than with undifferentiated schizophrenia.

Disorganized schizophrenics seldom complete meaningfully *MMPI–2* and will be assessed using behavioral observations during informal interactions. History shows a distinctly higher level of premorbid functioning in most instances at some time in the person's past. Catatonic schizophrenics are identified by peculiarities of posture and motor behavior. In addition to the *DSM* symptoms, clinical experience suggests that thought blocking may occur with catatonic disorder, and, further, that reduced postural flexibility may predate an episode and remain even after good mental recovery.

Schizoaffective Disorder. During its acute phase, this disorder is particularly challenging to distinguish from bipolar disorder with psychotic symptoms. Telling these disorders apart becomes easier after they are in substantial remission. Schizoaffectives are more likely on the *MMPI–2* scales listed for schizophrenia to show persisting signs of the underlying illness even when overt symptoms are in remission, that is, continued although lower level elevations are present on these scales. Recovered schizoaffectives also exhibit residual emotional lability. The *MMPI–2*s of bipolars who have recovered from psychotic features are unlikely to exhibit residual signs of a thought processing disorder. These facts recommend administering *MMPI–2* during remissions.

Delusional Disorder.   The *MMPI–2* literature gives mixed signals on the paranoid or delusional disorder. It leaves doubt about the value of *Pa* and *S+*, which are likely to elevate in schizophrenia. The clearest course of action in view of this is first to establish that nonbizarre delusions are present. The *MMPI–2* now becomes clinically useful by showing absence of psychotic elevations on *Sc, BIZ, 8BSE, I-RD*, and *W-PSY*. Moreover, persons with delusional disorder on the average function at higher levels than do those with schizophrenia.

Cognitive Disorders

Personality tests are not first line instruments for assessing the cognitive disorders. The *MMPI–2*, nevertheless, provides a number of scales that have value for assessing patient awareness of cognitive difficulties, specifying dimensions of the disorganized thought process and describing patient concerns. Scales recommended for exploring these issues are: *2MD, 8COG, TSC/A, 8BSE, W-ORG, NeurPsy*, and *I-DS*. No specific standard score values are suggested; rather, they are recommended to be used for clinical description.

A second use for the listed cognitive disorder scales is to screen for the presence of previously unsuspected cognitive difficulties. A pattern of several elevations will indicate the need for additional study. The presence of cognitive difficulties may well cause production of a less consistent record. Elevations of response consistency scales that appear earlier in this chapter will be used to corroborate cognitive difficulties. Records of high consistency inevitably raise questions about possible overreporting of cognitive difficulties.

Substance Abuse and Dependence

The *MAC* scale has been the subject of considerable research. In its *MMPI–2* version (*MAC-R*), newer items were added. Raw rather than *T*-scores are commonly used. Cutoffs vary by setting. The *APS* scale was developed after the *MMPI–2* revision and has been less studied. Both scales were developed by comparison of criterion groups, and both avoid inclusion of nearly all items that make explicit reference to substance abuse (exceptions: 382, 540). Thus, they are designed to function as subtle measures. Unfortunately, research has not made clear what their actual contribution is to identifying persons involved in substance abuse. The literature on them is well reviewed by Friedman et al. (2001).

Contrary to findings reported in chapter 8, clinical experience has shown the *MAC/MAC-R* to be a strong indicator of substance abuse and risk of substance abuse in persons with no history of abuse. Nevertheless, unacceptable levels of false positives have been encountered. Among those in a program for treating chemical dependency, occasional false negatives have also turned up.

A more useful approach has been to use an Addictive Activities (*AA*) scale (items and norms in Appendixes A and B) that was developed locally from Critical Inquiry Worksheet items (Appendix C). A positive indication on any of these 10 items is followed up with critical inquiry. These outperform *MAC-R* and *APS*.

Ultimately, whatever tools are selected for use, the assessing psychologist will need to follow *DSM–IV–TR* guidelines by inquiring into substances of abuse, course of disorder, whether or not dependence is present, severity of withdrawal episodes, legal and economic complications, the impact of abuse on vital life functions and health, prior treatment and results, patient followthrough when no longer in treatment, and circumstances surrounding relapse.

It has been productive also to approach the patient with the assumption that, despite the many downside features, the patient gets something out of using. Based on this assumption, inquiry is directed to finding out what is gained (e.g., good times, deadening of pain, social facilitation, tension reduction, as cover for engaging in other activities, excuse for acting out, etc.). The outcomes of use that the patient is pursuing can then become targets for treatment intervention.

Somatoform Disorders

First, *MMPI–2* scales offer screening level information, on the basis of which a more thorough health status workup may need to be completed. Chapter 10 clarifies the role of the psychologist in this regard. Beyond a screening function, the *MMPI–2* scales for somatic concerns cannot be used to infer illness or health as such—tasks for which they lack comprehensiveness of scope and depth of inquiry. Instead, they will be used to assess whether a somatoform disorder may be present.

Somatization. This is a diagnosis that will be assigned on the basis of the *DSM* specified complaints, and then only if the health status review fails to substantiate them. Scales that identify the tendency to complain about many and varied conditions include *Hs, HEA, TSC/B*, and *W-HEA*. Elevations above T65 point to possible somatization—the higher the level, the more likely.

Nevertheless, even at maximum raw score levels, no scale meets the specific criteria of *DSM–IV–TR*. Numerous gastrointestinal symptoms do support *DSM* Criterion B(2) matches. Only three pain areas (i.e., head, neck, and chest) appear in *MMPI–2*, but Criterion B(1) requires at least four. Zero items deal with Criterion B(3) for sexual symptoms. Thus, additional physical symptom inquiries will be required if this diagnosis is to be assigned, no matter how elevated the health scales.

Hypochondriasis. To the scales already cited, the following can be added to the previous ones when reviewing the possibility of hypochondriasis: *W-ORG, 8BSE, NeurPsy, I-DS, TSC/A, 3SC, 2PM*. That is, any bodily symptoms qualify for consideration. No specific number or type of complaint is relevant here. Hence, elevation (T65) on any of the four scales listed earlier or seven added here may call for additional workup. What further is necessary for this diagnosis is that the patient focuses excessive attention on a symptom and catastrophizes regarding it in the face of qualified medical opinion as to its actual significance. Unlike Somatization Disorder, the hypochondriacal patient may have one or more well documented physical problems. Complaints associated with them only lead to this diagnosis if the patient persists in misinterpreting them as ominous and reacting to the misinterpretations with worry and distress.

AXIS II AND ALLIED CONDITIONS

Social Maladjustment, Introversion, Alienation

The scales used for assessing these conditions were discussed relative to Social Phobia. The signals that they give for introversion are similar to those for Social Phobia (i.e., on *TSC/I, Si, SOD, W-SOC, Si1, Si2, 6P*), but the social anxiety component may not be as prominent (i.e., *3DSA, 4SI, 9IMP*, and *Impert* mean not lower than T45). Moreover, strong social alienation may be absent among introverts (*4SOA, 8SOA*, and *SoAlien* not expected to exceed T60).

HYP and *9PMA* may be low (T45) in these persons as a sign of their avoidance. If, however, *9PMA* exceeds T60, then shyness may be preventing the person from meeting a need for more social stimulation. Individuals with this combination of shyness and thwarted need for social stimulation may resort to using alcohol and substances that reduce shyness and facilitate social mingling.

The pattern for the socially maladjusted is likely to be higher than that for either introversion or Social Phobia on *TSC/I, Si, SOD, W-SOC, 4SOA, 8SOA, SoAlien*, and *6P* (mean close to T70). Note that these persons may harbor powerful feelings of alienation. Social anxiety indicators will be variable for these individuals, with some below T40 and others as high as T45. *Si1* and *Si2* may be as low as T55. They face the same conflict as introverts if their need for social stimulation exceeds their social anxiety. If social maladjustment and alienation are present, then they should be examined in light of the Psychosocial scales. Remarks can then be made in the report when maladjustment, social anxiety, and/or alienation are present.

Anger, Hostility, Suspicion, Cynicism, Resentment

These characteristics need not be reviewed if they have been accounted for by inclusion under Axis I. On the other hand, they may come in for initial analysis here. When *TSC/S* and *CYN* are T65 or above, the patient questions the motives and intentions of others, believing that they cannot be trusted. If, in addition, *Ho* is over T60, then this impression is reinforced; and if it is over T70, then the person is highly critical of others and feels disappointed with them.

Persons whose scores on *ANG* and *W-HOS* exceed T65 are irritable, prone to anger, quarrelsome, and at times have difficulty controlling hostile feelings. Those who score T65 or above on *TSC/R* are resentful, particularly of demands that others make of them. Those adults who appear neither angry nor hostile on *ANG* and *W-HOS* but who report resentfulness on *TSC/R* usually feel powerless and adopt a passive–aggressive stance. They express their discontent only in ways that they judge to be safe. This means behind others' backs. They will mutter caustic remarks inaudibly or unintelligibly. When asked what they said, they deny saying anything.

Virtue and Morality

When *3NA, 6N*, and *Trust* are between T58 and T65, usually along with *9AMO* T48 or below, an optimistic, trusting, uncritical outlook is reported. These scores result from attributing both honesty and reasonableness to others. The same scores for *3NA, 6N*, and *Trust* in combination with *9AMO* over T60 suggest that the person is experiencing a conflict over moral values. The conflict involves deciding whether or not it is more desirable to be honest and friendly or selfish and opportunistic. If *3NA, 6N*, and *Trust* surpass T66, then this may instead indicate denial of hostile or negative feelings. If so, scores on *ANG* and other scales in the preceding section will appear unusually low (below T40). When *L* and *5C* exceed T60, with *3NA, 6N*, and *Trust* at T66, defensiveness or denial is even more likely.

Behavior Controls and Norms Violations

Behavior Controls. The Impulsivity scales were introduced earlier in this chapter, and their role relative to two anger patterns appeared under Axis I. Now the Impulsivity scales—*Imp-B, Imp-I, Imp-A*, and *Imp-T*—are featured together with *8DI, R, O-H, Re*, and *9EI* indicators of behavior controls. Interfacing with them are *Pd, ASP, 9AMO, W-AUT, MAC-R*, and *APS* scales to represent the potential for norms violations.

The *8DI* and the four Impulsivity scales correlate positively with one another as measures of undercontrol when they are high ($M = $ T65) and overcontrol when low ($M = $ T40). When *8DI*'s elevation matches the other scales on the high end, this latter scale identifies concern and distress over dyscontrol. When the four are low, low *8DI* expresses the sense of being in control. Midrange scores (T45–T55) usually signify effective drive and impulse regulation.

The *9EI* scale cofluctuates positively with these five scales but especially with *Imp-I*, indicating poor judgment. A low score on *5C* further supports this interpretation. When *9EI* is elevated (T65) along with the other five, a sense of entitle-ment, limitations of self-awareness, and disregard for others make the under-controlled person's out of bounds behavior more arrogant and troublesome for others. When *9EI* is low (T40) along with the overcontrolled pattern, a more in-flexible style of instinctual management is often implied. Some overcontrolled persons avoid pleasurable activities, feeling that enjoyment means weakness.

The foregoing six scales correlate negatively with *R*, *O-H*, and *Re*. Low scores (T40) on these, along with the undercontrolled pattern, invite interpretation of the patient to include distinctly antisocial leanings. When the impulsivity scales indi-cate overcontrol, higher scores on *R*, *O-H*, and *Re* (T65) indicate rigidity of im-pulse control. When *Re* is markedly higher than *R* and *O-H*, this raises questions about the extent to which reporting is affected by self-enhancement.

Norm Violating Behaviors. The *Pd*, *ASP*, *9AMO*, and *W-AUT* scales signify antisocial behavior when elevated (M = T65) and relate highly positively to the *ANTI PDO* scale and highly negatively to Initiating vs. Guilt-Prone. Undercontrol plus antisocial elevation strongly suggests that norm violating be-havior can be expected. Low scores (M = T40) on the norm violating scales, espe-cially on *W-AUT*, when these accompany the overcontrol pattern indicate conformity and overconventionality. Alternatively, these signs may represent strong denial.

Gender and Sexuality

MMPI/MMPI–2 has in the past provided limited information relative to sexuality. Neither *Mf* nor *W-FEM* fulfills a role here. As a result of the *MMPI–2* revision, the Paraphilia/Pedophilia (*Pe*) scale required extensive modification and *I-SP* scale was lost to the *MMPI–2* revision. The *Pe* revision and a newer scale, Sexual-ity/Intimacy Failure (*Sexual*) to replace *I-SP*, are discussed in chapter 6. Both are promising experimental scales. *Pe* may be useful in forensic work with sex of-fenders. High scores on *Sexual* suggest for both genders a limited ability to com-municate with others, lack of interpersonal openness, and sexual difficulties. The scale relates negatively to *GM* ($r = -.42$), *GF* ($r = -.11$), and the Eriksonian-based intimacy scale, Involved vs. Disengaged ($r = -.54$). Low scorers assert that these are not problems.

The *GM* scale identifies behaviors associated more strongly with maleness and the *GF* scale those that relate more to femaleness. Higher *GM* scores have been found generally to have positive implications for both males and females (Butcher et al., 2001). Low scores turn out to be negative signs for both genders as well. Beyond feminine stereotype, the meaning of elevations on *GF* is less clear. Socio-economic background likely affects scores on these two scales. Firm interpretive guidelines await further study.

Self-Esteem

MMPI–2 identifies patients with low self-esteem by average elevations of T65 or higher on *LSE, W-MOR, I-SC*; below T35 on *So*; and below T45 on *5C*. Low self-esteem is expected to appear in particular with the various depressive spectrum disorders and social maladjustment. That is to say, it usually is seen as a companion to another identified disorder.

Dependency–Dominance

Low self-confidence and dependency are present when *Depnd* reaches T60. A more self-assured, dominant outlook is inferred when *Do* scores are greater than T60. Earlier these were measured by *I-De* and *I-Do*. After *MMPI–2* revision, the former is now of modest reliability and the latter is unreliable (Appendix B). Based on clinical experience, Levitt (1989; Levitt & Gotts, 1995) made inferences based on a difference between *I-De* and *I-Do* of T15, as well as inferences based on their absolute score levels. *Depnd* and *Do* scales are both more reliable than *I-De* and *I-Do* were previously. *Depnd* and *Do* correlate with each other ($r = -.62$) at a higher level than did the earlier scales ($r = -.14$). Thus a difference of T15 provides substantial support for using the T15 difference. For example, if *Depnd* is T55 and *Do* is T40, this is interpreted to mean dependency and low self-confidence, even though the absolute level of *Depnd* is below the T60 recommended earlier. The opposite holds for *Do* at T55 with *Depnd* at T40. *Re* is low (T40) in dependency and high with dominance (T60).

Family Relationships

Whenever *FAM, W-FAM,* or *4FD* exceeds T65, some family problem needs to be clarified through discussion with the patient. Implications of the finding for treating the patient will then be included in the assessment report.

DSM Personality Disorders

Chapter 6 describes the personality classification process. Adult patients with valid records who had received no psychotic or major affective diagnosis were examined for personality disorders. Any of these patients who produced a score on one or more of the Indiana *PDO* Scales at or above the 85th percentile were screened as positive for *PDO*s. Positively screened cases were next classified by specific disorder. Patients who screened as positive for *PDO*s were compared with a sample of those who produced no *PDO* score at or below the 72nd percentile on any of the 11 *PDO* scales. Methods for differentiating *PDO*s that resemble one another appear in chapter 9.

Screening with brief *PDO* scales can only approximate *DSM* criteria. In order to more fully evaluate matches, it is necessary to examine other *MMPI–2* scales that relate to the various criteria in *DSM–IV–TR* (2000) for each disorder. In some instances, other collateral data are needed that are unavailable from *MMPI–2*. Researched matches of *MMPI–2* scales to criteria are specified later.

Not all criteria need be met during confirmatory matching. The required number should be consulted for each *DSM* category. Nevertheless, it is expected that the patient record will show a patterning of scale scores that resembles many of the criterial attributes, and will usually exceed the number required for a *DSM* diagnosis. *Resemble* simply means that the profile of scale scores will follow the pattern of highs and lows for the disorder and will be at similar levels. Thus, the psychologist needs to focus both on scale patterning and score levels.

For patient records that otherwise match formal *DSM* criteria, component scale departures from the expected pattern challenge the tendency to pigeonhole patients. These variations invite appreciative description of individual patient characteristics that arise from the interaction of their differing constitutions and life experiences.

The *MMPI–2* scale levels suggested for each *PDO* are based on research with an inpatient population. The severity of their personality disorders may vary from the disorders of patients encountered in other settings. Thus, although the psychologist may have reasonable conceptual confidence in the scales used to match *DSM* criteria, patient severity may affect levels of scale elevation within the overall patterning. This limitation calls for further study with patients who differ from those studied in the present research.

Antisocial PDO. Persons with this disorder, on average, score over T70 on the *ANTI* screening scale. The core of the Anti *PDO*'s coping style shows up as misdirected initiative and regrets: *Initiating vs. Guilt-Prone* T40 & *4SA* T60. Criterially related signs of the Anti *PDO* are: Norm violating behaviors—*ASP* T65, *9AMO* T60, *O–H* T45; Authority conflict—*W–AUT* T60; Impulsivity and recklessness—*Imp-B* & *Imp-T* T65, exceeding *Imp-A* by T10; Irresponsibility—*Re* T35; Irritability—*Ho* T60; Callousness—*CYN* T60 & *Sadist* T55; Mistrust & deceitfulness—*Trust* T42, *TSC/S* T60, *Cared for vs. Neglected* T45; Controlled emotionality—*Panic, Imp-A* & *ANX* all T50, *ANG* & *2SD* T55. The following are some other characteristics: Denial of dependency—*Depnd* T50; Substance abuse—*MAC-R* T70; Minimal somatic preoccupation—*HEA* T50. The *Pd* scale relates more strongly to the Passive–Aggressive *PDO* than to the Antisocial in this population.

Paranoid PDO. Scores on the *PRND* scale screen positive around T68. The Prnd *PDO*'s core coping difficulty relates to a belief that people are uncaring and malevolent: *Cared for vs. Neglected* T36. Signs of a thought processing disorder resembling schizophrenia (e.g., *Sc, Pa, I-RD*) are only mildly elevated, averaging around T60. Criterial features are: Suspicions—*S+* & *TSC/S* T65; Mistrust of others—*Trust* T40 & *Cared for vs. Neglected* T36; Concerns about hidden meanings—*6PI* T75; Feeling alienated and under attack—*SoAlien* T62; Easily aroused to anger—*Ho* T62, *O-H* T40; Holds grudges, unforgiving, resentful—*TSC/R* T60; Judgment of others' motives impaired—*Imp-I* T63, exceeding mean of *Imp-B* and *Imp-A* by T5–T10. In seeming paradox, there is denial of social hypersensitivity (*6P* T50), which seems to say: "I am not overly sensitive. The problem is that others are causing me trouble." *MAC-R* often exceeds T65 among Prnds. Clinical interview is required to fill in this picture.

Narcissistic PDO.   Persons with the Narc *PDO* produce the lowest average elevation for a screening scale of any of the 11 *PDO*s. They can be identified at T65. Likewise, some of their essential qualities hide beneath the surface during casual contact. When they encounter disagreement or challenge to their fragile persona, however, their dark side asserts itself. Whereas *MMPI–2* scales do not correspond closely to the listed criteria, they do offer a more general match to the Narc *PDO*'s underlying burden of narcissistic pain, humiliation, and rage. Even then defensiveness causes these indicators to be understated. The full expression of their discontent is, hence, attenuated.

There is a less direct pattern that assists, nevertheless, in identifying this disorder: Minimization—Clinical scale mean under T60, *F* and *Sd* both T55; Pronounced denial of social maladjustment and anxiety—*SOD, TSC/I, W-SOC, Si, Si1, Si2, Impert* all under T50, *Involved vs. Disengaged* T48; But Denial contradicted by suspicion and mistrust—*TSC/S* and *6PI* T62, *Cared for vs. Neglected* and *Trust* both T42; And denial contradicted by low self-confidence—*Do* T38, *Depnd* T55, *Es* T42, *4SA* T63; Anger, hostility, and resentment—*ANG, W-HOS*, and *TSC/R* all T55; Lowered anger threshold for taking offense—*Ho* T62; Cynical lack of empathy—*CYN* T60 and *Sadist* T57; Impulsive, egocentric thinking—*5C* T42, *Imp-I* T60 that is T10 to T15 higher than *Imp-A*; Authority conflict—*W-AUT* T60; Social alienation and vulnerability—*SoAlien* T60 and *6P* T58. Striving to maintain the narcissistic self-image in the face of reactions to others results in the many tensions and contradictions seen in the Narc *PDO*. Elevations of *MAC-R* above T65 are common for this *PDO*.

Histrionic PDO.   Those who screen positive for Hist typically score above T70 on the *HIST* scale. Many of the *DSM* criteria for the Hist disorder require observation of the patient during interaction with the examiner and others. Some criteria matches occur: Interpersonal neediness—*W-HYP* T65, *9PMA* T60, *Depnd* T58; Claims of normal to hypernormal social relations—*Si, SOD, W-SOC, TSC/I, Si1, Si2, Impert, Sexual*, and *Involved vs. Disengaged* all averaging T50; Excessive emotionality—*Pt, ANX, TSC/T, Panic, D, DEP, TSC/D, W-DEP, 2SD, ANG, TSC/R* average T60 and *4SA* T65; Emotions undercontrolled—*O-H* T39 with *Imp-A* and *Imp-B* T60 and higher by T5 than *Imp-I*. Presentation and expressive behavior during interview can supply data on other criteria.

Borderline PDO.   Bord *PDOs* register one of the highest levels among the *PDOs* on their respective screening scales: *BORD* T78. Instability of emotions is seen in high levels on all scales in the Depressive and Anxiety Spectrum clusters (*M* = T70), with depression scales slightly higher. Intense dyscontrolled anger episodes occur (*ANG, W-HOS, Ho,* and *Imp-A* average T60, with *O-H* below T40). This mixing of powerful emotional states produces undifferentiated disturbances (*PK* & *PS* T70). These result in feelings of avolition (*8CON* T70 & *2PR* T65) and suicidal risk (*Suic-S* T70, *Suic-O* T65).

Behavioral impulsivity is high (*Imp-B* T65). Their efforts to stay connected with others involve excitement seeking (*W-HYP* & *9PMA* average T60), often involving risky behaviors. Thought Processing Disorders scales do not elevate (*M* = T55–T60), except for those indicating referential ideas (*6PI* T60), together with suspicion, mistrust, and illusions of betrayal (*Pa* and *TSC/S* T60, *Trust* T45). Moderately elevated Cognitive Disorders scales (T60–T65) link to dissociative tendencies and intrusive ideation. An immature sense of identity (*Ego Identified vs. Confused* T40) makes for unstable interpersonal relations (*SoAlien* T65, *Sexual* T60, *Involved vs. Disengaged* T40).

Passive–Aggressive PDO.   Persons screen positive on the *PAAG PDO* scale at T70. Criteria considered here are based on those specified for further study in the *DSM* (2000). These are resentful, hostile persons (*W-HOS* and *TSC/R* average T60–T65) who dwell on their dissatisfactions with life (*OBS* T60–T65, *2B* T70). They feel that they are entitled to more than they get (*9EI* T65). They suffer from low morale (*W-MOR* T60–T65) and feelings of regret (*4SA* T70). They feel powerless and insecure (*Do* T35, *Autonomous vs. Doubting* T40, *Depnd* T65). Thus, they feel unable to act directly against the sources of their frustration (*8CON* T65–T70, *2PR* T65), but they are ready at all times to act indirectly when opportunity offers (*Imp-T* T65, *O-H* T40). They believe that those in authority cause many of their problems (*W-AUT* T60). As a consequence of their view of life, their mood is chronically dysphoric and agitated (Depressive and Anxiety Spectrum Cluster scales T60–T65).

Dependent PDO.   Along with Bord *PDO*, the Dpnd *PDO* ties for having the highest mean scores on a screening scale: *DPND* positive at T78. A serious deficit of self-confidence accompanies their dependency (*Depnd* T70, *Do* T35, *Ego Identified vs. Confused* T35). They feel empty and helpless (*Autonomous vs. Doubting* T38, *Es* T35); fundamentally incapable of making a contribution in life (*Industrious vs. Inadequate* T35, *WRK* and *WA* both T65); and socially inept and anxious (*SOD, TSC/I,* and *W-SOC* average T65, *Impert* T40) without being as shy or avoidant (*Si1* and *Si2* T60). They seek, with minimal success, persons who will care for them. The unproductive search results in interpersonal disappointment and resentment (*SoAlien* and *TSC/R* T60) that are unsafe to express directly (*ANG* and *W-HOS* T50). They are more depressed (average scale T70–T75) than anxious (average scale T65–T70) and have low morale and paralysis of will (*LSE* and *W-MOR* T70, *8CON* T70, *2PR* T62).

Obsessive–Compulsive PDO.   A positive screen for this disorder results from *OBCP* scores around T70. These persons present themselves hypernormally with average range scores (T50–T55) on major affective disorder and mental illness scales, even when they are part of an inpatient population. This reflects their conventional conformist outlook, which otherwise is not represented among *MMPI-2* scales in explicit ways.

Characteristics that may match the conformist profile include: Guilt and low morale from rigid standards—*4SA* T62, *W-MOR* T58; Disappointment in personal accomplishments—*Industrious vs. Inadequate* T38, lower than other Psychosocial scales, which approach average; Restricted impulse life—Impulsivity scales averaging T55; Dissatisfactions and misgivings about the imperfections they perceive in others—*TSC/R, CYN, Ho, TSC/S* all near T60; Restriction of direct expression of either those angry feelings or of mean spiritedness (*ANG* and *Sadist* T50–T55). Nevertheless, they admit to obsessing (*OBS* and *I-OC* T60, *2B* T57), but in the absence of prominent phobias (*FRS* and *W-PHO* T55) or intrusive or disruptive ideation (*TSC/A* T50). This last set of findings suggests that mild obsessions are present that are not diagnostic of Obcp *PDO* and that do not correspond to specific criteria for Obsessive–Compulsive Disorder. The meaning of this is inconclusive inasmuch as both *OBS* and *I-OC* are mixes of items expressing behavioral rigidity, indecision, and worry, as well as a few that seem to express obsessions only approaching a match to *DSM* criteria. The *MAC-R* scale exceeded T65 for many of this group.

Avoidant PDO.   *AVDT* scale positively screens around T75. Hallmarks of avoidants are social anxiety and discomfort: *Si, SOD, W-SOC, Si1* at T60–T65; *Impert* at T40, *TSC/I* at T70; and *Si2* at T60. A higher *TSC/I* score level may result from its greater emphasis on low self-confidence (*Autonomous vs. Doubting* T38) and vulnerability (*6P* T58). A lower level for *Si2* may reflect their dependency (*Depnd* T65, *Do* T35), which makes their style of avoidance selective. That is, they cling to those on whom they depend, while avoiding new social contacts. Dependency needs create conflicts for their basic interpersonal style, and they can feel the pain of social alienation (*SoAlien* T62). These timid people feel less than robust, which increases withdrawal into introspective focus (*8EA* T65) and may foster somatic concerns (*HEA, TSC/B, W-ORG* all T60), or these latter concerns may be mood related.

They view themselves as interpersonally flawed (*Involved vs. Disengaged* T38) and castigate themselves over failed relationships (*4SA* T68). They brood over occupational inadequacy (*2B* T62, *GM* and *Industrious vs. Inadequate* T35,

WRK and *WA* T60). Mood is dysphoric (Depressive and Anxiety Spectrum scales all around T65). Self-esteem is seriously compromised (*LSE, W-MOR, I-SC* all above T65; *So* T35).

Schizotypal PDO. A *SCZY* screening cutoff of T70 identifies most of these persons. Ideas of reference (*6PI* T75), perceptual distortions (*8BSE* T65), dissociative experiences (*I-DS* T62), and both peculiar experiences and atypical patterns of thinking (*BIZ* T75, *I-RD* T65) are reported. They are extremely suspicious and mistrusting (*S+* and *TSC/S* both T65, *Cared for vs. Neglected* T35, *Trust* T40). They have limited interpersonal engagement (*SoAlien* T65). Their contacts with others prompt anxiety (*Impert* T45) and produce below average satisfaction (*FAM* and *W-FAM* T60–T65, *Sexual* T55). It is noted that there is some addiction risk (*MAC-R* T65). In order to be observed, some *DSM* criteria for this disorder require direct interaction between examiner and patient. Odd behaviors and peculiar speech, for example, cannot be inferred from *MMPI–2* scales.

Schizoid PDO. A screening cutoff on the *SCZD* scale of T70 separated these persons from the other 10 *PDOs* but resulted in false positives of about 50% of persons who exhibited affect to an extent that did not match *DSM* criteria for this disorder. The false positives were identified within the initially screened group when a further cutoff was set using the total number of *True* item responses made. Those exceeding 105% of CX norms (*True*: 232 for females, 223 for males) exhibited higher affect and, accordingly, were screened out. Thus, a two-stage screening procedure was required. Because this is an exceptional screening procedure, its complications are fully examined.

Patients now identified as Sczd corresponded closely to those selected by using the Morey et al. (1985) items. Sczd patients, on average, scored about one standard deviation lower on scales that elicit expressions of psychopathology and affect than did the patients who were removed by the second screening cut. The match is even stronger if Items *79, 157*, or *405* are answered True. The final Sczd group was used below for pointing out *MMPI–2* and *DSM* linkages. Some *DSM* criteria for Sczd are better studied by direct observation and interview.

Blandness, detachment from life, and low affectivity may be indicated by average to slightly below average scores on these relevant scales: *DEP, ANX, ANG, Dist* all T45–T50. Low scores on the first three of these could be artifacts of eliminating cases with high percentages of *True* responses. The *Dist* scale (T46) with five items keyed True and six False, however, was not subject to potential bias of that type. Lack of social interest is suggested by average scores on *SOD, TSC/I*, and *W-SOC*, with all falling near T50. The three scales are relatively balanced in terms of items being keyed True and False. If the cut on percentage *True* had affected scores, then *Impert* (T50), which is strongly negatively correlated with *SOD, TSC/I*, and *W-SOC*, would have been considerably higher. This is so because it has 12 of its 14 items keyed False. Based on these congruent comparisons relative to item keying, the possibility that these scores were biased by the second screening cut appears implausible and is rejected.

In addition to low social interest, social indifference is implied by below average scores for *6P* and *SoAlien* (i.e., both below T45). Below average scores on *9PMA* (T42) and *W-HYP* (T45) suggest below normal arousal and disinterest in or avoidance of excitement and risk (Graham, 1990). Indifference to social engagement is further attested by *Sexual* (T45) and *Involved vs. Disengaged* (T48) by being near midscore range.

A possibly problematic finding was that *L* was elevated (T62). If this were an overall sign of naïve magnification of personal qualities, then greater elevation would have been expected on the Wiggins *Sd* scale (T55). If it resulted from a naïve form of denial associated with higher False responding, then either *3NA* or *6N* should have been elevated, but neither was (T50–T55). Further observations relative to *L* are that *K* (T55) was average; *TRIN* (T56) and *VRIN* (T47), *RIncon* (T44), and the *RCon1* minus *RCon2* index (less than T2) all showed remarkable response consistency. These findings do not support a naïve defensiveness (Butcher et al., 2001) interpretation for mild elevation of *L* by Sczd persons. It is not inconceivable that persons who are as detached from life as they are may have more time and energy to devote to the kinds of activities encompassed by the *L* scale items.

The *SCZD* screening scale could not by itself single out Sczd *PDOs*. The reader hence was provided with both data and rationale supporting a two-stage screening process, using percentage True further to identify cases. In conclusion, Sczd *PDOs* identified by a two-stage screening process are bland, socially and emotionally detached, indifferent to social engagement, low in affectivity and arousal. They are disinterested in excitement, risk, and stimulation and may be avoidant of these. An unanticipated finding was mild elevation of *L*. Close examination of this in the context of other scales failed to support the view that it was the result of naïve defensiveness. Absent other leads in the literature, the possibility was suggested that Sczd persons' detachment may leave them more time for matters of the kinds covered by *L* scale items. Socially engaged persons likely find that other priorities cause them to neglect these kinds of details.

CONCLUSIONS

Linkages could be shown between *MMPI–2* scales and a number of *DSM* Axis I and II diagnoses. Matches to specific criteria were relatively close in some instances. In others, inferences could be made based only on similarities. Criteria for Major Depression, as one example, can be linked with reasonable accuracy to particular *MMPI–2* scales. Disorders omitted from discussion were found not to be especially amenable to diagnostic formulation through the use of *MMPI–2*.

Often it was noted to be necessary to supplement the *MMPI–2* scales with data gathered from observation, clinical interview, and use of informants. Some potential diagnostic uses of psychophysiological monitoring were discussed in relevant contexts. Although the Critical Inquiry method (Appendix C) was only occasionally mentioned in this review, it can be recommended as a simple and direct route for seeking clarifications. Assessment psychologists will employ additional procedures such as the *Rorschach* (chap. 11), Wechsler scales, and so on. Together with *MMPI–2*, they greatly enlarge the possibilities for identifying linkages to other *DSM* categories about which this chapter was silent.

Appendix A: Special Scales

NOTATIONS FOR COMPOSITION OF SPECIAL SCALES

Scale revisions based on item analyses are documented in their respective item listings using the following brief, direct codes:

C: An item was removed from a scale only if its inclusion diminished the scale's internal consistency in samples of 1,020 male and 637 female patients. Items cut/deleted appear italicized in parentheses following the list of their reliable item counterparts for all edited scales except Harris–Lingoes (see below).

Example: **True:** 22 85 130 (*C: 17 44*).

R: An item was rekeyed only if its reassignment increased its scale's internal consistency for both the male and female samples. Rekeyed items appear in boldface preceded by the code R in their appropriate new locations and are not relisted or cited in their original locations.

Example: **False:** 190 211 **R233** 259 294.

A: Additions were made to scales in only two circumstances: (a) original Harris–Lingoes items that are not in *Pd* (*4*) were reintroduced if they contributed to the *Pd* subscale's reliability or (b) if there was no acceptable substitute scale for an original scale that lost items when the *MMPI* was revised to *MMPI–2*. Specifically with respect to this second circumstance, Paraphilia (*Pe*), Dissociative Symptoms (*I-DS*), and Behavioral Impulsivity (*Imp-B*) were assigned replacement items. Other item losses due to the

MMPI revision were disregarded (i.e., no items were replaced). Harris–Lingoes (*H–L*) *Pd* subscale item add-backs and replacement items for *Pe, I-DS*, and *Imp-B*, which increased a scale's reliability in the patient samples, are coded in boldface in their proper newly assigned locations; unchanged *H–L* items are not listed.

Example: **True**: 61 93 **A148** 262.

If a potential add-back item did not improve a *H–L Pd* subscale's reliability, then it appears in parentheses and ordinary typeface where it would have been placed if it has contributed satisfactorily to the scale.

Example: **True:** (A367 non-fit).

Item compositions for other scales that are referenced in this book, but are not listed in Appendix A, can be found in the appendixes of *MMPI–2 Manual, Revised Edition* (Butcher et al., 2001), *Psychological Assessment with the MMPI–2* (Friedman et al., 2001), *The MMPI–2: An Interpretive Manual* (Greene, 2000), and *The MMPI–2 Restructured Clinical (RC) Scales* (Tellegen et al., 2003). These additional scales include the following: *VRIN, TRIN, FBack*, Superlative (*S*), traditional Validity and Clinical scales, new Content scales, *A, R, PK, PS, MAC-R, APS, GM, GF, Si1, Si2*, Harris–Lingoes, and Restructured Clinical Scales.

COMPOSITION OF SCALES AFTER ITEM ANALYSES AND EDITS

Tryon, Stein, and Chu Clusters

Autism & Disruptive Thoughts (*TSC/A*) (*n* = 20)
True: 16 30 32 48 87 122 221 268 308 311 316 325 327 328 341 394 448 471 472
False: 293

Body Symptoms (*TSC/B*) (*n* = 32)
True: 11 18 28 40 44 53 59 97 101 111 149 175 178 238 464
False: 2 3 20 33 45 47 57 91 141 148 152 164 176 179 208 224 295

Depression & Apathy (*TSC/D*) (*n* = 28)
True: 38 52 56 65 71 92 130 180 215 233 273 303 326 331 339 347 364 368 391 400 408 411 454
False: 9 43 75 95 388

Resentment (*TSC/R*) (*n* = 19)
True: 27 37 82 85 94 116 134 135 136 150 151 213 302 389 390 409 421 430 461
False: None

Social Introversion (*TSC/I*) (*n* = 26)

True: 46 73 127 158 161 167 185 243 265 275 285 289 337 446

False: 49 63 239 262 280 321 335 342 350 353 360 370

Suspicion & Mistrust (*TSC/S*) (*n* = 25)

True: 58 76 120 124 225 241 251 254 259 284 286 315 338 346 352 357 358 386
396 403 414 419 423 445 470

False: None

Tension, Worry, & Fear (*TSC/T*) (*n* = 35)

True: 15 23 31 39 89 146 154 170 172 196 218 274 290 299 301 304 305 317 329
334 367 395 415 420 424 438 441 442 444 463 469

False: 118 140 223 405

Harris–Lingoes Subscales

D1—Subjective Depression (*2SD*) (*n* = 27)

True: Same as original

False: (*C: 118 178 189 260 267*)

D2—Psychomotor Retardation (*2PR*) (*n* = 13)

True: **R29 R37 R55 R76 R134 R212**

False: (*C: 189*)

D3—Physical Malfunctioning (*2PM*) (*n* = 9)

True: (*C: 117 181*)

False: Same as original

D4—Mental Dullness (*2MD*) (*n* = 15)

True: Same as original

False: Same as original

D5—Brooding (*2B*) (*n* = 10)

True: Same as original

False: Same as original

Hy1—Denial of Social Anxiety (*3DSA*) (*n* = 6)

True: None

False: Same as original

Hy2—Need for Affection (*3NA*) (*n* = 11)

True: (*C: 230*)

False: Same as original

Hy3—Lassitude-Malaise (*3LM*) (*n* = 15)
True: Same as original
False: Same as original

Hy4—Somatic Complaints (*3SC*) (*n* = 17)
True: Same as original
False: Same as original

Hy5—Inhibition of Aggression (*3IA*)

Unreliable; Behavioral Impulsivity low score (−) replaces

Pd1—Familial Discord (*4FD*) (*n* =10)
True: **A190**
False: **A455** (*C: 214*)

Pd2—Authority Conflict (*4AC*)

Unreliable; Wiggins *W-AUT* high score (+) replaces

Pd3—Social Imperturbability (*4SI*) (*n* = 11)
True: **A262 A360 A452** (A55 non-fit)
False: **A275 A320**

Pd4—Social Alienation (*4SOA*) (*n* = 14)
True: **A55 A156 A277 A386** (*C: 113*) (A452 non-fit)
False: (*C: 129 157*)

Pd5—Self-Alienation (*4SA*) (*n* = 15)
True: **A65 A156 A386**
False: Same as original

Pa1—Persecutory Ideas (*6PI*) (*n* = 17)
True: Same as original
False: Same as original

Pa2—Poignancy (*6P*) (*n* = 7)
True: Same as original
False: (*C: 100 244*)

Pa3—Naivete (*6N*) (*n* = 9)
True: None
False: **R16**

Sc1—Social Alienation (*8SOA*) (*n* = 21)
True: Same as original
False: Same as original

Sc2—Emotional Alienation (*8EA*) (*n* = 10)
True: Same as original
False: (*C: 290*)

Sc3—Lack of Ego Mastery, Cognitive (*8COG*) (*n* = 10)
True: Same as original
False: Same as original

Sc4—Lack of Ego Mastery, Conative (*8CON*) (*n* = 14)
True: **R290**
False: Changed as noted in **True**

Sc5—Lack of Ego Mastery, Defective Inhibition (*8DI*) (*n* = 11)
True: Same as original
False: None

Sc6—Bizarre Sensory Experiences (*8BSE*) (*n* = 20)
True: Same as original
False: Same as original

Ma1—Amorality (*9AMO*) (*n* = 5)
True: Same as original
False: (*C: 263*)

Ma2—Psychomotor Acceleration (*9PMA*) (*n* = 10)
True: (*C: 206*)
False: Same as original

Ma3—Imperturbability (*9IMP*) (*n* = 5)
True: (*C: 155 200 220*)
False: Same as original

Ma4—Ego Inflation (*9EI*) (*n* = 7)
True: (*C: 61 211*)
False: None

Wiggins Content Scales

Authority Conflict (*W-AUT*) (*n* = 20)
True: 50 58 81 103 104 105 110 227 241 250 254 269 283 284 286 344 346 352
418
False: 266

Depression (*W-DEP*) (*n* = 33)

True: 38 52 56 65 82 92 94 146 196 233 234 246 252 277 301 303 305 341 364
396 400 407 408 450 451 454 463

False: 9 63 75 188 388 405

Family Problems (*W-FAM*) (*n* = 16)

True: 21 190 195 202 205 219 288 292 297 413 449

False: 83 90 125 276 455

Feminine Interests (*W-FEM*) Unreliable

Hypomania (*W-HYP*) (*n* = 21)

True: 15 122 156 169 213 218 226 242 244 267 304 308 330 366 389 393 420
422 428 439 444 (*C: 206 210*)

False: None

Manifest Hostility (*W-HOS*) (*n* = 23)

True: 27 37 68 76 98 116 134 150 151 256 302 323 324 332 358 386 406 410 414
419 423 430 461 (*C: 270 437*)

False: None

Organic Symptoms (*W-ORG*) (*n* = 32)

True: 18 40 97 101 147 149 168 172 175 229 247 296 299 472

False: 43 57 91 106 142 159 164 165 173 176 177 179 204 224 249 255 295 404

Phobias (*W-PHO*) (*n* = 26)

True: 154 170 317 320 329 334 367 392 395 397 435 438 441 442 458 468

False: 115 118 163 186 261 321 385 401 453 462

Poor Health (*W-HEA*) (*n* = 19)

True: 11 28 36 59 111 253 464

False: 2 20 33 45 47 117 141 143 152 181 194 208

Poor Morale (*W-MOR*) (*n* = 22)

True: 71 73 127 130 225 289 326 331 339 347 348 368 390 394 399 409 411 415
457 469

False: 109 239

Psychoticism (*W-PSY*) (*n* = 42)

True: 17 22 23 24 32 42 48 60 72 96 99 124 138 144 162 180 182 198 216 228
251 259 271 281 285 298 307 311 315 316 319 333 336 345 355 361 424
448 466 (*C: 61 113 211*)

False: 184 314 427

Social Maladjustment (*W-SOC*) (*n* = 26)

True: 46 158 161 167 185 243 265 275 337 357 391 446

False: 49 79 86 262 280 335 340 342 353 359 360 365 370 452

Indiana Personality Disorder (*PDO*) Scales (Rev.)

Antisocial *PDO* (*ANTI*) (*n* = 25)

True: 66 81 84 105 110 123 134 156 227 240 248 269 270 283 284 389 412 418
431 432 433

False: 34 126 266

Paranoid *PDO* (*PRND*) (*n* = 20)

True: 17 27 42 99 124 144 145 151 228 241 251 259 274 300 315 333 424 445

False: 63 314

Narcissistic *PDO* (*NARC*) (*n* = 23)

True: 17 19 22 42 110 153 227 248 254 256 271 285 286 289 300 302 345 347
350 358 410 448

False: 140

Histrionic *PDO* (*HIST*) (*n* = 17)

True: 23 25 112 146 169 189 226 242 302 308 389 393 444 469

False: 237 278 405

Borderline *PDO* (*BORD*) (*n* = 30)

True: 23 37 52 56 73 82 92 94 102 116 134 146 150 213 215 271 273 277 338
389 411 430 444 469, males only: 62

False: 9 34 372 388 405, females only: 62

Passive–Aggressive *PDO* (*PAAG*) (*n* = 28)

True: 15 31 37 38 55 85 98 134 135 145 178 190 202 212 225 233 286 288 308
325 364 419 423 461 472

False: 83 108 372

Dependent *PDO* (*DPND*) (*n* = 29)

True: 70 73 129 233 317 326 347 348 364 368 369 398 411 421 450 457

False: 43 61 95 109 120 157 206 214 239 318 335 440 452

Obsessive–Compulsive *PDO* (*OBCP*) (*n* = 24)

True: 55 87 120 135 136 193 196 211 212 268 290 297 309 313 328 351 356 396
402 403 415 442 447 470

False: None

Avoidant *PDO* (*AVDT*) (*n* = 20)
True: 73 127 130 178 185 273 275 277 289 310 326 386 390 411 446
False: 63 109 177 262 335

Schizotypal *PDO* (*SCZY*) (*n* = 19)
True: 24 32 42 72 99 124 138 144 145 241 259 311 315 316 333 361 466
False: 359 427

Schizoid *PDO* (*SCZD*) (*n* = 22)
True: 52 171 218 286 292 312 324 377 384 473
False: 54 57 99 309 391 440 449 450 451 479 482 547

PDO Distress (*Dist*) (*n* = 11)
True: 146 167 243 251 285
False: 79 95 157 208 321 405

Impulsivity Components Scales

Behavioral Impulsivity (*Imp-B*) (*n* = 18)
True: 37 82 84 85 105 134 150 169 202 240 322 362 412 431 540
False: 100 121 266

Ideational Impulsivity (*Imp-I*) (*n* = 20)
True: 17 22 50 66 81 89 123 145 190 227 248 283 284 309 346 348 393 436
False: 83 278

Affective Impulsivity (*Imp-A*) (*n* = 13)
True: 93 102 213 302 389 420 430 449 461
False: 63 79 157 372

Impulsivity Total (*Imp-T*) (*n* = 51):

Imp-T = [(Imp-B) + (Imp-I) + (Imp-A)]

Indiana Rational Scales

Severe Reality Distortions (*I-RD*) (*n* = 17)
True: 24 32 60 72 96 138 144 162 198 228 298 311 316 319 336 355
False: 427

Dissociative Symptoms (*I-DS*) (*n* = 10)
True: 23 72 168 182 229 308 311 **A530 A551**
False: 427

Obsessive–Compulsiveness (*I-OC*) (*n* = 8)
True: 55 193 309 313 327 328 356 408
False: None

Dominance (*I-Do*) (*n* = 12)
True: 120 157 214 239 318 350 365 403 414 416 423 452 (*C: 63*)
False: (*C: 70 446*)

Dependency (*I-De*) Unreliable; Dependency/Self-Doubt high score (+) replaces

Poor Self-Concept (*I-SC*) (*n* = 14)
True: 71 73 94 130 246 411 450, males only: 62
False: 61 78 109 237 239 318, females only: 62

Sex Problems Inventory (*I-SP*) Unreliable; Sexuality/Intimacy Failure high score (+) replaces

Critical Inquiry Scales

The following scales are based on the Critical Inquiry procedure (Appendix C), where most of their items appear.

Neuropsychological Signs (*NeurPsy*) (*n* = 14)
True: 168 172 182 229 282 298
False: 91 106 142 159 164 177 179 295

Addictive Activities (*AA*) (*n* = 10)
True: 264 387 487 489 511 527 540 544
False: 429 501

Suicide Subtle (*Suic-S*) (*n* = 13)
True: 65 92 234 306 379 407 454 505 512 526 539 546
False: 75

Suicide Obvious (*Suic-O*) (*n* = 6)
True: 150 303 506 520 524 530
False: None

Suicide Total (*Suic-T*) (*n* = 19); Suic-T = [(Suic-S) + (Suic-O)]

Physiological Reactivity/Panic (*Panic*) (*n* = 20)
True: 23 44 53 59 150 170 172 178 180 242 311 463 469 525 543 555
False: 47 164 208 564

Sado-Masochistic Signs (*Sadist*) (*n* = 18)

True: 27 68 134 150 256 270 323 324 332 379 407 414 419 425 443 478 530 548
False: None

Psychosocial Development Scales

Feels Cared for/Loved vs. Neglected/Disliked (*Cared for vs. Neglected*) (*n* = 20)

True: 278
False: 17 42 110 124 145 241 251 286 306 315 338 352 358 374 379 419 445 484 559

Autonomous/Self-Possessed vs. Self-Doubting/Shamed (*Autonomous vs. Doubting*) (*n* = 27)

True: None
False: 70 94 127 161 178 185 190 234 246 283 285 288 289 300 348 407 409 411 421 446 450 457 476 482 485 491 509

Initiating/Pursuing vs. Regretful/Guilt-Prone (*Initiating vs. Guilt-Prone*) (*n* = 29)

True: None
False: 19 27 35 50 52 82 84 85 98 105 123 189 209 225 240 284 324 373 386 390 393 396 403 430 431 433 451 470 513

Industrious/Capable vs. Inadequate/Inferior (*Industrious vs. Inadequate*) (*n* = 22)

True: 9 10 43 109 160 211 239 318 561
False: 31 38 71 73 89 130 326 347 377 503 517 554 566

Life-Goal Oriented/Ego Identity Secure vs. Directionless/Confused (*Ego Identified vs. Confused*) (*n* = 25)

True: 61 184 350 452 455 494
False: 54 87 129 291 371 375 376 380 394 399 425 454 483 504 516 519 526 528 549

Socially Committed/Involved vs. Disengaged/Lonely (*Involved vs. Disengaged*) (*n* = 17)

True: 78 280 481
False: 22 46 167 195 219 265 277 337 382 391 479 550 563 567

Other Individual Scales

Assertiveness (*Astvn*) Unreliable

Control (*Cn*) (*n* = 33)

True: 7 29 56 **R68** 84 93 103 122 134 151 169 203 215 218 260 267 286 301 **R329** 344 347 352 390 411 **R420** 423 456 469 (*C: 12 186*)
False: 83 100 159 223 455 (*C: 80 155 227 276 283 355*)

Conventionality (*5C*) (*n* = 9)

True: None

False: 19 26 27 68 76 104 107 120 254

Dependency/Self-Doubt (*Depnd*) (*n* = 26)

True: 73 80 127 129 146 153 175 190 219 227 309 326 331 348 364 368 369 386
390 398 421 446 457

False: 63 157 239

Depression, Subtle (*D-S*) (*n* = 15)

True: 117 181 (*C: 5*)

False: 29 37 55 68 76 134 178 189 212 221 226 238 267 (*C: 143 148*)

Dominance/Self-Confidence (*Do*) (*n* = 16)

True: (*C: 55 207 232 245 386 416*)

False: 31 52 70 73 82 172 202 227 243 275 309 325 399 412 470 473 (*C: 201 220
244*)

Ego Strength (*Es*) (*n* = 37)

True: 2 33 45 141 159 177 179 385 (*C: 98 169 189 199 209 213 230 245 323 406
413 425*)

False: 23 31 32 36 39 53 60 70 82 87 175 196 215 221 225 229 246 307 310 316
328 391 394 441 447 458 464 469 471 (*C: 119 128 236*)

Extreme Suspiciousness (*S+*) (*n* = 18)

True: 24 42 99 124 138 144 162 228 241 251 259 315 333 336 355 361 391 424

False: None

Hostility (*Ho*) (*n* = 46)

True: 19 27 46 50 58 76 81 99 104 110 124 136 145 205 225 227 241 248 251
254 259 265 286 306 315 338 346 347 352 357 358 386 393 406 414 419
423 425 436 443 445 452 457 466 470 (*C: 171 398*)

False: 372 (*C: 217 230*)

Imperturbability (*Impert*) (*n* = 14); Composite of 3DSA, 4SI, & 9IMP items

True: 262 360

False: 70 93 129 136 158 161 167 185 243 265 275 320

Mean Elevation (*ME*): ME is the *T*-score mean of the sum for Clinical scales 1 through 4
and 6 through 9, after *K*-correction.

ME = [(Hs + D + Hy + Pd + Pa + Pt + Sc + Ma)/8]

Overcontrolled Hostility (*O-H*) (*n* = 18)

True: 79 (*C: 67 207 398*)

False: 15 29 77 89 98 116 129 153 169 **R286 R305** 344 390 400 420 433 **R471**
(*C: 1 69 117 171 293 440 460*)

Paraphilia/Pedophilia (*Pe*) (*n* = 21)

True: 17 56 65 94 166 234 235 296 **A373 A377 A379** 396 425 **A480 A483 A485**
(*C119 C197*)

False: 12 49 121 148 343 (*C226*)

Psychogenic Rage (*Rage*) (*n* = 24)

True: 37 39 134 218 273 274 304 378 382 386 389 414 461 469 513 519 540 542
548

False: 3 140 372 405 564

Response Consistency 1st Half (*RCon1*) (*n* = 43)

True: 3 10 47 83 108 125 142 223

False: 15 21 22 24 30 31 32 37 38 54 73 82 92 96 104 124 130 134 135 136 138
145 167 195 212 215 234 241 248 259 265 273 274 281 283

Response Consistency 2nd Half (*RCon2*) (*n* = 43)

True: 295 318 383 388 404 405 455 561

False: 286 299 300 301 302 309 311 323 336 349 358 361 367 377 378 379 400
403 410 411 412 421 445 463 479 497 504 507 508 516 528 538 539 543
548

Response Consistency Pairs (*RConPr*) (*n* = 43)

True:			**Scale**
	3	388	*Dep*
	10	561	*Wrk*
	47	295	*Hea*
	83	455	*Fam*
	108	318	*Wrk*
	125	383	*Fam*
	142	404	*Hea*
	223	405	*Anx*
False:			**Scale**
	15	445	*Wrk*
	21	378	*Fam*
	22	539	*Trt*
	24	361	*Biz*
	30	463	*Anx*
	31	299	*Anx*
	32	508	*Biz*
	37	410	*Ang*

Response Consistency Pairs (*RConPr*) (*cont.*)

False: **Scale**

38	377	*Dep*
54	323	*Fam*
73	421	*Lse*
82	411	*Dep*
92	528	*Trt*
96	311	*Biz*
104	403	*Cyn*
124	286	*Cyn*
130	504	*Lse*
134	548	*Ang*
135	309	*Obs*
136	302	*Tpa*
138	336	*Biz*
145	379	*Fam*
167	479	*Sod*
195	300	*Fam*
212	507	*Tpa*
215	400	*Dep*
234	516	*Dep*
241	358	*Cyn*
248	412	*Asp*
259	543	*Biz*
265	367	*Sod*
273	301	*Anx*
274	497	*Trt*
281	349	*Sod*
283	538	*Cyn*

Pairs are coded in three ways: (a) per key above = self-enhancing (*RCon+*); (b) opposite key = self-effacing/downhearted (*RCon–*); (c) T–F or F–T = self-inconsistent (*RIncon*).

Sexuality/Intimacy Failure (*Sexual*) (*n* = 19)

True: 16 22 114 166 221 256 268 274 277 287 327 371 391 448 470, males only: 62

False: 12 34 121, females only: 62

Social Alienation (*SoAlien*) (*n* = 31)

Items drawn from 4SOA & 8SOA

True: 17 21 22 42 46 55 56 82 99 138 145 156 190 219 221 225 256 259 277 281 291 292 320 333 386

False: 12 90 276 278 280 343

Social Desirability Edwards (*So*) (*n* = 37)

True: 8 20 78 95 152 186 318 335

False: 31 39 48 54 127 136 146 158 168 172 221 238 243 270 273 288 289 299 300 301 306 320 324 338 349 368 415 420 469

Social Desirability Wiggins (*Sd*) (*n* = 20)

True: 49 100 184 201 206 207 211 220 257 345 416 439 (*C: 25 80 131 133 194 249 263 351 354 356 366 402*)

False: 29 41 77 93 183 203 326 341 (*C: 232*)

Social Responsibility (*Re*) (*n* = 26)

True: 100 160 266 (*C: 199 440 467*)

False: 7 27 29 32 84 103 105 145 169 201 202 235 275 358 412 417 418 430 431 432 456 468 470 (*C: 164*)

TRIN True (*TR-T*): Sum of keyed T–T response pairings

TRIN False (*TR-F*): Sum of keyed F–F response pairings

TRIN Sum (*TR-S*): = [(TR − T) + (TR − F)]

True (*True*): Sum across 567 items of all *T* responses

Trusting/Trustworthy (*Trust*) (*n* = 17)

Items drawn from 3NA & 6N

True: None

False: 16 26 58 76 81 98 104 110 124 151 213 241 263 283 284 286 315

Work Attitude (*WA*) (*n* = 33)

True: 15 17 31 38 42 48 50 71 98 225 227 233 273 281 299 309 346 364 368 394 399 403 445 454 (*C: 120 157*)

False: 3 9 10 75 174 188 318 **R330** 405

Appendix B: Contemporary Psychometric Properties of Scales and Methods for Estimating Standard Deviations

Scale	M/SD		Alpha Coefficients	
	Female	Male	Female	Male
Tryon, Stein, and Chu Clusters				
(Chu, 1966; Levitt, 1989; Stein, 1968; Tryon, 1966)				
Autism & Disruptive Thoughts (*TSC/A*)	5.24/3.41	5.24/3.27	.84	.85
Body Symptoms (*TSC/B*)	5.82/4.70	4.92/4.04	.88	.88
Depression & Apathy (*TSC/D*)	6.39/4.79	5.14/4.30	.90	.91
Resentment (*TSC/R*)	5.89/3.22	5.66/3.15	.82	.83
Social Introversion (*TSC/I*)	10.33/4.27	8.91/4.16	.86	.87
Suspicion & Mistrust (*TSC/S*)	9.71/4.07	10.39/4.01	.85	.85
Tension, Worry, & Fear (*TSC/T*)	10.26/5.12	8.32/4.68	.88	.89
Harris–Lingoes Subscales				
(Harris & Lingoes, 1968; Levitt & Gotts, 1995; see revisions in chap. 6)				
D1 Subjective Depression (*2SD*)	5.73/4.03	4.93/3.69	.87	.87
D2 Psychomotor Retardation & Suppressed Anger (*2PR*)	3.71/1.68	4.04/1.76	.68	.72
D3 Physical Malfunctioning (*2PM*)	1.60/1.30	1.29/1.19	.55	.55
D4 Mental Dullness (*2MD*)	2.57/2.27	2.42/2.15	.81	.81
D5 Brooding (*2B*)	2.49/1.96	1.83/1.79	.76	.76
Hy1 Denial of Social Anxiety (*3DSA*)	3.85/1.85	3.90/1.84	.71	.72
Hy2 Need for Affection (*3NA*)	6.15/2.29	5.96/2.30	.69	.66
Hy3 Lassitude-Malaise (*3LM*)	2.75/2.51	2.55/2.24	.82	.82
Hy4 Somatic Complaints (*3SC*)	3.24/2.55	2.49/2.09	.80	.79

(Continued)

Scale	M/SD		Alpha Coefficients	
	Female	Male	Female	Male
Hy5 Inhibition of Aggression (*3IA*)	Unreliable scale replaced by Behavioral Impulsivity			
Pd1 Familial Discord (*4FD*)	2.39/1.96	2.29/1.86	.72	.69
Pd2 Authority Conflict (*4AC*)	Unreliable scale replaced by Wiggins Authority Conflict			
Pd3 Social Imperturbability (*4SI*)	7.01/2.39	7.48/2.51	.71	.72
Pd4 Social Alienation (*4SOA*)	3.12/2.30	3.09/2.30	.75	.77
Pd5 Self-Alienation (*4SA*)	3.95/2.35	3.91/2.39	.74	.77
Pa1 Persecutory Ideas (*6PI*)	1.79/1.69	1.73/1.70	.82	.82
Pa2 Poignancy, Vulnerability (*6P*)	1.83/1.49	1.31/1.35	.61	.66
Pa3 Naivete (*6N*)	5.15/2.15	4.94/2.13	.72	.68
Sc1 Social Alienation (*8SOA*)	3.13/2.61	2.73/2.45	.77	.81
Sc2 Emotional Alienation (*8EA*)	0.59/1.02	0.50/1.01	.72	.73
Sc3 Lack of Ego Mastery, Cognitive (*8COG*)	1.20/1.67	1.31/1.69	.80	.82
Sc4 Lack of Ego Mastery, Conative (*8CON*)	2.23/1.89	2.23/1.80	.83	.83
Sc5 Lack of Ego Mastery, Defective Inhibition (*8DI*)	1.57/1.60	1.43/1.47	.73	.73
Sc6 Bizarre Sensory Experiences (*8BSE*)	2.07/2.22	1.89/2.07	.82	.82
Ma1 Amorality (*9AMO*)	1.38/1.15	1.69/1.24	.48	.51
Ma2 Psychomotor Acceleration (*9PMA*)	4.32/1.78	4.51/1.96	.55	.59
Ma3 Imperturbability (*9IMP*)	2.36/1.49	2.51/1.46	.53	.54
Ma4 Ego Inflation (*9EI*)	2.06/1.54	2.06/1.48	.61	.60

Wiggins Content Scales
(Greene, 1991; Levitt & Gotts, 1995; Wiggins, 1966)

Authority Conflict (*W-AUT*)	7.43/3.78	8.92/4.06	.78	.77
Depression (*W-DEP*)	7.23/4.83	5.89/4.40	.89	.89
Family Problems (*W-FAM*)	4.86/2.68	4.11/2.50	.79	.75
Femininity (*W-FEM*)	Unreliable and no suitable replacement scale available			
Hypomania (*W-HYP*)	9.09/3.08	9.09/3.24	.75	.77
Manifest Hostility (*W-HOS*)	6.96/3.57	7.47/3.55	.83	.83
Organic Symptoms (*W-ORG*)	4.99/3.85	4.55/3.53	.86	.87
Phobias (*W-PHO*)	8.66/3.96	5.77/3.45	.76	.76
Poor Health (*W-HEA*)	3.96/2.77	3.39/2.55	.72	.73
Poor Morale (*W-MOR*)	7.51/4.73	5.83/4.23	.86	.86
Psychoticism (*W-PSY*)	5.62/4.08	5.70/4.18	.90	.91
Social Maladjustment (*W-SOC*)	9.74/5.35	9.59/5.22	.85	.86

(Continued)

Scale	M/SD		Alpha Coefficients	
	Female	Male	Female	Male

Indiana Personality Disorder (PDO) Scales (Revised)
(Levitt & Gotts, 1995; see revisions in chap. 6)

Antisocial *PDO (ANTI)*	4.99/2.96	6.47/3.20	.77	.79
Paranoid *PDO (PRND)*	4.37/3.14	4.21/2.96	.82	.82
Narcissistic *PDO (NARC)*	7.04/3.43	7.16/3.38	.79	.80
Histrionic *PDO (HIST)*	5.77/2.43	4.83/2.50	.66	.71
Borderline *PDO (BORD)*	8.33/4.54	6.82/4.13	.87	.88
Passive–Aggressive *PDO (PAAG)*	7.35/4.23	7.61/4.13	.85	.87
Dependent *PDO (DPND)*	8.29/3.99	7.03/3.67	.82	.81
Obsessive–Compulsive *PDO (OBCP)*	9.11/3.44	8.56/3.38	.79	.79
Avoidant *PDO (AVDT)*	6.88/3.39	5.46/3.24	.83	.84
Schizotypal *PDO (SCZY)*	2.70/2.88	2.90/2.76	.82	.83
Schizoid *PDO (SCZD)*	5.70/3.03	6.15/3.26	.82	.84
PDO Distress *(Dist)*	4.36/2.08	3.48/2.12	.68	.72

Impulsivity Components Scales
(Gotts, Original Research Report, see chap. 7)

Behavioral Impulsivity *(Imp-B)*	3.39/2.46	4.60/2.51	.75	.76
Ideational Impulsivity *(Imp-I)*	5.83/2.90	6.13/2.93	.75	.77
Affective Impulsivity *(Imp-A)*	7.47/2.23	6.77/2.38	.70	.71
Impulsivity Total *(Imp-T)*	16.69/5.75	17.50/5.91	.86	.87

Indiana Rational Scales
(Levitt, 1989; Levitt & Gotts, 1995; see revisions in chap. 6)

Severe Reality Distortions *(I-RD)*	0.99/2.38	1.13/2.26	.82	.84
Dissociative Symptoms *(I-DS)*	1.19/2.18	1.03/1.99	.72	.75
Obsessive–Compulsiveness *(I-OC)*	1.96/1.71	1.94/1.71	.65	.61
Dominance *(I-Do)*	6.37/2.12	7.34/2.29	.64	.61
Dependency *(I-De)*	Unreliable scale replaced by Dependency/Self-Doubt			
Poor Self-Concept *(I-SC)*	3.15/2.13	2.43/2.03	.72	.72
Sex Problems Inventory *(I-SP)*	Unreliable scale replaced by Sexuality/Intimacy Failure			

Critical Inquiry Scales
(Gotts, Original Research Report, see chap. 7)

Neuropsychological Signs *(NeurPsy)*	1.69/2.21	1.49/2.13	.75	.71
Addictive Activities *(AA)*	1.04/2.28	1.74/1.76	.79	.74
Suicide Subtle *(Suic-S)*	1.02/2.85	1.01/2.00	.77	.83
Suicide Obvious *(Suic-O)*	0.22/1.15	0.16/1.20	.78	.75
Suicide Total *(Suic-T)*	1.24/2.57	1.17/2.62	.87	.86
Physiological Reactivity/Panic *(Panic)*	3.27/3.25	2.51/3.05	.85	.84
Sado-Masochistic Signs *(Sadist)*	2.79/2.17	3.50/2.31	.84	.75

(Continued)

Scale	M/SD		Alpha Coefficients	
	Female	Male	Female	Male

Psychosocial Development Scales
(Gotts, Original Research Report, see chaps. 7 & 8)

Cared for vs. Neglected	14.98/4.14	14.51/4.24	.80	.81
Autonomous vs. Doubting	20.08/4.99	21.69/5.33	.81	.82
Initiating vs. Guilt-Prone	20.38/4.59	19.22/5.08	.82	.82
Industrious vs. Inadequate	16.04/3.68	16.72//3.85	.76	.77
Ego Identified vs. Confused	19.72/4.45	19.97/4.56	.82	.81
Involved vs. Disengaged	12.34/3.30	12.34/3.61	.71	.77

Other Individual Scales

Assertiveness (*Astvn*) (Ohlson & Wilson, 1974)	Unreliable scale and no suitable replacement scale found			
Control (*Cn*) (Cuadra, 1956)	13.72/3.35	13.72/4.19	.80	.81
Conventionality (*5C*) (Levitt, 1989; Pepper & Strong, 1958)	5.72/1.87	5.15/1.98	.58	.56
Dependency/Self-Doubt (*Depnd*) (Derived from Levitt, 1989; Navran, 1954)	9.78/4.07	7.81/3.82	.84	.84
Depression, Subtle (*D-S*) (Wiener & Harmon, 1946)	9.92/2.29	9.38/2.48	.68	.67
Dominance, Self-Confidence (*Do*) (Gough et al., 1951)	11.47/2.74	12.01/2.82	.74	.73
Ego Strength (*Es*) (Barron, 1953)	28.66/4.12	30.28/3.67	.86	.88
Extreme Suspiciousness (*S+*) (Endicott et al., 1969)	2.02/2.73	2.18/2.50	.83	.82
Hostility (*Ho*) (Cook & Medley, 1954)	15.39/6.72	16.69/6.30	.89	.89
Imperturbability (*Impert*) (Items from 3DSA, 4SI, and 9IMP based on Levitt & Gotts, 1995; see chap. 6)	8.40/2.89	8.90/2.99	.76	.77
Mean Elevation (*ME*) (Levitt & Gotts, 1995; Modlin, 1947; see chap. 6)	50.00/10.00	50.00/10.00	.86	.88
Overcontrolled Hostility (*O-H*) (Megargee et al., 1967)	9.49/2.55	9.90/2.60	.75	.74
Paraphilia/Pedophilia, Males (*Pe*) (Toobert et al., 1959; revised, see chap. 6)	—	4.79/2.89	—	.81
Psychogenic Rage (*Rage*) (Gotts, Original research; see Appendix E)	7.08/4.33	6.46/4.03	.89	.90

Response Consistency Scales
(Gotts, Original Research Report, see chap. 7)

Response Consistency 1st Half (*RCon1*)	34.76/7.01	34.58/7.65	.87	.88

(Continued)

Scale	M/SD		Alpha Coefficients	
	Female	Male	Female	Male
Response Consistency 2nd Half (RCon2)	34.42/6.99	34.78/7.66	.87	.89
Self-Effacing, Downhearted (RCon−)	2.25/4.50	2.17/4.09	.87	.89
Self-Enhancing (RCon+)	28.51/7.74	28.63/7.96	.90	.92
Self-Inconsistent (RIncon)	12.24/4.00	12.20/4.10	.60	.63
Sexuality/Intimacy Failure (Sexual) (Gotts, Original Research; revised from Levitt & Gotts, 1995; see chap. 6)	4.09/2.78	4.10/2.72	.79	.80
Social Alienation (SoAlien) (Items from 4SOA and 8SOA based on Levitt & Gotts, 1995; see chap. 6)	5.87/3.89	5.46/3.79	.84	.86
Social Desirability Edwards (So) (Edwards, 1957)	28.70/5.16	30.16/4.56	.86	.88
Social Desirability Wiggins (Sd) (Wiggins, 1959)	6.71/2.52	7.61/2.72	.63	.63
Social Responsibility (Re) (Gough et al., 1952)	19.02/3.32	17.60/3.79	.72	.74
TRIN Components (Gotts, Original Analysis, see chap. 7)				
TRIN True (TR-T)	1.34/1.54	1.19/1.49	.59	.57
TRIN False (TR-F)	1.35/1.05	1.23/1.18	.14	.20
TRIN Sum (TR-S)	2.69/1.71	2.42/1.72	.40	.41
TRUE Sum (True) (Derived from Itemmetric Data of Butcher et al., 2001, across all 567 items)	220.12/40.01	211.71/42.38	—	—
Trustworthy/Trusting (Trust) (Items from 3NA and 6N based on Levitt & Gotts, 1995; see chap. 6)	9.55/3.31	9.28/3.21	.79	.76
Work Attitude (WA) (Tydlaska & Mengel, 1953)	8.28/4.43	8.08/4.33	.85	.87

DERIVATIONS FOR APPROXIMATING CONTEMPORARY NORMS

Itemmetric Data (Butcher et al., 2001) were entered into a file and then used to compute means for all edited or new scales. Corresponding standard deviations, however, cannot be derived in a similar manner. Regression studies were performed separately for male patients ($n = 1,020$) and female patients ($n = 637$) in order to determine if known standard deviations could be predicted from a best-weighted combination of the corresponding normative (CX) means, in combination with the two patient samples' means and standard deviations. Satisfactory prediction equations were obtained. That is, known standard deviations closely matched a large majority of predictions. The extent of the match can be appreciated by considering the multiple correlations that resulted: females, $R = .956$; males, $R = .953$. The prediction equations that produced these results in the inpatient samples were as follows:

Females

$$\text{CXFSigma} = [(\text{CXMean} \times .0950) - (\text{SampleMean} \times .0753) \\ + (\text{SampleSigma} \times .6797) + .2949]$$

Males

$$\text{CXMSigma} = [(\text{CXMean} \times .113) - (\text{SampleMean} \times .0420) \\ + (\text{SampleSigma} \times .5102) + .5373]$$

As can be seen by inspection of both equations, Beta weights assigned to the sample standard deviations were of paramount importance in determining the outcome. Differences between weights assigned to the female and male solutions were present but relatively minor in comparison with the respective weights assigned to the sample standard deviations. Intercepts also differed considerably between the female and male samples.

In the interest of considering the practical implications of the preceding, it will be useful to take in a ground level scan of some specific prediction results. This was accomplished by computing difference scores between known standard deviations and those predicted using the preceding formulas. For the aggregate of all 28 unrevised Harris–Lingoes Subscales, the mean difference for females was −0.20 standard deviations, with two thirds of the difference scores falling within plus or minus 0.30 (i.e., ranging from +0.10 to −0.50 SDs). These differences occur in the context of an average standard deviation of 1.92 for the 28 scales. More briefly stated for the males: mean difference was −0.22, range for two thirds of the differences was from +0.03 to −0.75, and mean standard deviation was 1.84. The possibility of significant divergences of standard deviations would of course directly affect efforts to calculate linear T-scores accurately. Thus, despite the overall quite favorable results seen in the high multiple correlations (R), the estimated standard deviations for the new and revised scales require future verification.

Failures of prediction also need to be mentioned. If estimates of the standard deviations for the eight Clinical scales had been made from the preceding equations, then 7 would have fallen within a reasonable tolerance of their actual CX statistics for both sexes. The exception is $Sc/8$, whose estimated standard deviation would have missed the mark for females and less so for males. Other scales for which a similar problem of inaccurate prediction occurred were: Si, F, CYN, TRT, A for both sexes; for males GM, So; for females only BIZ. Because the predicted standard deviations resulted in both underestimates and overestimates of the actual CX values, the results could not be further adjusted by formula as a means of increasing their accuracy.

Although none of the scales listed earlier was actually revised in the present research, the traits and styles that they represent offer clues as to the circumstances that may pose particular challenges to the use of sample statistics for estimating unknown standard deviations. It would appear that for scales measuring the extremes of psychopathology, character pathology, and response style, efforts to estimate standard deviations by this method may be less successful. Despite the drawbacks just considered here, the total set of results supported the present approach to estimating standard deviations from a sample. At the same time, it is necessary that the sample be of sufficient size to produce stable estimates and, furthermore, that it be representative of the substantive issues that are to be addressed.

Itemmetric data were used to estimate means for new scales and to adjust means for scales that were edited. It is important to note that estimated means may differ from true CX means by small, relatively negligible amounts, that is, by amounts affecting only the value of the means in the second decimal place. Such differences in mean value are due to the accumulation of itemmetric rounding of the original percentages of persons who answered *true* to each item. After obtaining the estimated CX means, they were combined with the female and male sample statistics for means and standard deviations and entered into the preceding regression equations. In this manner, CX standard deviations were estimated for those scales that were revised by item analysis, those that were developed during the research program reported here, and existing scales for which contemporary norms were otherwise unavailable. Thus the means and standard deviations reported in Appendix B were derived by application of the methods documented here. Further precision for these results could only have been achieved by recalculation of the standard deviations using the national norming database.

Different methods were required for estimating the CX equivalent means for the Response Consistency pairings (*RCon+*, *RCon–*, *RIncon*). Itemmetric data were assembled of CX true response percentages for the 43 item pairs. False keyed response values were obtained by subtracting item true percentages from 100. When they are converted from percentages to proportions, response percentages are, by definition, the same as response probabilities. Three probabilities were calculated for each item pair using the multiplication rule for the following combinations: *T–T*, *F–F*, and the sum $[(T–F) + (F–T)]$. Next, using the addition rule, probabilities were summed across the 43 pairs in accordance with the Response Consistency key to form *RCon+*. After reversing the key (i.e., all *true* now *false* and all *false* now *true*), the process was repeated to form *RCon–*. Once more the procedure was followed in order to combine all *T–F* and *F–T* response pairs, resulting in *RIncon*. Separate scores were calculated by gender.

The methods of calculation just described for the Response Consistency Scales were used to create and study the *TRIN* Components scores. Additional steps were considered, however, due to the presence in *TRIN* of three pairs of items that are counted both when answered *T–T* and *F–F*. These, hence, are not independent events. That is to say, although probabilities could be and were obtained in the usual manner for each of the three dually scored item pairs, the addition rule could not be applied directly to various combinations of *true* and *false* response pairs as was done for Response Consistency. Without having access to the normative *MMPI–2* database, estimating CX equivalent means for TRIN components posed unusual challenges. In order to circumvent this problem, sums of probabilities were computed separately for those TRIN responses keyed *true* and *false*. This resulted in the scores referred to here as TRIN True, TRIN False, and their sum TRIN Sum. Note that instead of subtracting TRIN False from TRIN True and adding a constant, the part scores were combined. The three resulting scales supported study of how these components interrelate and contribute to the composite TRIN score that is currently in use. This, however, precluded estimating reliabilities for TRIN Sum as was done for the other components.

Appendix C: Critical Inquiry

ADMINISTRATION PROCEDURES

Directions: Immediately following *MMPI–2* administration, while the patient is otherwise occupied, use a punched template that matches the answer form you are using to locate all keyed responses to the Critical Inquiry items. Mark throughout the worksheet's third column the numbers of any items that were answered according to the template key. Keyed direction appears in the second column of the worksheet. The first column of the worksheet identifies the category(-ies) to which the response may relate. Categories appear at the end of the worksheet. The fourth column suggests a symptom(s) possibly implied by the answer.

Also complete a quality control check at this time for items omitted or answered both *true* and *false*, noting those that the patient is to try again to complete. Then return the testing materials and ask the patient to review items omitted or answered both ways, saying for example, **"Look again at number _____. Would you say it is more true or more false of you?"** Transcribe spontaneous remarks offered during the quality control review and collect the finished answer form again, while leaving the test booklet with the patient.

Turn next directly to the Critical Inquiry procedure with words like these: **"Using the test booklet that you have, I want us next to review together some of your answers. Our review is important because it will help me better to understand your experiences and to learn how to help you."**

Specify in turn each item that you plan to review, **"Let's look first at number _____. You answered that** (Paraphrase here the patient's answer using the idiom of the item.)." Observe and continue: **"Tell me more about that."** Transcribe the reply. As you continue through the list of items to be reviewed and the patient catches on to the procedure, you will likely be able to simplify your questioning to: **"Now let's look at number _____. Tell me about your answer to that one."** You need not repeat the patient's *true* or *false* unless the patient needs a prompt. You may show the answer form if the patient denies a response. Accept this and note the denial. You may remark, **"Mistakes happen."**

If the patient requests to change an original answer at this time, agree to change your worksheet (i.e., not the answer form). Note the change it on the worksheet and transcribe any reasons given by the patient for why the earlier answer needed to be changed. Often at this time patients comment about having a problem understanding an item during their initial reading, particularly for items that: (a) have high lexile values (see Butcher et al., 2001, Appendix G), (b) involve direct or indirect forms of negation (e.g., *34, 177*), (c) are based on the qualifier that there is "no reason" or event to account for the experience (e.g., *226, 267*), or (d) confront the respondent simultaneously with alternatives, one of which may be true and another not true (e.g., *178, 208*).

CRITICAL INQUIRY WORKSHEET

Name _____ Date _____ Examiner_____

Code(s)	Key	Item	Possible Symptom(s)	Response/Evaluation
U	T	23	Emotional Dyscontrol	
P	T	24	Misperceptions, Blame avoidance	
P	T	32	Misperceptions, Dissociation	
D	F	34	Antisocial actions	
U	T	44	Autonomic instability	
U	F	47	Reactivity, Cardio-pulmonary sign	
U, N	T	53	Paresthesias	
U	T	59	Gastric distress, Autonomic reactivity	
P	T	60	Hallucinations	
S-S	T	65	Dysphoria	
P	T	72	Misperceptions, Dissociation	
S-S	F	75	Anhedonia	
N	F	91	Tics, Neuromuscular asynchrony	
S-S	T	92	Anhedonia	
P, Ad	T	96	Hallucinations	
P	T	99	Ideas of reference, Delusions	
N	F	106	Speech dysfluency, Dysphonia	
M	T/F	122	Flight of ideas	
D	T	134	Aggressive impulses	
P	T	138	Ideas of reference, Delusions	
N	F	142	Seizure disorder	
P	T	144	Ideas of reference, Delusions	

Code(s)	Key	Item	Possible Symptom(s)	Response/Evaluation
D, U, S-O	T	150	Dangerous compulsion _____	
N	F	159	Syncope _____	
P	T	162	Delusions _____	
N,U	F	164	Cerebrovascular or labyrinth problem, Panicky _____	
N, Ad	T	168	Substance induced blackouts, Seizure disorder _____	
U, P	T	170	Obsessions, Panic attacks, Incipient psychosis _____	
U, N	T	172	Intention tremor _____	
N	F	177	Neuro-motor dysfunction _____	
U	T	178	Autonomic overactivity _____	
N	F	179	Motor or labyrinth problem _____	
U, P, N	T	180	Cognitive problem, Psychosis, Panic _____	
N, Ad	T	182	Seizure disorder, Blame avoidance _____	
P	T	198	Hallucinations, Dissociation _____	
U	F	208	Somatic Focus, Reactivity, Dyspnea _____	
P	T	216	Ideas of reference, Delusions _____	
M	T/F	226	Euphoria _____	
P	T	228	Delusions _____	
N, Ad	T	229	Seizure disorder _____	
S-S	T	234	Fixed idea with depression or psychosis _____	
M, U	T/F	242	Dyscontrol of emotional arousal _____	
P	T	259	Ideas of reference, Delusions, Hallucinations _____	
Ad	T	264	Alcohol abuse or dependence _____	
D	F	266	Law infractions _____	
M	T/F	267	Euphoria _____	

Code(s)	Key	Item	Possi ble Symptom(s)	Response/Evaluation
N	T	282	Somnambulism	
N	F	295	Myasthenia, Paralysis	
N	T	298	Misperceptions, Hallucinations	
S-O, D	T	303	Suicide risk	
S-S	T	306	Alienation, Dysphoria	
P, U	T	311	Dissociation, Derealization	
P	F	314	Delusions, Ideas of reference	
P	T	316	Misperceptions, Dissociation	
P	T	319	Hallucinations, Tinnitus	
M	T/F	330	Hypomania	
P	T	336	Delusions, Ideas of reference	
P	T	355	Ideas of reference	
P	T	361	Delusions, Ideas of reference	
M	T/F	366	Insomnia, Hypomania	
S-S	T	379	History of physical abuse	
Ad	T	387	Alcohol dependence	
S-S	T	407	Strongly intropunitive	
Ad	F	429	Substance abuse	
S-S	T	454	Hopelessness	
U	T	463	Panicky foreboding	
P	T	466	Ideas of reference	
U, P	T	469	Panicky or psychotic fear of dyscontrol	
Ad	T	487	Cannabis abuse	
Ad	T	489	Substance abuse or dependence	

Code(s)	Key	Item	Possible Symptom(s)	Response/Evaluation
Ad	F	501	Substance abuse or dependence _____	
S-S, D	T	505	Suicide ideation _____	
D, S-O	T	506	Suicidal ideation _____	
Ad	T	511	Substance abuse or dependence _____	
S-S	T	512	Unresolved object loss _____	
D, S-O	T	520	Suicidal ideation _____	
D, S-O	T	524	Suicide attempt _____	
U	T	525	Excessive arousal _____	
S-S	T	526	Externality with helplessness _____	
Ad	T	527	Alcohol abuse or dependence _____	
M	T/F	529	Pressured speech, Circumstantiality _____	
D, S-O	T	530	Borderline behavior pattern _____	
S-S	T	539	Amotivational state _____	
D, Ad	T	540	Alcohol dyscontrol of aggression _____	
U	T	543	Obsessions, Panicky ideation _____	
Ad	T	544	Alcohol abuse with denial _____	
S-S	T	546	Preoccupation with death _____	
D	T	548	Rage reactions _____	
U	T	555	Phobic concerns _____	
U, D	F	564	Behavior dyscontrol _____	

GUIDE TO CRITICAL INQUIRY CODES

   Ad   Addictive signs

   D   Dangerousness to self or others & antisocial tendencies

M   Hypomanic or bipolar symptoms (*Caution*: normals often report; check both *T* & *F*)

N   Neuropsychological symptoms (*Note*: Symptoms frequently are reported by chemically dependent and psychotic persons.)

P   Delusional and psychotic symptoms (*Note*: Paranoid type answers given also by some nonpsychotics with character pathology and seen in chemical dependency; schizotypal, paranoid, and borderline personality disorders; and obsessive–compulsive disorder.)

S-O   Obvious suicidal statements and risk (*Note*: In addition to Axis I conditions, borderline personalities in crisis will respond in accordance with the key to many of these items.)

S-S   Subtle, passive signs of suicidal risk (*Note*: Depressed and psychotic patients and persons with poor morale and low self-esteem often report these symptoms.)

U   Unstable, panicky, decompensating (*Note*: Persons with elevated physiological reactivity and anxiety disorders often are identifiable by items in this category, irrespective of whether other reportable psychopathology is present.)

Appendix D: Inpatient Diagnostic Group Means

In preparation for the descriptive analyses that are summarized here, the sample of 1,020 valid adult records was further subdivided by diagnostic groups. Variables were developed that effectively removed all cases having psychotic or affective diagnoses from analyses of the *PDOs* and the substance abuse disorders for one set of sample descriptions. In a second division of the cases, all of those diagnosed with substance abuse disorders were removed from the sample before analyzing the psychotic and affective disorders. A third partitioning of the sample looked at those patients who were dually diagnosed with psychotic or affective disorders plus a substance abuse diagnosis. Fourth, the *PDOs* were separated for analysis from substance abuse, psychotic disorders, and affective disorders. Chapter 2 describes how diagnoses were gathered, made conformable to *DSM–IV*, and coded.

MMPI scores appeared to be unrealistically low for some of the scales that were selected for use in reviewing the *DSM* diagnoses. This was found to be true even for the better examples of *MMPI–DSM* matches that are reported in this appendix. Other attempted matches were far less defining or were represented by too few diagnosed cases in the sample for their results to be reported here. Those appearing here are, hence, the best of the matches. As can be observed, the scales and diagnoses related to one another below expected or acceptable levels.

The foregoing observations led to completion of a parallel series of analyses of the match of *MMPI* scales to *DSM* diagnoses. These analyses employed data from a file of 496 cases that had been separated by *AdjAll* from what are here referred to as the *Valid Records*. That is, these were cases for which one or more Validity scale scores fell beyond accepted limits. That sample is referred to here as the *Invalid Records*. The results of the analyses are displayed in matching arrays in order to facilitate comparison and contrast with results for the 1,020 Valid Records. Results of those comparisons are discussed later.

Descriptions of the diagnostically sorted Valid and Invalid samples were carried out using linear *T*-scores that had been assigned to *MMPI* scales. Findings for representative scales are presented in this brief appendix in order to illustrate these relations. As a result of the low and inconsistent relations found between *MMPI* and *DSM* diagnoses, the study focused in chapters 8 through 10 on selected *MMPI–2* Content and Clinical scales. These were grouped based on their intercorrelations into both trait oriented and diagnostically meaningful clusters, and psychosocial modality scales were interwoven with them.

The diagnoses examined were depression (Depr) and bipolar disorder (Bipol) by themselves and in combination with substance abuse or dependence (SubAb). The *SubAb* categories singled out were Alcohol and polysubstance (Polysub) dependence. These were studied alone and in combination with mental illness (MI). The composite MI category included all psychotic, depressive, bipolar, and anxiety diagnoses. The specific MI categories that were studied separately were schizophrenia (Schiz) and schizoaffective disorder (SzAff). They were further analyzed in dual diagnosis combination with SubAb. Finally, two *PDOs*—antisocial (Anti) and borderline (Bord)—were studied similarly.

DISCUSSION OF FINDINGS FOR DIAGNOSTIC GROUPS

Mean scores in Table D.1, Part I for *D, DEP*, and *3LM* are elevated but insufficiently so for persons diagnosed as having Depr. This nonmatch would cause many of the valid patient records to be classified as "not depressed." The Bipol situation is less acceptable than that for the Depr group. Bipol records would be

TABLE D.1
Mean Scores for Depressed and Bipolar Diagnoses

Scale	Depr	Depr+SubAb	Bipol	Bipol+SubAb
I. Means by Diagnostic Groups (Valid Records)				
D (2)	67.98	64.53	55.02	56.34
DEP	64.34	60.34	56.62	61.01
3LM	68.38	66.16	55.82	58.77
W-HYP	51.06	50.59	55.04	58.28
II. Means by Diagnostic Groups (Invalid Records)				
D (2)	76.71	79.73	68.75	71.32
DEP	81.24	86.41	70.99	80.69
3LM	80.72	84.90	74.05	78.63
W-HYP	61.91	63.78	67.69	78.63

classified as indicating neither depression or hypomanic elevation (i.e., *W-HYP* also too low). The Invalid record counterparts in Part II of Table D.1 fare better in terms of overall expected levels of elevation on the scales, while simultaneously showing too little differentiation between Depr and Bipol groups. The combination of SubAb with these disorders adds no clarity.

The *MAC-R* scale (Table D.2, Parts I & II), in relation to diagnosed substance dependence disorders, is not discriminating enough in either the Valid or Invalid sample. The *APS* scale was not tried here as an alternative to *MAC-R* because it was earlier found (chap. 8) to produce little score elevation across patient conditions. Moreover, the expected loading of antisocial trait (i.e., *ASP* too low) in the Polysub group was not substantiated. Only the *Re* scale produced an overall set of means that tended to follow an expected pattern across groups. Nevertheless, *ASP* and *MAC-R* scales are judged to be at least as credible as the diagnoses, so the findings could not be reconciled.

Findings for the Schizo and ScAff groups were altogether anomalous in relation to the *MMPI–2* scales (Table D.3, Part I). This was true both when the psychotic conditions were individually considered or when they were looked at in combination with substance abuse. Those scales reflecting a broader range of psychotic symptoms (*ScK* and *BIZ*) and more narrowly paranoid ones (*Pa* and *S+*) failed to relate in expected ways to the assigned diagnoses. Only in the sample of Invalid records (Part II of Table D.3) did these scales perform in an expected manner. Results obviously did not support using the diagnoses to evaluate the *MMPI–2* scales, nor did they support the converse.

Diagnoses of Anti and Bord *PDO* are at times assigned to patients based on reputation and the extent to which they create excess management problems in the inpatient milieu. Thus, the criteria may be applied rather loosely at times. It is, nevertheless, incredible that patients diagnosed as Anti would describe themselves on *ASP* and *W-AUT* as barely surpassing the mean of T50. Although the el-

TABLE D.2
Mean Scores of Patients Diagnosed with Alcohol and Polysubstance Disorders

Scale	Alcohol	Alcohol+MI	Polysub	Polysub+MI
I. Means by Diagnostic Groups (Valid Records)				
MAC-R	65.80	62.84	65.63	62.53
Imp-B	58.79	56.82	66.01	55.31
Re	40.37	43.90	36.93	45.12
ASP	55.82	54.15	58.59	47.85
II. Means by Diagnostic Groups (Invalid Records)				
MAC-R	67.83	65.23	69.62	70.68
Imp-B	71.17	72.72	80.00	77.18
Re	30.95	30.80	23.86	25.88
ASP	63.78	64.03	66.67	67.82

TABLE D.3
Mean Scores of Patients Diagnosed Schizophrenic and Schizoaffective

Scale	Schizo	Schizo+SubAb	SzAff	SzAff+SubAb
	I. Means by Diagnostic Groups (Valid Records)			
ScK	58.26	63.34	56.89	63.67[a]
BIZ	58.93	57.89	52.73	61.04
Pa	57.04	59.52	53.22	49.65
S+	55.51	60.78	52.47	62.61
	II. Means by Diagnostic Groups (Invalid Records)			
ScK	80.59	88.89	85.45	81.27[a]
BIZ	88.67	95.86	84.75	80.67
Pa	74.06	83.63	76.66	77.91
S+	75.06	77.67	68.66	72.60

[a]Small n's within the subsample render the means in this column potentially less stable.

TABLE D.4
Mean Scores of Patients Diagnosed as Antisocial and Borderline *PDO*

Scale	Anti PDO	Anti+SubAb	Bord PDO	Bord+SubAb
	I. Means by Diagnostic Groups (Valid Records)			
ASP	56.23	57.33	50.92[a]	55.76
W-AUT	54.86	56.93	46.50	56.41
LSE	55.56	54.92	67.46	54.76
2SD	54.65	58.68	65.39	58.23
	II. Means by Diagnostic Groups (Invalid Records)			
ASP	69.96	66.88	59.35[a]	64.32
W-AUT	63.97	64.31	55.82	63.46
LSE	79.33	71.78	73.19	68.28
2SD	78.35	78.73	82.83	77.34

[a]Small ns within the subsample render the means in this column potentially less stable.

evations for the Bord group on *LSE* and *2SD* in Table D.4, Part I are more credible, they are based on a small sample. The larger and more stable means for the Bord plus SubAb sample in Part I of the table are, on the other hand, totally out of keeping with Bord *PDO* diagnosis. As in some of the other preceding comparisons, means for the Invalid records come closer to matching expected score level but without successfully differentiating Bord from Anti *PDO* patients. As in the other comparisons, the co-occurrence of an addictive problem with the diagnoses failed to produce a marked increase in reported symptoms and distress such as would usually accompany a dual diagnosis condition.

It is possible that the problems encountered in matching *MMPI–2* scales and *DSM* diagnoses arose from their differing methodologies and frames of reference.

This possibility is neither particularly appealing nor plausible. The problems of gross mismatch may instead have resulted in part from the automatic application of quantitative exclusionary rules when Validity scale cutoffs were applied. The *AdjAll* correction admittedly did eliminate clinical judgment about the validity of the patient records. There is room of course to question the fidelity of the diagnostic assignments in this nonresearch hospital setting.

Prior attempts to establish close *MMPI/MMPI–2* score and codetype matches to *DSM* categories have been elusive and disappointing (Franklin et al., 2002; Pancoast et al., 1988; Wetzler et al., 1998). Whatever the cause may be for the present mismatch, it is incontestable. The remedy, as stated in chapter 8, was to conduct the study using diagnostic approximations created from multiple *MMPI–2* scales assembled into content clusters. That course of action carried with it the risk of the data being overly infused by the method specific variance associated with self-report (Campbell & Fiske, 1959). Further study will be needed to determine the extent to which that decision is supportable.

Appendix E: Psychogenic Rage

Other presentations of newer scales appear in chapter 7. An exception was made in the present case in view of the absence in the psychological and psychiatric literatures of a construct corresponding to *rage*, as it is conceptualized here. This appendix first presents an empirical background for this construct. The development of an *MMPI–2* scale to measure this construct is discussed.

THE *DSM* AND ANGER REGULATION

The psychogenic rage reaction is a condition that is neglected in the *DSM* series. That is to say, not all anger manifestations can be viewed as Axis II behavior, nor are they all adequately subsumed under the impulse control or mood disorders. Specifically, in the absence of intoxication or a psychotic disorder, there are persons whose anger overwhelms their rational processes on a fairly regular basis. The regularity of expression differs in these cases from the *DSM* recognized episodic pattern, Intermittent Explosive Disorder. This latter condition is detectable by *MMPI–2* scales measuring marked overcontrol of anger.

THE PSYCHOGENIC RAGE STATE

Unlike Intermittent Explosive Disorder, the anger response in susceptible persons regularly turns on the emergency survival system, triggering rapid increases in autonomic arousal and cascading endocrine activity. These persons act during rage episodes as if they temporarily disconnect from cortical control. It is as if their rational faculties have been captured by their glands. In this sense, they enter a state that usurps executive regulatory mechanisms in a manner resembling a panic attack. Psychophysiological monitoring of these persons during psychotherapy reveals grossly high electrodermal readings and heart rate increase to around 110–120 bpm. Although rages of psychogenic origin resemble the organic conditions itemized below by their physiological arousal, they differ by being kindled by thoughts and emotions. This is readily demonstrated by the observation that, when a psychogenic rage episode is in an early recruitment phase, it can be aborted by relaxation, distraction, and other methods.

ORGANIC CONDITIONS RESEMBLING RAGES

Similar manifestations are seen in toxic states (e.g., during intoxication produced by accidental ingestion of tobacco). Such toxic states usually clear in from 24 to 72 hours with use of supportive measures. Some individuals who are in a hypoglycemic state become extremely explosive and may behave aggressively. This state is readily reversed by administration of glucose and more slowly with other nutrients. Similar behavior may be seen also in acute schizophrenic and manic states. Beta adrenergic blockers have been shown to be effective in blunting the excessive arousal in these conditions. The controversial "further study" condition, Premenstrual Dysphoric Disorder (*DSM–IV–TR*, 2000) has been reported to be associated in some persons with extreme aggression. In these cases, it is variously treated with anxiolytics, antidepressants, and analgesics, among others. Post-ictal reactions in convulsive disorders, although rarely, may include severe aggression. All of the foregoing hyperarousal states arise from identifiable organic substrates. Unlike rages of psychogenic origin, their onset cannot be interrupted by relaxation and distraction.

AN *MMPI–2* SCALE FOR RAGE

The question raised was whether *MMPI–2* items and scales might provide clues regarding such patients, as they do for Intermittent Explosive Disorder. The *ANG, W–HOS, TSC/R, Ho, 2PR*, and *O–H* scales were reviewed critically. All capture only fragments of the rage construct. No *MMPI–2* scale was found that encompassed the constellation of characteristics seen in rage, nor was there a combination of scales that suited this assessment objective.

It became necessary to construct a scale to include elements gleaned from clinical experience with small numbers of these patients. They have a low anger threshold, leading to frequent angry outbursts. Further, they are partially adapted to high levels of chronic tension. For example, they are able to fall asleep at autonomic arousal levels that are experienced as highly distressing by others. From this high baseline of tension, small increases often destabilize their internal controls. Thus, their self-regulation is unreliable and inherently unstable. They are overly sensitive and ready to perceive threat and take offense. Their sensitivity permits a small incident to trigger a disproportionately enormous outburst. That is, their behavior is overdetermined and their reactions are grossly magnified.

Repeated searches of *MMPI–2* turned up 24 items (Appendix A). From them a scale was formed. The *Rage* scale's internal consistency was very satisfactory: .89 for females and .90 for males. Means and standard deviations, respectively, for the patient sample were: females, 11.21/6.19; males, 12.58/6.45. Means were computed and standard deviations estimated to match CX norms (Appendix B). Patient means exceeded the CX norms by .954 standard deviation for females and for males by 1.519 standard deviations.

Although anger control problems and arrests related to these were present in the sample, no definitive reference group of affected patients was available. Hence, preliminary findings were restricted to correlations between *Rage* and other *MMPI–2* scales.

Correlations with scales of interest relative to anger threshold and outbursts were *ANG* .87, *W-HOS* .83, *TSC/R* .86, *Ho* .73, *O-H* −.56. Unlike the Intermittent Explosive Disorder pattern of relations, low threshold for anger and undercontrol were demonstrated. Tension build up and instability were suggested by *W-HYP* .64, *9PMA* .61, *2PR* .75, *Panic* .73, *TSC/T* .81, *BORD PDO* .85. Excess sensitivity and readiness to perceive threat and to take offense appeared as *6P* .56, *TSC/S* .69, *Pa* .55, *S+* .56, and *6PI* .53. Loss of control showed up as predisposition to respond to impulse (*Imp-B* .69, *Imp-I* .62, *Imp-A* .81, *Imp-T* .84, *8DI* .65), with affective impulsivity being most prominent.

Rage's largest relation with a Psychosocial scale was with Initiating vs. Guilt-Prone ($r = -.80$), indicating particular difficulty in the area of initiative. The remaining five Psychosocial scales all related negatively to *Rage* but at much lower levels. It correlated .47 or less with Clinical scales *1, 2, 3, 4, 9*. Larger correlations were expected and obtained with Scales *6* and *7*, as already noted. A larger relation to Scale *8* (.61) appeared.

The foregoing relations were attributable in part to item overlaps between *Rage* and the comparison scales. The number of items overlapping the various scales were: *ANG* 10, *W-HOS* 5, *TSC/R* 4, *Ho* 3, *O-H* none, *W-HYP* 3, *9PMA* 1, *2PR* 2, *Panic* 1, *TSC/T* 7, *BORD* 7, *6P* none, *TSC/S* none, *Pa* none, *S+* none, *6PI* none, *Imp-B* 3, *Imp-I* none, *Imp-A* 3, *Imp-T* 6, *8DI* 2, *Initiating vs. Guilt-Prone* 2. It is evident that the overlaps were not numerous enough to account fully for any of the relations.

It was concluded that the *Rage* scale performed in keeping with its design, relative to relevant *MMPI–2* scales. The item composition of the scale is internally consistent. Further study is needed to establish its clinical utility for identifying rage reactions. Pending further study, it is regarded as experimental. It will likely be of value at least for screening for the presence of poorly controlled anger that is associated with hyperarousal and tension, instability, feelings of vulnerability, and impulsivity. It is hoped that this initial effort at defining *rage* as a neglected anger spectrum syndrome will result in others undertaking its study.

References

Acklin, M. W. (1993). Integrating the Rorschach and the *MMPI* in clinical assessment: Conceptual and methodological issues. *Journal of Personality Assessment, 60,* 125–131.

American Psychiatric Association. (1968). *Diagnostic and statistical manual of mental disorders* (2nd ed.). Washington, DC: Author.

American Psychiatric Association. (1980). *Diagnostic and statistical manual of mental disorders* (3rd ed.). Washington, DC: Author.

American Psychiatric Association. (1987). *Diagnostic and statistical manual of mental disorders* (3rd rev. ed.). Washington, DC: Author.

American Psychiatric Association. (1994). *Diagnostic and statistical manual of mental disorders* (4th ed.). Washington, DC: Author.

American Psychiatric Association. (2000). *Diagnostic and statistical manual of mental disorders* (4th ed., text revision). Washington, DC: Author.

Arbisi, P. A., & Ben-Porath, Y. S. (1995). An *MMPI–2* infrequent response scale for use with psychopathological populations. The Infrequency Psychopathology scale, *F(p)*. *Psychological Assessment, 7,* 424–431.

Arbisi, P. A., & Ben-Porath, Y. S. (1997). Characteristics of the *MMPI–2 F(p)* scale as a function of diagnosis of an inpatient sample of veterans. *Psychological Assessment, 9,* 102–105.

Arbisi, P. A., Ben-Porath, Y. S., & McNulty, J. (2002). A comparison of *MMPI–2* validity in African American and Caucasian psychiatric inpatients. *Psychological Assessment, 14,* 3–15.

Arbisi, P. A., McNulty, J. L., Ben-Porath, Y. S., & Boyd, J. (1999, April). *Detection of partial fake bad responding on the* MMPI–2. Paper presented at the 34th annual symposium on Recent Developments in the Use of the *MMPI–2* and *MMPI–A*, Huntington Beach, CA.

Archer, R. P. (1996). *MMPI–Rorschach* interrelationships: Proposed criteria for evaluating explanatory models. *Journal of Personality Assessment, 67,* 504–515.

Archer, R. P. (1997). MMPI–A. *Assessing adolescent psychopathology* (2nd ed.). Mahwah, NJ: Lawrence Erlbaum Associates.

Archer, R. P., & Krishnamurthy, R. (1993a). Combining the *Rorschach* and the *MMPI* in the assessment of adolescents. *Journal of Personality Assessment, 60,* 132–140.

Archer, R. P., & Krishnamurthy, R. (1993b). A review of *MMPI* and *Rorschach* interrelationships in adult samples. *Journal of Personality Assessment, 61,* 277–293.

Archer, R. P., & Krishnamurthy, R. (1999). Reply to Meyer on the convergent validity of the *MMPI* and *Rorschach*. *Journal of Personality Assessment, 73*, 319–321.

Ashton, S. G., & Goldberg, L. R. (1973). In response to Jackson's challenge: The comparative validity of personality scales constructed by the external (empirical) strategy and scales developed intuitively by experts, novices, and laymen. *Journal of Research in Personality, 7*, 1–20.

Baer, R. A., Wetter, M. W., & Berry, D.T.R. (1992). Detection of underreporting of psychopathology on the *MMPI*: A meta-analysis. *Clinical Psychology Review, 12*, 509–525.

Baer, R. A., Wetter, M. W., Nichols, D. S., Greene, R. L., & Berry, D.T.R. (1995). Sensitivity of the *MMPI–2* Validity Scales to underreporting of symptoms. *Psychological Assessment, 7*, 419–423.

Bagby, R. M., Nicholson, R. A., Buis, T., Radovanovic, H., & Fidler, B. J. (1999). Defensive responding on the *MMPI–2* in family custody and access evaluations. *Psychological Assessment, 11*, 24–28.

Bagby, R. M., Rogers, R., Nicholson, R. A., Buis, T., Seeman, M. V., & Rector, N. A. (1997). Effectiveness of the *MMPI–2* validity indicators in the detection of defensive responding in clinical and nonclinical samples. *Psychological Assessment, 9*, 406–413.

Bardwick, J. (1971). *Psychology of women: A study of bio-cultural conflicts*. New York: Harper & Row.

Barefoot, J. C., Dahlstrom, W. G., & Williams, R. B., Jr. (1983). Hostility, CHD incidence, and total mentality: A 25-year follow-up study of 255 physicians. *Psychosomatic Medicine, 45*, 59–63.

Barron, F. (1953). An ego-strength scale which predicts response to psychotherapy. *Journal of Consulting Psychology, 17*, 327–333.

Benjamin, L. S. (1993). *Interpersonal diagnosis and treatment of personality disorders*. New York: Guilford.

Ben-Porath, Y. S., & Butcher, J. N. (1989). Psychometric stability of rewritten *MMPI* items. *Journal of Personality Assessment, 53*, 645–653.

Ben-Porath, Y. S., Hostetler, K., Butcher, J. N., & Graham, J. R. (1989). New subscales for the *MMPI–2* Social Introversion (*Si*) scale. *Psychological Assessment, 1*, 169–174.

Berry, D.T.R., Baer, R. A., & Harris, M. J. (1991). Detection of malingering on the *MMPI*: A meta-analysis. *Clinical Psychology Review, 11*, 585–598.

Berry, D.T.R., Wetter, M. W., Baer, R. A., Larsen, L., Clark, C., & Monroe, K. (1992). *MMPI–2* random responding indices: Validation using a self-report methodology. *Psychological Assessment, 4*, 340–345.

Berry, D.T.R., Wetter, M. W., Baer, R. A., Widiger, T. A., Sumpter, J. C., Reynolds, S. K., & Hallam, R. A. (1991). Detection of random responding on the *MMPI–2*: Utility of the *F*, back *F*, and *VRIN* scales. *Psychological Assessment, 3*, 418–423.

Blackburn, R. (1968). Personality in relation to extreme aggression in psychiatric offenders. *British Journal of Psychiatry, 114*, 821–828.

Blackburn, R. (1972). Dimensions of hostility and aggression in abnormal offenders. *Journal of Consulting and Clinical Psychology, 38*, 20–26.

Blais, M. A., Hilsenroth, M. J., Castlebury, F., Fowler, J. C., & Baity, M. R. (2001). Predicting *DSM–IV* Cluster B personality disorder criteria from *MMPI–2* and *Rorschach* data: A test of incremental validity. *Journal of Personality Assessment, 76*, 150–168.

Bloomquist, M. I., & Dossa, D. E. (1988). Assessing family functioning with the *MMPI* family scales. *International Journal of Family Psychiatry, 9*, 19–27.

Boerger, A. R. (1975). *The utility of some alternative approaches to MMPI scale construction*. Unpublished doctoral dissertation, Kent State University, Kent, OH.

Bridges, M. R., Wilson, J. S., & Gacono, C. B. (1998). A *Rorschach* investigation of defensiveness, self-perception, interpersonal relations, and affective states in incarcerated pedophiles. *Journal of Personality Assessment, 70*, 365–385.

Buechley, R., & Ball, H. (1952). A new test of "validity" for the group *MMPI*. *Journal of Consulting Psychology, 16*, 299–301.

Buss, A. H., & Durkee, A. (1957). An inventory for assessing different kinds of hostility. *Journal of Consulting Psychology, 21*, 343–349.

Butcher, J. N. (1990). *The MMPI–2 in psychological treatment*. New York: Oxford University Press.

Butcher, J. N., Dahlstrom, W. G., Graham, J. R., Tellegen, A., & Kaemmer, B. (1989). *Minnesota Multiphasic Personality Inventory (MMPI–2). Manual for administration and scoring*. Minneapolis: University of Minnesota.

Butcher, J. N., Graham, J. R., & Ben-Porath, Y. S. (1995). Methodological problems and issues in *MMPI, MMPI–2,* and *MMPI–A* research. *Psychological Assessment, 7,* 320–329.

Butcher, J. N., Graham, J. R., Ben-Porath, Y. S., Tellegen, A., Dahlstrom, W. G., & Kaemmer, B. (2001). MMPI–2 *(Minnesota Multiphasic Personality Inventory–2). Manual for administration, scoring, and interpretation* (rev. ed.). Minneapolis: University of Minnesota.

Butcher, J. N., Graham, J. R., Williams, C. L., & Ben-Porath, Y. S. (1990). *Development and use of the MMPI–2 Content scales*. Minneapolis: University of Minnesota.

Butcher, J. N., & Han, K. (1995). Development of an *MMPI* scale to assess the presentation of self in a superlative manner: The *S* scale. In J. N. Butcher & C. D. Spielberger (Eds.), *Advances in personality assessment* (Vol. 10, pp. 25–50). Hillsdale, NJ: Lawrence Erlbaum Associates.

Calvin, J. (1975). *A replicated study of the concurrent validity of the Harris subscales for the* MMPI. Unpublished doctoral dissertation, Kent State University, Kent, OH.

Campbell, D. T., & Fiske, D. W. (1959). Convergent and discriminant validation by the multitrait-multimethod matrix. *Psychological Bulletin, 56,* 81–105.

Caron, G. R., & Archer, R. P. (1997). *MMPI* and *Rorschach* characteristics of individuals approved for gender reassignment surgery. *Assessment, 4,* 229–241.

Cernovsky, Z. (1986). Masculinity–femininity scale of the *MMPI* and intellectual function of female addicts. *Journal of Clinical Psychology, 42,* 310–312.

Christian, W. L., Burkhart, B. R., & Gynther, M. D. (1978). Subtle–obvious ratings of *MMPI* items: New interest in an old concept. *Journal of Consulting and Clinical Psychology, 46,* 1178–1186.

Chu, C.-L. (1966). *Object cluster analysis of the* MMPI. Unpublished doctoral dissertation, University of California, Berkeley.

Clopton, J. R. (1979). Development of special *MMPI* scales. In C. S. Newmark (Ed.), *MMPI clinical and research trends* (pp. 354–372). New York: Praeger.

Clopton, J. R., & Neuringer, C. (1977). *MMPI* Cannot Say scores: Normative data and degree of profile distortion. *Journal of Personality Assessment, 41,* 511–513.

Cohen, H., & Weil, G. R. (1975). *Tasks of emotional development test manual*. Brookline, MA: T.E.D. Associates.

Comrey, A. L. (1957). A factor analysis of items on the *MMPI* Hypochondriasis scale. *Educational and Psychological Measurement, 17,* 568–577.

Constantinople, A. (1973). Masculinity–femininity: An exception to a famous dictum? *Psychological Bulletin, 80,* 389–407.

Cook, W. W., Leeds, C. H., & Callis, R. (1951). *Minnesota teacher attitude inventory manual*. New York: Psychological Corporation.

Cook, W. W., & Medley, D. M. (1954). Proposed hostility and Pharisaic-virtue scales for the *MMPI*. *Journal of Applied Psychology, 38,* 414–418.

Costa, P. T., Jr., Zonderman, A. B., McCrae, R. R., & Williams, R. B., Jr. (1985). Content and comprehensiveness in the *MMPI*: An item factor analysis in a normal adult sample. *Journal of Personality & Social Psychology, 48,* 925–933.

Cronbach, L. J. (1951). Coefficient alpha and the internal structure of tests. *Psychometrika, 16,* 297–334.

Cuadra, C. A. (1956). A scale for control in psychological adjustment (*Cn*). In G. S. Welsh & W. G. Dahlstrom (Eds.), *Basic readings on the* MMPI *in psychology and medicine* (pp. 235–254). Minneapolis: University of Minnesota.

Dahlstrom, W. G., & Tellegen, A. (1993). *Socioeconomic status and the* MMPI–2*: The relation of* MMPI–2 *patterns to levels of education and occupation*. Minneapolis: University of Minnesota.

Dahlstrom, W. G., & Welsh, G. S. (1960). *An* MMPI *handbook: A guide to use in clinical practice and research*. Minneapolis: University of Minnesota.

Dahlstrom, W. G., Welsh, G. S., & Dahlstrom, L. E. (1972). *An* MMPI *handbook: Vol. 1. Clinical interpretation* (rev. ed.). Minneapolis: University of Minnesota.

Dahlstrom, W. G., Welsh, G. S., & Dahlstrom, L. E. (1975). *An* MMPI *handbook: Vol. II. Research applications* (rev. ed.). Minneapolis: University of Minnesota.

Davis, R. D., Wagner, E. E., & Patty, C. C. (1994). Maximized split-half reliabilities for Harris–Lingoes Subscales: A follow-up with larger *N*s. *Perceptual and Motor Skills, 78,* 881–882.

Dawes, R. M. (1999). Two methods for studying the incremental validity of a *Rorschach* variable. *Psychological Assessment, 11,* 297–302.

De Charms, R. (1968). *Personal causation. The internal affective determinants of behavior.* New York: Academic.

deGroot, G. W., & Adamson, J. D. (1973). Responses of psychiatric inpatients to the MacAndrew Alcoholism scale. *Quarterly Journal of Studies on Alcohol, 34,* 1133–1139.

Dembroski, T. M., MacDougall, J. M., Williams, R. B., Jr., Haney, T., & Blumental, J. A. (1985). Components of Type A, hostility and anger-in: Relationship to angiographic findings. *Psychosomatic Medicine, 47,* 219–233.

Drake, L. E. (1946). A social *I-E* scale for the *MMPI. Journal of Applied Psychology, 30,* 51–54.

Dreikurs, R. (1957). *Psychology in the classroom.* New York: Harper.

Duckworth, J. C. (1979). MMPI *interpretation manual for counselors and clinicians.* Muncie, IN: Accelerated Development.

Duckworth, J. C., & Anderson, W. (1995). MMPI *interpretation manual for counselors and clinicians* (4th ed.). Muncie, IN: Accelerated Development.

Duckworth, J. C., & Levitt, E. E. (1994). Minnesota Multiphasic Personality Inventory–2. In D. J. Keyser & R. C. Sweetland (Eds.), *Test critiques* (Vol. 10, pp. 424–428). Austin, TX: Pro-Ed.

Edwards, A. L. (1957). *The social desirability variable in personality assessment and research.* New York: Dryden.

Edwards, A. L. (1959). *Edwards Personal Preference Schedule.* New York: Psychological Corporation.

Edwards, A. L., & Edwards, L. K. (1992). Social desirability and Wiggins *MMPI* Content scales. *Journal of Personality and Social Psychology, 62,* 147–153.

Endicott, N. A., Jortner, A. S., & Abramoff, E. (1969). Objective measures of suspiciousness. *Journal of Abnormal Psychology, 74,* 26–32.

Erikson, E. (1963). *Childhood and society* (2nd ed.). New York: Norton.

Evans, C., & McConnell, T. R. (1941). A new measure of introversion–extroversion. *Journal of Psychology, 12,* 111–124.

Exner, J. E., Jr. (1993). *The* Rorschach*: A comprehensive system: Vol. 1. Basic foundations* (3rd ed.). New York: Wiley.

Exner, J. E., Jr. (2000). *A primer for* Rorschach *interpretation.* Asheville, NC: Rorschach Workshops.

Exner, J. E., Jr., Weiner, I. B., & PAR Staff. (2001). Rorschach interpretation program: Version 4 plus for Windows [Computer software]. Odessa, FL: PAR.

Faschingbauer, T. R. (1979). The future of the *MMPI.* In C. S. Newmark (Ed.), *MMPI clinical and research trends* (pp. 373–398). New York: Praeger.

Fisher, G. (1970). Discriminating violence emanating from over-controlled versus under-controlled aggressivity. *British Journal of Social and Clinical Psychology, 9,* 54–59.

Foerstner, S. B. (1986). *The factor structure and factor stability of selected Minnesota Multiphasic Personality Inventory (*MMPI*) subscales: Harris and Lingoes Subscales, Wiggins Content Scales, Weiner subscales, and Serkownek subscales.* Unpublished doctoral dissertation, University of Akron, Akron, OH.

Franklin, C. L., Strong, D. R., & Greene, R. L. (2002). A taxometric analysis of the *MMPI–2* Depression scales. *Journal of Personality Assessment, 79,* 110–121.

Fredericksen, S. J. (1975). *A comparison of selected personality and history variables in highly violent, mildly violent and nonviolent female offenders.* Unpublished doctoral dissertation, University of Minnesota, Minneapolis.

Fremouw, W. J., de Perczel, M., & Ellis, T. E. (1990). *Suicide risk: Assessment and response guidelines*. New York: Pergamon.

Friedman, A. F., Lewak, R., Nichols, D. S., & Webb, J. T. (2001). *Psychological assessment with the MMPI–2*. Mahwah, NJ: Lawrence Erlbaum Associates.

Gacono, C. B., Meloy, J. R., & Bridges, M. R. (2000). A *Rorschach* comparison of psychopaths, sexual homicide perpetrators, and nonviolent pedophiles: Where angels fear to tread. *Journal of Clinical Psychology, 56,* 757–777.

Gallen, R. T., & Berry, D.T.R. (1996). Detection of random responding in *MMPI–2* protocols. *Assessment, 3,* 171–178.

Ganellen, R. J. (1994). Attempting to conceal psychological disturbance: *MMPI* defensive response sets and the *Rorschach*. *Journal of Personality Assessment, 63,* 423–437.

Ganellen, R. J. (1996). Comparing the diagnostic efficiency of the *MMPI, MCMI–II*, and *Rorschach*: A review. *Journal of Personality Assessment, 67,* 219–243.

Gebhard, P. H., Gagnon, J. H., Pomeroy, W. B., & Christenson, C. V. (1965). *Sex offenders*. New York: Harper & Row.

Gotts, E. E. (1983). Home-based early intervention. In A. W. Childs & G. B. Melton (Eds.), *Rural psychology* (pp. 337–358). New York: Plenum.

Gotts, E. E. (1989). *HOPE, preschool to graduation: Contributions to parenting and school–family relations theory and practice. Final Report*. Charleston, WV: AEL, Inc. (ERIC Document Reproduction Service No. ED305146)

Gough, H. G. (1950). The *F* minus *K* dissimulation index for the Minnesota Multiphasic Personality Inventory. *Journal of Consulting Psychology, 14,* 408–413.

Gough, H. G. (1957). *California Psychological Inventory manual*. Palo Alto, CA: Consulting Psychologists.

Gough, H. G., McClosky, H., & Meehl, P. E. (1951). A personality scale for dominance. *Journal of Abnormal and Social Psychology, 46,* 360–366.

Gough, H. G., McClosky, H., & Meehl, P. E. (1952). A personality scale for social responsibility. *Journal of Abnormal and Social Psychology, 47,* 73–80.

Graham, J. R. (1987). *The MMPI: A practical guide* (2nd ed.). New York: Oxford University Press.

Graham, J. R. (1990). MMPI–2: *Assessing personality and psychopathology*. New York: Oxford University Press.

Graham, J. R. (2000). MMPI–2: *Assessing personality and psychopathology* (3rd ed.). New York: Oxford University Press.

Graham, J. R., Barthlow, D. L., Stein, L. A., Ben-Porath, Y. S., & McNulty, J. L. (2002). Assessing general maladjustment with the *MMPI–2*. *Journal of Personality Assessment, 78,* 334–347.

Graham, J. R., Watts, D., & Timbrook, R. E. (1991). Detecting fake-good and fake-bad *MMPI–2* profiles. *Journal of Personality Assessment, 57,* 264–277.

Grayson, H. M. (1951). *A psychological admissions testing program and manual*. Los Angeles: Veterans Administration Center, Neuropsychiatric Hospital.

Greene, R. L. (1978). An empirically derived *MMPI* Carelessness scale. *Journal of Clinical Psychology, 34,* 407–410.

Greene, R. L. (1991). *The MMPI–2/MMPI: An interpretive manual*. Needham Heights, MA: Allyn & Bacon.

Greene, R. L. (2000). *The MMPI–2: An interpretive manual* (2nd ed.). Boston: Allyn & Bacon.

Gronnerod, C. (2003). Temporal stability in the *Rorschach* method: A meta-analytic review. *Journal of Personality Assessment, 80,* 272–293.

Guilford, J. P., & Zimmerman, W. S. (1949). *Guilford–Zimmerman Temperament Survey Manual*. Beverly Hills, CA: Sheridan Supply.

Gynther, M. D., Burkhart, B. R., & Hovanitz, C. (1979). Do face-valid items have more predictive validity than subtle items? The case of the *MMPI Pd* scale. *Journal of Consulting and Clinical Psychology, 47,* 295–300.

Gynther, M. D., Lachar, D., & Dahlstrom, W. G. (1978). Are special norms for minorities needed? Development of an *MMPI F* scale for Blacks. *Journal of Consulting and Clinical Psychology, 46,* 1403–1408.

Hall, G.C.N., Bansal, A., & Lopez, I. R. (1999). Ethnicity and psychopathology: A meta-analytic review of 31 years of comparative *MMPI/MMPI–2* research. *Psychological Assessment, 11,* 186–197.

Hansen, J. C., & Campbell, D. P. (1985). *Manual for the* SVIB-SCII (4th ed.). Palo Alto, CA: Stanford University.

Hare, R. D. (1991). *Manual for the Hare Psychopathy Checklist—Revised.* Toronto: Multi-Health Systems.

Harris, R. E., & Lingoes, J. C. (1968). *Subscales for the* MMPI: *An aid to profile interpretation* [mimeographed]. San Francisco: Department of Psychiatry, University of California at San Francisco.

Hathaway, S. R. (1956). Scales 5 (Masculinity–Femininity), 6 (Paranoia), and 8 (Schizophrenia). In G. S. Welsh & W. G. Dahlstrom (Eds.), *Basic readings on the* MMPI *in psychiatry and medicine* (pp. 104–111). Minneapolis: University of Minnesota.

Hathaway, S. R., & McKinley, J. C. (1940). A Multiphasic Personality Schedule (Minnesota): I. Construction of the schedule. *Journal of Psychology, 10,* 249–254.

Hathaway, S. R., & McKinley, J. C. (1951). *Minnesota Multiphasic Personality Inventory manual* (Rev.). New York: Psychological Corporation.

Haven, H. J. (1972). *Descriptive and developmental characteristics of chronically overcontrolled hostile prisoners.* Unpublished doctoral dissertation, Florida State University, Tallahassee.

Hedayat, M. M., & Kelly, D. B. (1994). Relationship of *MMPI* Dependency and Dominance scale scores to staff's ratings, diagnoses, and demographic data for daytreatment clients. *Psychological Reports, 68,* 259–266.

Heilbrun, A. B. (1961). The psychological significance of the *MMPI K* scale in a normal population. *Journal of Consulting Psychology, 25,* 486–491.

Heist, P., & Yonge, G. (1968). *Manual for the Omnibus Personality Inventory.* New York: Psychological Corporation.

Hiller, J. B., Rosenthal, R., Bornstein, R. F., Berry, D.T.R., & Brunell-Neuleib, S. (1999). A comparative meta-analysis of *Rorschach* and *MMPI* validity. *Psychological Assessment, 11,* 278–296.

Hilsenroth, M. J., Handler, L., Toman, K. M., & Padawer, J. R. (1995). *Rorschach* and *MMPI–2* indices of early psychotherapy termination. *Journal of Consulting and Clinical Psychology, 63,* 956–965.

Honigfeld, G., & Klett, C. J. (1965). The Nurses' Observation Scale for Inpatient Evaluation: A new scale for measuring improvement in chronic schizophrenia. *Journal of Clinical Psychology, 21,* 65–71.

Jackson, D. N. (1975). The relative validity of scales prepared by naïve item writers and those based on empirical methods of personality scale construction. *Educational and Psychological Measurement, 35,* 361–370.

Jarneke, R. W., & Chambers, E. D. (1977). *MMPI* Content Scales: Dimensional structure, construct validity, and interpretive norms in a psychiatric population. *Journal of Consulting and Clinical Psychology, 45,* 1126–1131.

Johnson, J. H., Null, C., Butcher, J. N., & Johnson, K. N. (1984). Replicated item level factor analysis of the full *MMPI. Journal of Personality and Social Psychology, 47,* 105–114.

Jurjevich, R. M. (1963). Relationship among the *MMPI* and *HGI* hostility scales. *Journal of General Psychology, 69,* 131–133.

Keane, T. M., Malloy, P. F., & Fairbank, J. A. (1984). Empirical development of an *MMPI* subscale for the assessment of combat-related posttraumatic stress disorder. *Journal of Consulting and Clinical Psychology, 52,* 888–891.

Kelch, L. W., & Wagner, E. E. (1992). Maximized split-half reliabilities and distributional characteristics for Harris–Lingoes Subscales with few items: A reevaluation for the *MMPI–2. Perceptual and Motor Skills, 75,* 847–850.

Kessler, J. W. (1966). *Psychopathology of childhood.* Englewood Cliffs, NJ: Prentice-Hall.

Klerman, G. L. (1982). Practical issues in the treatment of depression and mania. In E. S. Paykel (Ed.), *Handbook of affective disorders* (pp. 438–451). New York: Churchill Livingstone.

Knapp, R. R. (1960). A reevaluation of the validity of *MMPI* scales of Dominance and Social Responsibility. *Educational and Psychological Measurement, 20,* 381–386.

Kohutek, K. J. (1992). Wiggins Content scales and the *MMPI–2. Journal of Clinical Psychology, 48,* 215–218.

Krishnamurthy, R., Archer, R. P., & Huddleston, E. N. (1995). Clinical research note on psychometric limitations of two Harris–Lingoes Subscales for the *MMPI–2. Assessment, 2,* 301–304.

Kuhn, T. S. (1970). *The structure of scientific revolutions* (2nd ed.). Chicago: University of Chicago.

Lachar, D. (1974). *The MMPI: Clinical assessment and automated interpretation.* Los Angeles: Western Psychological Services.

Lachar, D., & Alexander, P. S. (1978). Veridicality of self-report: Replicated correlates of the Wiggins *MMPI* Content Scales. *Journal of Consulting and Clinical Psychology, 46,* 1349–1356.

Lachar, D., Berman, W., Grisell, J. L., & Schoof, K. (1976). The MacAndrew Alcoholism scale as a general measure of substance abuse. *Journal of Studies on Alcohol, 37,* 1609–1615.

Ladd, J. S. (1998). The *F(p)* Infrequency-Psychopathology scale with chemically dependent inpatients. *Journal of Clinical Psychology, 54,* 665–671.

Lane, P. J., & Kling, J. S. (1979). Construct validity of the Overcontrolled Hostility scale of the *MMPI. Journal of Consulting and Clinical Psychology, 47,* 781–782.

Leary, T. (1956). *Multilevel measurement of interpersonal behavior.* Berkeley, CA: Psychological Consultation Service.

Leary, T. (1957). *Interpersonal diagnosis of personality.* New York: Ronald.

Lebovits, B. Z., & Ostfeld, A. M. (1967). Personality, defensiveness and educational achievement. *Journal of Personality and Social Psychology, 6,* 381–390.

Lester, D., Perdue, W. C., & Brookhart, D. (1974). Murder and the control of aggression. *Psychological Reports, 34,* 706.

Levitt, E. E. (1980a). *Primer on the* Rorschach *technique: A method of administration, scoring and interpretation.* Springfield, IL: Thomas.

Levitt, E. E. (1980b). *The psychology of anxiety* (2nd ed.). Hillsdale, NJ: Lawrence Erlbaum Associates.

Levitt, E. E. (1989). *The clinical application of* MMPI *special scales.* Hillsdale, NJ: Lawrence Erlbaum Associates.

Levitt, E. E. (1990). A structural analysis of the impact of *MMPI–2* on *MMPI–1. Journal of Personality Assessment, 55,* 562–577.

Levitt, E. E., Browning, J. M., & Freeland, L. J. (1992). The effects of *MMPI–2* on the scoring of special scales derived from *MMPI–1. Journal of Personality Assessment, 59,* 22–31.

Levitt, E. E., & Duckworth, J. C. (1984). Minnesota Multiphasic Personality Inventory. In D. J. Keyser & R. C. Sweetland (Eds.), *Test critiques* (Vol. 1, pp. 466–472). Kansas City, MO: Test Corporation of America.

Levitt, E. E., & Gotts, E. E. (1995). *The clinical application of* MMPI *special scales* (2nd ed.). Hillsdale, NJ: Lawrence Erlbaum Associates.

Levitt, E. E., Lubin, B., & Brooks, J. M. (1983). *Depression: Concepts, controversies and some new facts* (2nd ed.). Hillsdale, NJ: Lawrence Erlbaum Associates.

Lewak, R. W., Marks, P. A., & Nelson, G. E. (1990). *Therapist guide to the* MMPI *and* MMPI–2*: Providing feedback and treatment.* Muncie, IN: Accelerated Development.

Lilienfeld, S. O. (1999). The relation of the *MMPI–2 Pd* Harris–Lingoes Subscales to psychopathy, psychopathy facets, and antisocial behavior: Implications for clinical practice. *Journal of Clinical Psychology, 55,* 241–255.

Lindgren, T., & Carlsson, A. M. (2002). Relationship between the *Rorschach* and the *MMPI–2* in a Swedish population: A replication study of the effects of first-factor related test-interaction styles. *Journal of Personality Assessment, 79,* 357–370.

Lingoes, J. C. (1960). *MMPI* factors of the Harris and the Wiener subscales. *Journal of Consulting Psychology, 24*, 74–83.

Loper, R. G., Kammeier, M. L., & Hoffman, H. (1973). *MMPI* characteristics of college freshman males who later became alcoholics. *Journal of Abnormal Psychology, 82*, 159–162.

Lovitt, R. (1993). A strategy for integrating a normal *MMPI–2* and dysfunctional *Rorschach* in a severely compromised patient. *Journal of Personality Assessment, 60*, 141–147.

Lushene, R. E., O'Neil, H. H., & Dunn, T. (1974). Equivalent validity of a completely computerized *MMPI*. *Journal of Personality Assessment, 38*, 353–361.

MacAndrew, C. (1965). The differentiation of male alcoholic outpatients from nonalcoholic psychiatric outpatients by means of the *MMPI*. *Quarterly Journal of Studies on Alcohol, 26*, 238–246.

Mallory, C. H., & Walker, C. E. (1972). *MMPI O-H* scale responses of assaultive and nonassaultive prisoners and associated life history variables. *Educational and Psychological Measurement, 32*, 1125–1128.

Maslow, A. H. (1968). *Toward a psychology of being* (2nd ed.). Princeton, NJ: Van Nostrand.

McDowell, C., & Acklin, M. W. (1996). Standardizing procedures for calculating *Rorschach* interrater reliability: Conceptual and empirical foundations. *Journal of Personality Assessment, 66*, 308–320.

McGee, S. (1954). Measurement of hostility: A pilot study. *Journal of Clinical Psychology, 10*, 280–282.

McKinley, J. C., & Hathaway, S. R. (1940). A multiphasic personality schedule (Minnesota): II. A differential study of hypochondriasis. *Journal of Psychology, 10*, 255–268.

McKinley, J. C., & Hathaway, S. R. (1942). A multiphasic personality schedule (Minnesota): IV. Psychasthenia. *Journal of Applied Psychology, 26*, 614–624.

McKinley, J. C., & Hathaway, S. R. (1944). The *MMPI*: V. Hysteria, hypomania, and psychopathic deviate. *Journal of Applied Psychology, 28*, 153–174.

Meehl, P. E., & Hathaway, S. R. (1946). The *K* factor as a suppressor variable in the Minnesota Multiphasic Personality Inventory. *Journal of Applied Psychology, 30*, 525–564.

Megargee, E. I. (1966). Undercontrolled and overcontrolled personality types in extreme antisocial aggression. *Psychological Monographs, 80*, 3 (Whole No. 611).

Megargee, E. I. (1969). Conscientious objectors' scores on the *MMPI O-H* scale. *Proceedings of the 77th annual convention of the American Psychological Association, 4*, 507–508.

Megargee, E. I., Cook, P. E., & Mendelsohn, G. A. (1967). Development and validation of an *MMPI* scale of assaultiveness in overcontrolled individuals. *Journal of Abnormal Psychology, 72*, 519–528.

Megargee, E. I., & Mendelsohn, G. A. (1962). A cross-validation of 12 *MMPI* indexes of hostility and control. *Journal of Abnormal and Social Psychology, 65*, 431–438.

Meloy, J. R., & Gacono, C. (1995). Assessing the psychopathic personality. In J. Butcher (Ed.), *Clinical personality assessment: Practical approaches* (pp. 410–422). New York: Oxford University Press.

Meyer, G. J. (1996). The *Rorschach* and *MMPI*: Toward a more scientifically differentiated understanding of cross-method assessment. *Journal of Personality Assessment, 67*, 558–578.

Meyer, G. J. (1999a). The convergent validity of *MMPI* and *Rorschach* scales: An extension using profile scores to define response and character styles on both methods and a reexamination of simple *Rorschach* response frequency. *Journal of Personality Assessment, 72*, 1–35.

Meyer, G. J. (1999b). Introduction to the first Special Section in the Special Series on the utility of the *Rorschach* for clinical assessment. *Psychological Assessment, 11*, 235–239.

Meyer, G. J. (2001). Introduction to the final special section in the special series on the utility of the *Rorschach* for clinical assessment. *Psychological Assessment, 13*, 419–422.

Meyer, G. J., Finn, S. E., Eyde, L. D., Kay, G. G., Moreland, K. L., Dies, R. R., Eisman, E. J., Kubiszyn, T. W., & Read, G. M. (2001). Psychological testing and psychological assessment: A review of evidence and issues. *American Psychologist, 56*, 128–165.

Meyer, G. J., Hilsenroth, M. J., Baxter, D., Exner, J. E., Jr., Fowler, J. C., Piers, C. C., & Resnick, J. (2002). An examination of interrater reliability for scoring the *Rorschach* comprehensive system in eight data sets. *Journal of Personality Assessment, 78,* 219–274.

Meyer, G. J., Riethmiller, R. J., Brooks, R. D., Benoit, W. A., & Handler, L. (2000). A replication of *Rorschach* and *MMPI–2* convergent validity. *Journal of Personality Assessment, 74,* 1175–215.

Mezzich, J. E., Damarin, F. L., & Erickson, J. R. (1974). Comparative validity of strategies and indices for differential diagnosis of depressive states from other psychiatric conditions using the *MMPI*. *Journal of Consulting & Clinical Psychology, 42,* 691–698.

Miller, H. R., & Streiner, D. L. (1985). The Harris–Lingoes Subscales: Fact or fiction? *Journal of Clinical Psychology, 41,* 45–51.

Millon, T. (1987). *Manual for the Millon Clinical Multiaxial Inventory–II*, MCMI–II (2nd ed.). Minneapolis: National Computer Systems.

Modlin, H. C. (1947). A study of the Minnesota Multiphasic Personality Inventory in clinical practice with notes on the Cornell Index. *American Journal of Psychiatry, 103,* 758–769.

Monahan, J., Steadman, H. J., Appelbaum, P. S., Robbins, P. C., Mulvey, E. P., Silver, E., Roth, L., & Grisso, T. (2000). Developing a clinically useful actuarial tool for assessing violence risk. *British Journal of Psychiatry, 176,* 312–319.

Monahan, J., Steadman, H. J., Silver, E., Appelbaum, P. S., Robbins, P. C., Mulvey, E. P., Roth, L., Grisso, T., & Banks, S. (2001). *Rethinking risk assessment: The MacArthur study of mental disorders and violence.* New York: Oxford University Press.

Moreland, K. L., & Dahlstrom, W. G. (1983). Professional training with and use of the *MMPI*. *Professional Psychology: Research and Practice, 14,* 218–223.

Morey, L. C., Waugh, M. H., & Blashfield, R. K. (1985). *MMPI* scales for *DSM–III* personality disorders: Their derivation and correlates. *Journal of Personality Assessment, 49,* 245–251.

Morgan, B. W. (1968). *An introduction to Bayesian statistical decision processes.* Englewood Cliffs, NJ: Prentice-Hall.

Nash, M. R., Hulsey, T. L., Sexton, M. C., Harralson, T. L., & Lambert, W. (1993). Long-term sequelae of childhood sexual abuse: Perceived family environment, psychopathology and dissociation. *Journal of Clinical and Consulting Psychology, 61,* 276–283.

Navran, L. (1954). A rationally derived *MMPI* scale to measure dependence. *Journal of Consulting Psychology, 18,* 192.

Nichols, D. S. (1984). *The clinical interpretation of the Wiggins* MMPI *content scales.* Unpublished manuscript.

Nichols, D. S. (1987). *Interpreting the Wiggins* MMPI *Content Scales.* Minneapolis: National Computer Systems.

Nichols, D. S., & Greene, R. L. (1991, March). *New measures for dissimulation on the* MMPI/ MMPI–2. Paper presented at the 26th annual symposium on Recent Developments in the Use of the *MMPI (MMPI–2/MMPI–A)*, St. Petersburg Beach, FL.

Nichols, D. S., & Greene, R. L. (1995). MMPI–2 *Structural Summary interpretive manual.* Lutz, FL: Psychological Assessment Resources.

Norman, W. T. (1972). Psychometric considerations for a revision of the *MMPI*. In J. N. Butcher (Ed.), *Objective personality assessment* (pp. 59–84). New York: Academic.

Nunnally, J. C. (1967). *Psychometric theory.* New York: McGraw-Hill.

Ohlson, E. L., & Wilson, M. (1974). Differentiating female homosexuals from female heterosexuals by use of the *MMPI*. *Journal of Sex Research, 20,* 308–315.

Olmstead, D. W., & Monachesi, E. D. (1956). A validity check on *MMPI* scales of Responsibility and Dominance. *Journal of Abnormal and Social Psychology, 53,* 140–141.

Osberg, T. M., & Poland, D. L. (2001). Validity of the *MMPI–2* Basic and Harris–Lingoes Subscales in a forensic sample. *Journal of Clinical Psychology, 57,* 1369–1380.

Overall, J. E., & Gorham, D. R. (1962). The Brief Psychiatric Rating Scale. *Psychological Reports, 10,* 799–812.

Pancoast, D. L., Archer, R. P., & Gordon, R. A. (1988). The *MMPI* and clinical diagnosis: A comparison of classification system outcomes with discharge diagnoses. *Journal of Personality Assessment, 52*, 81–90.

Parker, K. C., Hanson, R. K., & Hunsley, J. (1988). *MMPI, Rorschach*, and *WAIS*: A meta-analytic comparison of reliability, stability, and validity. *Psychological Bulletin, 103*, 367–373.

Paulhus, D. L. (1984). Two-component models of socially desirable responding. *Journal of Personality and Social Psychology, 46*, 598–609.

Paulhus, D. L. (1986). Self-deception and impression management in test responses. In A. Angleitner & J. S. Wiggins (Eds.), *Personality assessment via questionnaires: Current issues in theory and measurement* (pp. 143–165). Berlin: Springer-Verlag.

Payne, F. D., & Wiggins, J. S. (1972). *MMPI* profile types and the self-report of psychiatric patients. *Journal of Abnormal Psychology, 79*, 1–8.

Pepper, L. J., & Strong, P. N. (1958). *Judgmental subscales for the* Mf *scale of the* MMPI. Unpublished manuscript.

Peterson, C. D., & Dahlstrom, W. G. (1992). The derivation of gender-role scales *GM* and *GF* for the *MMPI–2* and their relationship to Scale 5 *(Mf)*. *Journal of Personality Assessment, 59*, 486–499.

Piaget, J. (1967). *Six psychological studies* (A. Tenzer, Trans.). New York: Random House.

Piaget, J. (1972). *The child's conception of physical causality* (M. Gabain, Trans.). Totowa, NJ: Littlefield, Adams.

Piotrosky, C., Sherry, D., & Keller, J. W. (1985). Psychodiagnostic test usage: A survey of the Society for Personality Assessment. *Journal of Personality Assessment, 49*, 115–119.

Pokorny, A. D. (1968). Myths about suicide. In H.L.P. Resnik (Ed.), *Suicidal behavior: Diagnosis and management* (pp. 57–72). Boston: Little, Brown.

Polvi, N. H. (1997). Assessing risk of suicide in correctional settings. In C. D. Webster & M. A. Jackson (Eds.), *Impulsivity: Theory, assessment, and treatment* (pp. 278–301). New York: Guilford.

Raskin, R., & Novacek, J. (1989). An *MMPI* description of the narcissistic personality. *Journal of Personality Assessment, 53*, 66–80.

Rawlings, M. L. (1973). Self-control and interpersonal violence. A study of Scottish adolescent male severe offenders. *Criminology, 11*, 23–48.

Rosenthal, R., Hiller, J. B., Bornstein, R. F., Berry, D.T.R., & Brunell-Neuleib, S. (2001). Meta-analytic methods, the *Rorschach*, and the *MMPI*. *Psychological Assessment, 13*, 449–451.

Schlenger, W. E., & Kulka, R. A. (1987, August). *Performance of the Keane–Fairbank* MMPI *scale and other self-report measures in identifying post-traumatic stress disorder*. Paper presented at the annual meeting of the American Psychological Association, New York.

Schretlen, D. J. (1988). The use of psychological tests to identify malingered symptoms of mental disorder. *Clinical Psychology Review, 8*, 451–476.

Schretlen, D. J. (1997). Dissimulation on the *Rorschach* and other projective measures. In R. Rogers (Ed.), *Clinical assessment of malingering and deception* (2nd ed., pp. 208–222). New York: Guilford.

Schuerger, J. M., Foerstner, S. B., Serkownek, K., & Ritz, G. (1987). History and validities of the Serkownek subscales for *MMPI* Scales 5 and 0. *Psychological Reports, 61*, 227–235.

Shaw, M. C., & Grubb, J. (1958). Hostility and able high school underachievers. *Journal of Counseling Psychology, 5*, 263–266.

Shekelle, R. B., Gale, M., Ostfeld, A. M., & Paul, O. (1983). Hostility, risk of coronary heart disease, and mortality. *Psychosomatic Medicine, 45*, 109–114.

Smith, T. W., & Frohm, K. D. (1985). What's so unhealthy about hostility? Construct validity and psychosocial correlates of the Cook and Medley *Ho* scale. *Health Psychology, 4*, 503–520.

Spielberger, C. D., Jacobs, G. A., Russell, S., & Crane, R. S. (1983). Assessment of anger: The State-Trait Anger Scale. In J. N. Butcher & C. D. Spielberger (Eds.), *Advances in personality assessment* (Vol. 2, pp. 159–187). Hillsdale, NJ: Lawrence Erlbaum Associates.

Stein, K. B. (1968). The *TSC* scales: The outcome of a cluster analysis of the 550 *MMPI* items. In P. McReynolds (Ed.), *Advances in psychological assessment* (Vol. 1, pp. 80–104). Palo Alto, CA: Science & Behavior Books.

Stricker, G., & Gold, J. R. (1999). The *Rorschach*: Toward a nomothetically based, idiographically applicable configurational model. *Psychological Assessment, 11*, 240–250.

Sutker, P. B., & Allain, A. N. (1979). *MMPI* studies of extreme criminal violence in incarcerated women and men. In C. S. Newmark (Ed.), MMPI *clinical and research trends* (pp. 167–197). New York: Praeger.

Taylor, J. B., Ptacek, M., Carithers, M., Griffin, G., & Coyne, L. (1972). Rating scales as measures of clinical judgment: III. Judgments of the self on personality inventory scales and direct ratings. *Educational and Psychological Measurement, 32*, 543–557.

Tellegen, A., Ben-Porath, Y. S., McNulty, J. L., Arbisi, P. A., Graham, J. R., & Kaemmer, B. (2003). *The MMPI–2 restructured clinical (RC) scales. Development, validation, and interpretation.* Minneapolis: University of Minnesota.

Tesseneer, R., & Tydlaska, M. (1956). A cross-validation of a work attitude scale from the *MMPI*. *Journal of Educational Psychology, 47*, 1–7.

Thomas, A., & Chess, S. (1977). *Temperament and development.* New York: Brunner/Mazel.

Toobert, S., Bartelme, K. F., & Jones, E. S. (1959). Some factors related to pedophilia. *International Journal of Social Psychiatry, 4*, 272–279.

Tryon, R. C. (1966). Unrestricted cluster and factor analysis with application to the *MMPI* and Holzinger–Harman problems. *Multivariate Behavioral Research, 1*, 229–244.

Tydlaska, M., & Mengel, R. (1953). A scale for measuring work attitudes for the *MMPI*. *Journal of Applied Psychology, 37*, 474–477.

Vanderbeck, D. J. (1973). A construct validity study of the *O-H* scale of the *MMPI*, using a social learning approach to the catharsis effect. *FCI Research Reports, 5*, 1–18.

Viglione, D. J., Jr. (1996). Data and issues to consider in reconciling self-report and the *Rorschach*. *Journal of Personality Assessment, 67*, 579–587.

Viglione, D. J. (1999). A review of recent research addressing the utility of the *Rorschach*. *Psychological Assessment, 11*, 251–265.

Viglione, D. J., & Taylor, N. (2003). Empirical support for interrater reliability of *Rorschach* comprehensive system scoring. *Journal of Clinical Psychology, 59*, 111–121.

Ward, L. C., & Perry, M. S. (1998). Measurement of Social Introversion by the *MMPI–2*. *Journal of Personality Assessment, 70*, 171–182.

Webb, J. T., Levitt, E. E., & Rojdev, R. (1993, March). *A comparison of the clinical use of* MMPI–1 *and* MMPI–2. Paper presented at the meeting of the Society for Personality Assessment, San Francisco, CA.

Wechsler, D. (1955). *Manual for the Wechsler Adult Intelligence Scale.* New York: Psychological Corporation.

Wechsler, D. (1981). *Wechsler Adult Intelligence Scale—Revised manual.* New York: Psychological Corporation.

Wechsler, D. (1997). WAIS–III. *Wechsler Adult Intelligence Scale* (3rd ed.). *Administration and scoring manual.* San Antonio, TX: Psychological Corporation.

Weed, N. C., Ben-Porath, Y. S., & Butcher, J. N. (1990). Failure of the Wiener and Harmon Minnesota Multiphasic Personality Inventory (*MMPI*) subtle scales as personality descriptors and as validity indicators. *Psychological Assessment, 2*, 281–285.

Weed, N. C., Butcher, J. N., McKenna, T., & Ben-Porath, Y. S. (1992). New measures for assessing alcohol and drug abuse with the *MMPI–2*. *Journal of Personality Assessment, 58*, 389–404.

Weiner, I. B. (1993). Clinical considerations in the conjoint use of the *Rorschach* and the *MMPI*. *Journal of Personality Assessment, 60*, 148–152.

Weiner, I. B. (1998). *Principles of* Rorschach *interpretation.* Mahwah, NJ: Lawrence Erlbaum Associates.

Weiner, I. B. (2000). Making *Rorschach* interpretation as good as it can be. *Journal of Personality Assessment, 74,* 164–174.

Weiner, I. B. (2001). Advancing the science of psychological measurement: The Rorschach Inkblot Method as exemplar. *Psychological Assessment, 13,* 423–432.

Weiner, I. B., & Exner, J. E., Jr. (1991). *Rorschach* changes in long-term and short-term psychotherapy. *Journal of Personality Assessment, 56,* 453–465.

Weissman, M. M., Klerman, G. L., Markowitz, J. S., & Ouelette, R. (1989). Suicidal ideation and suicide attempts in panic disorder and attacks. *New England Journal of Medicine, 321,* 1209–1214.

Welsh, G. S. (1956). Factor dimensions *A* and *R*. In G. S. Welsh & W. G. Dahlstrom (Eds.), *Basic readings on the* MMPI *in psychology and medicine* (pp. 264–281). Minneapolis: University of Minnesota.

Wetter, M. W., Baer, R. A., Berry, D.T.R., Robison, L. H., & Sumpter, J. (1993). *MMPI–2* profiles of motivated fakers given specific symptom information: A comparison to matched patients. *Psychological Assessment, 5,* 317–323.

Wetter, M. W., Baer, R. A., Berry, D.T.R., Smith, G. T., & Larsen, L. H. (1992). Sensitivity of *MMPI–2* Validity Scales to random responding and malingering. *Psychological Assessment, 4,* 369–374.

Wetzler, S., Khadivi, A., & Moser, R. K. (1998). The use of the *MMPI–2* for the assessment of depressive and psychotic disorders. *Assessment, 5,* 249–261.

White, W. C. (1970). *Selective modeling in youth offenders with high and low* O-H *personality types.* Unpublished doctoral dissertation, Florida State University, Tallahassee.

White, W. C. (1975). Validity of the Overcontrolled Hostility (*O-H*) scale: A brief report. *Journal of Personality Assessment, 39,* 587–590.

White, W. C., McAdoo, W. G., & Megargee, E. I. (1973). Personality factors associated with over- and undercontrolled offenders. *Journal of Personality Assessment, 37,* 473–478.

Wiener, D. N. (1948). Subtle and obvious keys for the *MMPI. Journal of Consulting Psychology, 12,* 164–170.

Wiener, D. N., & Harmon, L. R. (1946). *Subtle and obvious keys for the* MMPI*: Their development* (Advisement Bulletin No. 16). Minneapolis, MN: Regional Veterans Administration Office.

Wiggins, J. S. (1959). Interrelationships among *MMPI* measures of dissimulation under standard and social desirability instructions. *Journal of Consulting Psychology, 23,* 419–427.

Wiggins, J. S. (1966). Substantive dimensions of self-report in the *MMPI* item pool. *Psychological Monographs, 80,* 22 (Whole No. 630).

Wiggins, J. S., Goldberg, L. R., & Applebaum, M. (1971). *MMPI* Content Scales: Interpretive norms and correlations with other scales. *Journal of Consulting and Clinical Psychology, 37,* 403–410.

Williams, R. B., Jr., Haney, T. L., Lee, K. L., Kong, Y. H., Blumenthal, J. A., & Whalen, R. E. (1980). Type A behavior, hostility and coronary atherosclerosis. *Psychosomatic Medicine, 42,* 539–549.

Wood, J. M., & Lilienfeld, S. O. (1999). The Rorschach Inkblot Test: A case of overstatement? *Assessment, 6,* 341–351.

Wood, J. M., Lilienfeld, S. O., Nezworski, M. T., & Garb, H. N. (2001). Coming to grips with the negative evidence for the comprehensive system for the *Rorschach*: A comment on Gacono, Loving, and Bodholdt; Ganellen; and Bornstein. *Journal of Personality Assessment, 77,* 48–70.

Woodward, W. A., Robinowitz, R., & Penk, W. E. (1980, March). *Predicting substance abusers' return to treatment from first admission personality scales.* Paper presented at the meeting of the Society for Personality Assessment, Tampa, FL.

Wrobel, T. A. (1992). Validity of Harris and Lingoes *MMPI* subscale descriptors in an outpatient sample. *Journal of Personality Assessment, 59,* 14–21.

Zalewski, C., & Archer, R. P. (1991). Assessment of borderline personality disorder: A review of *MMPI* and *Rorschach* findings. *Journal of Nervous and Mental Disease, 179,* 338–345.

Zuckerman, M. (1979). *Sensation seeking: Beyond the optimal level of arousal.* Hillsdale, NJ: Lawrence Erlbaum Associates.

Author Index

Subject Index